Mission
Religious Harmony

Mission Religious Harmony

Dr M. D. Thomas

GenNext Publication

Published by

GenNext Publication
5, Ansari Road, Daryaganj, New Delhi-110002
Phone: 011-47034999, 9811692060
E-mail: gennextpublication@hotmail.com

Distribution Network

gyanbooks.com

India, USA, Canada, UK, Australia, France

Institute of Harmony and Peace Studies
102, Floor 1, Plot No 155, Pochanpur, Sector 23, Dwarka, New Delhi-110077
Phone: 9810535378 (p), 8447925378 (p)
Email: mdthomas53@gmail.com (p), ihps2014@gmail.com (o)
Website: www.mdthomas.in (p), www.ihpsindia.org (o)

ISBN: 978-93-5663-423-7 (PB)

First Published, 2024

Printed at: Gyan Press, Delhi.

Mission Religious Harmony

Author: Dr M. D. Thomas

Contents

Foreword

Mission Religious Harmony is a valuable contribution of a scholar of religion and religious harmony, Dr M. D. Thomas, in the context of promoting inter-faith dialogue and strengthening inter-religious understanding. It is a collection of essays and articles by an engaged public intellectual who has been consistently involved in various initiatives of conversations about religious questions and controversies in a multicultural context.

Harmony is the most important precondition for a sane society. It is the most essential imperative for democratic nation-building in a multi-religious civilization. It creates spaces for approaching religion in historical as well as on sociological terms. Otherwise, religion becomes a convenient tool for 'othering' in day-to-day life through lack of information and understanding. It creates basis for 'politics' of religion, which is the most fertile ground for cultivation of communal hatred and fear.

Lack of harmony breeds misunderstanding, which in turn generates discrimination coupled with deprivations. There are enough historical evidences to prove that discriminations and deprivations together have been leading to social fragmentation and political separatism. No society can survive without justice and peace. There cannot be coexistence of freedom and injustice. Therefore freedom, justice, equality and integration go together. Any mission for harmony necessarily underlines these self-evident truths.

Most of the contemporary post-colonial societies are challenged by the memories of colonization and under-development. In case of India, the journey towards freedom demands coupling of three 'D's - de-colonization, development and democratization. During the freedom movement, the Indians were led by Gandhi and his followers to leave behind communalism through respect for all religions (Sarva Dharma Sambhav). It was further institutionalised by the Constitution of India in two ways - I) freedom of faith, and 2) equality among all citizens irrespective of caste, class, gender, languages, region and religion. There is need to continue our conversation about the importance of the idea of respect for all religions in a global setting of identity politics. This is an ideal which has to be practiced in personal life, family interactions, school system and community festivities as an integral part of democratic nation-building. Otherwise, quest for power may make us victim of hate and fear through various ways of 'othering' where abuse of religion is one of the most convenient ways.

It is not easy task. Religious diversity is a fact of our national cultural life. Unity in diversity is one of the most complex social ideas which needs missionary attitude whereas most of us treat it with benign neglect. 'Mission religious harmony' deserves a new centrality in the project of nation building in the 21st century in the age of globalisation. It is much more urgent for gen-next in India. Let us all welcome scholarly endeavours of concerned religious scholars like M.D. Thomas and engage with 'Mission Religious Harmony'.

Prof. Dr Anand Kumar

Former Professor of sociology at Jawaharlal Nehru University (JNU) and
President of Society for Communal Harmony (SCH), New Delhi

Preface

The word 'mission' derives from the Latin root 'missio' or 'missionem' meaning 'the act of sending' or 'mittere' meaning 'to send'. Obviously, the idea of mission evolved from Jesus Christ sending his disciples into diverse areas of the world with a command to preach his gospel or good news to one and all. The word mission took its origin in 1598 when the members of the Society of Jesus (Jesuits) sent its members abroad in line with the original command of Jesus. The term is most used in reference to Christian missions and centres. But it is also used in the classic sense to refer to any creed, ideology or project, as well.

Having had its origin in the Christian campus, the word 'mission' has travelled across the nations, communities and sectors of the world, thus becoming singularly popular among one and all. Accordingly, there are 'Buddhist Missions, Ram Krishna Mission, Rajeev Gandhi Mission, Space Mission, Mission 2024, mission mode, mission statement, and the like. Today, the word stands for commitment, dedication, quality, target, task, etc. It also connotes assignment, special job, duty, obligation, responsibility, scheme and undertaking. It refers to a commission from a divine or higher source, in the first instance. It includes the horizontal planes too, along with the vertical.

Mission is grounded in a divine charging, obviously so. But it is performed in the human context. The humans are its beneficiaries. 'Fully human, fully divine' thus goes the dictum. 'When something is performed to the humans, it is as well performed to the divine', as per the second golden rule stated by Jesus Christ. In other words, devotion to the divine is reflected in the commitment to the human and the natural world. Mission is geared towards the wellbeing of human beings and the entire creation. Commitment to the harmonious and peaceful living of the human world is the ultimate destination of mission.

The word 'mission' is essentially connected with 'vision'. Vision precedes mission. In other words, mission proceeds from vision. Mission follows vision, too, necessarily so. Vision and mission are complementary, one to another, like two sides of the coin. 'One completes the other' is the logic. Besides, mission has a unique role to play, in all circumstances. It is oriented to fulfil something. It celebrates a sense of special task. It is a calling. It carries with it a sense of purpose as well as a sense of motivation. The word 'mission' has a special feel in it. It has a dignity of its own right, as well.

Mission approaches life at a glance. In other words, it encompasses life in an integral manner, in all its dimensions and meanings. It upholds the universal values of life, both human and spiritual. It coordinates the humans with each other. It inter-relates the humans with the divine, as well. Mission takes care of the material as well as of the spiritual realm, at the same time. It also combines the vertical and the horizontal planes. Mission has a leaning towards religious outlook and social action at the same time.

Human society, the entire creation as well, is characterized by diversity. Diversity would imply being different as well as being many. Difference determines the uniqueness and dignity of every human person and other kinds of creation. Diversities include arenas of geography, climate, gender, language, caste, class, religion, culture, nationality, social mores, food habits, dress patterns and other traditions. Besides, difference or diversity is not a negative factor, but is a positive quality that enriches. It is geared towards unity and not division. Therefore, difference or diversity in all areas has to be honoured.

Religion, without doubt, is a significant reality in the human world. Different religious traditions evolved in the world thanks to the prophets and great persons of the world. These traditions emerged to be mighty systems with different theological theories and stipulations, along with myths, beliefs, fasts, pilgrimages, etc. In course of time, rigidity in the understandings caused a lot of exclusiveness and unsociability among them. The stiffness grew to even hostilities and mutual attacks, though in more or less degrees.

Hans Kung, a distinguished Catholic priest, theologian, author and President of the Foundation for a Global Ethic, states "No peace among nations without peace between religions! No peace among religions without dialogue between religions! No dialogue between religions without investigation of the foundation of religions!" (Hans Kung, Christianity: essence, history and future). Harmony among religions is the way to obtaining harmony among communities. Dialogue is the way to harmony and peace. Therefore, the foundations of religions have to be investigated.

The individualistic and separatist understanding of religion requires being revised. Addiction to religious observances has to be shed. Religion ought not to be used for dividing people. Religion has to focus on faith, which is the essence as well as the qualitative aspect of religion. The open and interactive characteristic of faith can help religion to be more elastic. The blind areas of faith and religion have to be transcended. Harmony and peace among religions is vital to social life that that has to be the orientation of religion, faith and related realities.

Mission has to be understood in the context of the entire colloquium of traditions of faith and ideology in the world. The Creator God has distributed his gifts all over the world, well, in all individuals, religious systems, communities and nations. Whatever the human society and nature have is the gift of the same Creator. They are the shared cultural heritage of the world human society, too. Therefore, the different faith traditions, ideologies, languages, cultures, etc are not 'yours and mine', but are 'ours'. 'One is mine in special and others are mine in general' is the way one has to understand and treat the legacies.

Harmony among religions calls for the collective ownership of the legacies of the human society. One should learn not only from the tradition one is affiliated to, but from all traditions. Appreciating, affirming and promoting what is good, true and beautiful in other faith traditions is also within the core mandate of the mission. Building constructive and positive relationships with people of other religious and social traditions is the focus of the mission. The initiatives of interaction and learning enhance mutual understanding, enrichment, harmony and fellowship.

What's more, water flows from a higher plane to a lower plane. The best of ones' faith values is spontaneously shared towards each other in this process. Consistent and collaborative efforts with persons of other faith backgrounds are geared towards making a better society and they are integral parts of the mission. Mission is undertaken not by just a particular religious group. It has to be performed jointly by persons of all affiliations of faith and ideologies. The collective consciousness of faith in oneself, in others and in God is the way to religious harmony. A radical change in attitudes and approaches is called for.

'Mission Religious Harmony' is a title that vouches to travel through the high ways, streets and corners of all religions and faiths. It is committed to explore the universal values that are the nerve hub of the human culture. It visualizes accomplishing harmony and peace among communities of all religious and secular affiliations. It is geared towards arriving at peaceful co-existence that leads to interaction, give and take and mutual learning. Inclusive thinking and harmonious living among people of all affiliations is the ultimate destination of mission religious harmony. 'I have a mission to you', 'you have a mission to me' and 'we have a collective mission towards the country and the larger society' is the logic of the mission.

The book 'Mission Religious Harmony' researches into the diverse themes of the title in question in an innovative way. A few of them explores the diverse facets of the dynamics of the mission under discussion. Most of the chapters discuss diverse aspects of harmony among religions and as a result among the various sections and sectors of social life. Yet a few of them are comparative studies between different religious branches of knowledge. They network and dovetail the characteristic nuances related to harmony and peace among religions, in view of a better neighbourhood, nation and society.

The book 'Mission Religious Harmony', yet again, is a singular series of essays on diverse themes related to the title in question. All the articles are well-researched with endnotes, making them studied, scholarly and authentic. These articles were written by the author at different times. A good number of them were published separately in diverse journals or books and the details of the respective publication are given at the end of the article, as well. Arranging the articles in to chapters and having it published as a book would benefit the larger public. That is the logic of this book.

This book is extremely privileged to carry a 'Foreword' by Prof. Dr Anand Kumar. He is Former Professor of sociology at Jawaharlal Nehru University and President of Society for Communal Harmony, New Delhi. He holds M. A. in Sociology from Banaras Hindu University, Varanasi, M. Phil. in Sociology from Jawaharlal Nehru University, New Delhi, and Ph. D. in Sociology from University of Chicago. He was Lecturer in BHU, Associate Professor and Professor at JNU and Visiting Professor at various universities in India and overseas. He is Former Member of Aam Aadmi Party and National convenor of Swaraj Abhiyan, a political organization, as well. I have the pleasure of placing on record my deep sense of admiration and gratitude to Prof. Dr Anand Kumar for blessing the book with an erudite, precise, brilliant and thought-provoking 'Foreword'. The good will, time and trouble he has measured out to me thus will ever be gratefully cherished.

GenNext Publications, New Delhi, with a national and international networking, has taken up with commitment the responsibility of publishing and disseminating the resourceful book to national and international circles. I am sure, the publisher will reach the book to academic, religious, multi-religious and social arenas as well as governmental and non-governmental institutions, especially in the wake of the acute communal and social shrinking across the globe. I have the joy of expressing my appreciation to Mr B. P. Garg and his team for the quality of publishing, along with the commitment to reach it far and wide and thus being part of the process of making this landmark volume a reality in India and the world over.

Before I conclude this 'Foreword', I wish to salute those who have made this volume possible in various ways. God the Creator has given me this precious life with all its resources, resourcefulness, opportunities and accomplishments. My lovely parents channelled life for me, nurtured me and helped me grow up. Jesus my Great Master has been an unfailing source of motivation, strength and companionship for me in life, par excellence. A series of great 'teachers and gurus' gave me a shower of inspiration in my life, in diverse ways and facilitated my further growth towards accomplishing certain heights. Quite a few good friends and well-wishers of mine supported me by standing by me in diverse ways, even against several odds of life.

With a deep sense of gratefulness, I offer this volume before God the Creator, my parents, Jesus the Master, teachers, Gurus, friends and well-wishers, by repeating the words of Mahatma Kabeer, "Meraa mujh meim kuchh naheen, jo kuchh hei so teraa; Teraa tujh ko saumptaa, kyaa laage hei meraa", well, in summary 'I present to you what is yours and not what is mine'!

What's more, my dear readers, if this book contributes at least a spark in the areas of 'missioning religious harmony' in the 'individual, social and spiritual realms of human life', I shall consider all the inspiration and efforts behind this volume worth the while. May the consciousness and commitment to the mission of religious harmony promote harmonious living and make our India and all countries of the world a better place for the humans and other beings to have their being!

Dr M. D. Thomas

01 January 2024

Founder Director
Institute of Harmony and Peace Studies, New Delhi

Chapter - 1

Mission as Promoting Harmony in Social Life

Introduction

Having a mission in life is the living sign of a purposeful human life. Facilitating such awareness is the right orientation of the institution of religion. This is the overall outcome of a faith-based life, too. Mission is always directed towards the other. The values of the great master Jesus are ethically rich and sublime and they deserve to be disseminated by means of deed and word as well as of personal experience. Individuals and communities of human composition, limited as they are in many ways, are prone to run into complex situations of disharmony of diverse sorts, especially in the global phenomenon of interactions. Reconciling the diversities of life and amicably settling the ever-sprouting tensions, conflicts and violence in social life emerge as the primary concern of the mission, along with all other good efforts that are being done. The multifarious factors of social life have to be harmonised. This requires humane ways that are spiritually charged. The religious theories and practices do not seem to produce the intended fruit. The sociological implications of human life as well as of religion itself have to be explored further. A culture of networking with one another, as individuals and communities, has to be fostered. A re-start seems necessary in order to activate the Christian mission in terms of a new understanding. Mission needs to be reinterpreted in a larger context. The hinge of the mission has to be 'promoting harmony in social life'. This paper attempts to consider some of the implications and dimensions of the mission in line with this perspective.

1. UNDERSTANDING CHRISTIAN MISSION ANEW

1.1. Inadequacy of the Traditional Patterns of Mission

The traditional patterns of the Christian mission, in spite of the best of intentions, were very much self-centred. That model was founded on the dictum 'outside the church there is no salvation'[1]. The approach of the mission then could be summarised in the following articulations. 'I have direct access to the eternal mysteries; you do not have it; and I want to assist you to have the same'[2]. 'On account of my faith in Jesus, I am saved; you are not saved; and I want to save you'[3]. In other words, 'I am ok; you are not ok; and I want to make you ok'[4]. 'I am the subject; you are the object; I have the mandate to perform a salvation operation on you'[5]. Accordingly, 'people of other faiths and ideologies were mere potential Christians'[6]. 'Conversion was necessary for salvation; it meant making the other like me; and I am the agent of conversion'[7]. All these phrases underline an absolutist understanding of one's faith and an exclusive attitude to people of their faiths and ideologies. They also smack of a cheap as well as high-handed way of saving others. Tragically enough, the above approach demoralises the unique role of the Divine Creator in ensuring each masterpiece of his creation its due destiny. Recognising the promptings of the Spirit in other faiths and accepting and respecting persons of other traditions as rich reservoirs of divine experience was unheard of according to the old mode of Christian mission. Obviously, this traditional attitude of the mission is out-of-date and stands in a dire need of radical change[8].

1.2. Meaning, Nuances and Implications of Mission

Mission is a task and an assignment entrusted by someone[9]. It is a duty or an undertaking. It is a commission from a higher source. It is the outcome of the realisation of having received a particular calling from above. Performing a special job for the other in particular and for the humanity in general is the engagement of the mission. Mission refers to a horizontal duty. It can be a religious obligation or a social responsibility. It is oriented to serving the other. It is intended for the wellness of the other. It is meant for facilitating the other for superior realisations and attainments in life. Mission tends to coordinate the humans with each other[10]. It endeavours to inter-relate the humans with the divine as well. It is a noble task that encompasses an integral approach to life. It takes care of the material as well as of the spiritual realm. It combines the vertical and the horizontal planes. Devotion to the divine is reflected in commitment to the human and the natural world. Mission has a leaning towards religious outlook and social action at the same time. It finds its way to the divine through the human. 'What is done to man or woman, in fact, is done to God himself'[11].

Mission approaches life at a glance, in all its dimensions and meanings. It upholds the universal values of life, both humanly and spiritually. Mission is geared towards making a more humane and a harmonious society.

1.3. Mission Grounded in the Command of Jesus

Christian mission is grounded in the life and teachings of Jesus Christ. Jesus, as God became man, incarnated the divine in all respects. He observed that a larger-than-life concept of religion distorts the perception of life. He realised that 'Sabbath is for the human being and not vice versa'[12]. He became deeply convinced that a radical change in the entire understanding of religion as well as of life was crucial. He attempted a revolutionary way of attaining the objective of bringing religion and life back into their track. Some of the citations of Jesus are unique articulations that stand out in the entire world of spirituality and morality. His command to his disciples were categorical – 'Love one another as I have loved you'[13]; 'Love your enemy'[14]; 'Do to the other what you would have him/her do to you'[15]; 'Love your neighbour as yourself'[16]; 'Father in heaven causes his sun to rise on the evil and the good and rain on the righteous and the un-righteous…be perfect as your heavenly father is perfect.'[17]; 'When you have done even to one of these little ones, you have done to me'[18]; 'We are like one body with many parts'[19]; 'Honour one another above yourselves'[20]. They apply to people of other faiths and even of no faiths as well as to people of Christian faith.

1.4. Mission Founded on the Documental Teachings of the Church

The convocation of the Second Vatican Council by Pope John XXIII was the symbol of a new awakening in the Catholic Church. This was nothing but the beginning of a revolution in the whole Christian tradition[21]. This can rightly be considered the greatest gift the Church has ever received in the history of her journey. It had a substantial difference in the self–understanding of the Catholic Church and its Christian faith. It had a major impact on the outlook of the Catholic Church on other Christian ideologies, other faith-based ideologies and on secular ideologies. This revolutionary change was certainly the result of a new and deeper understanding of the vision and mission of Jesus. It also highlighted a more positive and grown-up attitude towards other religious and non-religious traditions[22]. The five significant documents of the Second Vatican Council, such as AG, NE, GS and DH, *Redemtoris Missio*, Ecclesia in Asia, CBCI All India Seminar, Bangalore, 1969, CBCI Synod of Bishops, Calcutta, 1974, and the like, elaborate the implications of the above awakening to several details[23]. Dialogue and harmony among religions and faiths are firmly rooted in the essential missionary character of the Church. It is an integral part of the mission of the Church. 'The dialogue, which the Church proposes, is grounded in the logic of incarnation' (EA 29), says Ecclesia in Asia[24]. Obviously, this is the mainstream perspective of the Church today. These documents make a clarion call to a new way of understanding and living the mission pioneered by Jesus, in all its dimensions.

1.5. Mission as Articulated by the Statements of Popes

The documents of the Church are in fact guidelines from the Popes since the sixties of the 19th century, down the decades. Therefore, the statements of the Popes do not have in any way a water-tight separation from the official documents mentioned above. Moreover, the statements of the Popes are clear and condensed articulations of the Popes on the mission of the Church, especially on the mission to people of all faiths, ideologies and affiliations. "We have to look at what unites people rather than what divides them" (Pope John XXIII)[25]. "Man must meet man, nation meet nation, as brothers and sisters, as children of God" (Pope Paul VI)[26]."Religion has to be what God intended it to be – a source of goodness, harmony and peace" (Pope John Paul II)[27]. "By dialogue we let God be present in our midst, for as we open ourselves in dialogue to one another, we open ourselves to God" (Pope John Paul II)[28]. "Different religious traditions of India are a hope for a better future for the human family" (Pope John Paul II)[29]. "Religious collaboration offers the opportunity of expressing the highest ideals of every religious tradition" (Pope Benedict XVI) [30]. These selected citations from the Popes give a glimpse of the fact that the new understanding of the Christian mission is inclusive of all peoples and cultures of the world. They summarise the official documents, encyclicals and letters in a summary form and make the missionary path broad-based, clear and open-ended.

1.6. Mission According to the 'Catholic' Spirit

The word 'Catholic' means 'universal'[31]. It derives from the Greek *'katholikos'*[32]. The Christian ecclesiology has it that the word meant 'a communion of 23 Catholic Churches'[33], in a denominational sense. 'Catholicity' is considered one of the 'Four Marks of the Church'[34], the others being unity, sanctity, and apostolicity. Nevertheless, being 'catholic' in the communal sense is to diminish the meaning of the word. Reducing the catholic community to a mere 'sect' would mean violating the spirit of the word, too. 'To be catholic' is to have a 'universal' mindset. In order to be a catholic in the sense of being universal is to go beyond the boundaries of the catholic community in an inter-denominational and inter-religious and even non-religious way, like Jesus. Broadening one's horizons of life in an all-inclusive way is the 'catholic spirit' every disciple of Jesus is invited to live[35]. Down the centuries of its journey, the Church lost much of its 'catholic' spirit and developed a sectarian image in the context of polarised ideas and interpretations among the different Christian traditions. Besides, the spread of the Catholic Church advanced more in the quantitative dimension than in the qualitative. In the light of the revised understanding of the Second Vatican Council and the broadened horizons of the later decades, the original spirit of being 'catholic' has to be revived. Christian mission will then receive a welcome appeal beyond the boundaries. That would amount to say that the Catholic Church has to become more and more 'catholic' in its spirit and missionary style[36].

1.7. Mission in Relation to Other Faiths and Ideologies

The Creator is the original giver of life and has distributed diverse characteristics to all forms of life on earth. Whatever the nature and the human society have is the gift of the same Creator. They are the shared property of the world or the society. The different faith traditions, ideologies, languages, cultures, etc are not 'yours and mine'[37]. They are 'ours'. They are the common cultural heritage of the human society. One should learn not only from the tradition one is affiliated to, but from all traditions. 'One is mine in special and others are mine in general' has to be the way one understands and treats the colloquium of legacies[38]. Appreciating, affirming and promoting what is good, true and beautiful in other faith traditions is the right understanding of the mission. Building constructive and positive relationships with people of other religious and social traditions is the focus of the mission. The initiatives of interaction and learning enhance mutual understanding, enrichment, harmony and fellowship. The best of one's faith values are spontaneously shared towards each other in this process, like water flows from a higher plane to a lower plane. Consistent and collaborative efforts with persons of other faith backgrounds in view of making a better society are integral parts of the mission[39]. The right and uplifting orientation of the Christian mission is one that is undertaken jointly with persons of all affiliations of faith and ideologies[40]. A radical attitudinal change is called for.

2. SHIFT OF PARADIGM IN THE MISSIONARY STYLE CALLED FOR

2.1. From Theological to Multi-disciplinary Search

Theology has articulated Christian faith to unlimited degrees. It has elaborated the various dimensions of the Christian mission in all possible details and proportions. The contribution of theology in fostering the advancement of the mission is beyond the scope of being described in words. Of late, theology has ventured upon several innovative sectors, so much so that it seems that theology has not left anything unstated. While there is no denying the fact that theology has done a commendable job in broadening the horizons of religious thought, it has to be affirmed that theology is only one of the disciplines of knowledge. It articulates what religion stands for. There are hundreds of other disciplines that present various other angles of life and theology is not capable of conceiving those viewpoints[41]. Reality is multi-dimensional and all perspectives together picture the reality of life better. Understanding the reality in its entirety is still beyond the capacity of all perceptions put together. Mission has to be conceived and interpreted from the points of view of other disciplines, like biology, computer application, language, music, poetry, technology and arithmetic[42]. Mission has to be less theological and more multi-disciplinary in its search and outreach. The multi-disciplinary paradigm of the mission is more multi-sided and comprehensive[43]. It is capable of making the Christian mission more meaningful and effective.

2.2. From Theoretical to Practical Approach

Life is composed of both theory and practice. Theory sharpens the vision and practice makes the mission effective. Both components are complementary to each other as bone and flesh co-exist in a living body. They are the internal and external sectors of life. They have to correspond to each other. They have to go together, like a man and a woman who are wedded to each other. They are inseparable. One testifies the other. An exclusive approach wouldn't be justifiable at any rate. A purely theoretical way would lead one into empty abstractions. It would be like flying in the skies. Life is functional in the overall context. From that point of view, mission cannot be reduced to a communication of certain philosophy or theology. Teaching a set of doctrines and dogma cannot be the mission proper[44]. Performing a set of rituals for oneself and for others do not justify mission in the right sense of the word. Mission cannot be reduced to a mere intellectual exercise. Mission does not achieve its objective by replacing one religious ideology with another. Exchange of views and theories often does not bring any mutual agreement. The rational approach often ends up in frictions. Sharing of faith experiences would ensure better outcome for the partners[45]. Mission has to be more result-oriented. The focal point of the mission has to be imbibing and inculcating values of life. Its target has to be more spiritually tuned and focused on unity and togetherness. Purposeful endeavours are designed in terms of practicality. Mission today is conceived and approached more in terms of 'harmonious living together' by people of diverse persuasions[46]. Mutual sharing of spiritual and human experiences and collective engagement in humanitarian action for the wellness of the human society has to be its way forward[47]. Without doubt, backed by sound theories, missionary concerns have to be practical and functional, to the core.

2.3. From Religious to Inter-Religious and Multi-Religious Perspective

To understand mission in terms of one religion would mean making a close circuit, like a cobweb. That is a self-centred way of being religious. Making oneself and one's religion the centre of life is a highly dangerous drive. One can get overwhelmed by one's own religious perception and can tend to consider it right and that of others wrong. Claiming to have a privileged access to salvation or heaven is the outcome of such a wrong premise[48]. This mindset can drive one into a mania of converting people of other religious viewpoints into one's religion, so that they may be saved. Being 'inter-religious' in the missionary concept is a definitely step ahead[49]. It initiates a dialogical approach to the mission by exchanging faith-experiences between the two traditions concerned. This particular involvement between two religious traditions is on equal footing and mutuality is its spirit. Though this is vital in view of understanding the deeper implications of the religious traditions involved, it does not have space for involving all religious traditions. 'Multi-religious perspective' of the mission is obviously broader still and is all-inclusive[50]. While continuing deeper interaction in a one-to-one manner between two traditions, an all-embracing approach with all religious traditions would ensure better results in missionary endeavour. The values of Jesus will permeate in to all affiliations of faith in a spontaneous and interactive way. The endeavour also occasions learning from the specific values of other traditions, considering them at a glance. Multi-religious perspective takes care of the larger concerns of the mission with non-violent and effective dimensions of being religious[51].

2.4. From Religious to Non-Religious and Secular Mindset

Religion is certainly a great bestowment of the Creator upon the human society. Religion has brought lot of meaning to the lives of millions and millions of people. It has given its adherents motivation, inspiration and strength to live their lives, especially in times of hopelessness. All the same, it is a blatant fact that millions and millions of people on the other hand do not subscribe to religious theories, for reasons of their own. Some of them pursue a scientific and analytic path while others follow a non-theistic or non-religious way[52]. Therefore, reducing life to a religious position wouldn't be realistic or fair. Life has to be perceived from a non-religious angle as well. To be religious is only one of the ways of living one's human life. To be spiritual is the ultimate objective of human life. One does not have to be religious in order to be spiritual. The non-religious way is equally a path that leads one to spiritual fulfillment[53]. There are many natural ways of being spiritual. There are various secular ideologies that are highly noble and meaningful. A considerable per cent of people become good human beings in line with their non-religious precepts[54]. Those who have an aversion towards 'the secular' are under the grip of a major confusion. 'Secular' is not 'worldly', but is a broadened understanding of the 'Sacred'. Seeing the sacred wherever human eyes can reach is a fine spiritual perspective. This is a time-tested mystical way. Faith involves both religious and non-religious or secular mindsets[55]. It can be non-theistic as well as theistic. The understanding of and approach to Christian mission has to be widened in terms of worldviews that are non-religious and secular. That will enable the missioner in figuring out the multi-dimensional implications of human life. Reaching out to the non-religious and secular dimensions will ensure a more complete picture of life and a mission that is more meritorious and worth the while[56].

2.5. From Religion-centred to Life-centred Understanding

Religion has been playing a pivotal role in the history of human life. It has been evolving from its primitive forms to more developed and sophisticated forms. In course of time, most of the simple ideas of the founders of religions have become highly complicated abstractions and theories[57]. Many of the casual components of the original rituals have become inevitable imperatives of the religious practices. Several secondary aspects have taken the place of primary mandates. The market of religious traditions has become overpowered by an unhealthy spirit of cut-throat competition and rivalry, in terms of veracity and superiority[58]. Many clever persons use the religious sentiment of the common folk as a stepping stone to emerge as mini-gods. Politicians with vested interests use the religious sector for building up their vote bank[59]. The corrupt industrial and commercial sector uses it for pacifying their conscience that is disturbed by fraudulent practices. To say the least, religion seems to be considered the centre of human life. To add to the confusion, religionists hold on to the view that religion is the centre of their mission. It is high time to become realistic. 'Sabbath is for the human being', and not vice versa, says Jesus[60]. Except as a motivating force and the source of strength in life, religion cannot be the centre of the mission. Life is the centre of the missionary activity. Life is the gift of God. Religion is established for facilitating and enhancing life. People of religious and non-religious inclinations have to jointly address life-related issues and attempt to improve the quality of life and standard of societal well-being, while being rooted in the individual faith and ideological persuasions[61]. The true understanding of the mission has to be 'life-centred'.

2.6. From Exclusive to Inclusive Way

Religion, as a unique gift of God to the human society, has immensely contributed to the bettering of human lives and it continues to do the same. All the religious traditions have played their role in the global contexts as well as in the respective historical, social and cultural contexts of their regions and nationalities. Plurality of faith traditions is intended by God and they have to be part of the processes of serving human lives[62]. It is also true that each religion understands and approaches its religious heritage as unique and teaches it in a superlative spirit. Psychologically speaking, one cannot accept one's faith in a half-hearted manner as well. All the same, to understand one's religious tradition in an exclusive way would be literally naïve. That would mean understanding one's faith as a child understands one's parents as one's own. The exclusive understanding of faith considers one's faith as the only path to salvation[63]. It monopolizes God and the path towards him and deprives others of their legitimate religious right. A mono-track approach to religion can never do justice to the immense diversities of human existence. To be exclusive is to narrow down the understanding of truth to one opinion and experience only. The understanding of religion has to be broadened towards a perspective of all religions. An inclusive outlook of religion will broaden the horizons of the mission[64]. One has to have an inclusive attitude towards all traditions of faith and streams of thought, both inside and outside one's own religious affiliation. Inclusive frame of mind is the key that can operate multi-denominational, multi-faith and multi-ideological interactions in the missionary style[65].

2.7. From Hierarchical to Participatory Order

All forms of life, especially of human beings, have both individual and social dimensions[66]. Organisation is part of the social aspect of human life. Social order is unavoidable for a harmonious co-existence. One has to keep oneself within one's limits and not underrate the role of the other. Personal discipline is the foundation for order in the society. This is from an internal point of view. There has to be a mechanism for enforcing external discipline and ensuring arrangement[67]. There has to be certain hierarchical order in order to monitor such a mechanism. Accordingly, the Christian mission was undertaken by the hierarchical system established by the Catholic community. Although the members of the hierarchy are representatives of the entire community and they are at the service of the whole community, the members of the lay community that amount to more than 99 per cent can in no way be ignored. The Christian mission will be impoverished if it is monopolised by the hierarchy. The missionary mandate of living and sharing the values of Jesus is the duty of every Christian. Therefore, the active and full participation of the entire community is required for making the mission successful and effective as well as down-to-earth. The missionary activity has to be owned and participated by every member of the community[68]. The interaction and involvement of all members enriches the community and the mission as well. While recognising the great roles of the hierarchy, an open-ended and participatory approach to the missionary activity as well as administration has to be fostered[69]. Shared decisions and joint action with the lay persons is the social order that the catholic community has to pursue for the days that are ahead of us, especially in terms of the missionary concept and endeavour[70].

2.8. From Autocratic to Democratic Style of Leadership

To lead is to show the way. One who goes in front is the leader. A leader initiates a new process. He or she dares doing the right thing, especially when everyone else fails to do it. A leader is one who has the potential to start a new tradition. The degree of leadership in this sense may be more or less in persons. Every group requires someone to show the way. But, the leader should not tend to pretend that that is the only way and everyone has to follow it blindly. There are other dimensions of the way initiated by him or her. People of the community have the right to complement those aspects. Different people have diverse ideas and insights that are required for the wellbeing of the community[71]. Therefore, leaders cannot afford to be high-handed. The representative has no right to monopolise the entire show and dictate terms in the name of leadership. Autocratic ways would not bring lasting results as a rule. The spirit of equality and free flow of opinion are the signs of democracy[72]. The leader has to facilitate the emergence of grown up associates. Only self-governed partners can meaningfully interrelate and work together. Approach to the Christian mission needs to be revised in the light of the democratic principles of the Asian continent. One religious tradition has to allow and accommodate diversity of initiatives within it for facilitating the process of life in the respective community[73]. One religious tradition has not to monopolize the whole duty of leading the human society. Religious leadership is a process of facilitating the spiritual journey of the humans and that has to be done in a spirit of solidarity, shared responsibility and joint action with other religious traditions and non-religious and social ideologies[74]. The Christian mission has to further evolve towards such a democratic style everywhere, especially in the Asian context and more so in the Indian context.

2.9. From Paralleling to Networking Manner

Parallel lines do not meet. The two rails that form the track for the train to run its way are unaware of each other. The reason is because they are cut off from each other. To be unconnected from each other is to exist like islands[75]. To travel independent of each other is to travel like parallel lines. These tendencies are unsocial in character, especially among human beings and human institutions. Religion in principle is that which unites. But in practice we see that it unites only in a limited circle. On the whole, religious traditions seem to exist like islands[76]. Their missionary drives seem to progress like parallel lines. Some of them even tend to compete with each other. They slip into violations of the mutual courtesy lines. There are even instances of encroachment and aggression of the other because of over-enthusiasm and private interests. There are complaints of 'sheep-stealing' among religionists, too. Evidently, all these tendencies are aberrations of the real religious sentiment. Religion seems to be understood as if a private property of the respective groups[77]. The contents of the religions are complementary in nature and so religionists have to be inter-dependent. Networking is the catchphrase of the global worldview and modern life. Networking facilitates relatedness among communities. Networking with each other has to be the steering factor in religious traditions[78]. A 'spirit of togetherness' is the joint way forward for the partners of religious faiths[79]. Therefore, Christian mission has to be understood in a fashion that networks with other faith traditions in a spontaneous way.

2.10. From Static to Dialogical Mode and to Harmony of Faiths

A stagnant faith has no life in it. It is a dead one. It is no faith at all. The way one understands one's faith tradition has not to be a static one. Faith is a dynamic process. The way one lives one's religious values and shares with others also is a progressive reality. Religious mission is not distributing religious tenets in a capsule form[80]. It is not perpetuating a system of rituals and dogmas. It is essentially dialogical in its core dynamics. It is interactive, participatory, inclusive and dialogical. The dialogical process is geared towards the ultimate objective. The end result of life is 'harmonious living'[81]. Religious traditions have to ascend the ladder of mutual coordination and integration. They need to exchange their particular experiences of the divine as well as their specific insights. But this process of sharing is not an end in itself. It is oriented to harmony of faith traditions. Harmonious living together by faith communities is to be promoted. All faiths have to endeavour to attain this spiritual objective. The harmonious way is living in a spirit of togetherness. 'Harmony perspective of life' is the essence of religions and faiths[82]. The Christian mission has to broaden its perspective towards harmony of faiths. Such a universal outlook will add not only a new colour to its efforts but a new qualitative height in its human and spiritual dimensions[83].

3. FOSTERING HARMONY THROUGH DIALOGUE

3.1. The 'Harmony' Concept and Its Meaning

The word 'harmony' is from the art sector. It expresses itself the best in the world of music. The musical notes in play have to be based on a basic note. The melody, rhythm and tempo (*swar-taal-lay*) [84] between them have to be in right order. The singer, player and dancer have to be in perfect agreement with each other ('*Geetam vaadyam nrityam trayam sangeetamuchyate*') [85]. When these ingredients are in combination, there forms a musical effect of harmony. The Hindi word '*Samanvay*'[86] has two parts – '*anvay*'[87] (agreement, co-ordination, etc.) and '*sam*'[88] (on equal footing and totally).'Harmony' and '*Samanvay*' both together means 'integration, unity, balance[89], etc. Harmony is the vision and mission of life in the overall context. It is the spirit of life. It is the end result of life. The concept of harmony admits the pluralistic setting of life; it accepts the multi-disciplinary attitude to reality; and it lives the multi-dimensional perspective to religion. It pursues a holistic approach to the mission. Harmony celebrates a sense of completion and perfection in life. It has five steps, that are articulated by a five 'S' formula as *'panchsheel'* – *Sadbhaav* (good will), *Sambhaav* (equal footing), *Sammaan* (respect), *Sehyog* (co-operation) and *Samanvay* (harmony)[90]. The presence of these components in inter-personal and inter-community relations determines the quality of human life as well as its religious tuning. 'Harmony perspective of life' would mean seeing the entire life at a glance. The 'harmony' concept serves a solid foundation to a sound perspective of the mission[91].

3.2. The Dialogical Process

Dialogue is the social process through which harmony is attained. It means 'exchange of views or ideas between two or more'[92]. It would also mean interaction, friendly relations and cooperation between individuals and communities. It involves listening as well as speaking. It takes place on an equal footing and is open-ended. There is no superior or inferior in dialogue. The dialogical process refers to a 'non-dominating style of life'[93]. It implies 'being present to the other'. 'Getting related to the other' is the dynamics of mutual presence. In its deeper sense, dialogue means 'reflecting each other like a mirror'. Both parties in dialogue get an occasion to check one's human and spiritual fitness by looking at each other as if in a mirror. It is an opportunity to purify and enrich each other in all possible ways. The process of dialogue is 'walking together in life'[94]. It is also 'working together in life'[95]. It is 'making a joint pilgrimage to the same divine'[96]. Dialogue is a 'relational way of life'. It is being a brother, sister, friend, companion and co-passenger to persons of other affiliations of faith and ideology. Dialogical way would mean remaining connected to the other. It is a democratic attitude of living one's life. It is an exercise that is oriented to bridge-building between human beings and communities. Through dialogue, individuals and communities of different affiliations engage themselves in view of making a better society that is permeated by mutual understanding and fellowship. Dialogue is a shared way of life. The dialogical process initiates individuals and communities towards a network of harmonious living[97]. The style of life that suits the multi-dimensional plurality of Asia, and especially India, is the dialogical way. Only an inclusive, participatory, inter-active and dynamic way can adequately and effectively respond to the demands of the religious, cultural and other diversities of Asia and of India in special. Only a dialogical process of life can ensure the making of a better tomorrow that is characterised by the spirit of harmony in social life[98]. Christian mission, to be relevant for the times ahead, has to appropriate the dialogical way in its missionary approach[99].

3.3. The Harmony Model of Life 'One Body, Many Parts'

'One body, many parts', is a commonplace example. One of the leading authors of the Bible 'Paul' analyzes it and highlights the reality of 'essential relatedness among human beings' as well as the mystery of life[100]. The deeper implications of the reality from diverse angles speak volumes of the details of the harmony perspective of life. The parts of the body are different in their identity and are many in number. They perform different roles, but exist as one body. The different parts have equal duties and equal rights. All of them have their own singular importance and dignity, which is beyond the scope of being compared. One part cannot be replaced or suppressed by another. Joy or pain and achievement or failure of one part is shared and owned by all the parts. It is an 'existence in togetherness'. It is beauty in diversity and diversity in unity, at the same time. There cannot be a more powerful model for harmony among individuals and communities than the one under discussion[101]. This natural example of harmony invites the religious communities to endeavour for mutual appreciation, interaction and support that would ensure universal human solidarity and fellowship across all human-made limits[102]. Now the question is 'when is the Christian mission going to be re-fashioned after this natural, human and divine model that is universally intelligible, acceptable and applicable'?

3.4. Harmony Perspective of Life as a Higher Spirituality

'Harmony perspective of life' would mean networking the diversities of life[103]. It would mean accepting the universal values intrinsic to all faith traditions. It is surrendering to the eternal fact that the same Creator is the owner of all the resources of life, including the faith traditions. It would require considering them the shared property of the human race. It means thinking globally, nationally and regionally and acting locally at the same time. Harmony vision balances 'being rooted in one's tradition' and 'being creatively related to all other traditions'[104]. Harmony perspective of life is the real spirituality of life. Spirituality would mean 'being guided by the promptings of the Spirit'[105]. Spirit is like 'wind'. It blows when it pleases. Where it comes from and where it goes to cannot be predicted. Spirituality can never be identified with any particular religious tradition. Though persuasions of religion or faith are intended to facilitate spiritual experiences, they remain always on the way, on account of human limitations. Spirituality is not a ready-made product either. It is a dynamic and an ever-going process of life. Various spiritualities do not exist. The different religious traditions and social ideologies cannot claim to have independent spiritualities[106]. Only different dimensions of spirituality exist in the diverse religious traditions and worldviews. Spirituality, in the real sense of the word, is only one and it is beyond the reach of all individual perspectives and individual faith traditions. Those who are enslaved to the religious practices of their own traditions are bound to be deprived of being spiritual. One has to rise above the boundaries of one's religious beliefs, cultural affiliations, ethnic belongings and ideological leanings[107]. Harmony perspective of life initiates one to have a holistic glance at life and enables one to start one's spiritual journey in life. Fostering harmony among social, cultural and religious streams of life is the sublime mission that ensures the attainment of higher spiritual sensibilities[108]. Harmony perspective of life is a higher spirituality, as religious and non-religious traditions are spiritual initiatives and processes[109]. This was the lofty value of Jesus and the Christian mission has to imbibe this spiritual sense from him, in order to rise beyond the human-made boundaries, in view of decisively responding to the demands of the times[110].

4. MISSION AS PROMOTING HARMONY IN SOCIAL LIFE

4.1. Mission as Making a More Harmonious Society

There is an inner harmony that the Creator has bestowed on the whole creation. The human world has in it the spirit of that inalienable harmony of life. Negative energies and forces imbedded in the limitations of the creation and of the human beings disrupt the equilibrium of that harmony. Because disharmony is being created by the mutual friction of the human and natural units, the process of maintaining harmony has to actively go on. Promoting harmony in the diverse aspects of social life has to be the regular and sustained effort of human organisations, especially religious traditions[111]. Religious traditions are for human beings and not vice versa. They have to be at the service of the human society. 'Religion has to be what God intended it to be, a source of goodness, harmony and peace', observes Pope John Paul II[112]. Religion by its very nature has to foster harmony and peace. 'Making a more harmonious society' is the sublime work of the faith traditions at large. All human organisations, both collectively and individually, have to be involved in promoting harmony in social life. Christian mission is basically oriented to the wellbeing of the human society[113]. All the same, it is yet to emerge from its religion-centred missionary drive to the broader objective of making a more harmonious society. It has to permeate into the diverse areas of the society with a new style of leadership by way of facilitating harmonious and peaceful living[114].

4.2. Mission as Facilitating Collaboration with Other Faith-Based Organisations

Being firmly founded on the as above-mentioned common motto of all faith-based individuals, organisations and communities, sustained efforts are to be initiated for ensuring harmony in social life in the respective area of their operation. The goal of social harmony cannot be achieved single-handedly. Facilitating faith-based organisations to collaborate towards such a social orientation justifies the very relevance of faith in life[115]. Faith-based organisations have to be connected and networked with each other for guiding the destinies of the increasingly globalising society of today[116]. One has to get creatively related to other perceptions and communities of faith while remaining rooted in one's own[117]. Joining hands with other faith communities in order to foster harmony in social life is the grown up way of living one's faith. That justifies the relevance and utility of faith for the days and years to come. The Christian mission in particular has to strive towards such networking and collaborative style of promoting the values of Jesus.

4.3. Mission as Collaboration with the Civil Society

Religious outlook to life is only one of the two outlooks in life, the other being the non-religious perspective. The non-religious way of looking at life includes scientists, persons pursuing secular ideologies, persons who have lost faith in religious ideologies, and the like. Fostering harmony in the society is not the monopoly of the religious sector. The non-religious sector has to be honourably kept involved in the above process[118]. Moreover, there are lay persons who may be affiliated to some religious tradition or other but aren't directly involved with religion. They belong to all walks of life. The civil society includes people of diverse sectors and professions. They form the largest majority of the society. Among them are administrators, educationists, industrialists, businessmen, medical doctors, social activists and people of other service sections[119]. They also have a legitimate share in the making of the society. Since they are fully integrated in the details of social life in one way or other, they have a greater capacity to contribute towards the making of a harmonious society. Therefore, religionists should not attempt to go alone in leading the society towards a better tomorrow. They have to collaborate with the civil society in all details in the mission of promoting harmony in social life[120]. The Christian mission has to put in extra effort in making lay persons of the Christian community and people of the civil society active collaborators and leaders in advancing the missionary front.

4.4. Mission as Participating in the Administrative Process

The governmental machinery or administrative system is an unavoidable necessity in social life. Its duty is to maintain law and order or rule of law in the society. Its role is to facilitate the smooth flow of life. It has to ensure equitable distribution of resources and opportunities. It has to measure out justice to all. It has to think and legislate for the development and progress of the country. Whatever is the political system, inherited, autocratic or democratic, the concentration of power and resources can make the system self-centred. The system can slip in to mere governing and administering in terms of the benefits of the elected or selected functionaries. Therefore, faith-based organisations, the secular society, the elite, and the like have to keep negotiating with the governmental and administrative machinery from top to bottom[121]. Irresponsible ways of the elected representatives are to be challenged. Creative suggestions are to be provided to them. Making sure that the above system functions well is the duty of the citizens. Therefore, their active participation is unavoidable. Faith-based organisations, social activists, experts, scholars, and the like have to perform their responsibility of remaining involved in the administrative process. They have to assist the government and administrators at different levels to effectively perform their duties[122]. Faith-based organisations have to be networked for this purpose[122]. The Christian mission has to consolidate its human resources at all levels to interact with the administrative process of the respective country for promoting harmonious co-existence of peoples, of course motivated by the faith-based values[124].

4.5. Mission as Launching Forums for Promoting Harmony

'Harmony Forums' are to be launched for promoting harmony in social life. Well-meaning persons from all ethnic, linguistic, ideological and cultural communities and walks of life as well as faith-based organisations need to organise themselves into a task force. The coming together of leaders of religions and communities will certainly motivate the general public of the respective groups to come together[125]. Harmony Forums have to be comprised of persons from both governmental and non-governmental sectors. With persons committed to harmony in social life as members, the Forum can pioneer a new leadership for checking the anti-social behaviour of pathological individuals and organisations that are active in the society[126]. The Forum can play as a check on the administrative system for the effective implementation of people-oriented schemes. Harmony Forums need to be launched at different levels – city/town/village, *tehsil*, district, state and country. A team of co-coordinators could be elected for guiding the destinies of the activities of the Forum. The Forum shall have a plan of action for the respective levels, both on a short-term and a long-term basis. The Forum could collaborate with the government in emergency situations of communal disturbance, natural calamity[127], etc. On-going schemes for sensitising the public and mobilising goodwill have to be chalked out as well. These Harmony Forums could certainly contribute immensely to making the society more harmonious[128]. Could the Christian mission be launching such 'Harmony Forums' as a new missionary style? Could it conceive its discipleship to the great Master Jesus in such a radical fashion? Could it explore the details of living the missionary mandate in such a deep commitment to the fellow human beings, beyond all the human-made boundaries? Could it be 'role model' of a 'new paradigm of mission' that is permeated by a 'sublime culture' of 'the humans living together in harmony in a spiritual way'? [129] Could the Christian mission shoulder such new leadership of facilitating 'harmonizing forums' that live together, work together and journey together to the divine harmoniously, like the river that flows towards the ocean in a serene way?[130] Asia and India are jointly searching for the answers for such challenging as well as fundamental questions!

CONCLUSION

Life is an ever-evolving process of becoming human. Making better human beings and making them rightly oriented towards the ultimate end of life is the role of religion in the overall context. Religious traditions are intended to facilitate human beings to travel the journey of being spiritual. Fostering a humane spirit and thus contributing to making a better society summarises the task of religious traditions. The divine creative power is made alive again in such an approach to life. Religion and religious mission has to be reorganised in terms of social transformation and betterment of life. 'To be spiritual' is to be interactive with all religious streams and social affiliations. 'To be human' is to imbibe the universal spiritual values from all streams of faiths and ideologies. 'A spirit of togetherness' with all religious traditions and social ideologies is the core of the human civilisation that is infused by the divine. Facilitating the humans in the march 'towards a more harmonious society' is the shared mission of all individuals, traditions and communities on this planet. Such a composite culture is the heaven the humans are aspiring for attaining. Christian mission, especially in the light of the Second Vatican Council and that of the deeper realisations of the values and mission of Jesus, has to be transformed, revised, renewed and broadened in terms of 'promoting harmony in social life'. The 21st century is awaiting such a concept and style of the Christian mission, in view of finding itself relevant, meaningful, effective and worth-attempting as well as of doing justice to the ever-new good news of Jesus.

Endnotes

1. Francis, A. Sullivan, Salvation outside the Church: Tracing the History of the Catholic Response, Eugene, 2002, p. 02
2. *Ibid,* p. 23
3. *Ibid,* p. 149
4. *Ibid,* p. 58
5. *Ibid,* p. 63
6. *Ibid,* p. 93
7. *Ibid,* p. 107
8. Dana, L. Robert, Christian Mission: How Christianity Became a World Religion, New Jersey, 2011, p. 157
9. Angus Stevenson (Ed.), Oxford Dictionary of English, Oxford, 2010, p. 1133
10. Dana, L. Robert, Christian Mission: How Christianity Became a World Religion, New Jersey, 2011, p. 29
11. The Holy Bible, NIV, Michigan, 1994, Mt 25.40, p. 1128
12. *Ibid,* Mk 2.27, p. 1138
13. *Ibid,* Jn 15.12, p. 1228
14. *Ibid,* Mt 5.43, p. 1099
15. *Ibid,* Mt 7.12, p. 1100
16. *Ibid,* Mt 22.39, p. 1122
17. *Ibid,* Mt 5.45,48, p. 1099
18. *Ibid,* Mt 25.40, p. 1128
19. *Ibid,* I Cor 12.12-28, p. 1306
20. *Ibid,* Rom 12.10, p. 1291
21. Pat F. Rossi, Discourse in Dialogue: Reflections in Fundamental Philosophical Theology, Newcastle upon Tyne, United Kingdom, 2014, p. 94
22. *Ibid,* p. 96
23. Suhas Pereira, The Challenges of Vatican II for an Authentic Indian Catholic Church, Zurich, 2020, p. 194
24. *Ibid,* p. 74
25. Thomas Cahill, Pope John XXIII: A Life, London, 2002, p. 79
26. Claudia Carlen, The Papal Encyclicals: 1958-1981, vol.5, Ypsilanti, Michigan, 1990, p. 191
27. George Weigel, Witness to Hope: The Biography of Pope John Paul II, New York, 2005, p. 417

28. *Ibid,* 619
29. *Ibid,* p. 714
30. Anthony Cirelli and Pim Valkenberg (Ed.), Nostra Aetate: Celebrating Fifty Years of the Catholic Church's Dialogue with Jews and Muslims, Washington, D.C., 2016, p. 242
31. Michael Walsh, Roman Catholicism: The Basics, London, 2005, p. 17
32. *Ibid,* p. 16
33. *Ibid,* p. 19
34. *Ibid,* p. 23
35. *Ibid,* p. 109
36. Dana, L. Robert, Christian Mission: How Christianity Became a World Religion, New Jersey, 2011, p. 57
37. Maria Hornung, Encountering Other Faiths, New Jersey, 2008, p. 57
38. *Ibid,* p. 73
39. *Ibid,* p. 107
40. Anthony Cirelli, Pim Valkenberg (Ed.), Nostra Aetate: Celebrating Fifty Years of the Catholic Church's Dialogue with Jews and Muslims, Washington, D.C., 2016, p. 309
41. Wesley, J. Wildman, Religious Philosophy as Multidisciplinary Comparative Inquiry: Envisioning a Future for the Philosophy of Religion, New York, 2010, p. 30
42. *Ibid,* p. 37
43. *Ibid,* p. 53
44. *Ibid,* p. 107
45. *Ibid,* p. 113
46. *Ibid,* p. 158
47. *Ibid,* p. 159
48. Michael Amaladoss, Interreligious Encounters: Opportunities and Challenges, New York, 2017, p. 23
49. *Ibid,* p. 57
50. *Ibid,* p. 58
51. *Ibid,* p. 103
52. Anshuman, A. Mondal, Faith and Secularism, London, 2004, p. 13
53. *Ibid,* p. 24
54. *Ibid,* p. 53
55. *Ibid,* p. 57
56. *Ibid,* p. 63
57. Gavin Flood, Religion and the Philosophy of Life, Oxford, 2019, p. 23
58. *Ibid,* p. 53
59. *Ibid,* p. 103
60. Dana, L. Robert, Christian Mission: How Christianity Became a World Religion, New Jersey, 2011, p. 160
61. Gavin Flood, Religion and the Philosophy of Life, Oxford, 2019, p. 157
62. Maria Hornung, Encountering Other Faiths, New Jersey, 2008, p. 109
63. *Ibid,* p. 123
64. *Ibid,* p. 158
65. *Ibid,* p. 253
66. Gavin Flood, Religion and the Philosophy of Life, Oxford, 2019, p. 109
67. *Ibid,* p. 63
68. *Ibid,* p. 93
69. *Ibid,* p. 113
70. *Ibid,* p. 207
71. Anshuman, A. Mondal, Faith and Secularism, London, 2004, p. 53

72. *Ibid,* p. 63
73. *Ibid,* p. 93
74. *Ibid,* p. 95
75. Thomas, G. Plante, Religion, Spirituality, and Positive Psychology: Understanding the Psychological Fruits of Faith, Oxford, 2012, p. 23
76. *Ibid,* p. 53
77. *Ibid,* p. 63
78. *Ibid,* p. 107
79. *Ibid,* p. 1123
80. Michael Amaladoss, Interreligious Encounters: Opportunities and Challenges, New York, 2017, p. 33
81. *Ibid,* p. 53
82. Maria Hornung, Encountering Other Faiths, New Jersey, 2008, p. 127
83. *Ibid,* p. 129
84. Ashok Damodar Ranade, Perspectives on Music: Ideas and Theories, New Delhi, 2008, p. 11
85. *Ibid,* p. 17
86. Anindita, N. Balslev, On World Religions: Diversity, Not Dissension, New Delhi, 2014, p. 27
87. *Ibid,* p. 28
88. *Ibid,* p. 35
89. *Ibid,* p. 53
90. *Ibid,* p. 107
91. Maria Hornung, Encountering Other Faiths, New Jersey, 2008, p. 111
92. Angus Stevenson (Ed.), Oxford Dictionary of English, Oxford, 2010, p. 483
93. Simon Mary Asese A. Aihiokhai, Fostering Interreligious Encounters in Pluralist Societies: Hospitality and Friendship, London, 2019, p. 36
94. *Ibid,* p. 53
95. *Ibid,* p. 57
96. *Ibid,* p. 58
97. Anindita, N. Balslev, On World Religions: Diversity, Not Dissension, New Delhi, 2014, p. 108
98. Simon Mary Asese, A. Aihiokhai, Fostering Interreligious Encounters in Pluralist Societies: Hospitality and Friendship, London, 2019, p. 53
99. *Ibid,* p. 73
100. The Holy Bible, NIV, Michigan, 1994, 1 Cor. 12.12-28, pp. 1306-07
101. Maria Hornung, Encountering Other Faiths, New Jersey, 2008, p. 207
102. *Ibid,* p. 209
103. Eknath Easwaran, Your Life Is Your Message: Finding Harmony with Yourself, Others and the Earth, California, 2020, p. 27
104. *Ibid,* p. 29
105. *Ibid,* p. 33
106. *Ibid,* p. 35
107. *Ibid,* p. 39
108. *Ibid,* p. 47
109. Simon Mary Asese, A. Aihiokhai, Fostering Interreligious Encounters in Pluralist Societies: Hospitality and Friendship, London, 2019, p. 189
110. *Ibid,* p. 203
111. J. A. Scott Kelso, Learning to Live Together: Promoting Social Harmony, London, 2019, p. 33

112. George Weigel, Witness to Hope: The Biography of Pope John Paul II, New York, 2005, p. 203
113. Dana, L. Robert, Christian Mission: How Christianity Became a World Religion, New Jersey, 2011, p. 207
114. *Ibid,* p. 263
115. Maria Hornung, Encountering Other Faiths, New Jersey, 2008, p. 119
116. *Ibid,* p. 123
117. *Ibid,* p. 237
118. David Cortright, Laurel Stone and Melanie Greenberg (Ed.), Civil Society, Peace, and Power, London , 2016, p. 36
119. *Ibid,* p. 103
120. *Ibid,* p. 127
121. *Ibid,* p. 153
122. *Ibid,* p. 186
123. *Ibid,* p. 187
124. Simon Mary Asese, A. Aihiokhai, Fostering Interreligious Encounters in Pluralist Societies: Hospitality and Friendship, London, 2019, p. 203
125. Maria Hornung, Encountering Other Faiths, New Jersey, 2008, p. 203
126. *Ibid,* p. 207
127. *Ibid,* p. 211
128. *Ibid,* p. 212
129. *Ibid,* p. 223
130. *Ibid,* p. 230

Chapter - 2

Religious Harmony in the Asian Context

Introduction

Diversity is the hallmark of the entire creation, the human society in particular. Asia as a continent in general and India as a country in particular have the characteristic of diversity in an intense and elaborate form. The traits of being many and different, while are enriching on one hand, causes serious challenges in peaceful co-existence on the other. They require being addressed. This state of affairs calls for religion and faith to be interpreted and understood in an inclusive and larger way. The social utility of religion and faith has to be considered first and foremost. The foundations of harmonious living have to be strengthened. This essay discusses this concern under five titles, such as 'diversities in Asia, combating the challenges of the Asian context, exploring the larger implications of religion, advancing harmony among religions and broadening the foundations of harmonious living'.

1. DIVERSITIES IN ASIA

1.1. The Diversities of the Creation

The genius of the Creator is reflected characteristically in the diversities of life[1]. The entire creation witnesses to the immense aspects of this diversity. The galaxy of planets rotates around the sun in a faultless system. The sun during the day and the moon during the night add life and colour to human, animal and plant existence. The world of vegetation is in fact alluring. The flowers with diverse colours, shapes, sizes and fragrances fill the hearts of everyone. The mountains, the valleys, the trees, the plants, the rivers, the rains and the rainbow furnish an experience that is beyond the capacity of language to articulate. The world of animals brings thrill and support to human life. The world of human beings with its unlimited diversities of gender, ethnicity, language, ideology, food habit, dress pattern, profession, social customs and mores, religious traditions and cultures is indeed enchanting and mesmerizing[2]. They are numerous and are beyond the scope of being compared with another, even the item of the same species. One requires a poetical and aesthetic mind in order to discern, experience and enjoy the singular beauty in diversity. Every item in the creation in particular and the creation as a whole is a well-expressed proof for the amazing intelligence of the Creator[31]. The basic spirit of religion and faith present in the natural world of creation is the foundation for the spirituality the faith traditions claim to promote among human beings[3]. The missionary drive has to be well-situated in the context of the unlimited diversities.

1.2. The Interaction of Diversities in the Wave of Globalisation

The new wave of globalisation is a many-sided phenomenon with regard to its causes, effects and dimensions[4]. It has brought incredible achievements to the human civilisation and has to be considered a major blessing to the modern world. The world human society has become a global family. Information and technological know-how have developed and extended significantly. Geographical distances have reduced and travels far and wide have become very frequent. Market policies have been liberalised. Opportunities for social interaction and progress increased profusely. Networking with the other has become the catchphrase of the day. Any individual or community that dares to exist like islands or travel like parallel lines stands doomed to perish. Mutual connectedness, collaboration and integration are the basic ingredients of a meaningful human life as well as of the advancement of human culture today[5]. But, the phenomenon of globalisation is double-sided in its force. The spirit of nearness that made the entire world a cosmic village has become a spontaneous inclination, on the one hand. On the other hand, the wave of interaction has been forced upon everyone by the pressure of the situation. In either case, the realisation of having common elements in one another as regards language, ideology, tradition, faith and culture cannot be escaped from. Recognition of this factor fosters deeper interaction and harmony. The particular characteristics present in each of them drags them into an uneasy feeling, too. All the same, the dynamics of the phenomenon of closer interaction between cultural streams leave the partners in the battle field to explore the details of their individual and collective destiny, especially as regards one's faith and mission[6].

1.3. Multi-Cultural and Multi-Religious Context of Asia

Asia is the largest continent of the world. This is the most populated continent of the world, too. It hosts approximately two-thirds of the world population. It has a huge range of governmental systems, environments, regions, civilisations and peoples. Asian continent is unique in its characteristics in the entire landscape of the world. The immense dimensions of the social climate of the continent highlight the reality of human life that is significantly different from the rest of the continents. Diversity is the hallmark of the social fabric of Asia[7]. There are multifarious streams of cultures and religious traditions, in addition to the geographical, climatic, ethnic, racial, linguistic, professional, ideological, political and caste-class diversities[8]. A spirit of complementariness and mutual enrichment is the principle that can balance these differences in a harmonious way. Asian continent is greatly pluralistic. It has been the cradle of almost all the major religious traditions of the world[9]. Asia has perhaps the highest number of languages compared to those in other continents put together. Spiritual and aesthetic perspective of life as well as enormous dimensions of artistic expressions gives the continent a character that is its own. The Christian mission, though it emerged in the Asian soil, was articulated and developed in the western cultural setting[10]. It needs to be re-understood and re-interpreted right in the genius of the Asian purview. Despite the fact that lot of initiatives have been taken so far, much remains yet to be done.

1.4. The Indian Context of Pluralities

The characteristic of diversity that is true of Asia applies to India in an enlarged and multiplied manner. Indian subcontinent is a large section of the Asian continent. India could rightly be called the most pluralistic country in the world. *'Vividhtaa mein Ektaa'*[11], i.e., unity in diversity, is the catchword of the country. *'Vasudhaiv Kutumbakam'*[12] i.e., earth is one family, is its spirit. The Constitution of India can be stated as one of the best constitutions of the world[13]. 'Secular perspective of life' is its core message. The family and community values lived in India are well-acclaimed. There is wide range of diversity in ethnic traits, geographical conditions, climatic changes, ideologies, religious persuasions, artistic traditions, spiritual approaches, social customs, languages and dialects, political systems, economic situations, races, classes, castes, food habits, dress patters, cultures and value systems in India[14]. India stands out in the global context for the incalculable degrees and dimensions of plurality in social life. India is the only country in the world that has seventeen languages on its currency, not to mention the thousands of dialects[15]. The classical and folk traditions of dance and music are a regular festivity of its own right. India has been hosting the highest number of major and minor religious traditions since millennia[16]. Hindu, Buddhist, Jain and Sikh religious traditions emerged from India itself. Jewish, Zoroastrian, Christian, Muslim and Baha'i faith traditions came from outside. Many tribal and primitive forms of faith prevailed in India from time immemorial. India has evolved new faith traditions, like *Kabeer Panth*, *Ram Krishna Mission*, *Sai Baba Sect*, *Osho community*, *Nirankari sect*, *ISCON sect, Radha Swami, Brahmo Samaj, Brahma Kumari* group, Theosophical Society, *Swami Narayan Sect*, etc. *Satya Sai Baba, Ravi Shankar, Amritandamai* and others have initiated new streams of religious thought, too[17]. The foundational concepts of the country, such as 'unity in diversity' and 'global family spirit' thus become more articulate as time passes. The national moral fibre comes from the unique Constitution of the country and its secular perspective. Such multi-faceted differences in the country could be compared to a large garden of diverse flowers with a singular fragrance. To be a missionary in such an unparalleled country can in no way be founded on the carbon copy of imported themes[18]. A new concept, a new model and a new style is to be improvised and lived.

1.5. Complementariness of Diversity in Difference and Number

Obviously, diversity is the greatest characteristic the Creator has bestowed upon the creation. It has two intrinsic characteristics – being many and being different[19]. Being many refers to the numerical strength and is the direct outcome of the creative power of multiplying. Being different from the other is basic to all forms of existence. Only factory-produced goods can be uniform and they have no life in them. Being similar also admits difference in it. Both these characteristics apply to human beings in a special way and to other living beings and plants in a general way. The various living items in the nature are different from one another in shape, size, beauty, taste, fragrance, function, and the like. One plant is different from another plant. An animal is different from a human being. One species of animal is different from another species. Male is different from female. Human individuals and groups are different from one another in their ethnic traits, linguistic expressions, professional inclinations, cultural characteristics, ideological affiliations, social customs and mores, religious perspectives, life values, etc. Even identical twins have many differences. Difference in number as well as in quality makes diversity sensible[20]. They do not contradict each other in any respect. They are complementary to each other. Like a rainbow, they radiate a unique beauty in a spirit of togetherness. Thus, the diversity of number and difference is harmonised in a spirit of complementariness[21]. Such a characteristic vision and reality of existence of the human society in Asia and especially India persistently invite the missioner towards realising a superior concept and style of living and performing the Christian mission.

2. COMBATTING THE CHALLENGES OF THE ASIAN CONTEXT

2.1. The Challenges of Globalisation

The negative side of the phenomenon of globalisation poses many major challenges to human existence. It draws one's attention to certain distasteful consequences. There is no denying the fact that coming in contact with each other benefit individuals and communities of different languages, ideologies, traditions, faiths and cultures in terms of common interests. At the same time, the particular characteristics in them unsettle or threaten one another. The very interaction of diversities causes a sense of insecurity, especially in smaller entities[22]. The aspiration for self-fulfilment, the pursuit of excellence, individual success, etc. seem to end up in an attitude of competition, rivalry, communal distancing and aggressive ways. Political equations and commercial concerns contribute to multi-national enterprises. Individualistic considerations motivate coming closer to the other, all the more. But, encounters, conflicts, tensions and turmoil, in major or minor forms, is the upshot. Multi-nationals, majority communities, industrial pockets and political outfits start ruthlessly to rule over the society[23]. Smaller concerns, minority communities and weaker sections feel endangered and run the risk of being annihilated or pushed aside to the margins of the society. The selfishness and arrogance of the former causes in the latter a major crisis of identity and the consequent assertion of identity[24]. The religious sector is not unaffected of the dreadful situation. It has also aggravated the predicament. Such polarised standpoints cause confusion and unrest in the society. The chain of challenges posed by the mighty phenomenon of globalisation is to be addressed by honest, sustained and effective efforts for healthy interaction and mutually beneficial measures[25]. Only then, the alarming side-effects of globalisation can be countered. Christian mission has to consider this dilemma as a matter of serious concern. Christian mission have in order to improvise measures to combat this phenomenon[26]. In the wake of the impending tragedies, it has to re-understand its missionary drive.

2.2. Challenges of Communal Tensions and Atrocities

The social graph of the continent and the country is very much stained with wars, conflicts and violence in the name of caste, creed, tongue, ideology, etc[27]. This fact seems to defy the cultural fabric of both Asia and India. Because of the surrounding diversities, lots of people tend to lose their footing and start feeling anxious. And two types of reactions follow.

Some withdraw to their own shells as fundamentalists and communalists and others become fanatics and indulge in violence or terrorism[28]. One gets forcibly enslaved to a secluded world and the other tends to dominate over others by crook or hook. Both are barefaced pathological cases and have to be not only regretted but treated. But the latter create great havoc in the society through communal atrocities, riots and other tensions. The brutal atrocities perpetrated against the Christian community in Orissa in 2007 and 2008 and in other parts of the country in the last decade, the massive violence against the Muslim community in Gujarat in 2002 and the mindless massacre of the Sikh community in 1986 are striking examples of a pathological mindset in the Indian sub-continent[29]. History has it that similar instances take place in different parts of the continent in the name of nationality, regionalism, language, creed, caste, etc. Obviously, the carnage and vandalising terrorism have been orchestrated by certain misguided fundamentalist forces[30]. The colossal devastation of lives and properties and the consequent incalculable suffering, damage and shame are beyond all imagination. Threat from extremism, terrorism and aggressive ways appears to be a regular challenge. The militant masterminds behind the tragedies smack of a basic disorientation in life. The divisive tactics applied by them foretell an impending peril for the country, the continent and for the human society, too. Challenges to the celebrated cultural ethos of Asia and India seem to be steadily becoming intricate[31]. The communal tensions and atrocities present a clarion call before well-meaning citizens and human beings across all affiliations to rise, to gather and to join hands with a collective mission of combating the negative forces that are bent on breaking the life-web of the humans in the country and in the continent in to pieces[32]. Christian mission has to get awakened to these tragedies of the society. It cannot afford to evade the issue and proceed with a purely religion-centred missionary drive of saving souls[33]. It has to give an answer that can guide the destinies of combating the above foe.

2.3. The Dire Need of Cultural Integration

It is often a question of wonder how the multi-faceted diversities in Asia and especially in India stick together. This question seems to become a matter of deep concern in the milieu of the increasingly hostile challenges. There is a dire need to delve deep into the drastic implications of the black-lettered records in the annals of the continent and the country. The communal tragedies and other social maladies that have taken place need to be analysed and lessons need to be learned from[34]. First and foremost, the deplorable anti-social instances and tendencies are a sheer assault on a large number of individuals and organisations of all religious persuasions that pioneer honest efforts for promoting harmony among communities of all faiths and ideologies. Violation of other communities and breaking the courtesy line between the two has to be ended. The display of the unabashed audacity of majority communities and powerful bodies to attempt subjugating the minority communities and weaker groups to a second-class level requires to be arrested[35]. Desecration of the spiritual traditions and cultural values of the nation and the continent has to be stopped. Shattering of the secular and democratic fabric of the Asian continental and Indian national ethos has no longer to be tolerated[36]. Defiance of the Constitution of the country and its provisions, especially those of freedom of conscience, religion and equality, has to be dealt with strongly. Universal fundamental human rights as ensured by the UN Declaration have not to be violated any more[37]. Committing grave crimes against humanity like genocide should receive exemplary punishment or retributive restoration[38]. In order to uphold the social equilibrium by maintaining law and order in the society, sustained measures for cultural integration have to be monitored. Sincere effort for integration at the continental and national levels is the right responsive measure. The above problems, needs and aspirations of the Asian and Indian societies are very much dissimilar to other areas of the world. The challenges posed by the religious, ideological, regional and cultural plurality are beyond the scope of comparison, too. Therefore, being a member of the Asian society or being a citizen of the Indian nationality or being a member of the Christian mission is not the same as being so elsewhere[39]. To be a Christian or a Catholic and to be a missionary in Asia or in India has to be much different, in order to be relevant and effective[40]. From this angle, Christian mission requires a qualitative difference in its understanding and approach.

3. EXPLORING THE LARGER IMPLICATIONS OF RELIGION

3.1. The Words 'Religion' and '*Dharma*'

Religion derives from the Latin word *'ligare'*[41], which would mean 'to bind' or 'to connect'. *'Re-ligare'*, along with the prefix 're' that stand for 'again', would mean 'to connect/bind again' or 'to re-connect/re-bind' or 'to tie fast'[42]. Religion implies 'getting related' to the Supreme Power and to one another. With its two-dimensional relation, religion becomes an integral part of human life. 'Faith', though broader and simpler in its connotations, is a synonym for 'religion' in many of its dimensions. The Sanskrit word '*dharma*' means '*dhaaran karna*', which would mean 'to receive', 'to own', 'to feel responsible for', 'to feel bound', etc[43]. '*Dharma*' implies 'feeling bound by duty towards one's conscience or the divine power' and 'feeling responsible for one's life and that of others'. *'Dharma'* means 'duty', 'conscience' and 'nature', too. The *'nishkaam karma'*[44] advocated in *Bhagvat Gita* has direct bearing on the meaning of '*dharma*'. While following the whisperings of one's conscience is *dharma*, fulfilling one's responsibly towards others in diverse capacities is dharma, as well. Both words 'Religion and *Dharma*', in the general sense of the words, is a set of ideas, stories, symbols, beliefs and practices. They have often reference to a supernatural power. They can be theistic or atheistic in its basic position. Theistic standpoint also could accommodate monotheistic, tri-theistic, polytheistic, pantheistic and other combinations. At any rate, the perspectives and experiences of the practitioners of religion or dharma are geared towards attaining spiritual quality. Religion or *dharma* has emerged into such a large and complex system, and human beings by and large seem to be associated to it[45]. It appears that absorbing the essential meanings of the words 'religion', *'dharma'* and 'faith' and shedding the heavy load of the theological abstractions will help the Christian mission to be simpler and realistic.

3.2. Stages or Levels of Religion

Religion is a journey of life. It has five stages or levels, in line with the various observances and commitments. They could be understood as different rungs on the ladder of religion. The first from the bottom is 'Rituals'[46]. Rituals are sets of actions, often thought to have symbolic value. The second is 'Stories, Myths and Legends'[47]. They are ancient stories about gods and goddesses or fantastic adventures of heroes. They could be folk tales of ancestors intended to bind people together and are part of the collective consciousness of the people. The third is 'Doctrine-Dogma and Administration'[48]. Opinion or doctrine gets accepted as dogma and become a system of principles or tenets. Administration defends and contextualises them. The fourth is 'Spiritual experiences' or 'Religious experiences' that are known as sacred or mystical experiences[49]. They get altered into a state of consciousness that is the peak experience. The fifth and the final rung of the ladder of religion is 'Good behaviour'[50]. This is the result of all the four stages of religion. The focus of good behaviour is other human beings who are its beneficiaries. That is the proof of the utility of the observances of religion or dharma at different levels. To be religiously inclined in life would mean unceasingly to climb the rungs of the ladder of religion in order to arrive at the peak experience and its sublime result in life. Christian mission has to focus on the higher levels of religion and dwell on the final one in terms of making men and women 'humane' and 'more spiritual', even though 'less religious' may be[51].

3.3. Balancing the Specific and Common Elements in Religions

As human being has individual and social dimensions, so every religious system has both individual and social dimensions[52]. They are like two sides of the same coin and are complementary to each other. The individual aspect of religion is clear from the fact that the religious streams have originated from different sources – from different geographical areas, different times of history, different social backgrounds and different cultural settings[53]. The great men or women who were mediators of divine promptings were of dissimilar character. The quality of personal experiences and spiritual accomplishments of the seers and sages were beyond the scope of being compared with that of others. The contexts in which they had their earthly being were different, too. The human and spiritual values they upheld were unalike with that of others. The vision and mission of their lives characterised the genius of the respective religious tradition. Accordingly, each religious tradition developed its own specific traits. The matchless individual moral fibre present in each of them needs to be accepted and mutually benefited from. The specificity of each religious tradition, as reflected in its world view, perception, interpretations, regulations and practices, are sacrosanct and is not to be violated[54]. All these traditions have a role to play in the design of the Creator. All the same, the religious, social and cultural traditions have, at a wide spectrum, a common source and a common origin. That is their social aspect. They have a common existence or have a shared platform to exist[55]. They have a common destiny and destination to reach, as well. There have a large range of experiences that are similar to each other. They have a common ground to meet and a common search to make. They have to travel the path of life together and make a joint pilgrimage to the same source of life, the Creator. Religious traditions should be in creative interaction and fellowship with other religious affiliations[56]. There are various universal values that are present in all religious traditions that are capable of making human beings more humane and spiritual. The similarity in the symbols, theories and practices are to be further searched for[57]. There are elements of irreligion that all religious systems have and they need to be eliminated. The commonalities of the religious traditions facilitate the making of a well-knit country and a prosperous human society[58]. Christian mission has to foster building bridges between the religious traditions and reconcile their claims.

3.4. Religion as the Foundational Factor in Life

Bernard Shaw, a world genius thinker, observed "If you really want to do anything in life, you should have a religion"[59]. Manifestly, he does not advocate subscribing to a complex system of beliefs or doctrines and of performing a set of rituals. He intends to emphasise the fact that 'religion is the motivating factor in life'; 'religion is the source of strength for living one's life' and 'religion is that reality which gives meaning to life'[60].Religion is the sum and substance of one's experiences, attitudes and approaches. The way one thinks, speaks and behaves is religion. It is the foundational factor for one's life-commitments. One's vision and mission of life are grounded on religion or faith. Faith is the powerhouse of one's life[61]. Such a perspective of 'religion' articulates its deeper implications. It goes beyond the limits of all theistic-atheistic and denominational affiliations. It includes all individuals and communities of the human society. In this sense, religion or faith is fundamental to human existence. Besides, faith is the reality that keeps one rooted in the Creative Power. 'Being rooted' has both vertical and horizontal facets[62]. The main root of the tree goes vertically deep into the soil of the earth and the other roots horizontally. Accordingly, faith in the essentials of one's tradition is the vertical face and faith in the essentials of other traditions is the horizontal face[63]. The former is the primary element in faith and the latter is the secondary. But, being rooted in one's own tradition necessarily means being related to that of the other. Both together form the foundation of life. The Christian mission has to be revised so that it may delve deeper into the essentials of faith according to Jesus and at the same time emerge with an integrated perspective of all faiths, in order to attain a holistic grasp of life[64].

3.5. From Individual Identities to Shared Identities and even Beyond Identities

Human identity has three dimensions – individual identity, social identity and identity beyond identity[65]. 'Individual identity' is one's identity as an individual. Identity is basic to any form of existence and is one that cannot be shared with or substituted by anyone. Being conscious of that identity is the privilege of the humans. Being aware of one's interests, aspirations, accomplishments, gender, language, religion, ideology, social affiliation, cultural heritage, nationality, etc. is not only innate but is essential for any human life[66]. 'Social identity' is one's identity by virtue of one's social character. Every human being, in addition to his or her individual identity, has an identity that is common with others. That is his or her social identity. This is an identity that is shared with others. Belonging to the same family, same community, same neighbourhood, same profession, same ideology, same religion, same state, same country, same continent, same human society and the same creation are various facets of this shared identity. This common identity provides one with the realisation that one has in life multiple identities at the same time[67]. The growth of a human being is geared towards the consciousness of such a broader identity. 'Identity beyond identity' is transcending one's identity, both individual and social[68]. This is a spiritual quality and is not within the reach of the common man. Only persons of heavenly heights are capable of such attainment. All the same, it is within the extent of a majority of people to touch upon at least some aspect or other of that. Francis of Assisi is an unparalleled role model for this accomplishment. His prayer is acclaimed by people across all boundaries, "Make me a channel of your peace..."[69] because of its singular character of rising above all forms of individual and social identities. Certainly, the prayer is not only rooted in the genius of Christian values, but highlights the best of what is Christian. But, it crosses all religion-made boundaries and combines in it the essence of all systems of values. It proclaims the best of human and spiritual values in an unparalleled manner and has become acceptable to one and all. The Identity that abides beyond all identities is the culmination of all identities of human life[70]. That is the mark of the best of spiritual excellence a human being can attain. All the same, in the increasingly globalising world of today, identity-related confusions and problems are nothing but natural[71]. There is no disputing the matter that, first and foremost, one has to be awakened to one's individual identity and has to sustain it. But, not growing in consciousness towards one's superior identities make one stagnate in one's individual identity. No wonder, psycho-pathological aberrations like identity-complex, identity-clash, identity-crisis, etc. creep in[72]. Passionate assertions of one's identity and politics over one's identity are the consequences and they often end up in explosive tensions and violence that are detrimental to social life. Problems like poor self-image, self-marginalisation and tendency to make one identity absolute as well as unfair administrative policies need to be addressed[73]. Christian mission has to rise higher in its identity-consciousness and be committed to making a more liberated human society. Measures have to be appropriated in spreading more clarity in one's earthly identity and in broadening its horizons.

4. ADVANCING HARMONY AMONG RELIGIONS

4.1. Critical Approach to Religion

A critical approach to Religions is vital for justifying the social utility of religion, especially in today's times[74]. The effectiveness of the religious factor in life has to be assessed in terms of its vertical and horizontal expressions and also of the co-relation between them. The internal elements of the religious civilisations are to be preferred to the externals. One has to hold fast to the essentials and has to have the good sense and courage to part with the non-essentials. Focus has to be on the core elements of one's faith[75]. The extraneous details and bothersome stipulations are to be done away with. The superlative titles, comic dresses and luxurious habits of the religious leaders need to be simplified and their aspiration to become 'mini gods' has to be abandoned in view of the good of the human society[76]. Deep-seated superstitions, enslavement to corrupt practices and following certain perverted ways have to be eliminated. The entire religious system requires a radical process of simplifying and updating[77]. Genuine efforts for simpler life style and spiritual ways are called for. The religious systems in their original form were effortless movements. The messages of the Founders were as clear-cut and straight forward, as the common folk. But they have become too elaborate and sophisticated in the course of time. Theologians of the respective traditions have done a commendable job in articulating the initial vision of the Founder or the Sages. All the same, it is to be regretfully acknowledged that theologians have made the religious theories and practices so complicated that vast majority of the people fail to find any relevance in many of them[78]. Therefore, a critical attitude to religion is all the more necessary in modern times. This is inevitable for fostering dialogue and harmony among religions[79]. The missionary drive has much to do in making the religious systems easier, in enlightening people and in making people more dynamic in life.

4.2. The Horizontal Dimension of Religion

Religion has two dimensions – vertical and horizontal[80]. They can be called individual and social dimensions respectively. While the vertical deals with God or the Creator, the horizontal deals with human beings and the rest of the creation. Often, the vertical side gains more importance in religious traditions and the social dimension less. The Creator of life has absolutely no need of any adoration or praise from the created beings. Thanking the Creator for granting life is not very much important either. Living one's life within a discipline and in harmony with human and other beings and with the nature is more meritorious[81]. That would mean to state that the vertical duties of religion have to be harmonised with the horizontal implications[82]. Failing in one's duties towards one's fellow human and other beings is to defeat the effect of performing one's vertical obligations. The horizontal dimension of life underlines the fraternal implications of life as human beings. The fraternal idea of life is founded on the idea of the divine as 'father' or 'mother', i.e., 'parent' or 'Creator' or 'Life-Giver'[83]. It directly follows that every human being is a 'son' or 'daughter' of God and a 'sister' or 'brother' to the other. This is an understanding that surpasses the biological relation by blood and is charged by a spiritual sense. This horizontal relation makes life complete, along with the vertical one. Such an integrated idea blends both theory and practice. The fraternal implications of life are grounded on the filial experience of the divine, which is the sublime foundation of Christian spirituality[84]. The fraternal fashion of considering every one one's sister or brother beyond all borders facilitates a behaviour towards one and all that corresponds to the dignity of human beings[85]. It can go to the point of loving even the enemy and considering him or her a friend. Such a lofty behaviour justifies the ultimate usefulness and fruit of religion. The horizontal dimension of religion or faith is the real test of being spiritual as well as human in the right sense of the words. A preferential concern for and loving service of the weaker sections of the society is the extra-ordinary quality of being a spiritually accomplished human being[86]. The horizontal aspect of religion is a communitarian style of living one's life. In this respect, Christian mission unquestionably stands unique with all its schemes of service in diverse areas to people of all sections. But, it has to go much further in applying the fraternal spirituality into the sphere of harmony of faiths.

4.3. The Divine in the Other as a Spiritual Foundation for Social Responsibility

The vision of the *Upanishad 'Aham Brahmaasmi'*[87], which means 'I am Brahman', is so clear and uncompromising. Because of *'maayaa'*[88] (ignorance) one is not able to know that. When one is relieved of *'maayaa'*, one realises that one is the divine being oneself. The first chapter of the Bible[89] categorically states 'human being (man and woman) is created in the image and likeness of God'. Again, Paul in the latter half of the Bible[90] asks 'don't you know that you yourselves are God's temple and God's Spirit dwells in you?' The great mystic *Kabeer* exclaims, *'jit dekhoon, tit toon'*[91], i.e., 'wherever I look, Oh! God, you are there'. All these citations prove that the image and presence of the Creator is in all living beings, especially in human beings. One's faith has to assist one to recognise and experience the same. It is the awareness of this divine presence in human beings that motivates one to consider the other one's sister or brother. It is one's religion or faith that makes one accept him or her as a co-passenger in life and to feel responsible for the other[92]. One's religion or faith is the foundation for proving oneself as a brother or sister to the other by extending loving service, especially in times of dire need. The humanitarian services being extended by faith-based communities to persons across the communities and nationalities is motivated by such an elevated and harmonised perception of the divine and the human. Such an attitude seems to be innate to the Christian tradition on account of the vision and mission of Jesus[93]. Undertaking welfare schemes for the human society is the core value of any religion or faith. 'The services done to human beings are in fact done to God himself'[94]. There cannot be a double standard between one's relation with the divine being and with human beings. The Christian mission, relying on this incomparable strength, has to proceed to a leadership of eliciting harmony and collaboration among faith-based organisations for the welfare of the human society.

4.4. Promoting Universal Values of Religions

The universal values inherent in different religions are not to be considered 'yours and mine'. They are the common cultural and spiritual inheritance of the entire human society[95]. They are to be accepted, learned from and lived in a shared manner. The Buddhist Values like 'middle path, enlightenment, *nirvana*, eight-fold path and non-violence[96] contribute to the wellbeing of all. The Christian values like 'relational understanding of the divine, harmony of the vertical and horizontal dimensions of religion, social spirituality, ethical stipulations of love, forgiveness and service, and preferential service to the weaker section of the society'[97] are indeed values for all. The Hindu values *'nishkaam karma*, unity in diversity, oneness of the ultimate reality, welcoming noble thoughts from all directions, *Vasudhaiv kutumbakam*, synthesis of materialism and spiritualism', etc are not limited to one tradition. The Jain values like '*anekaantvaad*, plurality, relativity, nonviolence, *aparigrah*, live and let live' are imperatives for all. The Jewish values 'law-centred life and ethical monotheism', the *Nirankari* values like 'belonging to God, equality of genders and beauty in diversity'[98] are equally good for people of other traditions. The Parsi values 'good thoughts, good words and good deeds' (*Humata, Hukhta, Huvarshta*)[99] and the Shinto values 'following the ways of the Gods'[100] have clear messages for human uplift. The Sikh values like '*guru* concept, honouring scripture as *guru, langar, keertan* and service'[101] and the Tao values like 'the way or the path of life, the harmony of the opposites in *Yin-Yang*, idea of non-god and the natural way'[102] contribute to the treasure of human and spiritual values[103]. Universal human and spiritual values of diverse faith traditions have common characteristics that are capable of facilitating human unity[104]. Christian mission has to imbibe and promote the spirit of all these universal values, while being firmly rooted on the perspective of the great master Jesus.

4.5. Religious Communities in Harmony with Each Other

Relying on the basic meaning of religion and dharma as 'binding together in conscientious duty'[105], one has to broaden up one's commitment to faith to a circle of all religious traditions. Other religious ways are equally active responses to the Divine. No one faith vision has the complete answer to the needs, aspirations and problems of the world. No single faith perspective is capable of exhausting the divine experience. All faith perceptions together also cannot fully comprehend the divine reality[106]. Besides, much of the difference in faith traditions is a question of language only. Therefore, one has to be inter-lingual in order to be lingual. One has to be inter-ideological in order to be ideological[107]. One has to be inter-human in order to be human. One has to be inter-cultural in order to be cultural. One has to be international in order to be national. One has to be inter–religious in order to be religious. One has to be spiritual in order to be really human. One has to be humane in order to be spiritual, as well. One who knows only one thing knows nothing. One who knows only one language knows no language at all. One who knows only one's own faith does not know one's own faith also[108]. Knowledge, understanding and growth are comparative in nature. Enlightenment and wisdom are fruits of perfection, and perfection in life is grounded in the spirit of complementariness and interaction[109]. That would amount to say that harmony among faith communities is essential for the spiritual welfare of the human species[110]. Religious leaders have to be multi-religious in their outlook and have to involve themselves in an all-out campaign of promoting better relations and collaboration with other communities[111]. Networking with other faith persuasions purifies the understanding of one's own faith, enriches one's faith with other understandings and contributes immensely to harmony of faiths. A colloquium of all religions and cultures of the world is the fundamental form of religion[112]. Journeying towards cross-religious boundaries is the real sign of a living and worthwhile religion. Only harmony of faiths does justice to the *raison d'être* of religion[113]. Christian mission has to deepen and broaden its understanding of mission as well as of faith in order to encompass the large gamut of religious treasury the Creator has spread all over the world.

4.6. Religious Leadership for Social Transformation

Change is the inner dynamics of life. Where there is no change there is no life. To live would mean to keep changing. Change takes place gradually and degree by degree. It is a process. To go beyond the present form is to initiate change. Change is transformation. By and large, change is for the better. When a better form appears there is transformation[114]. Transformation of the society is societal transformation. Transformed individuals contribute to transforming the imperfect social structures. Change does not start with others. Change launches with oneself. The proof of the change in oneself is attempting to elicit change in others and in the society[115]. Commitment to the betterment of the society is leadership. A leader is someone who does the right thing even when no one else does it. To have right personal initiatives is the basic characteristic of a leader. Those who wait for someone else to set an example before they act are followers. Leaders create role models for making the type of society they want[116]. A leader has to break new grounds, travel new paths and be an evidence for the goal the path leads to. One's religion or faith has to facilitate one to have the mindset and calibre of a leader. Religious leadership is an innate quality. Real leaders are born. Genuine leadership is spiritual in its nature[117]. One's religious, moral and spiritual heights have to enable one to pursue a leadership role for social transformation. Social transformation would mean tuning the mindset of persons to be caring towards the other, especially the needy. Leadership supported by one's religion includes responding to the basic needs, balancing rights and duties, and ensuring socio-cultural interaction, peaceful co-existence and harmonious living[118]. Religious persons and communities have to spontaneously undertake such transforming leadership for the wellbeing of the society. They have to play responsible sociological roles together for the welfare of the entire society[119]. They have to contribute to the making of a better tomorrow. Christian mission has to transform itself into a new style of leadership by way of networking the human society and ameliorating human lives.

5. BROADENING THE FOUNDATIONS FOR HARMONOUS LIVING

5.1. Constitution of the Country as the National Sacred Scripture

Whatever that is written can be considered a scripture. Those scriptures that contain the sayings of great men and women or Founders of religious traditions have the status of a Sacred Scripture[120]. The faith of the followers of a particular tradition makes the scripture sacred. Sacred Scriptures are sacrosanct and inviolable. The sacredness of the scriptures contains in their capacity to inspire the readers[121]. They guide human lives with values that are universal and eternal. But secular writings also motivate and guide human beings. Those books and scriptures that are part of the world classics have a universal appeal beyond measure[122]. The Constitution of India is a book that has an unparalleled moral fibre[123]. That inspires and guides the citizens of the country. As people who belong to different religious communities, affiliation to Sacred Scriptures change. But as citizens of the same country all the people of India have 'The Constitution of India' as the common Sacred Scripture[124]. All the citizens of the country, irrespective of their religious persuasion, ideological leaning, social customs, ethnic-linguistic belonging and cultural upbringing, has to regard the 'Constitution of India' as the most sacred scripture of the country and abide by its values[125]. All the countries have their own constitution, which has to be considered sacred by the respective citizens[126]. This fundamental duty of the citizens takes care of the human and spiritual possibilities the Asian countries at large are aspiring for[127]. Christian mission needs to be awakened to this national duty in India and in other countries of Asia and inter-relate the Constitutional values of the country with values of the Bible.

5.2. Secular Perspective as the National Vision of Life in India

The genius of the Constitution of India is 'Secular perspective of Life'[128]. It summarises the entirety of the human and spiritual values the Indian society is invited to live by. Secular is not worldly or irreligious. Secular is 'non-attachment to one path'[129]. India has no one religion, no one language, no one culture and no one ideology, as its own[130]. Big or small, all communities have equal place in this country. All individuals and groups have opportunities for developing their potentialities and for living one's life to the fullest measure anywhere in the country. A 'composite culture'[131] is the fundamental identity of our country. A colloquium of the religious, social, cultural, ideological, ethnic, professional and linguistic streams is the esteemed treasure of our nation. All the individuals and communities have their due place as privileged citizens of this country. All of them are worthy of respect. All of them deserve opportunities for developing their own personalities and for living a dignified life. There is no small or great, in the real sense of the word. If there is anyone who claims to be stronger in number, wealth or power, it is his or her duty to see that the so called smaller and weaker are respectfully taken care of. There lies the central spirit of secularism as well as of religion. Besides, Secular Perspective of Life is a 'broadened understanding of the sacred'[132]. It de-centralises the sophisticated understanding of the geographically located presence of the Divine in the world, in the form of temples, churches, *masjids, gurudwaras*, and the like. It facilitates the seeker to see and experience the Divine everywhere. All the places, all the jobs and all the symbols are true dwelling places of the Divine[133]. The whole creation, all the living beings and especially human beings are the living and real temples of the Divine. This is what secular perspective is. This 'secular perspective of life', in one way or other, applies to all countries of Asia in spirit[134]. It supports and nourishes the harmony vision, which is foundational to life itself. Religions in India and in Asia have to promote such a secular and democratic spirit. The Christian mission has to pioneer such a secular attitude and find a new meaning in its future course of action.

5.3. Promoting Civic Sense

Civic consciousness is fundamental to being a citizen[135]. It is the fruit of being civilised, too. Therefore, citizens can never part with their duties as citizens. From this angle, no person or sector should attempt anything that disturbs the smooth flow of civic life in the society[136]. The religious sector should all the more be scrupulous about practicing their public duty. In this context, the propriety and modalities of the religious processions on the road at festival times should be re-considered[137]. They often make the entire traffic to a perfect standstill. They disturb the human needs, including emergency imperatives. They leave the road almost as bad as a long stretch of garbage heap[138]. These processions seem to be more a demonstration of the power of the given community than any devotional practice. Similarly, using microphone at night, in spite of the ruling against it by the Supreme Court of India, blocking the roads when VIPs travel, dirtying public places, etc. are violations of the civic sense and are to be refrained from[139]. Similar instances could be found in different countries of the Asian continent. Certain countries and cities of Asia are in fact role models in this respect, too. Behaviour at public place is a real reflection of one's spiritual sense as well as human culture and education[140]. Christian mission has to find a new direction along these routes. That will make the mission 'mission with a difference' in the most practical terms.

5.4. Progressing Together Towards a Better Society

Henry Wadsworth Longfellow, the most popular American poet of the 19th century in English Literature, in his poem 'A Psalm of Life' exhorts, 'But to act, that each to-morrow find us farther than to-day'[141]. One has to keep advancing in life in all respects. But, going alone is no progress, worth the name. Growing together in life is real progress. A culture of dialogue, interaction, collaboration, good relations and harmony has to be evolved for making it a reality. That would necessitate traveling together in life. For that, the driving force of the life-mission has to be 'Do to the other what you would have the other do to you'[142] and 'What you do to other human beings, especially to those that are weaker than Yourself, You do to God Himself'[143]. 'Leave the place better than you found it'[144] is the dictum that motivates one to strive for a better society. 'Making the society a better place to live in' is the ulterior purpose of life[145]. One has to ensure that there is nothing that is undone on the way of making one's personal life, family, neighbourhood, environment, community, country and the human society better than one has found it[146]. This has to be the way one looks at life. One's faith has to be such that furnishes vision, courage and strength for achieving the above objective of making a more harmonious society. Leaders and well-meaning people from all faith-based communities and the civil society need to be networked with each other in order to advance this fundamental objective towards realisation[147]. The diverse scriptures, cultures, traditions and sciences provide the humans with a firm spiritual foundation for facilitating a harmonious living together of all civilisations and ideologies[148]. Christian mission, for that matter, all the missions, has to mature towards such a height by fostering the spirit of progressing together along with values of other civilisations as well.

CONCLUSION

Religious harmony or harmony among religious communities is the ultimate destination of the phenomenon of religion. Diversities have to be harmonised with unity. Religious traditions not interacting with each other like parallel lines or remaining cut off from each other like islands do not make sense. All type of diversities on earth, in Asia in special, have to crisscross each other, in view of learning from each other and harmoniously and peacefully living together. Religion has to be transformed into a mission of promoting harmony and peace as well as inclusive thinking and larger outlook. Christian mission, with its larger reservoir of socio-spiritual values, has to pioneer such a noble task, especially for Asia. Religious harmony is forerunner of social harmony.

Endnotes

1. Robert McKim, On Religious Diversity, New York, 2012, p. 07
2. *Ibid,* p. 19
3. *Ibid,* p. 23
4. Hector Cuadra-Montiel, Globalization: Approaches to Diversity, Rijeka, Crotia, 2012, p. 03
5. *Ibid,* p. 57
6. *Ibid,* p. 93
7. Baogang He and Will Kymlicka, Multiculturalism in Asia, Oxford. 2015, p. 13
8. *Ibid,* p. 83
9. *Ibid,* p. 87
10. *Ibid,* p. 103
11. Dr Manoj Kumar Srivastva and Dr Santosh Kumar Singh, Society in India: Structure, Organisation and Change, Lucknow, 2022, p. 43
12. Vishakha, N. Desai, World as Family: A Journey of Multi-Rooted Belongings, New York, 2021, p. 37
13. *Ibid,* p. 53
14. *Ibid,* p. 107
15. Ramachandra Guha, Makers of Modern India, Cambridge, 2011, p. 466
16. *Ibid,* p. 467
17. Vishakha, N. Desai, World as Family: A Journey of Multi-Rooted Belongings, New York, 2021, p. 207
18. Michael Amaladoss, Interreligious Encounters: Opportunities and Challenges, New York, 2017, p. 33
19. Anindita N. Balslev, On World Religions: Diversity, Not Dissension, New Delhi, 2014, p. 27
20. *Ibid,* p. 63
21. *Ibid,* p. 98
22. Hector Cuadra-Montiel, Globalization: Approaches to Diversity, Rijeka, Crotia, 2012, p. 97
23. *Ibid,* p. 63
24. *Ibid,* p. 125
25. *Ibid,* p. 207
26. Dana, L. Robert, Christian Mission: How Christianity Became a World Religion, New Jersey, 2011, p. 160

27. Joseph Benjamin and Ram Dev Bharadwaj (Ed.), Conflict, Terror & Violence in Indian Society & Polity, New Delhi, 2022, p. 09
28. *Ibid,* p. 23
29. *Ibid,* p. 24
30. *Ibid,* p. 57
31. *Ibid,* p. 136
32. *Ibid,* p. 207
33. Maria Hornung, Encountering Other Faiths, New Jersey, 2008, p. 57
34. Baogang He and Will Kymlicka, Multiculturalism in Asia, Oxford, 2015, p. 53
35. *Ibid,* p. 58
36. *Ibid,* p. 103
37. *Ibid,* p. 209
38. *Ibid,* p. 211
39. *Ibid,* p. 278
40. Suhas Pereira, The Challenges of Vatican II for an Authentic Indian Catholic Church, Zurich, 2020, p. 194
41. Walter William Skeat, A Concise Etymological Dictionary of the English Language, New York, 1882, p. 143
42. *Ibid,* p. 144
43. R. S. Nathan, Hinduism that is Sanatana Dharma, Mumbai, 2000, p. 06
44. A.C. Bhaktivedanta Swami Prabhupada, Bhagavat Gita, Mumbai, 1990, 4.11, p. 209
45. Sadhu, Santinath, Encyclopedia of Philosophy of Indian Religion, New Delhi, 2001, p. 527
46. *Ibid,* p. 83
47. *Ibid,* p. 84
48. *Ibid,* p. 87
49. *Ibid,* p. 89
50. *Ibid,* p. 107
51. Suhas Pereira, The Challenges of Vatican II for an Authentic Indian Catholic Church, Zurich, 2020, p. 207
52. Victoria, S. Harrison, Religion and Modern Thought, London, 2007, p. 83
53. *Ibid,* p. 107
54. *Ibid,* p. 108
55. *Ibid,* p. 139
56. *Ibid,* p. 153
57. *Ibid,* p. 158
58. *Ibid,* p. 209
59. Michel Pharand (Ed.), Bernard Shaw on Religion, New York, 2016, p. 114
60. Victoria, S. Harrison, Religion and Modern Thought, London, 2007, p. 93
61. *Ibid,* p. 97
62. *Ibid,* p. 108
63. *Ibid,* p. 113
64. *Ibid,* p. 127
65. Bruce Haddock, Peter Sutch, Multiculturalism, Identity and Rights, New York, 2004, p. 107
66. *Ibid,* p. 109
67. *Ibid,* p. 110
68. *Ibid,* p. 113
69. Bee Teik Lee, Experiencing the Heart of Pastoral Counseling, Singapore, 2009, p. 274

70. Bruce Haddock, Peter Sutch, Multiculturalism, Identity and Rights, New York, 2004, p. 228
71. *Ibid,* p. 231
72. *Ibid,* p. 253
73. *Ibid,* p. 271
74. Ross Aden, Religion Today: A Critical Thinking Approach to Religious Studies, New York, 2013, p. 19
75. *Ibid,* p. 33
76. *Ibid,* p. 37
77. *Ibid,* p. 41
78. *Ibid,* p. 107
79. *Ibid,* p. 293
80. Elizabeth, M. Dowling and W. George Scarlett (Ed.), Encyclopedia of Religious and Spiritual Development, London, 2006, p. 53
81. *Ibid,* p. 69
82. *Ibid,* p. 79
83. *Ibid,* p. 107
84. *Ibid,* p. 153
85. *Ibid,* p. 211
86. *Ibid,* p. 233
87. Devdutt Pattanaik, Myth= *Mithya*: Decoding Hindu Mythology, Gurgaon, 2006, p. 23
88. *Ibid,* p. 26
89. The Holy Bible, NIV, Michigan, 1994, Gen.1.27, p. 2
90. *Ibid,* I Cor. 3.16, p. 1298
91. Shyam Sunder Das (Ed.), *Kabeer Granthaavalee, Sumiran Kou Ang 9*, Varanasi, p. 328
92. Elizabeth, M. Dowling and W. George Scarlett (Ed.), Encyclopedia of Religious and Spiritual Development, London, 2006, p. 207
93. Victoria, S. Harrison, Religion and Modern Thought, London, 2007, p. 207
94. The Holy Bible, NIV, Michigan, 1994,, Mt 25.40, p. 1127
95. Ross Aden, Religion Today: A Critical Thinking Approach to Religious Studies, New York, 2013, p. 109
96. Thich Nhat Hanh, The Heart of Buddha's Teaching, London, 2008, p. 46
97. Victoria, S. Harrison, Religion and Modern Thought, London, 2007, p. 76
98. Ross Aden, Religion Today: A Critical Thinking Approach to Religious Studies, New York, 2013, p. 19
99. Jenny Rose, 'Zoroastrianism—an Introduction', New York, 2010, p. 17
100. Thomas, P. Kasulis, Shinto: The Way Home, Honolulu, 2004, p. 53
101. Ranbir Singh and Surjeet Singh, The Sikh Way of Life, New Delhi, 2007, p. 23
102. Jean, C. Cooper, An Illustrated Introduction to Taoism: The Wisdom of the Sages, Bloomington, 2010, p. 08
103. Tara Sethia, *Ahimsā, Anekānta* and Jainism, New Delhi, 2004, p. 23
104. Michael, A. Meyer, Ideas of Jewish History, New York, 1987, p. 25
105. Kent, L. Koppelman, Values in the Key of Life: Making Harmony in the Human Community, New York, 2019, p. 13
106. *Ibid,* p. 15
107. *Ibid,* p. 16
108. *Ibid,* p. 23
109. *Ibid,* p. 26
110. *Ibid,* p. 39

111. *Ibid,* p. 43
112. *Ibid,* p. 109
113. *Ibid,* p. 156
114. Linda Woodhead (Ed.), Religions in the Modern World: Traditions and Transformations, New York, 2002, p. 276
115. *Ibid,* p. 277
116. *Ibid,* p. 279
117. *Ibid,* p. 280
118. *Ibid,* p. 302
119. *Ibid,* p. 303
120. Prahlad Rao, India's Futuristic Democracy-Threats of Constitutional Gaps and Digital Era, New Delhi, p. 98
121. *Ibid,* p. 101
122. *Ibid,* p. 103
123. *Ibid,* p. 107
124. *Ibid,* p. 108
125. *Ibid,* p. 126
126. *Ibid,* p. 129
127. *Ibid,* p. 137
128. Domenic Marbaniang, Secularism in India: A Historical Analysis, Bangalore, 2011, p. 33
129. *Ibid,* p. 56
130. *Ibid,* p. 78
131. *Ibid,* p. 106
132. *Ibid,* p. 122
133. *Ibid,* p. 176
134. *Ibid,* p. 207
135. Pradip, N. Khandwalla, Creative Society: Prospects for India, Noida, 2020, p. 302
136. *Ibid,* p. 303
137. *Ibid,* p. 304
138. *Ibid,* p. 309
139. *Ibid,* p. 311
140. *Ibid,* p. 313
141. T. Gregory Garvey, The Emerson Dilemma: Essays on Emerson and Social Reform, Athens, 2001, p. 197
142. The Holy Bible, NIV, Michigan, 1994, Mt 7.12, p. 1100
143. *Ibid,* Mt 25.40, p. 1128
144. Phil Geldart, Lead Yourself Lead Others, Ontario, 2015, p. 36
145. *Ibid,* p. 93
146. *Ibid,* p. 117
147. Anjan Chakrabarti and Stephen Cullenberg, Transition and Development in India, New York, 2013, p. 123
148. Baogang He and Will Kymlicka, Multiculturalism in Asia, Oxford, 2015, p. 293

Chapter - 3

Towards Harmony Among Religions

1. INTRODUCTION: RELIGION AND FAITH

'Religion'[1], beyond doubt, is a major phenomenon in human life and it is, arguably, both a positive force and a negative factor. Its off-putting dimension possibly has to be attributed to the high content of emotion it is charged with. In that case, it could be compared to the truck that carries petrol and diesel, with the caption 'highly inflammable'. It could also be like the bush 'touch me not'. The hyper-sensitive and over-reactive aspect of religion or faith is to be ascribed to the raw, illiterate and immature mental status of the so called believers of faiths, which, manifestly, is an obstacle to the state of harmony with other religions or believers[2].

'Faith'[3], by its very nature, is the internal aspect of religion and religion is the external aspect of faith, as well. Faith is very much free style in its disposition, where as religion is very much a complex system. While faith is more of a personal matter, religion is vastly a community affair. Faith could be stated as the qualitative aspect of religion and religion, the quantitative aspect of faith. Since faith is more basic and inclusive in its character, it has a better capacity than religion in being a uniting factor in social life[4]. At any rate, more often than not, faith and religion are used synonymously.

2. RISING ABOVE MYTHS ABOUT RELIGION

2.1. Religious identity is the basic identity in life!

The first myth people entertain as regards religion is that it composes the core identity of human beings in life. They believe that being religious is the ultimate value in life. Therefore, they consider religion the centre of life. Being Christian, Muslim, Sikh, et cetera, decides their worth in life. Their entire life is defined by religion and is stage-managed by the custodians of their respective religion. No wonder, 'no compromise with religious matters' is their 'gospel' in life[5]. In sum, religion and faith serve as the pivot of human life.

But, as a matter of fact, life is God's gift and is the most basic reality. Religion is only a secondary value. 'Sabbath is for the human being and not vice versa'[6], states Jesus, categorically so. Religion is for human beings. Life is and has to be the focal point of religion or faith. Religion is oriented to human lives and it has to be at the service of human lives. Enhancing the appetite, quality and meaning of life is the sole objective of religion or faith. Therefore, giving more importance to religion or faith than to life is a topsy-turvy of affairs.

'Being human' is the core nature of human beings and that is its identity, as well[7]. Religion may or may not be. If it is there, it has to produce result for life and that result is more important than religion itself. That is what Shree Narayan Guru of Kerala means as he observes, 'no matter what is your religion, it suffices if it makes you a good human being'[8]. Humanity is the real religion in life and faith in it constitutes the essence of human lives. 'Being a good human being' is the real identity of all human beings, irrespective of religious, ideological, cultural and social affiliations.

2.2. Religion is a private affair!

That 'religion is a private affair' is an idea that is very widely entertained and often repeated in public space[9]. The myth is possibly grounded in the fact that human beings take birth and die as individuals as well as live as individuals. It is also true that every individual is unique and he or she relates to God and to fellow humans differently. Pursuing a religion or not is a matter of individual choice, as well. No one has any business to interfere with any one in terms of one's religion. One's conscience should not be violated!

Nevertheless, there is a point in the above logic it is also equally true that there is nothing that is totally private in this world. Human beings are necessarily social beings in their character. An individual is born of two persons, who represent the society. An individual can live meaningfully only in the society. Besides, the question that contradicts the above argument is the fact that the largest and the most frequent of gatherings in the society are in the name of religion. In addition, if religion is a private matter, why is that people get unsettled by the change of religious affiliation or conversion of a certain individual! The individual aspect of religion cannot be pushed to the extent of denying the fact that religion is equally a social phenomenon[10].

Since human beings are essentially social animals, strengthening the social character of human life is the basic role of religion. All human behaviours have social implications, though may be more or less in degrees. Reciprocity is the principle of social life and relatedness is the way of being human beings. Caring for the other and of being of service to the other is religion proper. 'What is done to the other is what is done to God, the needy in special'[11], affirms Jesus. For that reason, religion shouldn't be a private affair, but has to be a motivating factor, in favour of a mutually engaging and meaningful social life.

2.3. My religion is for me and your religion for you!

The compartmentalised idea of religion seems to be supported by, if not grounded in, the words of the Quran, 'to you your religion and to me mine[12] (Quran 109.1-6). The religion I am born into is mine and I have nothing to do with other religions. Therefore, you believe in your God and I believe in mine. You pursue your religion and I pursue mine. It is as if your mother is yours and my mother is mine or you live your life and I live mine. Mixing up our religions would create confusion in us and in the society. In view of that, as we are born in to a certain religion, living our lives purely within the parameters of our own individual religious tradition is the supreme ideal for all believers! [13]

But such an isolated and insulted notion contradicts the truth that religion is the universal phenomenon of the human civilisation. All the founders of religions are representations of the same Creator. All the religious traditions are gifts of the same God. All religious traditions are the common cultural heritage of the human society[14]. It is outright wrong to consider any religious tradition the private property of a certain community. One's idea of religion and that of one's own religious tradition has to grow according to one's age, education and experience and touch upon the larger horizons of life.

Individualising and communalising religion is a crime against God and the humanity, at the same time[15]. Religions cannot be like islands, cut off from one another. Religions can never be like parallel lines that do not meet each other. Dividing the society along religious lines is not only un-constitutional but also an irreligious act, if not a sin. Conflicting and disruptive thinking in terms of 'I and he/she, we and they or us and them is a childish way and therefore has to be got rid of[16]. Such a mindset is symptomatic of retarded, undeveloped and pathological cases.

Further, all that is part of the created world is limited and so is not complete or perfect. All religious traditions emerged in a certain context of time and space. Even though there are timeless and universal elements in them, all of them are responses to a certain time and people. Consequently, all religious traditions are partial and incomplete. Along with the essentials, there are non-essential elements in all of them. And so, they are not contradictory, but are complementary to each other. The right way of looking at religions is 'all religious traditions are ours; one is mine in special and others are mine in general'[17]. A balanced diet requires various items of food for different vitamins. In a similar way, all religions have to be collectively owned and learned from by all.

2.4. Living and dying for one's religion merits heavenly reward!

Lots of people hold the strong opinion that religion is the ultimate value in life. They consider that whatever one's religion teaches is absolutely and exclusively right. As a result, they tend to become over-enthusiastic about the tenets of their religion. Believing in and living for even the smallest teachings of the religion often becomes an unmanageable passion for them, so much so that very many of them are ready even to die for one's belief, right or wrong[18]. The funniest part of the story is that they think that dying while defending the teachings of one's religion is a praiseworthy thing and becoming a martyr thus is sure to merit heavenly reward!

It is obvious to a sound thinking that a misplaced passion for religion is out of place. Living for religion is disorientation. Dying for religion, that too, unnecessarily and unwisely, is not intended by God and it is not only unmerited, but also is idiotic[19]. On the other hand, there are lots of persons who are not inclined to the religious stipulations, but are governed by greater concerns of life. In addition, pro-life efforts, especially in terms of other human beings, have to motivate one's appetite to live and willingness to die, if need be. Causes that are geared towards meaningful human lives have to receive divine inspiration and human values have to guide the destinies of the passion one has for religion[20].

2.5. Hating and even killing others in the name of God is justified!

Those people who claim to have a religion perceive life, God and others in a certain way. Considering themselves right and even cocksure of their theories, they treat those who do not subscribe to their beliefs as heretics, heathens or pagans or *kaafir* and hate them as if they are enemies of God. And it naturally follows that 'applying *jihad* on *kaafir* and *kuffar* (non-Muslim) and killing them is pleasing to God', as Quran 9.5 states[21]. Accordingly, hating and even killing others in the name of God is justified!

But, if truth be told, it is not that those who do not believe in what we believe do not believe in anything at all. Every person believes in something or other, which sustains his or her life meaningfully. It doesn't stand to any reason that those who do not believe in a certain theory are bound to go to hell, and so they have no right to exist and they have to be eliminated. What's more, to think that my belief alone is right, my belief is for all and all have to accept my belief, or in other words, 'my belief is at the centre of the world', smacks of a self-centred and sick mindset[22].

Further, belief is a personal conviction and freedom of belief is a fundamental human right. It is enforced by the Constitution of India as well as the Charter of the United Nations. Violating this human right, to the point of hating and even killing others, is a defiance of the Constitution and the UN Charter of human behaviour. It is also an infraction of the Quranic stipulation 'there is no compulsion in religion' (Quran 2.256)[23]. No one should be forced to become Muslim, for that matter, Christian, Vedic, Jain, and the like, as well. Also, hating others, worse still, killing others in the name of God is a fatal anomaly. God is a positive force that motivates the humans to love others and to foster their lives, and not otherwise. Belief in God, in the right sense of the word, is an element that is proactive towards promoting fellowship among the humans[24].

2.6. Killing even one's own in the name of religion brings honour!

People of this mindset entertain the theory that one's religious belonging is sacrosanct and that changing the same for any reason is wrong. Religion is definitely a higher value than love. Love is valid only when it is between persons of one's own clan, tribe, community or religion. If one violates this norm in the realm of love, he or she, even if one is own daughter or son, is destined to lose one's right to live. Love is not allowed to spill over religious campuses. If it does, it is right to take law into one's hands and to punish the culprits, even to the point of death[25]. That makes the so-called 'honour-killing' by the parents themselves justified, in favour of a certain imaginary honour!

However, to a sane mind, love is the most central value in life. Religion is only a supplementary value in life. Love has to be the result of true religion. Eliminating even one's children who crossed the borders of religions in the name of love can never restore any fictitious honour to anyone. Instead, killing one's son or daughter, any human being for that matter, in the name of religion, especially when he or she is genuinely in love with the counterpart, brings never-ending shame to the family, clan, religion or community, and to the human society, as well. In actual fact, that religion, which refuses to recognize and support genuine love or becomes an obstacle on the way has to be identified as fake and be discarded at one stroke[26].

2.7. Theological confusions, like 'only/last/most ancient (*sanaatan*)/ fulfillment'

Even though theology has done a remarkable job in articulating the diverse religions, it is theology that is responsible for the characteristic divisions among them. The exaggerated theological abstractions have enlarged the differences among them and made them unbridgeable, as if next to impossible. The theological confusions, like 'only, last, most ancient (*sanaatan*) and fulfillment', which have created a superior-inferior mindset among religions have to be squarely looked at, assessed and transcended, so that believers can stay tuned to each other in a fraternal way, as they walk together to the same divine in the spirit of a shared pilgrimage[27].

Exclusivist and inclusivist perspectives are positions that are polarised to each other. Exclusivist' believers exclude others. Their attitude is 'I am ok, others are not ok'. They remain secluded, as if living in an island. 'Only' is their catch phrase. 'Inclusivist' believers are open to include others. But, they are at the centre, truly right, though they agree that there is something partially right with others, too. Their attitude is 'I am ok; you are also ok, to some extent'. 'Also' is their slogan. Even though the inclusive position is to be very much preferred to the exclusive one, self-importance and superior feeling suggests that it requires improvement[28].

Absolutist and relativist points of view are extreme positions on either side. 'Absolutist' believers enlarge and laminate their faith to a hundred percent and zero other believers down. They survive in an insulated world of superiority. Their attitude is 'I am ok, you are not ok'. 'Fully' is their watchword. 'Relativist' believers consider faiths as plural[29]. They follow their path and allow others to follow theirs. '*Anekaandvaad*'[30] of Jain philosophy is a case in point here. Their attitude is 'I am ok, you are ok'. But, despite the fact that there is recognition of the other on equal footing, this position is a free-lanced and unconnected outlook to life. This could be compared to travelling like 'parallel lines' that do not meet. 'Pluralist' believers hold that 'there are many paths and all paths are right. 'All are ok' is their attitude[31].

Though there is something right about this position, pluralists are not harmonised. Pluralism is to be revised in terms of making it harmonised among their constituents. 'Mutually inclusive pluralism' or 'harmonious pluralism' or 'interactive pluralism' is the best position that justifies a dynamic and dialogical faith or religion[32]. All the same, this is an ideal position and is rarely found anywhere. Efforts have to be regularly geared towards such a truly grown up and interactive faith or religious system, which advocates 'inclusive thinking and harmonious living' among the human communities.

3. REALISATIONS OF THE CHRISTIAN COMMUNITY

3.1. Second World Council of Vatican / '*Nostra Aetate*' (In our time)

The Second World Council of Vatican in the 60s of the 20th century, in its landmark document *'Nostra Aetate'* (In Our Time), came up with a historic realisation and exclaimed, 'we cannot call God our Father, if we treat any people as other than sisters and brothers'[33]. 'There is no basis for any discrimination, in theory or practice, between individual and individual, or between people and people'[34]. 'Church reproves, as foreign to the mind of Christ, any discrimination against people or any harassment of them, based on race, colour, condition in life or religion[35]. This realisation was the outcome of a great spiritual spark and awakening, as a result of 20 centuries of pursuing the mission of Jesus world over.

The following are some of the ground-breaking statements that emerged from the above realisation. 'Different religions are different answers to the unsolved riddles of life'[36]. 'All religions have evolved well-defined concepts and answers to questions'[37]. 'There is a search for what is common among people and what brings them together'[38]. 'Humanity forms but one community'[39]. 'All people share a common origin, common existence and common destiny'[40]. These pronouncements not only made the Council a unique event for the world, but also initiated 'a culture of interfaith thinking and living'[41] for the humans, so much so that people of all religions and communities, by and large, have taken inspiration from it.

The decisive mandate and roadmap that came down from the above Council to the Christians is to 'enter into discussion and collaboration with members of other religions'[42], necessarily so. They have to 'together preserve and promote peace, liberty, social justice and moral values'[43]. They have also to 'acknowledge, preserve and encourage (promote, persuade and support) the spiritual and moral truths in people of other religions, cultures and traditions'[44]. Since 'the common roots are the spiritual ties that link the people'[45] and that we 'have a common spiritual heritage'[46], the maxim for the way forward is 'do not teach anything that is not in tune with the spirit of Christ'[47]. The clear plan of action for a believer in Jesus Christ was to 'make sincere effort for mutual understanding'[48] and to 'encourage and further mutual understanding and appreciation'[49] among people of all communities and civilisations. Obviously, the brighter future of the Christian community, of the entire country and the society as well, is inherent in this great command of love that is grounded in the mission of Jesus the Master and the Son of God.

3.2. Biblical Foundations

The insightful realisation of the above Council is deeply beached at the eternal divine and human wisdom of God the Father that was powerfully embodied and channelised by Jesus. Bible is the unfathomable reservoir of motivation and strength for the genuine Christian mission that evolves from the above insight, as well. 'God created man in his own image… male and female he created them'[50]. 'You yourselves are God's temple and that God's Spirit dwells in your midst'[51]. 'Whoever does not love does not know God, because God is love'[52]. Besides, 'He (God the Father) sends sunshine and rain on the righteous and the unrighteous'[53] and, therefore, 'be perfect, therefore, as your heavenly Father is perfect'[54].

Furthermore, 'all stem from one stock created by God'[55] and 'God's providence, goodness and saving designs extend to all humankind'[56] are foundational truths that are grounded in the creative design of God. 'Conduct yourselves well among gentiles'[57] and 'live at peace with all people'[58] are directives that are focused on the behaviour of Christians among people of other faith-based communities. Jesus pronounces the golden code of behaviour that suits his disciples in relation with people of all civilisations, 'unless your righteousness surpasses that of the Pharisees and the teachers of the law, you will certainly not enter the kingdom of heaven'[59] and expressed before his Heavenly Father the culmination of his all-inclusive aspiration in life 'that they all may be one'[60].

3.3. Insights from Popes

Firmly rooted in the teachings of Jesus recorded in the Bible and taking off from the runway of the above Council, several Popes articulated outstanding insights in line with the revised vision and mission of Christian life. 'We have to look at what unites people, rather than what divides them', stated Pope John XXIII[61]. 'What *we* all *have* in common is greater *than what separates* us', he continued[62]. Pope Paul VI furthered the vision in the Meeting of Religions, Bombay, January 1964, stating 'we don't have to meet only as tourists, but as pilgrims and start a journey searching for God, not in buildings of stone, but in the hearts of humankind'[63].

Advancing the relay race of the new vision of the Council initiated by Popes John XXIII and Paul VI, Pope John Paul II travelled far and wide in promoting better relations with people of all faiths and made enormously significant pronouncements during his elaborate period of papacy. He stated in a Meeting of Religions, New Delhi, 1999, 'different religious traditions of India are a hope for a better future for the human family'[64]. 'Religion should be what God intended it to be, a source of goodness, harmony and peace', he affirmed in a Meeting of Religions, New Delhi, 1999[65]. His statement was really categorical as regards the interactive dynamics of divine-human relations when he said in a Public Meeting, Madras, 1986, 'by dialogue we let God be present in our midst, for as we open ourselves in dialogue to one another, we open ourselves to God'[66]. Yet again, he highlighted the eternal grounding interaction in a Meeting of Religions, New Delhi, 1999, as he avowed, 'dialogue is an act of love, which has its roots in God himself'[67].

In recent times, Pope Francis, through his progressive, open and outright insights, captured the imagination of the entire world, especially of people of all faiths, ideologies and cultures as well as of the Christian community. He challenged Christians during a Mass in Cuba, 2015, 'being a Christian entails promoting the dignity of our brothers and sisters, fighting for it, living for it'[68]. During a general audience, St Peter's Square, Vatican City, 2015, he gave a thorough shock to the outdated custodians of the Church, saying, 'dogmas and rituals are not the centre of the concerns of the church, but human beings'[69]. He furthered his critique of the closed door culture of the Church, wherever it is present, by the words, 'Churches, parishes and institutions with closed doors must not call themselves a church; they must call themselves museums'[70]. 'Interreligious dialogue is an indispensable condition for peace and a duty for all believers', he emphasised in a Meeting of diverse religious communities, Bosnia-Herzegovina, 2015[71].

4. Harmony AMONG RELIGIONS

4.1. Harmony – Implications and Applications

The word 'harmony'[72] comes from the art sector. It would plainly mean 'the combination of simultaneously sounded musical notes to produce a pleasing effect'[73]. When applied to the social context, it is a pleasing agreement of relations among persons in a certain group, may it be a family, institution, community, nation or the society in general. Harmony is not a readymade thing, but is a dynamic and ever-evolving process in social life. It involves five steps on the ladder that assists one ascend towards and arrive at the destination. They are 'goodwill (*sadbhaav*), equality (*sambhaav*), respect (*sammaan*), cooperation (*sahyog*) and harmony (*samanvay*)'[74].

Harmony has to be applied to the pleasing and complementary combination of the 'enriching difference' and the 'spirit of togetherness' in social life. The most vivid and powerful paradigm for the illustration of this harmony is 'rainbow', that celebrates diverse colours and shades of colours as a combined reality of 'one and many', as, two in one[75]. In the context of religions harmony signifies recognising their 'common origin, common existence and common destiny'[76]. It believes in all religious traditions as the 'gift of the same Creator' and the 'common cultural heritage of the human society'[77]. The diversity among them is to be benefited from and unity among them has to be celebrated, as two sides join together to make one coin.

4.2. Faith, interfaith and harmony among faiths

The word 'faith'[78] means 'belief, trust, confidence, conviction', and the like. Markedly, it is secular in its essence. It can be religious and non-religious, simultaneously. It exists in one who believes in God. It can exist in a scientist, an agnostic, a humanist, as well, who may not believe in such a God. It is inclusive of ideologies, cultures, experiences or convictions. It highlights the quality of perception, thought, experience and commitment in the author of faith[79]. It refers to the values and standards one holds on to in life and the principle that guides one in life.

Faith is an integrated discipline, by way of a balanced combination of three dimensions – faith in God, faith in other human beings and faith in oneself[80]. Faith in God is 'spiritual faith', faith in the other is 'social faith' and faith in oneself is 'individual faith'. Again, self-confidence is the fruit of individual faith, staying tuned to the society is the fruit of social faith and elevating the individual and social faith to the divine is spiritual faith. Faith is complete only when these three components are together. The three dimensions of faith are complementary to each other, as well.

Faith is not an isolated or insulated reality. Thousands of drops come together to form a flow of water. Likewise, several ideas, feelings, insights, views and experiences jointly compose a faith. Faith is necessarily an interactive and collective phenomenon. In other words, faith is a relational reality, like 'one body with many parts'; the dynamics of the former resemble the latter[81]. Only when faith becomes a shared happening it can be called a living faith. The degree and extent of interaction decides the excellence and worth of faith in one's life, too. Looking at faith in general as well as one's own faith in special from the angle of the other enriches faith itself.

Faith is essentially oriented to interfaith. 'Interfaith'[82] would mean 'faith meets faith' or 'believer meets believer'. When the quality of faith in a certain believer meets the quality of the faith in another believer, the process of harmony among faiths or religions is initiated. In other words, faith is a partnership of faiths. Partnership calls for rising above the individual levels. For example, while travelling in a 'flight', the divisions and demarcations of the world do not figure out anywhere. Everything appears 'at a glance'. The lesson that emerges from this instance is that 'differences' figure out only 'on the surface' and in higher altitudes there is a sense of equality and unity and that is the proof of a full-blown faith[83]. In the process of securing a larger faith, the divine and the human both become larger as well as deeper and higher, as well.

4.3. Dos for Harmony among Religions

'Unity in diversity'[84] is the characteristic feature of life in the world, in Asia in special and in India in very special. Diversity would mean being 'more than one' and being 'different', in one go. The poles of 'one' and 'many' require being harmonised. Difference that is inherent in diversity is not a negative quality, but is an enriching factor. Difference has to be engaged with and to be benefitted from[85]. Only then, the spirit of harmony among religions as well as other arenas can be promoted.

A 'culture of interaction'[86] is the call of the hour. Interaction has to be facilitated to regularly going on between seniors and juniors (inter-generational dialogue), between leaders and the common folk, among the past, present and future, among different religious communities, among different ideologies, among different cultures, between the rural and the urban life styles, between science and religion, between academics and grass roots, between the mainstream and the margins, and the like. Such an interactive culture will ensure inclusive thinking, integrated and harmonious living, which will advance all-round development, balanced growth and collective progress in life.

'Vasudhaiva Kutumbakam'[87] (the earth is but one family) is perhaps the greatest ideal for the humans to live as a family. But, *'udaarcharitaanaam'*[88] (being generous and open) is the conditional requirement for making the 'family culture' a reality. Co-existing peacefully among one another is the beginning of harmony. The 'spirit of living together' has to be fostered. The process of 'sharing with' the other the best of one's values has to be blended with that of 'sharing in' the best of the values the other has[89]. Willingness to learn from each other, walk with the other and work with the other will usher in a culture of making a shared pilgrimage to the same divine and of committing to making a better society, both at one fell swoop. These 'do's' will contribute substantially to fostering harmony among religions.

4.4. Do not's for Harmony among Religions

By way of 'do not's', misuse of religion for personal and political gains has to be checked. Religion with politics is the most unholy combine in the world and they require being separated. Mixing up religion with patriotism creates confusion and that danger needs to be avoided. Discriminating religious communities in the name of religion and in terms of minority and majority communities is a crime against divinity and humanity at the same time[90]. Fake *baabaas* and magicians pollute religion and they have to be ousted from the religious sector. Empty shows of religious rituals have to be curtailed. Religion should not be a 'nuisance factor' to social life, as rightly cautioned by *Sonu Nigam* and *Javed Akhtar*[91]. Religious subsidiaries like '*azaan*, bell, microphone, procession, fireworks, etc.' have to be edited to the minimum size of the need.

Entertaining prejudice against other religious communities is a sickness and measures have to be devised for treating such menace. Negative, derogative and overblown remarks on other religions have to be refrained from. Inflating religious issues and propagating lies about others and creating conflicts in the name of religion are diabolic in its essence and require being abstained from. One has to be aware that the 'instinct to survive, extend, dominate and rule over' is at the heart of religion and that instinct runs religion for the most part[92]. Often, the dynamics of money and power hijack religion and make it what it is not supposed to be. Political and economic overtones disfigure religion very much. A high percentage of religious custodians are illiterate, untamed and raw in their instincts and this state of affairs needs improvement.

Moreover, religion has an overdose of myths and superstitions, exaggerated theological abstractions and ritual obsessions and that has damaged religion and religions all over the world and continues to do so often in worse ways, especially in India[93]. It is an investigated fact that, for the most part, it is the elements of ignorance, guilt-feeling, fear and greed that govern the behaviour of the believers in the religious sector and not the right motives. The Directive Principles of the Constitution advocate the application of scientific temper in religion and life. *Pandit Jawaharlar Nehru*, the first Prime Minister of India, underscored and profusely emphasised the reinforcement of scientific temper, too. Only scientific temper can clear up the mess in the religious sector and promote the real development and progress of the so-called religious country that India is[94].

CONCLUSION

People of all faiths and ideologies have a mission in life. 'Seeing God on every human face', in the creation as well, is the core faith the humans must have. 'Making the family of God on earth' is the common mission of people of all religious and other communities in life. The spirit of 'sharing with' and 'sharing in' has to be combined as the complementary dynamics of the shared faith and mission of the humans. That calls for abiding by the perception of life advocated by Poet Basheer Badr, *'khudaa mujhe aisee khudaayee na de, ki apne siwaa kuchh dikhaayee na de'*, which means 'Oh God, do not give me such selfishness, spirituality or mission that does not allow me to see anything but myself or my own'.

Mahatma Kabeer cautions, *'bahtaa paanee nirmalaa, bandaa gandaa hoi; Saadhoo jan ramtaa bhalaa, daag na laage koi'*. One has to keep journeying to the other, like the 'flowing water', to the larger and higher horizons of life. Interaction and flow ensures purity in thought, word and deed and that is the secret of a dynamic, ever-blossoming and meaningful life, with divine implications and human applications. 'Making a good human being' is the ultimate utility of religion, which will facilitate people of all faiths, religions, ideologies and cultures to the shared mission in life, in line with the last message of Lord Robert Baden Powell, 'leave this world a little better than you found it'!

Endnotes

1. Angus Stevenson (Ed.), Oxford Dictionary of English, Oxford University Press, New Delhi, 1998, p. 572
2. Victoria, S. Harrison, Religion and Modern Thought, London, 2017, p. 11
3. *Ibid,* p. 17
4. *Ibid,* p. 11
5. Alister, E. McGrath, Christian Theology: An Introduction, West Sussex, U.K., 2011, p. 43
6. *Ibid,* p. 63
7. Carl Sterkens, Interreligious Learning: The Problem of Interreligious Dialogue in Primary Education, Leiden, Netherlands, 2010, p. 203
8. Sadhu Santinath, Encyclopedia of Philosophy of Indian Religion, New Delhi, 2001, p. 527
9. Victoria, S. Harrison, Religion and Modern Thought, London, 2017, p. 39
10. *Ibid,* p. 40
11. *Ibid,* p. 53
12. Mary, E. Ali, Through Three Miracles: Pulling the Sail in Together and Resetting "The Middle of the Political Spectrum", Pennsylvania, 2013, p. 90
13. *Ibid,* p. 132
14. M. Zuzanna Smolenska (Ed.), Embracing the Other: Philosophical, Psychological, and Historical Perspectives on Altruism, New York, 2019, p. 13
15. *Ibid,* p. 15
16. *Ibid,* p. 53
17. *Ibid,* p. 14
18. Vijay, K Bhatia, Ms Anne Wagner (Ed.), Diversity and Tolerance in Socio-Legal Contexts: Explorations in the Semiotics of Law, Burlington, USA, 2019, p. 14
19. *Ibid,* p. 26
20. *Ibid,* p. 56
21. Mary, E. Ali, Through Three Miracles: Pulling the Sail in Together and Resetting "The Middle of the Political Spectrum", Pennsylvania, 2013, p. 53
22. *Ibid,* p. 145
23. *Ibid,* p. 112
24. *Ibid,* p. 156
25. Vijay, K Bhatia, Ms Anne Wagner (Ed.), Diversity and Tolerance in Socio-Legal Contexts: Explorations in the Semiotics of Law, Burlington, USA, 2019, p. 53
26. *Ibid,* p. 57
27. *Ibid,* p. 59
28. *Ibid,* p. 63
29. *Ibid,* p. 61
30. *Ibid,* p. 107
31. *Ibid,* p. 119

32. *Ibid,* p. 126
33. Edward Bristow, Edward W. Bristow (Ed.), No Religion is an Island: The *Nostra Aetate* Dialogues, New York, 1998, p. 13
34. *Ibid,* p. 14
35. *Ibid,* p. 15
36. *Ibid,* p. 16
37. *Ibid,* p. 17
38. *Ibid,* p. 18
39. *Ibid,* p. 19
40. *Ibid,* p. 23
41. *Ibid,* p. 29
42. *Ibid,* p. 39
43. *Ibid,* p. 42
44. *Ibid,* p. 43
45. *Ibid,* p. 63
46. *Ibid,* p. 64
47. *Ibid,* p. 71
48. *Ibid,* p. 72
49. *Ibid,* p. 23
50. The Holy Bible, NIV, Michigan, 1994, Gen. 1.27, p. 2
51. *Ibid,* 1 Cor 3.16, p. 1298
52. *Ibid,* 1 Jn 4.8, p. 1396
53. *Ibid,* Mt 5.45, p. 1099
54. *Ibid,* Mt 5.48, p. 1099
55. *Ibid,* Acts 17.26, p. 1262
56. *Ibid,* Acts 14.17, p. 1257
57. *Ibid,* Jn 4.8, p. 1396
58. *Ibid,* Rom 12.18, p. 1291
59. *Ibid,* Mt 5.20, p. 1098
60. *Ibid,* Jn 17.21, p. 1230
61. Thomas Cahill, Pope John XXIII: A Life, London, 2002, p. 79
62. *Ibid,* p. 96
63. Paul, M. Collins, Christian Enculturation in India, New York, 2007, p. 157
64. George Weigel, Witness to Hope: The Biography of Pope John Paul II, New York, 2001, p. 619
65. *Ibid,* p. 519
66. George Weigel, Witness to Hope: The Biography of Pope John Paul II, New York, 2001, p. 619
67. *Ibid,* p. 630
68. Pope Francis, The Infinite Tenderness of God: Meditations on the Gospels, Maryland, 2016, p. 109
69. By Gill K. Goulding CJ, A Church of Passion and Hope, New York, 2015, p. 127
70. By Gill K. Goulding CJ, A Church of Passion and Hope, New York, 2015, p. 127
71. http://en.radiovaticana.va/news/2015/06/06/pope_says_Inter-faith_dialogue_is_a_duty_for_all_in_bosnia/1149623
72. Angus Stevenson (Ed.), Oxford Dictionary of English, Oxford University Press, New Delhi, 1998, p. 572
73. *Ibid,* p. 573
74. Ramchandra Verma (Ed.), *Maanak Hindee Kosha*, Vol. 5, Allahabad, 1993, p. 280
75. Max Weber, The Sociology of Religion, 1993, p. 07
76. *Ibid,* p. 23

77. *Ibid,* p. 53
78. Terence Patrick Dolan (Ed.), A Dictionary of Hiberno-English: The Irish Use of English, Dublin, 1998, p. 88
79. Carl Sterkens, Interreligious Learning: The Problem of Interreligicus Dialogue in Primary Education, Leiden, Netherlands, 2010, p. 203
80. Dottie Pennington Smith, You Can Do It!: Learning to Manage Life's Difficulties with God's Help, Bloomington, 2011, p. 327
81. Max Weber, The Sociology of Religion, 1993, p. 137
82. Terence Patrick Dolan (Ed.), A Dictionary of Hiberno-English: The Irish Use of English, Dublin, 1998, p. 207
83. Alf Hiltebeitel, *Dharma*: Its Early History in Law, Religion, and Narrative, New York, 2011, p. 59
84. T. K. Suman Kumar, India, Unity in Diversity, New Delhi, 2007, p. 08
85. *Ibid,* p. 53
86. *Ibid,* p. 217
87. Hiro G. Badlani, Hinduism, Path of the Ancient Wisdom, New York, 2008, p. 336
88. *Ibid,* p. 116
89. Paul Tillich, Dynamics of Faith, New York, 2001, p. 22
90. *Ibid,* p. 93
91. https://www.hindustantimes.com/music/sonu-nigam-s-old-azaan-tweets-surface-again-he-says-it-is-time-for-us-all-to-come-together/story-AZjjV6O2Gn9r75Az5Nke9O.html
92. T. K. Suman Kumar, India, Unity in Diversity, New Delhi, 2007, p. 97
93. *Ibid,* p. 103
94. *Ibid,* p. 147

Chapter - 4

Relations with People of Other Faiths

INTRODUCTION

Faith is integral to human life on earth. But it is not the same for all individuals and groups. Therefore, there is always the 'other' in the sector of faith, as in other realms. Now, do I dare to reduce the other to a potential 'me' or do I have to consider the reality of another entity other than me and enter into friendly relations with him or her? Well, there is a call for unlearning and relearning the way we conceive God and live our faith and enlarge the horizons of our lives, lest the divine, along with the human, get fragmented or shrunk and lost. At the end of the day, the social character in the humans demands 'friendly relations' with people of other faiths. These are some insights this article vouches to examine, explore and explain.

1. NOTIONAL CONSIDERATIONS

The notions connected to relation, relations, relationship and the social character that make them possible, along with their basic or inner sense compose the base of our discussion on the main title above. Notional considerations unearth in brief and make clear the implications of the key words in question.

1.1. Relation or Relations

'Relation or relations'[1] could be described as 'connection between two or more things'. It is the 'various connections, association, involvement, alliance or friendship in which persons are brought together'. It is 'the way people, groups, countries, etc. feel about or behave towards the other'. In other words, it is 'social, political or personal connections or dealings between or among individuals, groups, nations', and the like. As per the focus of the relation, relation could be personal relations, foreign relations, public relations, business relations, social relations, and the like.

1.2. Relation/s and Relationship

Relation/s and relationship have the following nuance between them. 'Relation' refers to the 'way to the connection or the way things are connected', while 'relationship'[2] refers to the 'connection itself or the sense of relation'. The difference is not spacious. But, while 'relations' describe larger contexts, like countries, cities, companies and large families, 'relationship' is used for smaller groups of people, making things more personal or human. For instance, relation, in science, refers to the 'interconnections between and among the parts of a system', like neuron in the brain cells. Relationship, in databases, is a 'situation that exists between two relational database tables'.

1.3. Relations and the Social Character of Life

Relation or relations is rooted in the 'social character' of life. Manifestly, the social fibre admits degrees, dimensions and gradations. The humans stand atop in the 'collective sense'[3], which is the core shared element in them that cannot be parted with, as 'homo sapiens', rational animals or social beings. That amounts to state that 'relation or relations' is the direct outcome of the social character. While human beings are born and they pass away as individuals, they are born from the society, live in the society and even for the society. Only together, can the humans make the best 'social sense' out of their lives.

2. THE BACKDROP OF THE THEME IN QUESTION

The theme in question has a significant backdrop that paved the way for evolving a Christian and a truly catholic thought in the Catholic tradition. This thought launched a family culture, in the larger context, for the Catholic and Christian mission to take off its course for the future. The backdrop presents the highlights of the Second Catholic World Council, along with its document *'Nostra Aetate'*, and its radical implications, and critiques their prospects along with its setback in the course of its journey ahead.

2.1. The Second Catholic World Council of Vatican

The sixties of the twentieth century made history anew and thus marked a new beginning, not only for the Catholic Christian community, but also for the other Christian communities and people or communities of all faiths, religious or not religious. The Catholic Church emerged then as an adult and pioneered the 'new wave of inter-faith relations or dialogue' in the history of the world. *'Nostra Aetate'*[4], meaning 'in our time', was the name of that momentous document, which thoroughly shook the entire religious world, the secular world as well, with a distinctive 'culture of inter'. 'Interface, interaction, interchange and cross-border relations' are a few of the catchphrases of this core culture of the believers, humans as well.

2.2. Christianity Back to Its Roots

Pope Francis, the most brilliant and down-to-earth pope of the modern times, observed, 'the Second Vatican Council was a serious attempt to take the Church back to its roots'[5]. The roots of Christianity would mean 'the human-divine person of Jesus Christ and his amazingly sublime values', which ceaselessly glow with a sense of 'good news', by way of a loving openness to and acceptance of one and all, beyond all borders. The document, along with the entire Council, was a clarion call for a 'restart' and a 'refresh' of Christianity. It could even be said as 'the second coming of Jesus' and therefore 'the second phase of Christianity'. 'A new way of being Christian' was its revitalising maxim that emerged from the above epoch-making event. 'Being a humane Christian' in the plural world was the call of the hour, too.

2.3. *Nostra Aetate* and Its Genius

The ground-breaking and thought-provoking realisation *Nostra Aetate* presented before Christians, all human beings as well, reads thus, "if Christians treat other individuals, groups and peoples in a manner that is not befitting sisters and brothers, they have no right to call God their Father"[6]. That makes it mandatory for Catholics to extend 'fraternal behaviour' to people of all faiths and affiliations. Discriminating persons on any ground would be a major violation of the Christian faith in God the Father, whom Jesus revealed, as one who sends sunshine and rains on the good and the evil alike[7]. The breach of the above ethics would land Catholics and Christians the tragic fate of finding themselves out of the campus, as rendered faithless. That would amount to state that Christians have to necessarily engage in friendly dialogue or interaction with people of all communities, religious and not religious as well as Christian and other. Such is the revolutionary genius of the above document.

2.4. Credits in the New Dimension and Style of Mission

It is heartening to note that, taking impetus from the Council, several Councils at the Pontifical level and Commissions at the national level of the Church (CBCI in India) were launched, for promoting dialogue with people of other religions as well as Churches[8]. Several Institutes and Commissions were established by Congregations and Dioceses, too. Seminaries started courses on 'ecumenical and inter-religious dialogue' and hundreds of scholars emerged, who wrote several books and articles on the diverse areas of the theme. Lots of sessions of interaction were organised, involving leaders and members of all communities of faith, too. Some individuals and institutes made outstanding contribution in the area, at local, national and international levels, noticeably so. These efforts motivated lots of people in other communities to initiate similar efforts, as well, efforts that were perhaps more applied to the social context than ever before[9].

2.5. A Theoretical Setback in the New Mission

All the same, it has to be admitted with deep regret that on the whole the Christian community at the level of the leadership took a 'back seat' in this great mission. A bird's eye view of the reasons could be the following. The new area of the mission was to engage in 'dialogue, inter-religious dialogue or interfaith dialogue'. The word 'dialogue', used independently, sounded too classical or ambiguous. 'Inter-religious dialogue' had too much of a theological connotation and so was understood to be the business of theologians. Theologians, by way of theorising it, seem to have complicated it more than necessary, unfortunately so. 'Inter-faith dialogue' was slightly simpler, but still was thought of as something only scholars or leaders could attempt[10]. As a result, the above mission was not owned by most heads and members of the Catholic and even Christian community, either for not understanding it properly or for finding it difficult or not to the taste or to the ultimate advantage of doing what a screw driver could do.

2.6. Practical Prospects of the Mission of Relations

The main title of this article, 'relations with people of other faiths', suggests clearly a Christian mission, human mission too, within the reach of every person. Promoting friendly relations with all human beings has various degrees, grades, levels and dimensions and one of them or some of them can suit all peoples, irrespective of gender, age, education, position, class, caste, creed, and the like. 'Good human relations' is everyone's cup of tea and people of all persuasions will equally relish it, as well. Language is the door to enter into the world of the other, and therefore, proficiency in the national and/or regional language/s of the country will go remarkably a long way in fostering relations with people of any affiliation or level who would come on one's way in life. However, it is the mindset of the believer that matters, how he or she conceives faith, God, other, life, mission, and the like. Travelling the path oneself will reveal to the Christian and all believers that the lasting prospects of promoting friendly relations are highly promising[11].

3. CONTEXTUAL CHALLENGES

Context is the situation in which everything happens. It causes certain things to happen, too, which otherwise perhaps wouldn't happen. Context is often precarious and it challenges those who are within the area and places a persuasive invitation to creatively respond to it. The current times are painfully aware of the corona virus. But it is more than relevant to consider the many-sided context of our mission, in terms of a series of viruses other than corona, like social virus, political virus, religious virus and ethical virus. All these viruses are vibrant in our country and in the society at large, and they are heavily destructive, each in its own way, to human life and, I suppose, are more death-defying than corona. No wonder, our mission has to be reconceived and refashioned to suit the demand of the context, in view of enhancing the relational quality of the life of the humans as well as of making the mission worth the while.

3.1. The Corona Virus

The respiratory corona virus, with the pet name Covid 19, has shaken the entire human world. It has shattered its self-confidence and sense of dignity, to a great extent. It has leveled every one, like death, to equal footing, without considering religious or not religious, catholic or protestant, Christian or Muslim, male or female, rich or poor, high or low, black or white and big or small. The single criterion that made some sense to corona virus was the 'power of immunity'. The Himalayan lesson that comes across to the humans across the globe from the corona virus is to 'stay united as brothers, sisters, neighbours and friends' across the human-made borders and be of help to each other in remaining healthy and well[12].

3.2. The Social Virus

While a fine-tuned social character is the distinction of being human beings, on the one hand, the sheer violation of the very same social sense is the brutal virus that haunts the humans, every moment of their lives, on the other. 'Discriminating' human beings and 'dividing' them in the name of ethnic background, gender, language, colour, caste, class, creed, rite, dress patterns, food habits, ideology, culture and tradition explain how the social virus eats up the human qualities of the humans. The derailed mindset of considering high and low, black and white, right and wrong, mine and yours, us and them, and the like, is the deep-seated social perversion that is bent on plundering all that is 'humane' on earth and on leaving the humans bankrupt of human sense[13]. This age old and yet ever new social virus requires being treated with effective vaccine/s, lest the humans cease to be social beings. Any mission can make sense only then.

3.3. The Political Virus

The political virus in the human society is as old as the human society. The four-sided 'instinct to survive, extend, dominate and rule over' is the basis of this virus. It grows by advertising oneself as the best option for all, canvassing the blind support of the people, liquidating all that is different and opposite and thus by monopolising the entire show. The politically loaded people are clever enough not to fail in exploiting the leading religious system, the media and the economic pockets as the scaffolding to climb up and construct their kingdom. The deadly phenomenon advances by being authoritarian and autocratic, by taking over all autonomous institutions and by literally ruling over as nothing less than God incarnate, declaring all the different voices anti-state and foul[14]. In the process, the citizens are sure to be befooled to all details and turned upside down, helpless and in shatters, except those who worship the self-appointed gods in reign. For all obvious reasons, there is no single-doze medicine for this political virus. But a missioner has to be aware that one has to perform the mission of life in such an insecure and challenging political scenario.

3.4. The Religious Virus

The phrase 'religious virus' would sound ironical. Yes, indeed it is. Religion is supposed to be the ladder for the believers to climb up the rungs of heaven. But when it goes off the track, it becomes a mere license to play with 'power and money' and enjoy all that the world can offer, in the name of God, mostly for the higher ups. The common believers are very much left with the fate of being domesticated and reduced to fall a prey to the whims and fancies of the custodians and to keep touching their feet for blessings, to survive or to prosper. The nexus with politics makes it easy for all these to happen, especially for the majority religious wing. Aggressive evangelism, along with violation of the freedom of conscience, thought and expression, both within and outside, clearly smacks of the weak spiritual sense in the religion[15]. When the country and the world have lots of instances to prove such occurrences, it is too obvious that the religious virus requires being diagnosed and treated. 'Physician, heal yourself' is a thought for the way.

3.5. The Ethical Virus

The ethical virus is too apparent in the social life around to deny, unless one opts to close one's eyes by all means. By and large, the ethical fibre of the humans seems to keep eroding progressively in the public sphere of the so called developed and globalised world, rather than getting strengthened. *'Satyamevjayate'*[16] is the esteemed axiom of the nation as well as an esteemed ideal of most religions. The Father of the nation,

Mahatma Gandhi, had the guts to experiment with truth. But, to his utter shame, experiment with lies, by way of telling, propagating and acting on half-truths and full lies, seems to win the game at the end of the day, in religion, too. The environment of the country, of the larger society, too, shows up as acutely short of values, nobility, integrity and a sense of right and wrong, due to the terrible hollowness of conscience and ethics. The religious sector appears to be more part of the problem than of the solution[17]. In such a sad state of affairs, what could be the response of a diligent human being, religious or other, is a question that requires keen attention by everyone, who is conscious of shouldering a mission in life.

4. CONCEPTUAL MOTIVATIONS

The basic role of the concept is to motivate and inspire the humans in a certain direction, purposefully so. An idea can change the world. In fact, only an idea can evoke real change in human beings. Law and fear of punishment, along with goody-goody instructions, can do only temporary patchworks. Only a motivated human being can pursue an idea, a thought, an ideal, a vision and a mission. Good sense, along with guts and calibre, keeps the mission clearly geared towards the destination, too. Achieving the objective would necessitate being informed, equipped, enlightened, energised and empowered to shoulder a mission and to translate the same in to the various routines of lives. It is a motivated concept that facilitates the above process into fulfilling an effective mission. The current concept is socially motivated and it is strongly inclined to promoting 'good relations with people of other faiths and affiliations', irrespective of the fact there is a world of difference in the way individuals, families, institutions, communities and nations conduct themselves.

4.1. Relations – Friendships and Partnerships

In line with the linguistic and notional implications cited above, a few of the crystal forms of relation could be 'acquaintance, friendship, partnership and fellowship' among believers of all faiths and associations. Relations branch out into 'interpersonal, inter-family, inter-institutional, inter-community, inter-national relations', along with its major and minor offshoots, like 'inter-faith, inter-religious, inter-ideological, inter-linguistic, inter-gender, inter-age, inter-caste, inter-class, inter-tribal and inter-cultural' relations[18]. Relation/s is an attitudinal mindset, in which sentiments of 'goodwill, respect, appreciation, esteem, understanding, love, care, help, cooperation', etc guide the destinies of friendship with other believers, thinkers and followers. Relation or friendship can prosper only on equal footing, which is above considerations of superior and inferior, right and wrong, good and bad, powerful and weak and rich and poor.

Good relations are 'inclusive, interactive, participatory, collaborative and harmonious' in character and they usher in friendships and partnerships in life. What is required is a talent for building bridges.

4.2. The Other – Friend, Brother/Sister, Better Half

The 'other' is he or she who exists or is present in addition to me[19]. He or she is not the same as me, but is clearly different from me. Male and female are a case in point. Male is not female and female is not male. Both are different from each other. Both reflect the divine image. Even as clearly defined individual human beings with different identity, dignity and role, they share the same human nature. In a similar fashion, the other has a different faith, ideology, perception of life, and so on, along with a clear identity and dignity, but either of them shares the same human nature. They are not enemies to each other, and not meant to be. They are intended to be friends and companions, as extension of one's own being. The difference in each other is not a negative factor, but is an element of enrichment. The 'others' together, like the colours in the rainbow, make sense collectively, true to their social quality[20]. The reciprocal value in being brotherly-sisterly/friendly, even better half, one to another, is what defines and qualifies the other.

4.3. People – Family, Community, Nation, Society

Human beings exist as individuals and groups, at the same time. Groups can be family, institution, institute, organization, forum, community, nation and society, along with its sub-units. 'People' is composed of a collection of individuals, small or big[21]. Every individual who joins the group is an 'other'. Living alone in the physical sense does not mean being cut off from the people, family, community or society. Living together in a group does not guarantee being a family, community or a society, too. 'Staying tuned to each other' with a unity of purpose and mutual bonding, leading to relation or friendship makes the difference[22]. The dignity and merit of being a people, family, community, nation or society is inherent in balancing the equation between 'one and many', like 'one body with many parts', which is a perfect blend of rights and duties. The spirit of 'unity in diversity' and 'diversity in unity', as a collection of several 'other's, defines the moral fibre of being 'a people, a family or a community'[23].

4.4. Faith – Inter-faith, Harmony among Faiths, the Divine in Full

More often than not, faith is understood to be the sole property of the religious sector. But, as a matter of fact, it is not so. Everyone has a faith, religious or other. Faith is larger than religion. Faith is a perception, an idea, a conviction, a trust, a commitment to the power above, a devotion to one's conscience, and the like[24]. A scientist or a thinker also is dedicated to the supreme energy or knowledge beyond him or her. Faith is plural and three-sided in its character. It has individual, social and spiritual facets, as faith in oneself, faith in the other and faith in God, all existing as one shared but single reality[25]. It is inclusive, relational, interactive, collaborative and complementary, necessarily so. The spirit of being one, as in a concert, articulates what faith is all about. Therefore, faith can exist meaningfully only in unison and it is geared towards 'interfaith, multi-faith, all faiths and harmony among faiths'. 'Sharing with' the other the best of my values, along with 'sharing in' the best values of the other' is the dynamics of faith[26]. Only when one is able to live the 'ethics' of such 'collective sense' in faith, one's hearts, minds and spirits will be large enough to contain God or the divine, in the real sense of the term, or in full. Well, divinity, along with humanity, is much larger than religion and even faith. That is the logic of life, human life in special.

5. THE MISSION OF EXTERNAL RELATIONS

The idea of the 'mission' has evolved from the Christian world, to be more exact, from Jesus Christ who, with a singular vision, performed a unique and universal mission in the world. While being a Jew, he emerged beyond the Jewish religion, beyond religion itself, blending all that the human and divine realities can contain. A brother and friend to one and all, a man for all seasons and a revolutionary to that effect, he became an unparalleled paradigm for the mission of making good relations with one and all, outstandingly so. The mission of external relations has to be applied to every person, community and context, in favour of strengthening the relational network of the family of God across the globe.

5.1. The Foundational Values and Directives of Jesus

Jesus stated in a crystal-clear way the human, relational and reciprocal 'culture of inter', 'do to the other what you would have him or her do to you'[27]. This 'golden rule' governs the dynamics of inter-personal, inter-family and inter-community relations, irrespective of all differences. Further, Jesus summarised all his values of love into a paradigm of human-divine blend, 'whatever you did to one of the least of these sisters and brothers of mine, you did to me'[28]. The relations with the humans, even the so called least, are balanced with the divine world, that too, on an equal footing in effect. Pope John Paul illustrated the dynamics of this culture further when he addressed People of Other Religions (Madras, 1986), "By dialogue, we let God be present in our midst, for as we open ourselves to one another, we open ourselves to God"[29]. Being open to one and all, without discrimination and leading to good relations, is the Christian and human way to approach God, the God of all, positively so, and definitely not otherwise.

5.2. Latest Papal Guidelines for the Christian Mission of Social Relations

In the recent encyclical '*Fratelli Tutti*'[30], meaning 'fraternity and social friendship', Pope Francis underscores the mission of promoting relations with everyone in an outstanding way. The above words were coined by Saint Francis of Assisi to address his brothers and sisters and they intensely radiate the flavour of the 'good news' of Jesus Christ, markedly so. Further, the Joint Declaration of Pope Francis and *Sheikh Ahmed el-Tayeb*, Grand Imam of *Al-Azhar*, in Abu Dhabi, 2019, reads "God has created all human beings equal in rights, duties and dignity, and has called them to live together as brothers and sisters"[31]. The brotherly and sisterly sentiments reflected therein make a clarion call to transcend all sorts of difference, distance and otherness and to touch upon the realm of social friendship, beyond all human-made borders. This maxim summarises all the sublime values Jesus lived and taught.

5.3. 'Making the Family of God the Father on Earth' – the Umbrella Outcome of the Mission

Grounded in the filial experience of God as 'Father', Jesus became fraternally incarnate to every person, as an elder brother, a Master, a friend, a companion, a healer, a giver of life, and the like, all these roles in the spirit of 'he does all things well'[32]. In point of fact, the mission Jesus launched was truly catholic and all-embracing, 'making the family of God the Father on earth', the 'mission par excellence' and a 'mission with a difference', for Catholics, Christians and for all faiths, for all times as well[33]. Therefore, all human beings are daughters and sons of the same Heavenly Father and are sisters, brothers and friends, one to another. That would amount to conclude that 'promoting friendly relations with people of all faiths, ideologies and cultures' is Christian mission, in the larger context. All other dimensions and details of the Christian mission have to be conducted in such a way that this larger ethics is not violated and ultimately accomplish the 'paternal-filial-fraternal' style of family relations of God the Father on earth[34]. Commitment to the larger mission of making a 'family of families', a 'community of communities', a 'nation of nations' and a human society that is 'charged with the divine nerve' is the call of the hour[35].

CONCLUSION

'External relations' define the larger social fibre of nations, communities, families, institutions and individuals. Establishing, maintaining and promoting friendly relations with all 'others' is the litmus test of a faith that is worth being had, too. The ethics of good relations, leading to 'fraternal friendship and cooperation' with people of all communities, especially well-meaning persons, in view of making a better nation and society, is the right response to the challenging context of the bitterly viruses as well as the rightly motivating insights and divinely charged human values of Jesus. The Christian community is called to rise above tendencies of making 'islands', 'parallel lines' and 'cobwebs' as well as of 'cutting the limbs to suit the ready-made churchy coat', in the name of the mission of Jesus. Rather, it will do well delving deep and large in to the ocean of the human and environmental world of the very same Creator of all, God the Father, after the fashion of Jesus Christ.

Endnotes

1. Sirshree, Celebrating Relationships: Bring Love, Life, Laughter in Your Relations, Pune, 2015, p. 07
2. *Ibid,* p. 08
3. *Ibid,* p. 17
4. Edward Bristow (Ed.), No Religion is an Island: The *Nostra Aetate* Dialogues, New York, 1998, p. 07
5. Andrew Singleton, Religion, Culture & Society–A Global Approach, London, 2014, p. 44
6. Rafael Luciani, Synodality–A New Way of Proceeding in the Church, New Jersey, 2022, p. 43
7. The Holy Bible, NIV, Michigan, 1994, Mt 5.45, p. 1099
8. Suhas Pereira, The Challenges of Vatican II for an Authentic Indian Catholic Church, Zurich, 2020, p. 31
9. *Ibid,* p. 57
10. Mark, D. Chapman, Vladimir Latinovic (Ed.), Changing the Church–Transformations of Christian Belief, Practice and Life, Gewerbestrasse, Switzerland, 2020, p. 209
11. *Ibid,* p. 302
12. Gerard Delanty (Ed.), Pandemics, Politics, and Society: Critical Perspectives on the Covid-19 Crisis, Boston, 2021, p. 57
13. *Ibid,* p. 103
14. *Ibid,* p. 107
15. *Ibid,* p. 126
16. Sonia Singh, Defining India: Through Their Eyes, New Delhi, 2019, p. 36
17. *Ibid,* p. 109
18. Sirshree, Celebrating Relationships: Bring Love, Life, Laughter in Your Relations, Pune, 2015, p. 97
19. *Ibid,* p. 38
20. *Ibid,* p. 153
21. Nancy Snow (Ed.), In the Company of Others: Perspectives on Community, Family, and Culture, London, 2019, p. 33
22. *Ibid,* p. 57
23. *Ibid,* p. 63
24. Ghoulem Berrah, Our Common Faith: A Plea for Interfaith Harmony, Aventura, Florida, 2019, p. 13

25. *Ibid,* 33
26. *Ibid,* 57
27. The Holy Bible, NIV, Michigan, 1994, Mt 7.12, p. 1100
28. *Ibid,* Mt 25.40, p. 1128
29. George Weigel, Witness to Hope: The Biography of Pope John Paul II, New York, 2001, p. 619
30. Pope Francis, *Fratelli Tutti*: On Fraternity and Social Friendship, New York, 2020, p. 03
31. Dane Munro, Ian McIntosh, Nour Fara Haddad (Ed.), Peace Journeys: A New Direction in Religious Tourism and Pilgrimage Research, Newcastle upon Tyne, United Kingdom, 2020, p. 59
32. The Holy Bible, NIV, Michigan, 1994, Mk 7.37, p. 1158
33. Rafael Luciani, Synodality–A New Way of Proceeding in the Church, New Jersey, 2022, p. 109
34. Jordan Nyenyembe, Fraternity in Christ–Building the Church as Family, Nairobi, 2005, p. 10
35. Paul, M. Collins, Christian Enculturation in India, New York, 2021, p. 157

Chapter - 5

Mission among the Peoples—An Interactive Paradigm of Good News

INTRODUCTION

The 'sense of mission' that emerges from one's faith is the focal point in life. But the missioner has to be equipped with the know-how of the concept, context, style and the beneficiaries of the mission. A one-sided and solo approach, as in 'mission to the people' would fall short of the intended purpose, if not backfire. 'Mission among the people' is a style that is inclusive, collaborative and complementary. As a result, it evolves from among all the constituent members and assures the optimum outcome. Having reviewed the framework of the mission and the inadequacy of the one-sided mission, as suggested by 'mission to the peoples', this paper analyzes the participatory and all-inclusive style of 'mission among the peoples', highlighting its implications and brilliant prospects as applied to life.

1. THE FRAMEWORK OF THE MISSION

The first part of the paper describes 'the framework of the mission' and in the process, explains the nuances of the concepts, such as 'mission, diversity, difference, individuality and privacy, the social character and relatedness and people/community'.

1.1. Mission

Mission[1] is a 'special task or undertaking'. As commissioned by the 'higher power', it is a 'calling from above'. 'Reaching out to one and all as well as far and wide' is its larger implications, while an intense commitment to the cause confirms its deeper meanings. Mission is grounded in the vision, universally conceived but locally applied. A 'sense of mission'[2] is the core of the mission. It motivates one towards investing oneself to the cause in hand, with the 'whole heart, mind and spirit'. The 'quality' of the mission performed has a direct bearing on its higher and larger outcome. The altitude and magnitude of the mission acquired is the scale of the credit the missioner accords the one who has empowered him or her. The sense of mission is the yardstick of the purposefulness of the mission, as well.

1.2. Diversity

'Diversity'[3] would mean a wide variety of something. It implies two things, 'being many' or more than one and 'being different' from the other. Diversity is the mastermind of the Creator and is perhaps the most incontestable reality of the universe. It applies to the entire creation, planets, vegetation, animals and human beings. In the human cultures, it makes a world of difference, though in a very subtle manner. Ethnicity, gender, language, food taste, dress pattern, ideology, social mores, cultural streams, faith perceptions, spiritual sensibilities, and the like, determine the distinctiveness of the diverse human editions. The collective sense, as in 'one body and many parts', emerges from the diverse expressions of the human nature. It contributes also to the higher reality of 'unity' in diversity. It makes diversity meaningful and purposeful, too. The missioner has to apply himself or herself to the vast and many-sided context of diversity.

1.3. Difference

Difference[4] is the distinguishing mark in diversity. It is the distinctiveness of a person, thing too, that makes one special or unique. It is this difference that justifies the relevance of one's existence. Difference does not have any negative connotation, but is always positive in its element. It is an enriching and creative factor. 'Male-female' is a case in point. Difference affirms the specific, un-interchangeable and singular roles in each unit. Difference stands for the brilliance of life, especially of the humans. It is never contradictory but is complementary, one to another, as 'made for each other'. 'One completes the other' is the logic of difference. The quality of difference makes interaction among the diverse components necessary and relevant. The missioner has to situate himself or herself in the framework of diversity of individuals and communities, as regards the mission in hand.

1.4. Individuality and Privacy

An 'individual' is a person who exists as a separate and distinct entity. Individual could be an institution, too. 'Individuality'[5] is the state or quality of being an individual. As a person, an individual is separate from other persons or people and he or she possesses his/her own needs, goals, rights and responsibilities. The character of being a particular person distinguishes him or her from others of the same kind, especially when strongly marked. An individual or a group is endowed with 'privacy'[6], which is a 'space to oneself', can be rightfully commanded. It could be a special place or a piece of information inherent to oneself. Privacy is a fundamental right to be protected by the Constitution of India, as per the historic judgment by the Supreme Court of India, on 24 August 2017[7]. The mission has to honour the individuality, dignity and the sacred space of the person or community in hand while performing his or her mission.

1.5. The Social Character and the Relatedness

Frederick Engels, in his classic ecological work 'The Part Played by Labour in the Transition from Ape to Man', observes "in nature, nothing takes place in isolation. Everything affects and is affected by every other thing"[8]. The diverse and numerous processes of 'motion and interaction' in play govern the dynamics of the unfathomable mystery of the creation as well as the whereabouts of the wisdom of the Creator. 'Everything is connected to everything else' is the wisest paradigm of human relatedness. It is the refined social character of the humans that makes relatedness a reality. Human beings are individuals, as they are born and as they pass away from this world. But they are and have to be necessarily social beings as they live in the society, to all details. Therefore, mission can be really accomplished only in a shared manner, lest it violates the essential social sense and reciprocal relatedness of life.

1.6. People / Community

On account of the social fibre, human beings compose groups, like families, communities, organisations, nations and society, along with its sub-units. Collection of individuals makes 'people'[9] or communities, with different traditions of ethnic origin, caste, creed, ideology and culture. Living together in a group demand abiding by certain ideologies and traditions, along with 'staying tuned to each other'[10] within the group. Definitely, a different community is not to be cut off, like an island or lake. It is not to be travelling like parallel lines, too, having hardly anything to do with it. All the same, all communities or people have a uniqueness and dignity that cannot be violated in any disguise. The missioner has to abide by the framework of the rights and duties of individual communities or people, while performing the mission one is assigned to accomplish.

2. THE BACKDROP: 'MISSION TO THE PEOPLES'

The second section of the paper discusses 'the backdrop: mission to the peoples'. 'Mission to the Peoples, its larger musings, its institutional pedestal, its colonial mindset, its one-sided approach and towards larger prospects' are the titles that are covered in it.

2.1. Mission to the Peoples (MTP)

'Mission to the Peoples', popularly known in its Latin rendering *'missio ad gentes'*[11], has been mostly the missionary style of the Christian community from its inception. It refers to the mission Jesus inaugurated and the Church was commissioned to perform, too. Without doubt, it is more or less the very same mission the Christian has to perform for all times. The Second World Catholic Council has discussed the mission under this title profusely too. But, as a matter of fact, 'mission to the peoples' is roughly the summary of the mission the Church has been performing till then[12]. While recognizing all the merits of this missionary style, the Council redefined the mission in the sense of 'mission among the peoples'. 'Mission among the peoples' is the focal point of the Council as a 'new style' of accomplishing it, well, an 'interactive way'. The due recognition of the larger and plural context of the mission and the collaborative and shared style of accomplishing it made the mission new and its style different. For the rest, the mission is the same.

2.2. MTP – Its Larger Musings

The decree 'mission to the peoples' *(missio ad gentes)* revised the traditional maxim of the Church 'there is no salvation outside the Church'[13], which meant 'an exclusive right over the saving grace of God'. Further, a broader perception of people of other Christian and religious communities led to larger musings, like 'accepting them as co-members of the same group of humans', 'being united with them in a sense of esteem and love', 'being familiar with the national and religious traditions of fellow beings', 'sharing in their cultural and social life', 'learning the treasures God has distributed among the nations of the earth', 'acknowledging the presence of God in other traditions', 'recognition of living according to one's conscience', 'absorbing their ways and culture', 'sincere and patient dialogue with them', and 'collaborating with people of other organisations, denominations and faiths'.

2.3. MTP – Its Institutional Pedestal

The pastoral intention of 'mission to the peoples' was 'founding new churches'[14]. This intention smacked of a scheme of extending the boundaries of the Church. This 'institutional and hierarchical pedestal' of pre-eminence meant a strategy or intent of 'converting' the other to one's fold. This intent further meant 'violating the conscience and the fundamental right of the other' and thus 'treading on the toe of the other', which is not approved by Jesus, positively so. It is 'uncomfortable with religious and social pluralism'. Such a self-coiled mindset utterly defeats the human and spiritual niceties distinctive of the sublime mission inherited from Jesus. The institutional pedestal of 'mission to the peoples' and its thrust areas are grounded in 'discredited missiological approaches' and are harmful to the mission, along the lines of Jesus[15].

2.4. MTP – Its Colonial Mindset

'Mission to the peoples' is grounded in the 'centrality of salvation' by Jesus and Christianity. Considering oneself as 'exclusive, superior and unique' as well as 'definitive, normative and absolute' is certainly a 'holier than thou' theological attitude, which was accumulated over the millennia[16]. To consider people of other faiths 'potential Christians' is to violate the fundamental duty of respecting the individuality and dignity of the other. Such 'imperial and colonial overtones' oriented to 'conquering and displacing the other' shows up a political outlook and highhandedness on people of other convictions and affiliations. A colonial mindset in the mission of Jesus is not only belittling the noble missionary goals and is objectionable in the larger context[17].

2.5. MTP – Its One-sided Approach

'Mission to the peoples' is a one-way activity, like 'riding the horse whose sides are blocked'[18]. It attempts to export, transfer and transplant a faith in a certain cultural setting to another place. It suffers from a 'giver-complex', which treats people of other faiths as mere objects and belittles them. There is absolutely no denying the fact that Jesus commands an unparalleled standing in the entire world and he taught with a gleaming authority, unlike other teachers of law[19]. His ethical values, palpably so, stand out as singular across all traditions of values, too. However, Jesus and his values do not approve, not even the least, the exclusive divine right to exist and to extend. Nay, such a claim violates extremely the basic Christian ethos the Church is professed to live. A self-righteous and un-negotiable notion of faith is totally one-sided and does not correspond to the noble and serene way Jesus lived and taught. The overbearing concepts of 'mission to the peoples' seem to disregard the undeniable fact that 'God was already there in the world before the Christian missioners arrived'[20].

2.6. Towards Larger Prospects

There is no denying the fact that 'mission to the peoples', along with *Nostra Aetate*, made a considerable momentum in fostering better relations with people of diverse religious and cultural affiliations. Mission studies developed new branches, like 'interfaith dialogue', 'comparative religion' and 'cultural adaptation', along with scholars, books, articles, courses in religious institutes, sessions with other believers, chairs and departments of religious studies, institutes, councils, commissions and other initiatives[21]. All the same, 'mission to the peoples' received the centre stage in most circles and in course of time, it mostly overpowered the missionary style of the Christian community. Consequently, much of the enthusiasm and activities pioneered by *Nostra Aetate* dwindled for reasons like, hesitance in losing comfort zones and larger demands of the new mission[22].

3. MISSION AMONG THE PEOPLES: THE NOTION AND ITS GROWTH

The third part of the paper elucidates 'mission among the peoples: the notion and its growth'. The sub-points analyzed are 'the notion, the beginnings, the underpinnings, the journey, the larger application and the democratic and secular implications'.

3.1. The Notion

The title 'Mission among the Peoples' is the English derivative of the Latin phrase *'Missio Inter Gentes'*[23], meaning 'mission between or among the nations or the peoples'. It could also imply 'trans, across or beyond' the peoples, since meeting of two or more is oriented towards creating a new effect. In other words, 'Mission among the Peoples' is a mission 'of the people, by the people, for the people, with the people, from the people and among the people'. That would amount to state that, in this sense, mission is a collective reality, involving all the constituent members. It 'emerges or evolves from among the people' as a natural process, as well.

3.2. The Beginnings

Mission among the Peoples, as a term in Latin *'missio inter gentes'*, was first proposed by 'William R. Burrows', who was a research scientist and professor of missiology in the World Christianity Programme at New York Theological Seminary and Managing Editor Emeritus of Orbis Books, Mary knoll, New York, in 2001[24]. It was systematically developed by Prof. 'Yonathan Yun-Ka Tan', Professor of Australian Catholic University, Sydney, a distinctly seasoned specialist of missiology, and, as a concept, was approved and advanced by the 'Federation of Asian Bishops' Conference'[25].

3.3. The Underpinnings

The underpinning of the concept could be located in the final statements of all the plenary assemblies of FABC from 1974 to 2000. The concept was published in FABC Papers 109, in 2004, in the article, titled *'Missio*

Inter Gentes: Towards a New paradigm of the Mission Theology of the Federation of the Asian Bishops' Conference'[26]. This essay surveys the principal aspects and foundational principles of the FABC's theology of mission – a 'threefold dialogue with the myriad of Asian religious traditions, Asian cultures and the teeming masses of Asian poor and marginalised'[27]. Observably, the underpinnings of the new thought have an ecclesial and official status and are exceptionally historic, impressive and convincing.

3.4. The Journey

The concept further journeyed and acquired wider clarity, taking and thrust by diverse conferences, publications, researches and field engagements. 'International Association of Catholic Missiologists' explored the nuances of the theme through a conference on '*Missio Inter Gentes*: Challenges and Opportunities', held in Nairobi, in 2013[28]. Institute of Missiology and the Study of Theologies beyond Europe, WWU, University of Munster, had an international theological colloquium on '*Missio Inter Gentes*: the Future of Christian Mission in Asia', in 2014[29]. Divine Word Institute of Mission Studies, Manila, launched a journal with the name '*Missio Inter Gentes'* in 2015[30]. In addition, several inter-faith activists and missiologists have been engaged in researching the area further.

3.5. The Larger Application

Law has been considered in terms of its plural and complex nuances, by ways of law between states as 'law among people'. Faculty of Law, McGill University, Canada, launched 'McGill Journal of International Law & Legal Pluralism' in 2016 for inventing international law in an inclusive, collective and incisive way[31]. The journal is intended to be an open forum for debating, exploring and exchanging the shades of law in social life. It is committed to an informed, constructive and collaborative redefinition of law in the context of diversity across the nations. The initiative of McGill University is a paradigm by itself in applying religion and religious perceptions to secular disciplines and contexts of life.

3.6. Democratic and Secular Implications

'Mission among the Peoples' implies all that the word 'democracy' could ever imagine. In principle, it stands for 'power (*kratos*) of the people (*demos*)', which is scheduled to result in 'collective governance', willed by one and all[32]. Further, 'mission among the peoples' highlights the 'all-inclusive' character of 'secularism', envisioned in the Constitution of India. The implications of both democracy and secularism vibrantly boost up the spirit of a mission to be accomplished by and among all its beneficiaries, who have a complete share in the entire process of the mission. The democratic and secular framework ensures every constituent member of his or her dignity, freedom, right, duty, voice, role, and the like, in making the mission a collective engagement, in the interests of one and all[33].

4. MISSION AMONG THE PEOPLES: ITS CHRISTIAN GROUNDING

The fourth segment of the paper considers 'mission among the peoples: its Christian grounding'. It covers sub-themes 'the second catholic world council of Vatican, *Nostra Aetate*: the thought-provoking realisation, *Nostra Aetate*; a culture of interaction, the many-sided Christian foundation, the core values of Jesus and the illuminating papal pronouncements'.

4.1. The Second Catholic World Council of Vatican

The Second World Council of Vatican of the Catholic community made history anew, in the sixties of the twentieth century, by launching the 'new wave of inter-faith relations'[34] in the history of the world. With a 'new way of being Christian'[35] as the thrust, it was a 'restart' of the understanding of Christian life and mission. In other words, "the Second Vatican Council was a serious attempt to take the Church back to its roots", as Pope Francis observes[36]. 'Back to the roots' would mean 'Jesus and his values', which is the core of the Christian mission. It 'redefined the vision and mission of Jesus' and that of the Church, initiating the 'second phase of Christianity' thus. No doubt, the Council struck a 'note of unity' within the Catholic Church, in the Christian community, among all religious traditions and in the entire human society, all in one[37]. This was the plinth area of 'mission among the peoples'.

4.2. *Nostra Aetate*: A Thought-provoking Realisation

Nostra Aetate[38], meaning 'in our time', was the incredible document thunder-stormed by the above Council. The thought-provoking realisation it presented to Christians in particular and the world in general had direct reference to the very foundations of Christian faith. 'If Christians treat other individuals, groups and peoples in a manner that is not befitting sisters and brothers, they have no right to call God their Father'[39]. That would amount to state that Catholics and Christians are bound to think as large as the world and to engage in fostering relations, fellowship and collaboration with people of all communities, lest they lose their filial status with God and cease to be Christians, even believers. Being 'catholic' by way of 'all-inclusive'[40] was the call of the hour. The highly demanding realisation of *Nostra Aetate* of the Second World Council of Vatican paved the way for 'mission among the people' at the centre stage of Christian life and mission.

4.3. *Nostra Aetate*: A 'Culture of Interaction'

The ground-breaking realisation of *Nostra Aetate* has initiated a 'culture of interaction or dialogue and fellowship'[41] in the Christian mission, brilliantly so. The most major indicator in this missionary mode is the recognition of a 'common origin, a common existence and a common destiny'[42] with people of all religious and other persuasions. Christians are called upon to 'acknowledge, preserve and encourage the spiritual and moral truths found among people of other faiths'[43], along with their 'social life and culture'. Therefore, an 'interactive faith, equal footing, shared mission and a complementary life' are a few pillars of this many-sided culture of interaction. Thus, it follows that 'mission emerges from among individuals, families, communities, nations and civilisations', of course in the given context, as 'mission among the peoples'.

4.4. The Many-sided Christian Foundation

The Christian idea of God as 'Father, Son and Spirit'[44] is a Trinitarian monotheism of being 'one-in-three' and 'three-in-one'. The notion of human beings as 'created in the image and likeness of God'[45] and as 'divine abodes' or 'living temples of God'[46] strike a parallel with the divine reality. Therefore, the Christian dynamics of life are three-faceted and mutually related, as among oneself, the other and God. The 'parable of the talents'[47] suggest investing oneself towards a life in full, in line with the life mission of Jesus[48]. 'Doing to the other what one would have the other due to one'[49] is the golden rule for inter-human ethics of behaviour. 'What is done to the human beings is what is done to God as well'[50] is human-divine dynamics. The idea of 'mission among the peoples' is firmly grounded in the triangular setting of Christian life and it justifies the dignity of the humans, along with the fatherly character of God, both in one shot.

4.5. The Core Values of Jesus

The core values of Jesus are universal and all embracing. 'Pursuit of perfection as non-discrimination' as the ultimate spiritual goal[51], 'loving enemies[52] as well as one another'[53], 'forgiving the other unconditionally'[54], 'washing the other's feet[55] and serving them by 'doing good to the other'[56], 'considering one another as friends'[57], 'reaching out to the weak'[58], being 'good news' to one and all[59], 'honouring the other above oneself'[60], 'being a brother or a sister to everyone'[61], after the fashion of Jesus and fulfilling the culminating aspiration of Jesus 'Father, that they all may be one'[62] compose the core values of Jesus, par excellence. These values substantiate 'mission among the peoples', crossing all boundaries, of their own accord.

4.6. Illuminating Papal Pronouncements

Popes delivered several instructive and stimulating pronouncements on the lifestyle of interaction during the course of the last fifty years. Pope John XXIII emphasised, 'we have to look at what unites people, rather than what divides them'[63] and 'what *we have* in common is greater *than what separates* us'[64]. Pope Paul VI exclaimed in Meeting of Religions in Bombay, 1964, 'we…have to meet…as pilgrims and start a journey searching for God…in the hearts of humankind'[65]. Pope John Paul II in his public meeting in Madras, 1986, categorically stated thus, 'by dialogue we let God be present in our midst, for as we open ourselves in dialogue to one another, we open ourselves to God'[66]. At his Meeting of Religions in New Delhi, 1999, he definitively added that 'religion should be what God intended it to be, a source of goodness, harmony and peace'[67]. Pope Francis in his General audience, at St Peter's Square, Vatican City, 2015, advocated ironically an open state of mind, 'Churches, parishes and institutions with closed doors must not call themselves a church; they must call themselves museums'[68]. These insights illustrate the interactive and inclusive character of faith and mission, as summarised by 'mission among the peoples'.

5. MAP – AN INTERACTIVE PARADIGM OF GOOD NEWS

The fifth section of the paper examines 'map – an interactive paradigm of good news'. It discusses titles like 'interactive dynamics of the mission, the mission that evolves, faith becomes inter-faith and multi-faith, the Asian genius of the mission, making the family of God the father on earth, the paradigm of good news and mission among the peoples: a paradigm par excellence'.

5.1. Interactive Dynamics of the Mission

What is special in 'mission among the peoples' is the joining element 'between, among, with, through or across' persons or communities, as the case may be, in line with the 'culture of inter' launched by *Nostra Aetate*. The interface, interaction and crossing point between or among individuals or communities, along with their perceptions, faiths, attitudes, ideologies, cultures, traditions, approaches, concerns, etc, compose the interactive dynamics of the mission. Faith is the basic component that regulates the 'dynamics of inter' as an 'exchange and sharing'[69]. The 'interactive mode' functions as a 'two-way or multi-way' process of 'partnership' on a 'common footing'[70]. As a participatory, collaborative, complementary and harmonious way, the mode ensures the dignity of all the constituents of the process. The interactive dynamics is characteristic of mission among the peoples.

5.2. A Mission That Evolves

Interaction or dialogue between, among as well, always proceeds to a third or higher element. When persons from diverse backgrounds, convictions, interests and persuasions, meet, they are bound to evolve towards one another and together beyond themselves. Mission thus becomes a 'mission to one another'[71] and they emerge jointly to larger and higher proportions, well, towards the human and divine realms. Evolving beyond prejudices, fixed positions and vested interests will prove to be mutually enriching and elevating. The 'shared journey'[72] of faith and mission becomes an 'ever-evolving and collective reality' among or between them. This is the common crossing of co-pilgrims, justifying the reality of the 'pilgrim Church'[73]. Such an open-ended, all-inclusive and innovative dynamics of 'mission among the peoples' brings in new vistas, not only in the areas of faith and mission but also in the entire gamut of human life.

5.3. Faith Becomes Inter-Faith and Multi-Faith

Faith is plural, inclusive and multi-faceted in its character[74]. It is like tens and thousands of drops of water come together to make a flow possible. Faith is formed as a result of such a process. It is a perception, outlook, trust, belief, understanding, sentiment, conviction, attitude, commitment, and the like, that is rooted in one's consciousness and conscience. It motivates one towards performing a mission in life, towards the other, the family, the community, the nation and the society. When 'faith meets faith', faith becomes interfaith, and multi-faith when many faiths meet[75]. In fact, there aren't many faiths, but many dimensions of the same faith, which focus on the same divinity and humanity. Therefore, those dimensions have to be inter-related, necessarily so. That amounts to state that individuals, communities and traditions have to meet each other and interact and thus advance the process of a multi-faith way of living one's life. This is what 'mission among peoples' is all about.

5.4. The Asian Genius of the Mission

The concept 'mission among the peoples' has emerged from the Asian milieu; it is applied to its 'rich diversity and plurality of religions, cultures and philosophical world views'[76]. It has distinctively an Asian approach to carrying out the Christian mission that is sensitive to the integrity and dignity of the diversities, spread even over the entire globe. The mission is not super-imposed, but is completely applied to the given context and people. All the beneficiaries of the mission have a full share in the entire process of the mission, too. The style of the mission is beached at the shared faiths that 'all traditions and cultures are gifts of the same Creator' and all beliefs and cultures as the 'common cultural heritage of the human society'[77]. There is no 'mine and yours' or 'ours and theirs', but 'all are ours; one is mine in special and others are mine in general'. It professes the sublime maxim 'all faiths and cultures have a mission to fulfill to other faiths and cultures'. 'Sharing with'[78] the others one's values, along with 'sharing in'[79] the values of other traditions, is mission mode of 'mission among the peoples'.

5.5. Making the Family of God the Father on Earth

Considering 'God as Father' on relational terms is the brilliance of Christianity, thanks to the revelation of Jesus. This idea makes it possible for the entire world of human beings to gather under 'one umbrella' as one family or an integral whole. 'Making the family of God on earth' is the esteemed mission of a Christian and it involves humans of all communities and nations[80]. The culture of being the divine-human family is one of 'staying tuned to each other, sticking together, walking together and working together'[81], in the 'spirit of solidarity and interaction'. Considerations of high and low, familiar and strange, superior and inferior and friend and enemy cannot stand the ground of this family. Being rooted in the filial experience in relation to God, the sisterly and brotherly expressions to one and all is the strength of this culture. Making a 'family of families, a community of communities' out of people of all faiths, ideologies, cultures and civilisations is the out-and-out mark of the missioner. Facilitating such a Christian spirit of 'God with us'[82] is the esteemed outcome of 'mission among the peoples'.

5.6. The Paradigm of 'Good News'

The word 'good news' or 'good spell' comes from the word 'gospel', which in turn derives from the Greek word 'evangelion'. In the ordinary sense, 'good news' is 'something or someone pleasant, fortunate and positive'[83]. The 'values of Jesus elevate and save the humans'. This 'good news' has to be proclaimed to 'all creation'[84], to all cultures, in all times and to all sorts. 'Sharing the values of Jesus with other persons in a pleasing manner' makes it 'good news' for them. To 'stay united to the humans' and to 'get connected to God' is the result of this good news, too. Imposing upon the other a well-formulated dogma or a solemnly performed ritual need not be good news for the other. 'Being good news, one to another' would boost up a 'spirit of togetherness, solidarity and harmony'[85] with one and all. Becoming partners in faith and co-pilgrims in life will multiply the good news, which will facilitate both or all to 'going beyond' towards larger and higher proportions in life. The style of mission 'mission among the peoples' advocates has the mettle of manufacturing in the hearts of the peoples a series of 'good news'.

5.7. Mission among the Peoples – A Paradigm Par Excellence

Firmly grounded in his filial experience with God the Father, Jesus literally became 'all things to all people'[86]. He reached out to the human beings who came across to him as 'an elder brother, a Master, a friend, a companion, a healer, a giver of life', and the like, all these roles in the spirit of 'he does all things well'[87]. 'Mission among the peoples' proposes to incarnate this style of advancing and accomplishing the mission of Jesus and of the Church, which, in essence, is markedly different from 'mission to the peoples'. The truly inter-faith and multi-faith mission, brilliantly master-stroked by the Second Catholic World Council of Vatican, is a truly 'catholic, universal and all-embracing' paradigm[88]. That would amount to state that with the sublime mission of celebrating the family of God on earth, Father on earth' at its core, 'mission among the peoples' is a 'mission par excellence'[89] and a 'mission with a difference'[90], for Catholics, Christians and for all faiths, for all times as well. Mission among the peoples is geared towards 'fraternal and friendly relations' with people of all faiths, ideologies and cultures and is charged with the paternally divine nerve[91].

CONCLUSION

The mission mode of 'mission among the peoples' is grounded in the 'logic of incarnation'. It makes incarnate a 'culture of inter', by way of inter-personal, inter-faith, inter-ideological, inter-cultural and inter-traditional relations. It is a shared mission, a mission to one another and a mission to the country and the society together. The blend of 'sharing with' with 'sharing in' strikes a balance among the diverse communities of faith, ideologies and cultures. It safeguards and enhances the freedom, rights, duties, integrity and dignity of every individual, community and entity. Individual persons and the various streams of faiths and cultures advance the collective journey of life, in an interactive style between and among the constituent members. As they share their distinctive elements unto the enrichment of each other, they are geared for celebrating the 'culture of being the family of God on earth'. 'Mission among the peoples' is the expressway towards crisscrossing the human similarities and commonalities, guided by the divine energy, like 'the rail engine that runs by the electric wire laid above'.

Endnotes

1. J. Andrew, What is Mission?: Theological Explorations, Minneapolis, USA, 2000, p. 13
2. *Ibid,* p. 33
3. Beatrice, S. Brown, Case Studies in Evangelism: Effective Principles in Reaching Others, New York, 2008, p. 13
4. *Ibid,* p. 83

5. Ernst Wolff, Shaping a Humane World, Bielefeld, 2014, p. 62
6. *Ibid,* p. 96
7. Ratna Kapur, Gender, Alterity and Human Rights: Freedom in a Fishbowl, Massachusetts, 2018, p. 33
8. Friedrich Engels, The Part Played by Labour in the Transition from Ape to Man, Moscow, 1963, p. 16
9. Ernst Wolff, Shaping a Humane World, Bielefeld, 2014, p. 93
10. *Ibid,* p. 106
11. Austin Flannery (Ed.), *Ad Gentes Divinitus*: Decree on the Church's Missionary Activity, Dublin, 2014, p. 07
12. *Ibid,* p. 33
13. *Ibid,* p. 29
14. Wallace, M. Alston, The Church of the Living God: A Reformed Perspective, London, 2002, p. 61
15. *Ibid,* p. 96
16. Austin Flannery (Ed.), *Ad Gentes Divinitus*: Decree on the Church's Missionary Activity, Dublin, 2014, p. 33
17. Ray, Vander Laan, Early Church Discovery Guide: Becoming a Light in the Darkness, Michigan, 2008, p. 153
18. *Ibid,* p. 223
19. The Holy Bible, NIV, Michigan, Mt 7.29, p. 1101
20. Wallace, M. Alston, The Church of the Living God: A Reformed Perspective, London, 2002, p. 33
21. Edward Bristow, Edward W. Bristow (Ed.), No Religion is an Island: The *Nostra Aetate* Dialogues, New York, 1998, p. 13
22. *Ibid,* p. 57
23. Jonathan, Y. Tan, *Missio Inter Gentes*: Towards a New Paradigm in the Mission Theology of the Federation of Asian Bishops' Conferences (FABC), Mission Studies, 21.1, 2004, p. 88
24. *Ibid,* p. 09
25. Stanley, D. Brunn, The Changing World Religion Map: Sacred Places, Identities, Practices and Politics, London, 2015, p. 1859
26. *Ibid,* p. 1901
27. Jonathan, Y. Tan, *Missio Inter Gentes*: Towards a New Paradigm in the Mission Theology of the Federation of Asian Bishops' Conferences (FABC), Mission Studies, 21.1, 2004, p. 88
28. Emma Wild-Wood, Peniel Rajkumar, Foundations for Mission, Eugene, 2014, p. 93
29. https://www.uni-muenster.de/imperia/md/content/fb2/d-praktischetheologie/missionswissenschaft/studienwoche/kurzbio_ref.__2__docx.pdf
30. Jonathan, Y. Tan, World Christianity: Perspectives and Insights: Essays in Honor of Peter C. Phan, New York, 2016, p. 118
31. https://www.mcgill.ca/law/channels/event/launch-inter-gentes-mcgill-journal-international-law-legal-pluralism- 264055
32. Jonathan, Y. Tan, World Christianity: Perspectives and Insights: Essays in Honor of Peter C. Phan, New York, 2016, p. 87
33. *Ibid,* p. 143
34. David, J. Bosch, Transforming Mission: Paradigm Shifts in Theology of Mission, New York, 2011, p. 109
35. *Ibid,* p. 113
36. *Ibid,* p. 117
37. *Ibid,* p. 122

38. Edward Bristow, Edward W. Bristow (Ed.), No Religion is an Island: The *Nostra Aetate* Dialogues, New York, 1998, p. 19
39. *Ibid,* p. 59
40. Jonathan, Y. Tan, *Missio Inter Gentes*: Towards a New Paradigm in the Mission Theology of the Federation of Asian Bishops' Conferences (FABC), Mission Studies, 21.1, 2004, p. 107
41. *Ibid,* p. 143
42. *Ibid,* p. 147
43. Jonathan, Y. Tan, World Christianity: Perspectives and Insights: Essays in Honor of Peter C. Phan, New York, 2016, p. 57
44. The Holy Bible, NIV, Michigan, Jn 15.26, p. 1228
45. *Ibid,* Gen. 1.27, p. 02
46. *Ibid,* 1 Cor 3.16, p. 1298
47. *Ibid,* Mt 25.14-30, p. 1127
48. *Ibid,* Jn 10.10, p. 1220
49. *Ibid,* Mt 7.12, p. 1100
50. *Ibid,* Mt 25.40, p. 1128
51. *Ibid,* Mt 5.45,48, p. 1099
52. *Ibid,* Mt 5.44, p. 1099
53. *Ibid,* Jn 13.34, 35, p. 1226
54. *Ibid,* Lk 23.34, p. 1201
55. *Ibid,* Jn 13.14, p. 1225
56. *Ibid,* Lk 10.25-37, p. 1180
57. *Ibid,* Jn 15.15, p. 1228
58. *Ibid,* Lk 15.3-7, p. 1188
59. *Ibid,* Mt 4.23, p. 1097
60. *Ibid,* Rom 1.12.10, p. 1282
61. *Ibid,* Jn 10.30, p. 1221, Mt 25.40, p. 1127
62. *Ibid,* Jn 17.21, p. 1230
63. Thomas Cahill, Pope John XXIII: A Life, London, 2002, p. 79
64. *Ibid,* p. 96
65. Paul M. Collins, Christian Inculturation in India, New York, 2007, p. 157
66. George Weigel, Witness to Hope: The Biography of Pope John Paul II, New York, 2001, p. 619
67. *Ibid,* p. 519
68. http://www.catholicnewsagency.com/news/churches-families-must-be-places-of-welcome-pope-says-13552/
69. Emma Wild-Wood, Peniel Rajkumar, Foundations for Mission, Eugene, 2013, p. 158
70. *Ibid,* p. 159
71. Jonathan, Y. Tan, World Christianity: Perspectives and Insights: Essays in Honor of Peter C. Phan, New York, 2016, p. 97
72. *Ibid,* p. 103
73. *Ibid,* p. 142
74. Jonathan, Y. Tan, *Missio Inter Gentes*: Towards a New Paradigm in the Mission Theology of the Federation of Asian Bishops' Conferences (FABC), Mission Studies, 21.1, 2004, p. 87
75. *Ibid,* p. 93
76. *Ibid,* p. 98
77. *Ibid,* p. 146
78. Stephen, B. Bevans, Roger P. Schroeder, Roger Schroeder, Constants in Context: A Theology of Mission for Today, New York, 2004, p. 283

79. *Ibid,* p. 287
80. James Joseph Buss, C. Joseph Genetin-Pilawa (Edi.), Beyond Two Worlds, New York, 2014, p. 174
81. *Ibid,* p. 203
82. *Ibid,* p. 186
83. *Ibid,* p. 269
84. The Holy Bible, NIV, Michigan, Mark 16.15, p. 1160
85. Elochukwu, E. Uzukwu (Ed.), Mission for Diversity, London, 2020, p. 161
86. The Holy Bible, NIV, Michigan, 1 Cor 9.22, p. 1303
87. *Ibid,* Mk 7.37, p. 1158
88. Elochukwu E. Uzukwu (Ed.), Mission for Diversity, London, 2020, p. 173
89. Daniel Lee Hill, Gathered on the Road to Zion: Towards a Free Church Ecclesio-Anthropology, Eugene, 2021, p. 57
90. *Ibid,* p. 132
91. *Ibid,* p. 209

Chapter - 6

Universal Fibre in Christianity

INTRODUCTION

Religion, of its own accord, is a universal phenomenon. Therefore, the character of universality is and has to be inherent in all religions. The more the fibre of universality in a religion, the more universal appeal it commands. As a matter of fact, religious traditions vary in their content and degree of universality. Believers of religions have to primarily focus on the universal values present in the respective tradition of their persuasion. They have to continuously endeavour to make the foundations of their faith broader and broader, towards a multi-faceted universal fibre, as well. At the same time, they have to imbibe the universal elements of belief that are intrinsic to other religious cultures. As a matter of fact, faith is all about making its adherents transcending the boundaries, in view of growing towards horizontal magnitudes and vertical altitudes, both simultaneously. Where does Christianity stand in terms of the quality and quantity of universal fibre, which is capable rendering human lives humanly and spiritually fit to travel the path of eternity, in line with the universal standards of religion as well as the aspirations of the humans? This article attempts to explore and elaborate in brief the answer to this question, by attempting to travel the divine and human corridors of Christian vision and mission of life.

1. THE CHRISTIAN IDEA OF GOD AND ITS UNIVERSAL IMPLICATIONS

1.1. God as 'Trinity'

Christianity is a theistic and monotheistic religion, obviously so. In spite of the fact that it believes in a 'one and the only' God, it propounds a 'tri-theistic'[1] or 'Trinitarian' combination of 'one-in-three' and 'three-in-one'. To be precise, there are 'three persons' in God, namely, 'Father, son and spirit'. They are equal in dignity, status and divine character. Their individual and social qualities are perfectly blended and therefore they form 'one God' and they are eternally in the spirit of mutual 'communion'[2]. Manifestly, the Christian idea of God is characterised by the worldwide reality of multiplicity coupled with union as well as by a wide-ranging base for the human society.

1.2. Triune God – Symbolic Meanings

The triune[3] idea of God in Christianity has several symbolic meanings. The number 'three', being considered a 'perfect number', refers to God as 'perfection', 'fullness' or 'hundred per cent'. As the least number representing many, 'three' is a 'magic number', too. It signifies 'community' and the spirit of 'communion' that makes a community. It is a relational term and connotes 'relation' and 'relationship'. As largely a familial phrase, it is grounded in the idea of a 'family', which is the smallest unit of the human society. It would imply that 'God is a family', after which fashion human beings are a family too. The multi-faceted connotations of the triune notion of God, no doubt, enrich the broad-based perception of the divine reality.

1.3. Tri-theistic God – Similarities in Other Traditions

The tri-theistic notion of God in Christianity matches the bipolar characteristic of 'one and many', which is the most fundamental truth of the universe. It agrees with the proverbial dictum of 'unity in diversity'[4] or the aesthetic axiom of 'beauty in difference' that is seen applied to the context of the human society and the world in general, in Asia in special and in India in very special. It also corresponds to the three-dimensional notions of God in the Vedic tradition, like *'brahma, vishnu, mahesh'*[5], *'satyam, shivam, sundaram'*[6] and *'sat, chit, anand'*[7] as well as in the *'om mantra'* of *'shanti, shanti, shanti'*[8]. It concurs with the view of number 'three' in 'triple *talaaq*'[9] in the Islamic tradition and similar perceptions in other religions, as well.

1.4. God as Father

Christianity considers God 'Father' or 'like a father'[10], who is the first person of the trinity. The term 'father' is inclusive of motherly qualities, too. Father of the creation would mean its 'source of life', which gives, nourishes and sustains it with love. He loves his children, without any condition. He takes care of them with a 'sense of equality and fairness' and with a 'sense of all', certainly with a special concern for the weaker ones. He does not discriminate even between the good and the evil. He sends his sunshine and the rains to both, in an equal measure. Even in defections, he forgives, overwhelmed by total love, it is as if nothing wrong has taken place. He is head of the 'large divine family' of human beings, along with the entire creation. The notion of God as Father in Christianity, without a shred of doubt, defies all divisive considerations, in terms of religious and other affiliations.

1.5. God as Son

'Jesus Christ' is the second person of the Godhead and is 'Son of God'[11] the Father, who incarnated himself in the form of a human being. While on earth, Jesus stayed totally 'tuned' to the Father and experienced his 'oneness' with him, from birth to death and even to life eternal. He had him in full figure always before his eyes, fully listened to his word, considered doing his will his food, implored him to forgive his offenders, commended his spirit in his hands at last and thus portrayed to the world the brilliant stature of his Heavenly Father. His mission in life was 'making the family of God on earth'[12] and he fulfilled this mission to the details, by promoting the spirit of being a sister or a brother to one another. Playing such a messianic role, Jesus, as the Son of God, presented himself as the living 'carbon copy' of the Father on earth. He communicated to the world the welcome 'good news' that 'all human beings on earth are sons and daughters of the very same Father' whose Son he is.

1.6. God as Spirit

Spirit[13] is the third person of the holy trinity of God. It derives from the first and the second persons of God, in an equal way. It interconnects the Father and the Son and is the eternal bond between the two. It is the symbol of not only the completion of the triune God, but also of total communion among the persons of God. In addition, spirit signifies the invisible character of God, because God is spirit and therefore he cannot be seen. Spirit is like the breath, too. The process of creation involved infusing the breath of the spirit. Spirit is like the breeze, as well. No one knows, cannot even imagine, how, when and where it comes from and wither it goes. It cannot be held or controlled. What's more, spirit is energy and is the motivating power. It organises and gives direction to human and other lives on earth. All these characteristics apply to the person of the Spirit and the same crosses all the boundaries the religious and other communities have erected on earth among them.

1.7. Transcendent God in Immanent Form

The Christian idea of God is a perfect blend of transcendence and immanence[14]. The idea of God as Father brings the divine, which in principle is far and beyond the human realm, within the reach of the humans in a familial and a familiar way. The fatherly God can easily be approached in the spirit of filial freedom. His justice is combined with unconditional love and overwhelming forgiveness. He has a preferential concern for the weaker, the sidelined and the deprived. In addition, the idea of God as Son and incarnation of the Father in Jesus Christ further makes the distant God immanent, near, tangible and realistic in the human form. The Father is replicated and presented in Jesus, in all his details and in the language of the humans. While Jesus Christ the messiah makes the invisible God the Father fully visible, he could be related to in all possible human categories, by way of one's spiritual pursuit. Furthermore, Spirit, like the electric wire above the rail track, the touch or feel of which makes the human journey charged and energised and is carried forward to its destination. In the mutual dynamics between transcendence and immanence, the divine image and likeness are found reflected in the humans and thus God spontaneously becomes a natural reality in human lives, beyond all borders.

1.8. God as Relation

The Christian language of God is relational, to be precise, familial. The notion of both Father and son connote relation, that too, the most fundamental relation in the vertical line. The fatherly relation of God to human beings could easily be responded to by filial relation. Among all the relational categories, 'father' is the widest and it is like a 'large umbrella', which can gather the whole humanity, and even the whole creation, in one single fold. The filial relation of Jesus as Son to the Father could be imbibed by human beings, too, in order to rightly situate themselves in their spiritual orientation. Jesus, as the incarnation of God the Father, stands as a paradigm of multi-faceted relation. He brings the Father into diverse relational offshoots, in order to suit the various aspirations the humans cherish. As Son of God, he is elder 'brother' to all human beings, who are younger brothers or sisters to him. He is teacher or '*Guru*', par excellence, and the humans could relate to him as students or disciples. He called his disciples 'friends' and therefore, he is a friend to everyone. He was a 'healer'[15] to those with infirmities. He said, 'I shall be with you always'[16] and one could accept him as a true 'companion'[17] in life. All these relational faces of Jesus as well as Father are variations of God as relation.

1.9. The Universal Implications of the Christian Idea of God

The Christian idea of God, in all its dimensions, is profoundly loaded with open and universal characteristics. The implications as well as language, terminology and categories are all-inclusive and therefore apply to people of all affiliations of faith and ideologies. As the universal fatherhood of God could be acceptable to one and all, so could the filial devotion to him epitomised in Jesus be appealing to one and all, beyond all boundaries, in their spiritual pursuit. The tri-theistic idea of God honours diversity on one side and facilitates unity to the point of an in-depth communion. Similar perceptions elsewhere affirm its in-built wider sense and symbolic meanings, too.

Furthermore, while the terms 'father and son' transcend male connotations and include female qualities, on one hand, the entire perspective of the divine includes also the entire creation as well as people of non-theistic ideologies, on the other. The relational and familial approach to the divine makes the religious engagement interesting and the same motivates meaningful human relations. The effective translation of the transcendent God into immanent God makes him not only realistic but also sensible and approachable to one and all. The spiritual character of God stands above comprehensively as the motivating constituent of human life across all horizons. What's more, the divine language that rises beyond the borders of ethnicity, gender, caste, class, creed, profession, language, ideology, culture, and the like, ushers in a collective spirituality of filial experience from the humans across all affiliations.

2. THE SOCIAL IMPERATIVES OF CHRISTIAN FAITH AND ITS UNIVERSALITY

2.1. Christian Ethics and Its Universal Scale

Christian values are considerably universal in its implications and applications, so much so that they compose a landmark ethics for the world human society. They are – human beings are 'created in the image of God'[18] and are 'divine abodes' or 'living temples of God'[19], the word Jesus means Emmanuel or 'God with us'[20], 'do to the other what you would have him or her do to you'[21], 'God does not discriminate'[22], 'be perfect as the heavenly father is perfect'[23], 'love your neighbour as yourself'[24], 'love your enemies'[25], 'love one another as I have loved you'[26], 'he does all things well'[27], 'forgive one another without condition'[28], 'you also should wash one another's feet'[29], 'I call...you friends'[30], 'reach out to the weak'[31], be 'good news' 'to one and all' [32], 'honour the other above yourself'[33] and 'be a brother/sister to everyone, like Jesus'[34], 'when you did it to even the least of my brothers and sisters, you did it to me'[35], 'we are like one body with many parts'[36] and 'if you do not love your neighbour whom you see, you cannot love God whom you have not seen'[37]. These values that are specifically Christian are enormously charged with a universal bearing and they scale an all-embracing compass, distinctly so.

2.2. Christian Spirituality and Its Holistic Character

The Christian spirituality is not an engagement with the spirit of the other world or one that is cut off from the body. It is the pursuit of human life that is fully integrated in and applied to the social context. It is holistic and multi-faceted and it involves all the aspects of human life, like physical, intellectual, emotional, social and cultural. It is totally grounded in the values and teachings of Jesus, as well. It is mainly three-faceted and has a mutually related dynamics involving life – oneself, the other and God. The first aspect would mean investing oneself towards attaining 'life in its full measure', in line with the purpose of the incarnation and mission of Jesus[38] and his parable on the 'talents'[39]. 'Doing to the other what one would have the other due to one'[40] is the second dimension of the spiritual outlook of a Christian. The third spiritual element of Christian spirituality is 'when you did to one of the least of my sisters and brothers, you did it to me'[41]. That would mean 'what is done to the human being is what is done to God himself'. Christian spirituality is not an observance of a set of rituals, but is a triangular cycle of life and a three-dimensional attainment of the divine in the natural course of human life. Therefore, it applies to the human society in a universal manner, as a collective spirituality of the humans. As an all-inclusive human-divine dynamics, it defies boundaries of religions and promotes an interactive and holistic culture that suits the social character of human and other forms of life.

2.3. Fraternal Framework of Human Life and Its Universal Language

The entire narrative of God in Christianity is relational, functional and applied to the human context, of course, within the setting of the entire creation. Human beings reflect the 'image of God' and they are the real 'divine abodes'. Therefore, 'what is done to them is what is done to God'. Such a divine-human dynamics gives a very substantial foundation for a fraternal framework of human life. It perfectly blends the horizontal and vertical dimensions and proportions of human life, as well. Such a perspective translates the theory of God into the practical life of the humans. The fraternal framework of the idea of God as Father would mean that human beings are 'sons and daughters' of the Heavenly Father and 'brothers and sisters' to one another, irrespective of the diversity of religious and other affiliations. Fraternal experience of life in the horizontal context is an upshot of the filial experience of life in the vertical. Considering other human beings one's brothers or sisters in a universal manner is the way to make the entire humanity and the creation 'the family of God' and, in fact, that is the spiritual way of 'being human', in the ultimate context. The life of a Christian cannot be conceived outside the fraternal spirit of love and service to one and all among human beings, including the creation. The fraternal culture of human life inaugurated by Jesus has unlimited universal possibilities, in favour of the wellbeing of the human society, when lived honestly.

2.4. Paradigm of 'One Body, Many Parts' and Its Bifocal Dynamics

The chief interpreter of the story of Jesus and one of the main writers of the New Testament, Paul by name, presents 'one body, many parts'[42] as a highly telling paradigm for the bifocal dynamics of life. The paradigm is nothing less than a fundamental key to the understanding and unfolding of the mystery of life, especially that of human beings, that too, from the divine perspective. The example is just commonplace, but its inner implications highlight the wide scope for its global application. The parts of the body are different in their identity as well as are many in number. They perform different roles, but exist as one body. The different parts have equal duties and equal rights and are complementary to each other. All of them have their own singular importance and dignity, which is beyond the range of being compared. One part cannot be replaced or suppressed by another. Joy or pain and achievement or failure of one part is shared and owned by all the parts. It is an 'existence in togetherness'. It is 'beauty in diversity'[43] and 'diversity in unity'[44], at the same time. I don't think, there can be a more powerful paradigm than this for 'harmony' among individuals and communities across all affiliations at the global level.

2.5. An Interactive Faith and Its Inclusive Applications

The Second World Council of Vatican[45] of the Catholic community launched an interactive faith in the 60s of the 20th century. It emerged with an adult application of the universal standing of Christian ethos in terms of its relations with other religious and social communities, positively so. This epoch-making event marked the new wave of 'inter-faith relations'[46] in the history of the world. The foundational document '*Nostra Aetate*'[47] (in our time) reads thus, 'if Christians treat other individuals, groups and peoples in a manner that is not befitting sisters and brothers, they have no right to call God their Father'. This would amount to losing their filial status with God as well as ceasing to be Christians and believers, tragically so. Therefore, Catholics and Christians are bound to think as large as the world and to engage in fostering relations, fellowship and collaboration with people of all religious, ideological, cultural, social and national communities. In other words, believing in God as Father would clearly mean staying tuned to people of all religious and humanistic ideologies and remaining actively committed to making a family of God on earth, along with all of them. This is because, far from being an isolated or insulated entity, faith is a relational and reciprocal occurrence, just like a flow of water that is composed of tens and thousands of drops. Such an interactive faith, for sure, is capable of according Christianity with the most universal outlook and ethics, all the more so.

2.6. Harmony with Other Faiths, Ideologies and Cultures – Major Christian Decrees

Several pronouncements of the Popes on harmony among faiths have been categorically articulate and across-the-board in their implications. Convening the Second Vatican Council in 1962, Pope John XXIII declared, 'we have to look at what unites people rather than what divides them'[48]. 'We...have to meet as pilgrims and start...searching for God...in the hearts of humankind,'[49] added Pope Paul VI at the Meeting of religions at Bombay, India, in 1964. He continued then, 'man must meet man, nation meet nation, as brothers and sisters, as children of God.'[50] Pope John Paul II, during his visit to Manila in 1981, exhorted, 'Christians will... join hands with all men and women of good will and work together in order to bring about a more just and peaceful society, in which the poor will be the first to be served'.[51] During his first visit to India, he stated at Madras in 1986, 'by dialogue we let God be present in our midst, for as we open ourselves in dialogue to one another, we open ourselves to God'.[52] 'Either we learn to walk together in peace and harmony or we drift and ruin ourselves and others,'[53] he affirmed at World Day of Prayer for Peace at Assisi, 1986. 'Dialogue is an act of love, which has its roots in God himself,'[54] he emphasised during his second visit to India at New Delhi, in 1999. 'Different religious traditions of India are a hope for a better future for the human family'[55], he further stated then. He caught the imagination of people of all religions as he pronounced categorically then that 'religion should be what God intended it to be, a source of goodness, harmony and peace'.[56] What's more, Pope Francis took inter-religious dialogue to new directions when he re-defined it in the words 'accompaniment' and 'the journey together'.[57] All these Papal pronouncements are grounded in the statement of Ecclesia in Asia, 26, that 'the dialogue, which the Church proposes, is grounded in the logic of the incarnation'.[58]

2.7. Service of the Humanity, Especially the Deprived, and Its Catholic Spirit

The social service schemes pioneered and monitored by the Christian community, world over, is grounded in the fraternal imperatives that emerge from the values of Christianity as the spiritual motivation. A Christian has no short cut to attain God. Attaining eternal salvation is no easy way, either. His or her way to God the Father is necessarily through his or her neighbour who are children of the same Father, not only in the Christian community but also widely spread over all the diverse communities of faith, ideologies and nations in the world. A Christian is ordained to reach out to the oppressed and the deprived[59] in a preferential way. This is based on the option Jesus initiated for 'the lamb that got lost and searching and finding which was the priority of the 'good shepherd'[60], because he believed in having 'all the hundred'[61], after the heart of the Heavenly Father. Accordingly, Christianity stands out among all religious traditions for its elaborate schemes for social change and transformation. While educational[62] development was pioneered by schools, colleges and universities in the cities, towns and villages, medical[63] and health-related enterprises were ventured by hospitals, dispensaries and health centres in rural and urban areas. Projects of housing, clothing, feeding, non-formal education, literacy, adult education, etc, in view of social change at the grassroots have been undertaken by social service centres[64]. The making of an egalitarian society was geared at by special schools[65] and centres for the physically disabled, mentally challenged, orphans, old and abandoned, deprived, and the like. Mother Theresa[66] is a major icon in this sector. Massive efforts for social awakening have been campaigned in view of fostering interfaith interaction, inter-community relations[67], national integration and social cohesion, through interactive, participatory and harmonious living among religious and non-religious communities. All these attempts for social transformation are motivated by Christian faith and are spiritually charged by the 'catholic' vision and values of Jesus Christ. They are extended to people of all groups without any discrimination, as well.

2.8. Functional Feature of Religion and Its Wide-Ranging Significance

'The Sabbath was made for man, not man for the Sabbath'[68], states Jesus. To apply this wisdom in the larger context, 'religion is for the human being and human being is not for religion'[69]. The latter portion of the axiom refers to the topsy-turvy of affairs in life and the former fraction sets the orientation of human life in the right perspective. Life is the gift of God, is God-given and is and has to be at the centre of life. Religion[70] is human-made and has to be at the service of life, and not more than that. Religion is meaningful so far as it enhances the quality of human life and gives meaning to it. Life is the ultimate reality, whether of this world or beyond, but religion is a relative reality only. In other words, religion is merely a functional entity. It is like a 'ladder', which makes sense when it helps one ascend higher human and spiritual altitudes. Religion is useful when it facilitates human beings grow towards horizontal proportions as well as elevates them towards vertical directions in life. This basic and universal philosophy of Jesus applies to all religious, ideological, social and cultural traditions in the world, manifestly so.

2.9. Christian Values in the Global Space

Christian values have acquired lots of space in the global and national civilisations and networks of administration, on account of the all-embracing and developmental element in it. United Nations Organisation launched eight 'Millennium Development Goals 2000'[71] for the world and it addressed concerns of the poor, hungry and sick; children and mothers; and gender, education and environment, in an integral way. In the 17 'Sustainable Development Goals 2015-2030'[72], it advanced its focus on the details of the above and more areas and vouched to promote values of inclusiveness, growth, human rights, equality, progress, wellbeing, sustainability, accountability, collaboration, responsibility, transformation, partnership, peace, and the like, with the commendable pledge that 'no one will be left behind'[73]. The Constitution of India[74], its preamble in particular, underscores sovereignty, republic, secularism, democracy, justice, equality, freedom, dignity, fraternity, etc, in the social, economic, political and other areas. It is not difficult to see that most of the values highlighted by MDG, SDG, Indian Constitution and many other national Constitutions greatly reflect Christian values in letters or in spirit. It could also be stated without exaggeration that the major space in the transformational schemes of the world Christianity has been occupying has to be attributed to the 'universal fibre'[75] of the values, ethics and ethos Jesus Christ conceived, lived and taught, and Christianity has been attempting to live and promote for the last twenty plus centuries, the world over.

2.10. Universality of the Social Dynamics of Christianity

The horizontal framework of human life is the social dynamics of Christianity and it is firmly rooted in the divine-human dynamics of life. 'No one has seen God', but Jesus made the invisible God visible, not only by his own person as the Son of God but also by his universal outlook that includes one and all. His Heavenly Father who does not discriminate even between the righteous and the unrighteous was his model and he presented himself as God incarnate in the form of a 'brother and friend' to all human beings. He made the pursuit of the divine easy and realistic by launching a fraternal system of human life where 'what is done to the human beings is what is done to God himself', because the humans reflect the image of the divine and radiate a feel of the divine and living temples. Responding to such a system of values and taking care of one's brother and sister in the spirit of love and service 'beyond all borders' is the way of 'being a Christian'. Even after giving everything the humans require, God does not require or want anything in return from human beings. All that he wants is 'take care of the fellow humans', the weaker and those on the margins in special. 'Do to the other what you wish the other do to you' is the horizontal ethics, which automatically takes care of the vertical ethics of spiritual elevation. Such a 'social dynamics' is the 'divine-human Christian ethos' and it speaks volumes as a 'universal ethos of the humans' on earth, as characteristically phrased in India *'Vasudhaiv Kutumbakam'*[76].

CONCLUSION

'Universal fibre' is the golden thread that inter-connects the entire human family, across the borders of ethnic traits, gender, language, race, caste, class, creed, region, nation, ideology, culture, food tastes, dress patterns, and the like. The universal character is also reflected in the inter-twining of the divine-human dynamics of human life. The Christian ethics and ethos, grounded in the life, vision, teachings, values and mission of Jesus, blends the vertical-horizontal, divine-human, human-human and internal-external dynamics of life, exceptionally well, not only in terms of the theoretical devotion but also in terms of the practical life, in the spirit of loving service. The social imperatives of Christian life match the idea of God and they are applied into the human life, to the details. While it has to be humbly granted that the 'Christian mission of all-inclusive love and service' is still in the process of being improved and perfected, both in its qualitative and in quantitative proportions, it has also to be recognised incredibly that the 'universal fibre' in Christianity is decidedly comprehensive in its vision, scope and network, both at the divine-human and human-human dynamics and stature.

Endnotes

1. Timothy, George, God the Holy Trinity: Reflections on Christian Faith and Practice, Michigan, 2010, p. 17
2. *Ibid,* p. 56
3. *Ibid,* p. 33
4. Rajendra Vora, Suhas Palshikar, Indian Democracy: Meanings and Practices, New Delhi, 2004, p. 102
5. Bansi Pandit, Explore Hinduism, Loughborough, 2010, p. 39
6. *Ibid,* p. 40
7. *Ibid,* p. 42
8. *Ibid,* p. 43
9. Salman Khurshid, Triple *Talaq*: Examining Faith, New Delhi, 2018, p. 11
10. Timothy George, God the Holy Trinity: Reflections on Christian Faith and Practice, Michigan, 2010, p. 18
11. *Ibid,* p. 19
12. Charles Anderson Godby, Jr, God's Kingdom on Earth: A History of Mankind, Bloomington, 2005, p. 23
13. Timothy, George, God the Holy Trinity: Reflections on Christian Faith and Practice, Michigan, 2010, p. 18
14. Keith Ward, The Christian Idea of God: A Philosophical Foundation for Faith, Cambridge, 2016, p. 39
15. *Ibid,* p. 27

16. The Holy Bible, NIV, Michigan, 1994, Mt 28.20, p. 1134
17. Timothy, George, God the Holy Trinity: Reflections on Christian Faith and Practice, Michigan, 2010, p. 27
18. The Holy Bible, NIV, Michigan, 1994, Gen. 1.27, p. 02
19. *Ibid,* 1 Cor 3.16, p. 1298
20. *Ibid,* Mt 1.23, p. 1094
21. *Ibid,* Mt 7.12, p. 1100
22. *Ibid,* Mt 5.45, p. 1099
23. *Ibid,* Mt 5.48, p. 1099
24. *Ibid,* Lk 10.27, p. 1180
25. *Ibid,* Mt 5.44, p. 1099
26. *Ibid,* Jn 13.34, 35, p. 1226
27. *Ibid,* Mk 7.37, p. 1145
28. *Ibid,* Lk 23.34, p. 1201
29. *Ibid,* Jn 13.14, p. 1225
30. *Ibid,* Jn 15.15, p. 1228
31. *Ibid,* Lk 15.3-7, p. 1188
32. *Ibid,* Mt 4.23, p. 1097
33. *Ibid,* Rom 12.10, p. 1291
34. *Ibid,* Jn 10.30, p. 1221, Mt 25.40, p. 1128
35. *Ibid,* Mt 25.40, p. 1128
36. *Ibid,* 1 Cor. 12.12-26, pp. 1306-07
37. *Ibid,* Let. of Jn 4.20, p. 1396
38. *Ibid,* Jn 10.10, p. 1220
39. *Ibid,* Mt 25.14-30, p. 1127
40. *Ibid,* Mt 7.12, p. 1100
41. *Ibid,* Mt 25.40, p. 1128
42. *Ibid,* 1 Cor. 12.12-28, pp. 1306-07
43. Frank J. Matera, New Testament Theology: Exploring Diversity and Unity, London, 2007, p. 59
44. *Ibid,* p. 68
45. Walter, M. Abbott, SJ, Documents of Vatican II, New York, 1966, p. 07
46. *Ibid,* p. 36
47. Walter M. Abbott, SJ, Documents of Vatican II, New York, 1966, p. 04
48. Thomas Cahill, Pope John XXIII: A Life, London. 2002, p. 79
49. Paul M. Collins, Christian Enculturation in India, New York, 2007, p. 157
50. *Ibid,* p. 158
51. George Weigel, Witness to Hope: The Biography of Pope John Paul II, New York, 2001, p. 619
52. *Ibid,* p. 619
53. *Ibid,* p. 623
54. *Ibid,* p. 629
55. George Weigel, Witness to Hope: The Biography of Pope John Paul II, New York, 2001, p. 639
56. *Ibid,* p. 637
57. Harold Kasimow and Alan Race (Ed.), Pope Francis and Interreligious Dialogue: Religious Thinkers Engage with Recent Papal Initiatives, London, 2018, p. 217
58. https://www.ewtn.com/library/papaldoc/jp2asia.htm
59. Holy Bible, NIV, Michigan, 1994, Lk 19.1-10, p. 1193; 16.19-31, p. 1190; 15.1-32, pp. 1188-89; 5.30-32, p. 1170; 23.24, p. 1200; 23.34, p. 1201; Mt. 5.43-48, p. 1099; 18.1-5, p. 1115; Jn 8.1-11, pp. 1216-17; I Cor. 1.26-29, p. 1297

60. *Ibid,* Jn 10.11, p. 1220
61. M. D. Thomas, Moolya Bible Ke, Varanasi, 2016, Samarpan, p. v., p. 23
62. Chacko Aerath, George Menachery, Christian Contribution to Nation Building: A Third Millennium Enquiry, Michigan, 2009, p. 80
63. *Ibid,* p. 89
64. *Ibid,* p. 90
65. *Ibid,* p. 93
66. Christie, R. Ritter, Mother Teresa: Humanitarian & Advocate for the Poor, Minnesota, 2011, p. 46
67. Chacko Aerath, George Menachery, Christian Contribution to Nation Building: A Third Millennium Enquiry, Michigan, 2009, p. 139
68. The Holy Bible, NIV, Michigan, 1994, Mk 2.27, p. 1138
69. Jesse Bering, The God Instinct: The Psychology of Souls, Destiny and the Meaning of Life, Boston, 2013, p. 91
70. Alf Hiltebeitel, Dharma: Its Early History in Law, Religion, and Narrative, New York, 2011, p. 59
71. UN Millennium Project, UN Millennium Development Library: Health Dignity and Development: What Will it take?, London, 2000, p. 13
72. Stephen Browne, Sustainable Development Goals and UN Goal-Setting, London, 2017, p. 11
73. *Ibid,* p. 67
74. P.M. Bakshi, The Constitution of India, New Delhi, 2011, p. 01
75. David Hockey, Developing a Universal Religion: Why One Is Needed and How It Might Be Derived, Ontario, 2003, p. 53
76. *Mahopanishad* 6.72, Swami Bharati Krishna Tirath, Vedic Metaphysics, New Delhi, 1978, p. 134

(Published in Universal Religion and Education: Practitioners' Perspectives (Book) – published by Faculty of Education, Banaras Hindu University (BHU), Varanasi, pp. 63-80 – in November 2018)

Chapter - 7

Vaishnavism and Christianity—Inclusive Characteristics

1. KEY CONCEPTS

1.1. Vaishnavism

'Vaishnavism'[1] is one of the philosophical traditions of Hinduism. It stands different from Shaivism, Smartism and Shaktism. The followers of Vishnu are called Vaishnavites or Vaishnavas. They follow differentiated monotheism, called henotheism[2], which is a belief in one God without denying the existence of others. Vaishnavas compose the largest community among Hindus.

The key figure in Vaishnavism is Vishnu and he is accessed through his ten incarnations. The word *'Vishnu'* means 'one who is all-pervading'. Vishnu is one among the Trinitarian[3] God-head of Hinduism. *Brahma* and *Mahesh* or *Shankar* are the other counterparts. *Rig-Veda* holds Vishnu as the supreme deity and the foundation of all existence. *Katha Upanishad*[4] describes *Vishnu* as the chief living being amongst all living beings and the one who grants the desires of all other sentient beings. That proves the importance of Vishnu.

The two main focuses of Vaishnavite veneration are *Krishna* and *Rama*, who are usually considered God. Other deities are in relatively subordinate positions. *Vaishnavas* are inclined to be 'personalists', who are associated with the devotional or *bhakti* traditions. There are several schools of thought (philosophy) and *bhakti* traditions (*sampradaya*) of Vaishnavism, as well. *Diksha*, the process of initiation by a *Guru*, *Mantra*, that is repeated by the disciple as an act of worship of Vishnu or one of his *avatars* and *Japa* as a repetitive prayer by the disciple are a few of the salient features of Vaishnavas.

1.2. Neo-Vaishnavism in Assam

Neo-Vaishnavism[5] is a movement of liberal and simple faith that emerged with *bhakti* or devotion as its core. It evolved with the Alwars of South India and then spread to the entire country. It occurred at a time when the priestly and the ruling class of the Hindu society got corrupted with empty ritualism and the consequent social degradation. This was accessible to people of all castes and classes and thus contributed to a new value system of equality. The movement awakened a socio-religious regeneration of the country. *Kabeer, Ravidas, Meerabai, Basweshvar, Vaman, Tukaram*, and the like were stalwarts of this revolutionary movement. Sankardev pioneered this reformatory movement in Assam in a singular fashion.

1.3. The Concept of *Vaishnav* held by Poet *Narsinh Mehta* and liked by *Mahatma Gandhi*

This is one of the most popular Hindu Bhajans, written in the 15th century by poet *Narsinh Mehta*, in Gujarati. This *bhajan* was included in the daily prayer of Mahatma Gandhi. The *bhajan* speaks of what the life, ideals and mentality of *Vaishnav jan* have to be.

'Vainshnav jan to tene kahiye je, Peed paraayi jaane re; Par-dukhkhe upkaar kare toye, Man abhimaanna aane re'. Sakal lok maan sahune vande, Nindaa na kare keni re; Vaach kaachh man nishchal raakhe, Dhan-dhan janani teni re. Sam-drishti ne trishna tyaagi, Par-stree jene maat re; Jivha thaki asatya na bole, Par-dhan nav jhaalee haath re. Moh-maaya vyaape nahi jene, Dridh vairaagya jena man maan re Ram naam shoon taali laagi; Sakal tirath tena tan maan re. Van-lobhi ne kapaT-rahit chhe, Kaam-krodh nivaarya re; Bhane Narsaiyyo tenun darshan karta, Kul ekoter taarya re[6].

One who is 'a *Vaishnav*, knows the pain of others; Does good to others, without letting pride enter his mind'. A *Vaishnav*, to lerates and praises the entire world. Does not speak ill of others, Keeps his promises, actions and thoughts pure; our mother is blessed indeed. 'A *Vaishnav* sees everything equally', rejects greed and avarice; respects women as he respects his own mother, though his tongue may tire he will utter no untruth, Never touches the property of others. A *Vaishnav* does not succumb to worldly attachments, he has renounced lust of all types and anger; the poet *Narsi* will like to see such a person, by whose virtue, his entire family gets salvation.

1.4. Christianity

'Christianity' is a monotheistic religion based on the life and teachings of Jesus Christ. The word 'Christianity' emerges from the word 'Christ', which in turn derives from the Greek 'Christos' and the Hebrew *'Masiah'* meaning 'the anointed one'. The followers of Jesus Christ are called 'Christians'. According to the core belief of Christians, Jesus is the Son of God, fully divine and fully human; he is the saviour of humanity, who was prophesied in the Old Testament. Therefore, he is Jesus Christ or Messiah.

Christianity is the largest religion of the world. The Christian tradition had been one and undivided from the first century onwards. Eastern Orthodox Church and Protestant denominations emerged from Christianity when it split from the Roman Catholic Church in the 11th century and during the Reformation of the 16th century respectively. The original Catholic Church composes the largest portion of Christianity till date, too.

1.5. Catholicism

Catholicism[7] is the faith, practice and system of the Catholic Church. The word was first used in the second century. The word then was supposed to mean 'all-embracing, integral, including a wide variety of things, relating to the historic doctrine and practice, orthodox', etc. It was later used to refer to a single and visible communion, separate from others. The core spirit of Christianity is inherent in the word '*catholic*'. *It* derives from the Latin root *'catholicus'*, which derives from the Greek *'katholikos'*, *meaning* 'whole', 'general', 'universal' and 'all-embracing'. It also means 'broad' or 'liberal' in scope or 'comprehensive'. It suggests 'belonging to the Roman Catholic church' as a community and underlines an 'all-inclusive mindset' in spirit.

2. MUTUALLY INCLUSIVE CHARACTERISTICS

2.1. Theistic Perspective

2.1.1. Theism

The term 'theism'[8] derives from the Greek *'theos'* meaning 'god'. Theism conceives a conscious being that exists of itself and is the cause of all things. It recognizes a power that is superior to human beings and accepts total or ultimate surrender and subordination to it. It describes the nature of the deity, its relationship with the universe, etc. In its specific sense, theism considers God as personal, present and active in the dynamics of the world and the universe. Theism has diverse forms, such as monotheism[9], deism[10], henotheism[11], pantheism[12] and polytheism[13]. Atheism[14] does away with beliefs in the existence of gods or even the absence of gods. Agnosticism asserts knowledge and declares any deity unknown or unknowable. The ideology that sees and interprets life from the angle of theism is theistic perspective. Theistic perceptions are not one either. The wise saying of the *Upanishads* goes thus, *'Ekam sat viprah bahudha Vadanti'*. There is only one God, but wise men describe it differently.

2.1.2. Theism in Hinduism

It is difficult to articulate the nature and type of theism in Hinduism[15]. Basically, there is a trinity called *Brahma, Vishnu* and *Mahesh*. Their roles are generation, operation and destruction, respectively. Among them, Vishnu takes incarnation in different forms. Ten incarnations of Vishnu are stipulated. There is a pantheistic idea of God that believes that God is present in everything. In the overall context, Hinduism admits that there is only one God. But, specifically speaking, there are thirty three crores of gods and goddesses, meaning countless. In other words, God has innumerable forms.

Vaishnavism presents God in the incarnate form. This is a personal idea of God. One could choose God as *'ishtdevtaa'* or *'ishtdevee'*. One, few or all forms of God could be appropriated by the believer, of course, in more or less degrees. God can be personalised through *bhakti* or devotion. God could be considered in any form. Master, husband, wife, son or daughter, mother, father, etc are the main forms in which the God incarnate is approached in *bhakti*. *Naamjap* or taking the name of God is the usual way of awakening the awareness of God in the devotee.

2.1.3. Theism in Christianity

Christianity is out and out into theism. In the general sense, it holds 'monotheism', i.e., belief in one and the only God. But, in the specific sense, the Christian perspective of God is 'tri-theistic' or 'trinitarian[16]'. It refers to a combination of 'one-in-three' and 'three-in-one'. There are 'three persons' in God, namely, 'Father, son and spirit'. They are equal in dignity and status. The divine character of each of them stands intact. But, they form only one God. The individuality of each person remains. There is perfect communion among them, as well. The individual and social qualities are found in them perfectly blended. Triune God in Christianity, in fact, is unity in diversity, to use the Indian language.

Further, in the Christian perspective, God is Father, first and foremost. Though the term 'father' is from the male gender, it has no male connotation at all. It includes female qualities, too. In clearer terms, it is better to say 'God is like a father'. In other words, God has fathered the creation. Father is the source of life. He gives, nourishes and sustains life with love. Love is his fundamental character. He loves his children, without any condition. He takes care of them with a sense of equality and with a sense of all, certainly with a special concern for the weaker ones. He does not discriminate between the good and the evil, too. He sends his sunshine and the rains to both, in an equal measure. Even in defections, he forgives, overwhelmed by love, as if nothing wrong has taken place. He is perfect by nature. He is united with all human beings, relishing the freedom of his children. He eternally celebrates his 'large divine family' with all the human beings, along with the entire creation.

'Jesus Christ', who is one of the three persons in the Godhead, is God himself, as well. He is 'the Son of God', on clearer terms. Jesus could be brought into one's personal life in diverse forms. As Son of God, he is the elder 'brother' and one could be his younger brother. He is the teacher or 'Guru' and one could approach him as disciple. He called his disciples 'friends' and therefore, he is the friend of all. One could hold him as one's 'friend'. He said 'I shall be with you always' and one could accept him as one's 'companion', who travels with one every moment of one's life. Jesus could thus be personalised in diverse ways.

2.1.4. Comparative Features

Theism or belief in God is a common characteristic in both traditions. In the overall picture, the 'monotheistic' idea of God applies both to Vaishnavism and Christianity, though in slightly different ways. The 'personalised approach to God' is a common characteristic, though there is variation in details. 'Intimate interaction with the incarnate form of God' is another shared feature. Vaishnavism engages with only one of the three dimensions of God, whereas the closely knit triune concept of God stands singular in the Christian world.

The implications of theism are of greater significance and they are equally valid in both Vaishnavite and Christian traditions. Belief in a higher power indicates having a point of reference above us. That would mean playing the second fiddle in life, allowing the Creator to play the first one. It denotes one's humble mindset, which motivates total surrender to that superior being, as well. This is the first implication of theism in either system. Secondly, faith in the visible or symbolically visible form of God evokes devotion towards the divine and serves a motivating foundation for a life that intimately connected to God. In a nutshell, faith in God plays back to diverse arenas of human life as a sustained source of meaning. In other words, theistic faith serves an ethical fibre, a refined conscience and a spiritual boost in the lives of the humans.

2.2. GOD OF INCARNATION

2.2.1. The idea of Incarnation

Incarnation suggests 'the idea of God coming to the earth and involving himself in the affairs of men'. It would mean 'embodiment in the flesh by a deity, spirit or quality'. It is the manifestation of God in human flesh. The traditional understanding of incarnation is 'the intervention of super-beings in human history', even fictional characters.

2.2.2. Incarnation in Vaishnavism

Vishnu is the God of universal preservation in the Hindu trinity, the other two being *Brahma* as creator or generator and *Mahesh* or *Shankar* as destroyer. Among these, only *Vishnu* takes *avatar* and the word 'incarnation'[17] refers to *Vishnu* alone. *Vishnu* seems to have taken ten *avatars*, which is called *'dashaavtaar'*. Etymologically, the word *'avtaar'* means 'descent' and *'das'* means 'ten'. *Vishnu* incarnates on earth, time to time, in view of 'eradicating evil forces and of restoring the *dharma* as well as of liberating the worthy ones or devotees from the cycle of births and deaths'. Vaishnavism admits God taking incarnation in the form of animals, as well.

2.2.3. Incarnation in Christianity

Incarnation[18] is the core doctrine of Christianity. The Christian idea of incarnation stands different by way of 'God taking human form'. It is the embodiment of God the Son in human flesh as 'Jesus Christ'. 'God became flesh, assumed the human nature and became man in the form of Jesus Christ' is the central belief of a Christian[19]. Jesus is the Son of God and the second person of the Trinity, the other persons being the Father and the Spirit. The divine and human natures of the Son of God has been perfectly united in Jesus and he is both truly God and truly man. This remains the foundational position of Christianity. Besides, in Christianity incarnation takes place only once and that has taken place in Jesus Christ and in the human form only.

2.2.4. Comparative Features

God in an incarnate form is a common phenomenon in both Vaishnavism and Christianity. Making the invisible God visible to human beings is the role of incarnation. Manifesting the divine characteristics to the humans is its function. Incarnation makes it easy for the humans to get a feel that God is with them. The celebration of the presence of God makes life meaningful, too. These are converging elements in the above religious systems. Incarnation only in the human form in an unrepeatable way is characteristic of Christianity, keeping the dignity of incarnation integral. Vaishnavism holds plurality of incarnation and in multiple forms. This is the main diverging point between them in the comparative survey.

The idea of God incarnate in Christianity in the person of Jesus Christ presents a God who is at the service of human beings. It is the picture of a God, who washes the feet of his devotees; who searches and finds the lost sheep and celebrates joy; who dies and rises for them; and who loves and forgives without any condition. In all these examples God sets a perfect ideal for a human behaviour that can compose a life that is righteous and harmonious. What is special about God incarnate in Vaishnavism is the loving devotion to God in whatever form that gives a firm foundation for human life. It also makes God accessible of all, without any discrimination. The transformative aspect of God-experience is the most significant element in both systems of faith.

2.3. DIVERSITY OF DIVINE QUALITIES

2.3.1. The Idea of Diversity of Divine Qualities

The very idea of diversity in divine qualities is grounded in the logic of incarnation. The concept of incarnation presents diverse characteristics of God. The divine characteristics are spiritual values and spiritual values are, in its turn, human values. One single incarnation also manifests various qualities of God. Various incarnations reveal multifarious qualities of God, too.

2.3.2. Diverse Divine Qualities in Vaishnavism

The word *'Vis'* or *'Vishnu'*[20] means 'to enter', 'to settle', 'to pervade', etc. The derived meaning of *'Vishnu'* is 'the one who is present everywhere', 'the one who enters everywhere', 'the one who pervades everything' and 'the one who is free from fetters and bondages'. The incarnation of *Vishnu* as '*Rama*' presents the quality of *'maryaadaa purushottam'*[21] (the ideal man as the one who remains in his limits; and who symbolises an ideal world in the name of *'ramraajya'*). In folklore, '*Rama*' is the personification of graciousness and courage as well as obedience to sacred law'. He is also a symbol of 'good winning the evil over'. Similarly, '*Krishna*' means 'all-attractive' or a 'combination of attraction and bliss'. *Krishna* also stands for an idea of God who is fun-loving and playful; who drives the chariot of human life to the performance of his duty at all costs (*nishkaam karma*)[22]; and who supports the falling, as in *'cheerharan'* and *'govardhan parvat'*. The ten incarnations symbolise different attributes of God.

2.3.3. Diverse Divine Qualities in Christianity

Christianity sees God as a person. This is the first quality. Diversity in the persons of God is another quality. 'One-in-three' or 'three-in-one' is the specific way of articulating it. This can even mean immense qualities of God. God is transcendent in the sense of being far and beyond the reach of the humans. His immanence is clear in his being near. God is a relational reality. He is father or like a father, rendering the scope of being approached with a filial freedom. He is love, justice, knowledge, forgiveness, service, equality, preferential concern for the weaker, and the like. God's image and likeness are reflected in every human being, by virtue of the creation. His dwelling places are human beings. As many human beings are there, so many qualities of God could be counted, as smaller versions of incarnations.

2.3.4. Comparative Features

God's presence in the creation in an all-pervading manner is a common feature. The immanence of God in his smaller and greater forms of incarnation is another general quality. The application of divine qualities to human beings is yet another characteristic. The involvement of God in the day-to-day affairs of human life is a shared phenomenon. God is the supreme ideal in life. He is like a mirror, in which the humans can check their human and spiritual fitness. He is the origin and destiny of the humans. He is life companion of every human being, as well.

2.4. *BHAKTI* MOVEMENT AS A CLASSLESS DIVINE DRIVE

2.4.1. The idea of *Bhakti*

Bhakti or devotion contains commitment or loyalty to God or to his representation. It involves also affection or attachment to God at its core. *Bhakti* is a divine drive. Affiliation to classes and castes does not matter. It becomes a movement both with regard to the intensity of experience in the individual and to the extensiveness of the same in terms of the involvement of a large number of people. Human mind makes it a means to reach out to God when it looks for consolation or assistance to solve the complexities of life. It is part of the religious history of the world. India has it that its medieval period witnessed a thoroughgoing wave of movement of *bhakti*, when its religious world was badly afflicted with corrupt practices.

2.4.2. *Bhakti* in the Vaishnavite-Neo-Vaishnavite Traditions

Vaishnavism expressed itself in *bhakti* or devotion to Vishnu and his ten incarnations. Krishnaism, *Gaudiya* Vaishnavism, International Society for *Krishna* Consciousness, *Swaminarayan* Hinduism and *Eksarana Dharma* are a few of the versions of *Vaishnava bhakti* movements. The Vaishnavite *bhakti* movement pervaded the entire country in the middle ages through *Kabeer, Nanak, Chaitanya Mahaprabhu, Ravidas, Ramanand, Basveswar, Vaman*, and the like. The Neo-Vaishnavite[23] offshoot of *Sankardev* made a drastic impact over the religious, social, political and cultural arenas of Assam in the 15th-16th centuries.

Sreemant Sankardev[24], born of the *Kayasth* caste, with his versatile endowments as scholar, poet, playwright and socio-religious reformer, emerged as a leader of his own right. His *bhakti* sprouted out of his pain of separation on account of the death of his wife. His pilgrimage to places of religious importance round the country took him towards *bhakti* to *Narayana*, who is one of the incarnations of *Vishnu*. He focused on *'daasyabhakti'*. *'Eksarana Dharma'*[25] was the name of his *bhakti*. He established *'sattras'* as a complex of religious activities, monasteries and prayer houses. *Keertanghar* or the prayer hall had only *'Dasama'*, the scripture, and no idols. The *bhakti* of *Sankardev* had a significant social and cultural appeal.

2.4.3. *Bhakti* in the Christian Tradition

Bhakti movement is not innate to Christianity. But there are movements that are similar to it. One is Pentecostalism and another is charismatic movement. Both Pentecostalism and Charismatic movement are renewal movements within Christianity. Both have similar characteristics, such as focus on the Holy Spirit and confessing a deep and experiential faith in Jesus. There are free style approaches to religion and faith that stand different from highly systematic and organised ritual performances. They appeal to the general public all the more and produce good results in terms of spiritual conversion that transform human behaviour in life.

The term 'Pentecostal'[26] derives from the word 'Pentecost', which is the Greek name for the Jewish Feast of Weeks. In the Christian context it stands for the event of the descent of the Holy Spirit upon the followers of Jesus Christ, as described in the second chapter of the Book of Acts. Pentecostalism focuses on a direct and a personal experience of God through the baptism of the Holy Spirit. It accepts Christ as personal Lord and Saviour. It motivates the Christian to live a Spirit-filled and empowered life. This empowerment includes the use of spiritual gifts, such as speaking in tongues and divine healing, too. It emerged in the early 20th century, energised by revivalism and expectation for the imminent Second Coming of Christ. Pentecostal Movement comprises of over 700 denominations and a large number of independent churches, with no central authority. However, many denominations are affiliated with the Pentecostal World Fellowship. Pentecostalism influenced Catholic and protestant churches. Charismatic movement is the result of this influence.

The term 'charismatic'[27] derives from the Greek words *'charis'*, meaning 'grace', and *'mata'*, meaning 'gifts'. Gifts of the Holy Spirit are its focus. These spiritual gifts are called *'charisms'* in the biblical language. Charismatic movementis an offshoot of Pentecostalism and is centred on the use of spiritual gifts. This movement traces its roots to 1906 and began in 1960 among Protestants. Roman Catholics adopted it around 1967. It is an interdenominational Christian renewal movement and is one of the most popular and fastest-growing forces within the Christian world today. Speaking in tongues and miracles of healing is part of the spiritual frenzy the movement arouses. Most meetings are for praying and spirited singing, dancing, shouting 'in the spirit' and raising hands and arms in prayer. Anointing the sick with oil also is often part of the worship service.

Personal Devotion to Jesus is a very down to earth approach to devotion in the Christian context. It has varied forms. Firstly, Jesus revealed God as father. He manifested himself as Son of God, too. Therefore, one way of devotion to Jesus is holding on to Jesus as one's elder brother. Secondly, Jesus is known to be a unique teacher of the world. He is a great Master, who even washed the feet of his disciples. One could approach him as his Master. Thirdly, Jesus presented himself as the great healer of all sicknesses. One could accept him as the healer of one's sicknesses. Fourthly, Jesus called his disciples 'friends'. One could accept Jesus as one's friend. Fifthly, Jesus said that he is the 'way'. One could take him as 'co-traveler' in life or the 'companion' in one's life journey. There could be yet similar ways of expressing one's devotion to Jesus. The common focus is all these devotional approaches are experiential ways that establish a deep relationship with Jesus.

2.4.4. Comparative Features

Both Vaishnavite and Christian approach to *bhakti* or devotion is personalised in nature. They are oriented to innovative and free style ways. They also are deeply experiential in their character. They bring forth qualitative results for one's personal and social life. The devotional approaches in both traditions give the devotee a new meaning in life. Quality faith is at the core of these devotional styles. Genuineness and transparency in devotion are reflected in both traditions. Both have social implications, too. Result-oriented disposition to religion and faith is another common character. By way of differences, Vaishnavite devotion assumes the role of a servant or wife in reaching out to God as master or lord and Husband respectively. Christian tradition reached out to God in a filial way, as son or daughter. Vaishnavite tradition admits rituals like *'naamjap'*, whereas Christian tradition is more in terms of attitudinal experiences. Again, Vaishnavite *bhakti* more individual-centred and Christian devotion is more socially oriented.

2.5. Social Transformation

2.5.1. Social Transformation

Social transformation refers to an act or a process that awakens change in the individual or the society. The alteration in appearance or character is usually for the better. Variables are replaced in terms of the values held. The altered value or behaviour acquires a social status, even different from that is inherited from his or her parents. Individual or group of individuals facilitates large scale social change in the cultural areas of social life. The former is social transformation on the individual level and the latter, on the level of the social system.

Social transformation involves interpersonal negotiation and engagement with the people. It awakens a shift in the collective consciousness of a society. The external stimulus could be religious, royal, academic or even individual. Intentional social transformations occur at the level of nations, communities, groups and individuals. A revision of assumptions, beliefs, attitudes, values, paradigms, strategies and measures are involved in the process.

2.5.2. Social Transformation in Vaishnavism

The fruit of *bhakti* movement was reflected in its social implications. As an egalitarian divine drive, *bhakti* tradition strongly advocated non-discrimination based on caste, class, gender, etc. Excepting a few luminaries born in Brahmin families, like *Gyaaneshwar* and *Tulseedaas*, most of the stalwarts evolved from suppressed backgrounds. The only thing that mattered to the devotee was his or her relation to God, as a 'servant with the Master' or a 'wife with the husband'. Sankardeva, like other revolutionary *bhakti* saints, rejected discriminatory caste system in an outright manner. Born in the low caste *'Kayasth'*, he boldly appointed non-brahmins also as heads of *sattras* or places of prayer. This provided an inbuilt opportunity for Brahmins and non-brahmins to mingle together. Other than this measure to uphold human dignity, *Sankardeva* could not take up social reforms, due to the deep-seated domination of the Brahmins.

As regards equality of women, *Kanaklata*, the granddaughter of *Sankardev*, played an important role in managing *satras*. Other than that, there wasn't any effort in transforming the male-dominated society towards a better participation of women in social life. Other *bhakti* saints also seem to have been discouraged by the scandalous instances in the Buddhist *sanghas* and found themselves helpless against deep-rooted discriminatory practices as well as abuses.

Neo-Vaishanvism of *Sankardeva* was centred around *Narayana* and refused to accommodate other perspectives and cults. Due to this rigidness, it failed to accommodate the people on the hills and remained confined to the *Brahmaputra* valley. Though there are a few exceptions to this fact among the tribals and muslims, neo-vaishanvism did not make any radical changes in social transformation. But, the '*naamghar*'[38] or '*keertan ghar*' or '*sattra*', as a large prayer hall, built in the traditional style, was a unique type of institution, where congregational prayer, religious discourses and discussions on life-related matters were conducted. This was like self-governed parliament or cultural centre at the grassroot level and was a landmark contribution of *Sankardev*.

2.5.3. Social Transformation in Christianity

Christianity stands out among all religious traditions for its exceptional perspectives and elaborate schemes for social transformation. The significant impact of Christianity in facilitating social awakening and change is acknowledged worldwide. The whole world has benefited from the same, India in particular, too. Schools, colleges and universities in the cities and towns cover the educational area of service. Hospitals, dispensaries and health centres in the cities display the picture of service in the medical and health area. The social service centres that undertake schemes of housing, clothing, feeding, non-formal education, literacy, adult education, etc are efforts for social change at the grass roots. The special schools and centres for the physically disabled, mentally challenged, orphans, old and abandoned, etc are commendable efforts for making a society that is inclusive as well as transformed. The efforts for social awakening in terms of dialogue and harmony among religious and non-religious communities contribute to fostering inter-community relations, national integration and social cohesion. All these attempts for social transformation are motivated by the Christian faith, which has the spiritually charged vision and teachings of Jesus.

2.5.4. Comparative Features

Social transformation is a common denominator in both Christianity and Vaishnavism or Neo-Vaishnavism. Vaishnavism doesn't have a basic inclination for social transformation. Only Neo-Viashnavism has some elements of social change, that too, in a limited context. The efforts for social transformation in Christianity are fundamental to its faith and are elaborate and comprehensive in nature. Vaishanvite faith and *bhakti* are primarily oriented to individual transformation. Christian faith and devotion is for the most part directed towards social renewal and uplift. While Vaishnavite *bhakti* takes care of the liberation of the individual, first and foremost, Christian faith and worldview combines not only the individual and societal but also the human and the divine elements of life. Therefore, social transformation in Christianity, especially in terms of the weaker sections, is the ultimate focus of faith. Vaishavism, as conceived and interpreted by *Narsinh Mehta* and liked by *Mahatma Gandhi*, i.e., 'knowing the pain of others' and 'doing good to them', has lot of scope to be developed.

3. CONCLUSION

Sri Narayan Guru[29] of Kerala, a great poet, philosopher and social reformer, who has contributed immensely to the making of the modern Kerala, who organised the first ever inter-caste dining and inter-faith meet in Alua, Kerala, in 1894, has a very valuable message for us. He says, *'majhab ho koi bhee, insaan bhalaa so bhalaa'*. That means, 'whatever be your religion, be a good human being'[30]! Jesus adds to this, 'Sabbath is for man, and not vice versa'[31]. Religion is for the human being and human being is not for religion. Life is the gift of God and religion is at the service of life. 'Becoming a good human being' is the basic logic of religion. One's faith needs to motivate one to become good human beings and to become active instruments of transforming the society.

This short survey of the inclusive characteristics in Vaishnavism and Christianity has to nourish us with a mindset that prompts a realisation that the religious traditions the humans are affiliated to are mutually inclusive and complementary. They are the gift of the same creator and are the common cultural heritage of the human society. They are not yours and mine. They are ours. One is mine in special and the others are mine in general. Comparison in terms of superior and inferior and competition in terms of hegemony over the other defeat the fundamental logic of our belonging to it. The common denominators and similarities invite us for a shared journey of life. Differences, dissimilarities and specialties have to motivate us to learn from each other, enrich each other and grow further together in the divine-human as well as individual-social dynamics of life.

A divinely enthused human wisdom of life has to evolve and emerge in us, as a result of our engagements and experiments with religion, faith and *bhakti*. An all-inclusive mental frame is the outcome of this exercise. Inclusive thinking has to lead us to harmonious living with communities of all affiliations and persuasions. A joint commitment to making a better country and the society is the ultimate drive that will guide the destinies of religion, faith and life, in the days and years ahead of us, in the 21st century and beyond.

Endnotes

1. Vensus, A. George, Paths to the Divine: Ancient and Indian, Washington, 2008, p. 226
2. Brain Bumann, Divine Knowledge: Buddhist mathematics according to anonymous Manual of Mongolian astrology and divination, Leiden, Netherlands, 2008, p. 50
3. C. T. Benedict, One God in One Man, Bloomington, 2007, p. 318
4. Katha Upanishad 2.2.13, Steven Rosen, Krishna's Song: A New Look at *the Bhagavad Gita*, Westport, 2007, p. 72
5. M. D. Muthukumaraswamy, (Editor), Folklore as Discourse, Chennai, 2006, p. 81
6. Diamond Pocket Books, Bhajan, Lokgeet or Aartian, New Delhi, 2005, p. 63
7. Katy Gerner, Catholicism, Tarrytown, 2008, p. 05
8. Erwin Fahlbusch, Geoffrey William Bromiley (Ed), The Encyclopaedia of Christianity, Volume 2, Michigan, 2001, p. 199
9. Erwin Fahlbusch, Geoffrey William Bromiley (Ed), The Encyclopaedia of Christianity, Volume 2, Michigan, 2001, p. 524
10. *Ibid,* p. 199
11. *Ibid,* p. 199
12. *Ibid,* p. 77
13. *Ibid,* p. 524
14. *Ibid,* p. 137
15 Sabapathy Kulandran, Grace in Christianity and Hinduism, Cambridge, 1964, p. 115
16. C. T. Benedict, One God in One Man, Bloomington, 2007, p. 318
17. Farooqui Salma Ahmed, Salma Ahmed Farooqui, A Comprehensive History of Medieval India: From Twelfth to the Mid-Eighteen Century, New Delhi, 2011, p. 199
18. John Hick, The Metaphor of God Incarnate: Christology in a Pluralistic Age, London, 1993, pp. 03-04
19. Holy Bible, NIV, Michigan, 1994, John 1.14, p. 1206; Col 2.9, p. 1342; Phil 2.7-8, 1336-37
20. Lisa Greathouse, Vishnu, California, 2010, p. 20
21. Devdutt Pattanaik, Seven secrets of Vishnu, Chennai, 2011, p. 159
22. Arjunsinh, K. Parmar (Editor), Critical Perspectives on the Mahabharata, New Delhi, 2002, p. 111
23. Satish Chandra, Medieval India: From Sultanat to the Mughals-Delhi Sultanat (1206-1526), New Delhi, 1997, p. 215
24. Byomakesh Tripathy, Sristidhar Dutta (Editor), Religious History of Arunachal Pradesh, New Delhi, 2008, p. 363
25. Kali Prasad Goswami, Devadaasee: Dancing Damsel, New Delhi, 2000, p. 19
26. William, K. Kay, Pentecostalism, London, 2009, p. 08
27. William, K. Kay, Pentecostalism, London, 2009, p. 185
28. Jyoti Prasad Rajkhowa, Sankaradeva, His Life, Preachings, and Practices: A Historical Biography, Guwahati, 2003, p. 288
29. Thummapudi Bharathi, A History of Telugu *Dalit* Literature, Delhi, 2008, p. 49
30. Swami Satchidananda, Sri Narayan Guru – the Universal Guru, Chapter 12
31. James Morison, Mark's memoirs of Jesus Christ: a commentary on the Gospel according to Mark, London, 1873, p. 72

(Published in Third Millennium (Quarterly Journal), Rajkot, Vol. XX, No. 04, pp. 49-62 – in October-December 2017)

Chapter - 8

Non-Violence in the Bible: Dimensions and Implications

INTRODUCTION

A discussion on 'Holy Books and Violence' may raise the eyebrows of thinking people. There is no doubt about the fact that the title suggests a basic self-contradiction. But, considering the religious, political and social contexts in which these holy books have been produced, anyone would affirm that it does make sense. Repeated instances of communal turbulences and violence in the society assert its relevance, too. The incontestable history of terrible wars and massacres in the name of religion that the world has witnessed, along with its lingering hangover of painful memories, makes it necessary for well-meaning people to analyze the content of these so called holy books. How could the holy books, in the real sense of the word, contain divine sanctions and descriptions of brutal violence? Or is it that the readers and the interpreters of the books lost sight of the intention of the author and the fundamental orientation of the books as a call from violence to nonviolence? Aren't the religionists responsible for not learning enough from the positive ideals enshrined in the sacred scriptures? Isn't it vital for the world of today to imbibe the core universal values of the sacred scriptures in order to ensure a nonviolent and more harmonious living for the humans of tomorrow? Against the backdrop of these concerns and questions, this paper attempts to explore the deeper dimensions and implications of nonviolence in the Bible, in line with the vision, mission and teachings of Jesus Christ, and brings to light some of the multi-faith possibilities for a harmonious and spiritual way of human living.

1. VIOLENCE AND NONVIOLENCE: CONCEPTS AND CONTEXTS

1.1. Violence

Violence[1] is the expression of force. It is a compelling action. Physical aggression is its usual form. Intention to cause pain or harm is intrinsic to aggression or violence. It is generally geared against another person. Violation of the will of the other is its essential component. Violence can be done against oneself also, when one's own will is infringed upon. Violence can be against animals, too. Especially when done to human beings, it includes hitting someone, causing bodily harm, pain or death, waging war and genocide. It can be the destruction of non-living objects also. In such cases, it is used as a tool for expressing anger, protest, retaliation, manipulation, etc. Violence can be non-physical as well, psychological, mental, moral, verbal, etc. as the context may be.

1.2. Violence Caused by Natural Calamities

The phenomenon of natural calamities occurs in nature on their own accord. Horrifying events like earthquakes, floods, volcanic eruptions, landslides, fires, spontaneous tree limbs falling, winds, hurricanes, tornadoes and ice storms keep happening. We cannot say that the creator God sends such disasters in order to destroy or cause havoc in human lives or in the creation. The colossal suffering and the struggle for preserving life that all forms of life – the plants, trees, animals and especially human beings – undergo is beyond the capacity of imagination. The desperate clinging to stronger items for support is a painful sight to see. These natural disasters cause untold violence and misery. But such violence cannot be in any way attributed to human beings or God[2]. One would think why this violence is not prevented by the creative power. The limitation of the created world has its answer. Could violence in nature be a sign of violence in human beings and in the human society? Human beings are part of nature and the creation. All the same, does violence in nature justify violence in human life? Human beings have to attempt making better provisions for minimizing the natural disasters and their consequences.

1.3. Domestic Violence Caused by Human Beings

Domestic violence is spousal abuse or wife-beating or intimate partner violence. It occurs when a family member, partner or ex-partner attempts to physically or psychologically dominate over another. It also includes violence between cohabitants and non-married intimate partners. Domestic violence occurs in all cultures; people of all races, ethnicities, religions, sexes and classes. It is perpetrated by both men and women.

Domestic violence has many forms, including physical violence, sexual abuse, emotional abuse, intimidation, economic deprivation and threats of violence. Violence can be criminal and includes physical assault (hitting, pushing, shoving, killing, etc.), sexual abuse (unwanted or forced sexual activity) and stalking. Passive, subtle and veiled abuses like victimisation, neglect, etc. also are included in domestic violence[3]. Recent understanding of domestic violence includes also feminism and women's rights. Both women and men can be victims of domestic violence.

1.4. Public Violence Caused by Human Beings

Since the systems of the human society have their limits, being dissatisfied with them is a normal thing. Dissatisfaction can make human beings angry. Expressing the anger thus arising is also legitimate. But appropriating illegal and illogical ways is certainly a sub-human behaviour. People get together and mob-mindedness and blind reaction cause immeasurable amount of violence in the society. Violence caused by human beings is projected as bearing the name of religion, caste, ideology, profession, culture, class, ethnic traits, nationalities, and the like. Family violence, communal violence and reactionary violence are deliberately caused by people who have pathological egos, individual or collective[4]. Often communal disturbances and riots are caused by politicians and fundamentalist religious leaders who have vested interests. Communal violence, sometimes inter-communal violence, is perpetrated across ethnic lines and membership in a particular ethnic group is made as the criterion for victimising someone. Communal violence, as seen in South Asia, includes genocide as a sub-category and proceeds to mindless massacres.

1.5. The Aftermath of Violence in the Society

Whatever is the reason for and the type of violence, the untold misery of diverse sorts that follows remains a question mark for the human culture. It goes without mention that a large number of human beings become victims of violence. According to a study, over 1.6 million people worldwide and on a yearly basis lose their lives as a result of violence. Violence seems to be one of the leading causes of death for people aged 15-44 years, 14% of them among males and 7% among females[5]. A much larger portion of people get injured and are condemned to suffer from a range of physical, sexual, reproductive and mental health problems. Violence also places a massive burden on the economy of individuals, families, institutions, communities, countries and societies for guaranteeing curative, defensive and preventive measures. Productivity and progress get appallingly affected, too. The equilibrium of social life is badly disturbed. Moreover, eyebrows rise against the relevance and effectiveness of God, religion, education, values, government and of the dignity of the human person.

1.6. Violence Recoils on Itself

Violence begets violence. It is a phenomenon that recoils on itself. It generates violence in an enlarged manner. A slight violence may be retaliated for in a very outsized quantity. Verbal violence can ignite physical violence. Wounding one organ of a body can be paid for by even the loss of life. Aggression with one individual can cause the destruction of the entire family or clan[6]. People can be punished for their sinfulness in great measures. One violent act can cause a series of violent acts and normally one pays a huge price for even smaller forms of violence. Experience of life substantiates the wisdom of the axiom, "If a man digs a pit, he will fall into it; and if a man rolls a stone, it will roll back on him" (Proverbs 26.27, p.745). The Psalmist adds, "He, who digs a hole and scoops it out, falls into the pit he has made. The trouble he causes recoils on himself; his violence comes down on his own head" (Psalms 7.15-16, p. 613). These profound insights assert categorically that violence is not the means for fulfilling one's desires, plans and demands. It is no solution to the problems of dissatisfaction on account of injustice, oppression and even violence itself. It only can cause graver violence, discord and misery that ultimately hurt and even ransack the entire society in different ways.

1.7. Violence is a Matter of Perception

There is a radical question that arises regarding violence. How does one judge something as violence or not? Are all violent acts really violent in the ultimate context? The criterion of violence in the long run is the way one perceives it. It is a measurable phenomenon. It is to be understood in terms of the historical context in which it emerges and the overall outcome of the act. Psychologists find persons reacting differently to physical acts that are seemingly violent. State policies vary in countries as regards capital punishment. The executioner is not conclusively perceived as violent. Besides, the understanding of violence is dependent on the aggressor-victim relation. Violence could be a reaction against victimization, as in the case of the Israelites of the Old Testament. It is not that violence is justified[7]. The ancient Hebrew people recognised their own past as slaves in Egypt and realised that their predicament was one of the scapegoat victims. That is why the Psalmist of the Old Testament laments from the victim's perspective. The victims did not proceed to violent acts of retaliation against the oppressor. However, their realisation caused bitter thoughts and feelings in them, without their being aware of it. Though these thoughts and feelings could be grouped under the category of violence, could this violence be considered a pure violence? There is a different reality involved in this phenomenon. It is difficult to say anything categorical about this situation. Therefore, appears that some space has to be left for one's perception of violence, as long as it directly does not hit someone or do not get aggravated.

1.8. Violence for Self-Defence

Violence is often pursued as a measure for self-defence. Self-defence can be in immediate response to the ongoing violence, by way of preventing the harm that is being inflicted or by way of reacting to the pain caused. It can be anticipatory also, by way of a precaution against the approaching violence. The use of violence is often as an antidote to shame or humiliation. It can be motivated by dignity and pride and be intended for defending one's honour, especially among males who misunderstand capacity for violence as a sign of manliness. Defensive use of force or aggression is not considered violence, even in cases where the amount of force used is significantly greater than otherwise[8]. Countries have a responsibility to defend their respective citizens from aggression from outside forces. Self-defence in case of a direct attack could be justified even when violence is applied and when all other roads for escaping the danger are exhausted. It would mean restraining the attacker and hindering him or her from further attacks. Self-defence has to be applied to defend oneself, one's family, one's dear and near ones, any victim of violence if one happens to be present on the occasion.

1.9. Nonviolence

The word 'violence'[9] is direct in the system of language and 'nonviolence' negatively is worded. For that matter, whether violence is more natural to life or not is a point of dispute. Obviously, non-violence is the negation of violence or aggression. It rejects the use of physical violence. It is a doctrine, a policy or a practice of rejecting violence in favour of peaceful tactics as a means of gaining anything. It is a positive philosophy of life. It can be a strategy for social change as well. Nonviolence is not passive acceptance of oppression or armed struggle. Nonviolence is a power within that is capable of discovering the means of combating violence. It is the reluctance to cause pain and harm to others and consciously refraining from it. It is sensitiveness to the wellbeing of others. It is overcoming discord by concord. The mode of nonviolent action can become an effective substitute for violence as a way of securing redress of wrongs. It is a style of life that advocates overcoming evil by good. It is a way of confronting the power of the world with the power of the supernatural spirit.

1.10. Nonviolence as the Spirit of Human Culture

Among prehistoric humans, there is archaeological evidence for both contentions of violence and peacefulness as primary characteristics of life.

Violence seems to be inherent in the humans. But there are also lots of natural mechanisms for checking and overcoming conflict, for channeling aggression and for cooperating with others. Peaceful ways appears to be more natural than aggressive tendencies. At any rate, nonviolence is definitely part of the higher human self. It is the inbuilt law of nature. Even animals do not normally attack its species without any reason. They violate the lives of other species of animals only for their survival. Though certain forms and some degree of violence is part of this limited world, life in its higher aspects is nonviolent in spirit[10]. The spirit of nonviolence is all the more a human quality. Normally human beings are friendly in their mental texture. They like meeting other human beings. The social character in human beings makes it impossible for the humans to live alone. The humanisation process becomes effective only in company with others. This human phenomenon does not work in an attitude of violence against the other. The struggle for existence and pathological aberrations, like pride and greed, make human beings aggressive towards the other. But the basic orientation of the humans is towards peace and wellbeing of all. This is like the law of gravity. Nonviolence leads to further nonviolence and to fuller life. It leads one to the human qualities of love, justice and peace. Nonviolence is humanly transforming. That is why Jesus, the champion of nonviolence and peace, says, "If you hold to my teaching, you are really my disciples. Then you will know the truth, and the truth will set you free" (Jn.8:31-32, p. 1217). Transcending oneself towards the spiritual realm is the process of freedom. That is the real culture of the humans.

1.11. Violence in the Sacred Scriptures

'Violence in Sacred Scriptures or Holy Books' is a phrase that contradicts itself. It is really shocking to observe that there is elaborate description of violence in the Sacred Scriptures. To observe that violence is given divine sanction can make one feel breathless. But, as a matter of fact, according to a rough calculation, if not two-thirds, at least a major portion of the Sacred Scriptures of the world put together is contaminated by violence of diverse sorts, mainly bloody violence[11]. There is brutality, adultery, fornication, corruption, murder, massacre, cheating, destruction, pride, enmity, hatred, jealousy, fundamentalism, fanaticism, communalism, and the like. One could very rightly wonder 'what is holy about these books!' The central theme of the Hebrew Scriptures, the Old Testament of the Christians, is violence. There is over two-thirds of the Bible, including some portions of the New Testament of the Christians, discussing violence or threats of violence. We find an angry God who takes revenge for evil-doing or sanctions violence (Ezekiel 21.31, p. 959). The Hindu Scriptures, like Mahabharata and Ramayana, is full of war, direct and indirect. Though the motive of violence is presented as doing what is right, the means used is horrifyingly violence. Likewise, the Quran has a strong orientation toward religious violence. God seems to attack and incite to violence far more than he blesses and he is projected as promoting religious terrorism. The Qur'an contains a number of verse references that address states of war. Similarly, the holy books of other religions also have sanctions of violence and their descriptions, in more or less degrees.

1.12. Nonviolence in the Sacred Scriptures

Sacred Scriptures of all faith traditions have a strong message for nonviolence in a considerable portion of them, though in a more or less manner. Holy books are holy because of their orientation for the positive values of human life. The worth of the sacred scriptures is only to that extent to which they contribute to making the human life more nonviolent through its stress on spiritual values. Nonviolence guards the honour of the people under one's responsibility. It would mean risking one's life, even for the sake of others. Nonviolence applies to thought, word and deed. It is extended towards human beings and towards all other living beings. The understanding and implementation of '*ahimsa*' in Jainism is more radical, scrupulous, and comprehensive than in any other religion. *Avesta* stresses on 'pure thoughts, words and actions' that cannot but be nonviolent. *Dhammapada* has compassion as its genius. The gist of the Quran is peace[12]. The New Testament of the Bible is all for love and service. Nonviolence is a way of life for spiritually tuned people. Nonviolence believes that the universe is on the side of justice. All Sacred scriptures have nonviolence as their core message. Well, it takes courage to draw motivation and strength from them and live a nonviolent life.

2. NONVIOLENCE IN THE BIBLE – DIMENSIONS

2.1. Nonviolence in the New Testament versus Violence in the Old Testament

The very name 'Old Testament' and 'New Testament' indicates a contrasting character in them. The God of the Old Testament is one of justice. The God of the New Testament is a God of goodness. And that is the God of Jesus Christ. Roughly three forth of the Old Testament is the description of violence and related miseries, either caused by human beings or seemingly willed and sanctioned by God. The New Testament understands it with a broadened perspective, beyond the literal meaning. It imbibes illumination and inspiration from it, in view of proceeding beyond the Old Testament itself. The episodes are taken with a new interpretation and meaning. In the Christian context, the Old Testament is only a preparation for the New Testament[13]. The old law is being revised and replaced by a new law. The significantly violence-dominated Old Testament story is being reconstructed with a New Testament that is permeated by benevolence and love. The New Testament celebrates the spirit of nonviolence mostly. The entire message of the New Testament is one of nonviolence, with its diverse implications. The central part of the New Testament idea of nonviolence coils around the life, experience and teachings of Jesus Christ.

2.2. Nonviolence as Grounded on Jesus' Experience of God as 'Father'

The basic relation between the creating and created realities is symbolised by the word 'father'. The word stands for the widest relational category of life and covers all relational categories found in other faith traditions. It is like a large umbrella that brings together the entire creation in one single fold. Human beings, therefore, are empowered to relate to the divine in a very personal manner. The understanding of 'God as Father' is rooted in the personal experience of Jesus. The filial experience of Jesus (Mt 3.17, p.1096; 17.5, p.1114; Jn 5.19, p.1211; Jn 14.9,10,11 p.1227; Jn 15.1, p.1227; 17.10,11, p.1230; Lk 10.22, p.1180; Lk 23.34,46, p.1201)[14] is broadened (Mt 6.4, 6,8,18,26,30,32, p.1099; Mt 10.29-31, p.1105; Mt 20.1-16, p. 1118) to include the entire human effort to reach out the divine. Experiencing oneself as the son/daughter of God would mean understanding God as Father. This filial experience is a spirituality of freedom that elevates one from the state of a mere creature/servant to the status of a son/daughter of God (Jn 15.15, p.1228). This experience is open to all the sectors of the society and is beyond the borders of gender, caste, class, creed, profession, language, culture, and the like. The Christian understanding of God as Father is fundamental to human life and it offers great possibilities of multi-faith and human implications of a higher plane.

2.3. Nonviolence of Jesus Founded His Fraternal Attitude to Others

The fraternal attitude of Jesus to his fellow human beings emerges from his filial experience of God as Father. Both these realities are basically inter-linked. The vertical relation expresses itself in a horizontal one. Both together make the idea of God a perfect blend of theory and practice. The filial experience facilitated a realisation that all human beings are 'the sons and daughters of the same God' and so are brothers and sisters in a universal manner. Such a spiritual way of being human enables one to love even one's enemy and not to discriminate between one's friend and enemy, as Jesus did on the cross as well as in life. The culture of being fraternal, beyond the boundaries of the virtuous and the unrighteous, (Mt 5.43-48, p.1099) is one that is of high spiritual quality. Establishing loving relationship with every human being one meet in life and being of all possible service to him/her across all boundaries is what is meant by the new culture of fraternal love. Being a disciple to Jesus or being a Christian would mean nothing but this. Such a fraternal style of life has unlimited universal possibilities and implications for a neighbourly and brotherly way of living one's life and for the wellness of the society.

2.4. Nonviolence in the Life of Jesus

Although it is difficult to reconcile the nonviolence of Jesus with the violence performed at God's behest in the Old Testament, Jesus lived the principle of nonviolence to the nub before he preached it. Various instances could be highlighted from the personal life of Jesus to this effect. One illustration regarding the defence of Jesus' life is so striking in which he is seen rejecting violence outright. When he was being seized and arrested, one of Jesus' companions could not tolerate this. He reached for his sword, drew it out and struck the servant of the high priest, cutting off his ear. Jesus exhorted him to put his sword back in its place and made a caution "all who draw the sword will die by the sword" (Matthew 26. 50-52, p.1130). The ethics of nonviolence lived by Jesus now is not a foolish idea of a visionary fanatic. It is a sane submission to the God of heaven and earth. There is an everlasting wisdom that is intrinsic to it. The resurrection of Jesus is the tangible sign for this fact. It stands as a powerful sign that the nonviolent way will ultimately prevail. The new age inaugurated by the private and public life of Jesus was intended to dethrone the principalities and powers of the world and to destroy death itself (I Cor 15.24, p.1309). The nonviolent style of life is the proof that demonstrates the fact the new age is begun. The good news he preached is fulfilled in the hearing of those present then (Lk 4.18-21, p.1168).

2.5. Non-Violence in the Teachings of Jesus

Jesus was a great teacher. He taught the method of nonviolence in life. Even the opponents of Jesus, the Pharisees and the Scribes, recognised that Jesus taught with authority as no one else did, "Teacher, we know that you speak and teach what is right, that you do not show partiality but teach the way of God in accordance with the truth" (Lk.20.21, p.1195). Jesus was often called 'rabbi' or 'teacher'. Like other itinerant preachers or teachers of his time, he traveled about with a group of students, who are called 'disciples'. True to the role of a teacher, he guided his followers, encouraged them, challenged them, questioned their preconceptions and urged them on to the wisdom of nonviolence. He taught a new law, an entirely new way of life, the way of divine justice and nonviolence. The centerpiece of the teachings of Jesus on nonviolence is the 'Sermon on the Mount', which can be called his formal 'manifesto of nonviolence'. Matthew begins with the 'beatitudes' that enlist a series of blessings for the disciple of Jesus who travels the path of nonviolence. This upside-down vision of life declares the poor, mournful, meek, hungering and thirsting for justice, merciful, pure in heart, peacemaking and willing to be persecuted for justice's sake blessed. These qualities of nonviolence make one eligible for a great reward in heaven (Mt.5.3-12. p.1097) as well as transform the imperial culture of violence in the world. The 'Sermon on the Mount' is the foundation of the great ethic of nonviolence lived and advocated by Jesus. This teaching of Jesus on the nonviolent way of life is capable of establishing God's reign on earth as in heaven (Mt 6.10, p.1099).

2.6. Revised Version of the Old Testament Laws Regarding Strict Justice and Retaliation

The nature of God Jesus knew from his experience and the picture he portrayed in his teachings was of a loving Father, which was entirely different from that of the Old Testament. Therefore he could not accommodate the Old Testament laws that had stipulations of severe justice. He revised them and reinterpreted them for his disciples. Some of the harsh phrases of the Old Testament law were – "eye for eye" (Mt 5.38, p. 1098), "tooth for tooth" (Mt 5.38, p.1098), "do not break your oath" (Mt 5.33, p. 1098), "love your neighbour and hate your enemy" (Mt 5.43, p.1099), "do not commit adultery" (Mt 5.27, p.1098), "do not murder" (Mt 5.21, p. 1098) and "anyone who divorces her wife must give her a certificate of divorce" (Mt 5.31, p.1098). Jesus reinterprets the Old Testament 'tit for tat' laws in a positive manner, with a characteristic authority 'but I say to you'. Analyzing the historical setting of the laws, one would find that the tendency was to engage in counter-violence that would escalate dramatically – you take my eye, I'll take your life; you kill my family in retaliation, my family kills your tribe, etc. In such a situation, there is no denying the fact that the above laws limit violence. But, the laws weren't positive yet, by being indicators for eliminating violence. The new law of Jesus applies to the victim of violence so that he or she may not aggravate violence by retaliating. He also empowers him or her to be a catalyst of arresting violence for the oppressor by the strength of his or her moral stamina. Nevertheless, the nonviolent way does not mean being a passive doormat in any way. It is a creative and positive action that confronts the oppressor with spiritually and invites him/her to change. It is a different style of response altogether.

2.7. Nonviolent Alternatives Suggested by Jesus

The popular dictum of science goes 'there is an equal and opposite reaction to any action'. But 'reaction' is an un-reflected one and is of the physical plane. Human action, in the right sense of the word, is a 'response', which is positive. Even the negative action of violence is to be positively responded to. Punishment and revenge after the initial offence are retaliatory measures and are negative. Jesus campaigns for creative alternatives. Some of the radically positive responses of Jesus are worded as follows and they speak for themselves concisely and impressively. "But I tell you, love your enemies and pray for those who persecute you" (Mt 5.44, p.1099), "anyone who is angry with his brother will be subject to judgment" (Mt. 5.22, p.1098), "do not resist an evil person. If anyone strikes you on the right cheek, turn to him the other also; if someone wants to sue you and take your tunic, let him have your cloak as well. And if someone forces you to go one mile, go with him two miles; Give to anyone who asks you, and do not turn away from the one who wants to borrow from you' (Mt 5.38-42, p. 1098), "All men will hate you because of me, but he who stands firm to the end will be saved. When you are persecuted in one place, flee to another" (Mt 10.22-23, p.1105), "if you are offering your gift at the altar, and there remember that your brother (or sister) has something against you, leave your gift there in front of the altar. First go and be reconciled to your brother (or sister); then come and offer your gift" (Mt.5.23-24, p.1098) and 'do not look lustfully at another woman' (Mt.5:27-28, p.1098). Jesus proposes nonviolent resistance to evil and promotes a new and third alternative to the methods of passive acceptance or active involvement in nonviolence. The antithesis of Jesus is the command to practice unconditional love beyond the margins of all divisions. His alternatives are pro-life measures, like doing well and practicing unconditional love.

2.8. Nonviolence According to Jesus as an Advocacy for Nonviolent Revolution

Nonviolence in the New Testament of Jesus is a revolution of nonviolence. It is a not in any way a passive peace. It is not violent revolution, either. The core of the New Testament of Jesus Christ is fundamental change in the attitude of human beings, in relation to God the Creator and in relation to other human beings. This attitudinal change has a preferential reference to the poor, the disadvantaged, the sinful and the so called low caste. New Testament is a powerful voice against the unjust forms and systems of violence – the soldier who kills the projected enemy, the revolutionary who assassinates the adversary, the privileged proprietor who ill-treats his workers, the haves who have caused the sad plight of the have-nots or do nothing for them, the affluent sections that perpetuate poverty, the unjust economic structures that produce suffering and starvation for others, the established order that systematically murders the innocent under the shield of hierarchical and nonsensical privileges, the self-righteously religious persons who discriminate and stamp on the lowly, the powerful who exploits the weaker sections, and the like. The revolution of nonviolence is geared towards challenging the very logic of the unjust systems of the society[15]. The advocacy of Jesus is a timely and strong voice for the dignity of the trampled as well as a championing step for the basic right to live.

2.9. Nonviolent Revolution as an Active and Positive Measure

The nonviolent campaign of Jesus cannot be reduced to mere passivism. It is an activist movement of direct confrontation with self-indulgent social structures that are fundamentally compatible with his call for non-resistance. The style of confrontation makes the difference. The nonviolent campaigns are sloping towards joyful celebrations of victory. They respond to violence, brutality, prison and death non-violently but actively. Jesus' cleansing of the temple provides the clearest evidence. Jesus engaged in aggressive resistance against evil when he marched into the temple, drove the animals out with a whip, overturned the money tables of the businessmen and denounced their defiling of the temple. He certainly did not kill and probably did not whip the moneychangers, but he clearly and muscularly resisted their evil in a dramatic act of civil disobedience. Jesus denounced the Pharisees as 'blind guides, fools, hypocrites and a brood of vipers'. He uttered harsh public words condemning them for their many errors, including their preoccupation with tithing on small matters and their neglect of more important things such as justice and mercy (Mt 23.1-38, pp. 1122-25). He questioned the soldier who unjustly struck him on the cheek and did not submit meekly to the unjust act, "If I said something wrong, testify as to what is wrong. But if spoke the truth, why do you strike me?" (John 18.23, p.1231). Jesus respected the authorities at his trial. But several instances prove that his nonviolent love was not a passive one in any way. Jesus retained a nonviolent spirit all throughout the process of his arrest, jailing, trial, torture and public execution. But he was positive, strong and active in his ways of loving, forgiving and tenderly inviting the oppressors to conversion. Jesus was a perfect 'role model of nonviolence', especially in his last days when he had to face untold violence.

2.10. Nonviolence in Jesus Calls for a Fundamental Transformation of Life

The nonviolence of Jesus is an earnest invitation to an agonizing realisation of the disoriented and deep-seated political, religious and economic establishments. It is a summons to an active repentance over the incalculable pain and harm inflicted upon the victims. It is also a firm campaign for transforming the above unjust structures. It would proceed to picket, boycott, obstruct and paralyze the institutionalised structures of scandal. The cross of Jesus is the foundation for the nonviolent revolution of the New Testament. Nonviolent resistance would mean challenging the oppressor with a gentle firmness that underlines God's love even for him and inviting the oppressor to repent and change, even while opposing his evil actions[16]. The nonviolent movement can appear as irrelevant and as an impossible ideal. The nonviolent movement is definitely not a 'quick fix' solution of the problem or a short-term treatment. It is amazingly effective as a long run way, after the fashion of the suffering and death on the cross of Jesus and of his resurrection, as powerfully presented by the New Testament. The nonviolent battle of Jesus is a protest against the affluence that is built on poverty and starvation elsewhere. It is a campaign against the multinational corporations engaged in injustice. It is a clarion call to repentance from the sin of economic injustice, religious superiority, social prejudice and discrimination. It demands nothing less than a fundamental transformation of one's life for the better and in favour of others and God.

2.11. Jesus as the Good News of Nonviolence

Violence in the world is always a 'bad news', even though it may sound 'good news' to the disoriented and self-indulging people. The blatantly violent ways depicted on the pages of the Old Testament is a 'bad news', too, as well as on the pages of other religious scriptures. The New Testament message of nonviolence pioneered by Jesus is 'good news' of the highest order. The Gospels tell the story of nonviolence in the life of the 'peacemaking Jesus' and his nonviolent alternatives to the impulsive and violent ways of the world. The Jesus of the New Testament practices nonviolence and invites people to follow his way to the God of peace[17]. The 'good news' of nonviolence is a call to appropriate humane ways of relations among one another. Jesus embodies nonviolence and 'Jesus style' stands out amidst the world of widespread violence and confusion. Jesus reveals the nature of the divine as nonviolent, generous and loving in all details. Jesus reveals to us 'what God really is'. The Gospels in particular and the New Testament in general present Jesus as the image of God's active nonviolence, against the violence-ridden background of the Old Testament. Jesus also facilitates a way out of the world's cycle of violence. Jesus incarnates nonviolence. He lived, taught and advocated it powerfully. He emerged as a 'ever-living sign of active nonviolence' for all times. He inaugurated the reign of the nonviolent and loving God. He continues to remain as an ever-new 'good news' of non-violence that can usher in a more 'humane' style of life in this earthily life.

3. NONVIOLENCE IN THE BIBLE – IMPLICATIONS

3.1. Nonviolence as Self-Emptying in Incarnation

The mystery of incarnation of God in Jesus is very vividly presented in the Gospel according to John. 'Word was there in the beginning, it was with God, it became flesh and made his dwelling among human beings. Thus, the glory of the Father's Son was revealed in full grace and truth' (Jn 1.1-14, pp. 1205-06). This is the story of God's nonviolent and pro-active response to human limitation and sinfulness. The tale of incarnation announces the way God sanctifies human life and becomes present in the details of earthily life. 'God became man' invites 'human beings to become God'. This is a nonviolent but active and conscious process of emptying oneself on either side. The voluntary way of self-emptying in order to become divine is a spontaneous and nonviolent process, necessarily through one's fellow human beings. Therefore, 'the incarnation of Jesus Christ' challenges the humans to resist inhuman behaviour and every act of violence. Incarnation binds the humans morally and spiritually to refrain from hurting or killing another. The God of peace is involved in either process. Incarnation is an invitation to humane and spiritual ways; it is a journey of nonviolence. To be incarnated into the spirit of nonviolence is the path of personal transformation in life. The mystery and reality of the incarnation of Jesus is an incontestable invitation addressed to the humans to be incarnations of nonviolence and peace, through thoughtful and fine acts of loving service of one's sisters and brothers. The self-emptying process of incarnation is the 'grace' that is offered by the incarnate Word of God. The manner of such high-ranking spiritual attainment is living the down-to-earth message of Jesus "if anyone would come after me, he must deny himself and take up his cross and follow me. For whoever wants to save his life will lose it, but whoever loses his life for me will find it" (Mt 16.24-25, p.1114). Nonviolence means to lose oneself from the angle of the world and to gain from the angle of God.

3.2. Nonviolence as Total Surrender to the Will of God

After the piercing but elevating prayer in Gethsemane, Jesus experienced total union with his Heavenly Father. He felt fully resigned to the will of the Father. When his sense of self is completely surrendered, no violence from any quarters could affect him. Though, humanly speaking, he suffered deep pain in his body, he might not have had any suffering or resistance in his heart and spirit because of total surrender of the self in nonviolence. His prayer speaks volumes, "Abba, Father, everything is possible for you. Take this cup from me. Yet not what I will, but what you will" (Mk 14:36, p.1156; Mt 26.42, p.1128; Lk.22.42, p.1198). At his trial before the Sanhedrin, the high priest, all the chief priests, the elders and the scribes accused him; yet, he was silent and made no answer to their charges (Mk.14.61, p.1157). They struck him, slapped him on the cheek and spat at his face (Mt 26.67; Mk 14.65; Lk 22.63). They stripped him and put a scarlet robe on him and making a crown of thorns they put it on his head and put a reed in his right hand. And kneeling before him they mocked him, saying 'Hail, King of the Jews'. And they spat upon him, and took the reed and struck him on the head (Mt 27.28-30). Jesus remained totally yielded to the will of the Father. His prayer after being crucified is an eternal proof of his spirit of wholehearted nonviolence in terms of his persecutors, "Father, forgive them, for they know not what they are doing" (Lk 23.34, p.1201). This prayer of forgiveness was followed by his final prayer of offering himself, before he breathed his last, "Father, into your hands I commit my spirit" (Lk 23.46, p.1201). That was the culmination of nonviolence and total surrender to God and will ever remain the most sublime human quality in life as well as the highest spiritual attainment any human being could ever make. Jesus portrayed the nonviolent and loving heart of God. He showed how to live and die a perfect nonviolent human being, in spite of all odds. He proved in a lofty way 'to what level a human being can rise in loving and forgiving one's fellow beings', even under the most violent and pressing circumstances. Jesus overcame violence, attained victory over it and set an outstanding model of human transformation at the price of one's own life.

3.3. Nonviolence as Walking the Way of Nonviolence

Nonviolence is a narrow path. Few are those who opt for walking that path. Violence is a wide path. Generally people are inclined to travel that path. But the path of nonviolence is the surest way to being spiritual and eternal. Jesus articulates this phenomenon when he says, "enter through the narrow gate. For wide is the gate and broad is the road that leads to destruction, and many enter through. But small is the gate and narrow the road that leads to life and only a few find it" (Mt 7.13-14, p.1100). Entering by the small gate of nonviolence and journeying along the narrow road ahead is a target that is achievable and it has to be attempted with the whole heart, mind and spirit. From the first day of his public life, Jesus had been exhorting his disciples to walk the narrow path of nonviolence. He challenged the lies and false gods of the empire. He exposed the inner emptiness and hypocritical ways of the religious leaders of the time in severe words (Mt 23.1-39, pp. 1122-25). He was steadfast to witnessing to the truth of nonviolent ways, to all the details. Prophets are called upon to walk the talk of life, even in their struggles, in perfect communion with the divine. Jesus was called a prophet. Telling the truth was his prophetic duty and he did it applying it to nonviolent ways of life. At the beginning of his mission, Jesus announced, "the time has come. The kingdom of God is near. Repent and believe in the good news!" (Mk 1.14-15, p.1136). This was an invitation to denounce all ways that leads to oppression, violence, slavery, sin and death and to appropriate ways that lead to the acceptance of God's reign, i.e., to a nonviolent style of living one's life.

3.4. Nonviolence as Becoming like Children

Nonviolence is a mindset that is invariably found in children. It is a natural attitude for them. Children are spontaneous and simple. They are humble and unassuming. They are pure of heart and straight forward. They are honest and dependent on the elders. They have no sense of vengeance or retaliation. Nonviolence is a state of mind that is comprised of all these qualities and many more like them. That is why Jesus says, "I tell you the truth, unless you change and become like little children, you will never enter the kingdom of heaven" (Mt 18.3, p.1115). He cautioned his disciples to entertain a reverential attitude to children because of their angelic character, "see that you do not look down on one of these little ones. For I tell you that their angels in heaven always see the face of my Father in heaven" (Mt 18.10, p.115). Jesus elaborated the child-like qualities that are required to live a meaningful life. "Do not worry about your life, what you will eat or drink; or about your body, what you will wear" (Mt 6. 25-34, p.1100). He asks, "Who of you by worrying can add a single hour to his life? Since you cannot do this very little thing, why do you worry about the rest? ...For the pagan world runs after all such things, and your Father knows that you need them. But seek His kingdom and these things will be given to you as well" (Lk.12:25-32, p.1184). When one is free of these worries and anxieties and place confidence in God, one becomes totally nonviolent like children. As human beings grow older, they get corrupted with evil thoughts and actions and that is the source of violence. "For from within, out of men's hearts, come evil thoughts, sexual immorality, theft, murder, adultery, greed, malice, deceit, lewdness, envy, slander, arrogance and folly. All these evils come from inside and make a man unclean" (Mk 7.21-23, p.1145). That is why Jesus invites his disciples to be nonviolent in every way like children. Jesus, who is 'gentle and humble of heart' (Mt 11.29, p.1106), is the model for adults to imbibe child-like qualities. Nonviolence is childlike purity of heart that radiates divine features. The so-called grown-up persons have much to learn from children.

3.5. Non-Violence as Loving Others

Christianity is known to be a religion of love. This statement is rooted in the Bible, especially in the New Testament message of Jesus. 'Loving others' is the identity of a Christian or a disciple of Jesus. In the discussion on the greatest commandment in life, Jesus affirms the age-old teaching of the tradition as 'loving the Lord your God with all your heart, soul, mind and strength' and 'loving your neighbour as yourself' (Mk 12.29-31, p.1153). Jesus did not keep these two commands in two different directions. He combined them into one single command with two aspects, like a coin with two sides. One side is a proof that the other side exists. One aspect completes the other. He brought perfect clarity to the inter-relation of these dimensions of love. One cannot do without the other. Claiming to love God and not loving one's brother is a big lie; it amounts to being a murderer, who would be deprived of eternal life (1 Jn 4.19-21, p.1396; 1 Jn 3.15, 1305). The initiative of love is from God and human love is just an appropriate response to it. The evidence of one's state of love is the presence of God within one (1Jn 4.7-12, p.1396). That is why Jesus declares that 'laying down one's life for one's sisters and brothers' is the irrefutable evidence for one's love' (Jn.15.13, p.1228). The culmination of Jesus' teaching on love is "A new command I give you: love one another. As I have loved you, so you must love one another. By this all men will know that you are my disciples, if you love one another" (Jn 13.34-35, p.1226; Jn 14.21-22, p.1227; 14.27, p.1227). Loving others, God and human beings combined, is the real testimony of one's nonviolent state of mind.

3.6. Nonviolence as Loving One's Neighbours

A neighbour is a person who is placed next door. To be neighbour is a double-faceted experience. There is mutuality and inter-relatedness that are essential to it. The word rules out considerations of caste, class, creed, language, ethnic characteristics, nationality, profession, ideology, socio-economic status, etc. The reality of neighbourhood can in no way accommodate any sort of violence or aggression. When Jesus says, 'love your neighbour as yourself' (Mt 22.39, p.1122), he is opening a new world that is pervaded by humane and spiritual qualities. One's own self is dear to everyone. That is the example for considering others dear. Loving self and loving others are two sides of the same act of loving. One cannot do without the other. As the other is a neighbour to me, so am I a neighbour to the other. The bridge is to be travelled from either side. Being a neighbour to the other in the ultimate outcome has the implication of being nonviolent to him or her. A complementary spirit of nonviolence to one another is the great mandate of Jesus. The Parable of the Good Samaritan (Lk 10.20-37, pp. 1180-81) narrated by Jesus raises the question 'who is my neighbour?'. It presents a man who fell into the hands of the robbers and was unattended by a priest and a Levite, but was taken care of to all the details by a Samaritan, who proved to be a real neighbour to the wounded man. The legal experts realised what it means to be a neighbour. Jesus commanded them to 'go and do likewise'. Considering every human being one meets in life as one's neighbour, recognizing in him or her one's sister or brother, friend, companion, etc, and extending to him or her gestures of love, especially in times of need, is the new law that Jesus composed for a nonviolent style of life (Lk 10.27, p.1180; Lev 19.18, p.134; Mt 5.43, p.1099, Mt 19.19, p.1117; Mt 22.39, p. 1122; Mk 12.31,33, p.1153; Lk 10:27, p.11870; Rom 13:9, p.1291; Gal 5:14, p.1327; Jas 2:8, p.1380). In fact, loving one's neighbour, 'every one' in other words, is a step much ahead of nonviolence.

3.7. Nonviolence as Loving One's Enemies

'Loving one's enemies' is an idea that is characteristically of Jesus Christ. It stands out as a unique way in the entire world of human and spiritual pursuit. 'Loving one's neighbour and hating one's enemy' is the usual way. This was the practice in the tradition of the Old Testament also. People have a strong tendency to discriminate between those who are one's own and those who are not one's own. But, Jesus could not see in this practice anything humanly or spiritually meritorious or worth the while. He launched a new tradition altogether when he said, 'love your enemies' and 'pray for those whose persecute you'. Only then, one qualifies for 'becoming the children of the Father in heaven'. The logic for this new law is what Jesus learned from the Father in Heaven from his personal experience. 'The Father in Heaven makes his sun rise on the evil and on the good and sends rain on the righteous and on the unrighteous'. 'Loving those who love one has nothing special about it and has no claim of reward attached to it, because even the evil-minded human being does it'. The model for loving one's enemies is 'the Heavenly Father who is perfect', who extends his love even to the enemy (Mt 5.43-46, p.1099). One should do good to those who hates one and treat one badly (Lk 6.27-28, p.1170). Jesus invites his disciples to go beyond still by 'turning the other cheek also' before the offender. The style of Jesus in approaching violent persons is not one of retaliation, but one of suffering, patience, doing well, etc. Jesus' method of dealing with evil is one of love and that is a divine style. The New Testament concept of nonviolence reaches its culmination in the 'Jesus way' of loving one's enemies.

3.8. Nonviolence as Forgiving Others

As the popular maxim goes, 'to err is human, to forgive is divine'. The created existence has its limits. Shortcomings are part of human life. Interpersonal dealings can have various flaws. Mutual relations can collapse. Forgetfulness, selfishness, greed, need, corruption, misunderstanding, pride, distortions in thinking, etc., can disrupt the equilibrium of human life in several ways. If there isn't a mechanism in life for amicably settling them and bringing life back to its rails, life will be impossible. Life will be meaningless, as well. It will end up in violence, destruction and chaos. Besides, the higher and spiritual dimensions of human life make life relevant. That requires one to be farsighted, large-hearted and noble; that calls for transcending the trivialities of life as well. There comes the role of forgiveness. Jesus insists on this as the spiritual way of life. He lived it in full and advocates it powerfully. He exposed the dynamics of relating to the divine when he said, "if you are offering your gift at the altar and there remember that your brother has something against you, leave your gift there in front of the alter. First go and be reconciled to your brother; then come and offer your gift" (Mt 5.23-24, p.1098). When Peter asks how often he must forgive a brother who wrongs him, "as many as seven times?", Jesus responds, "Not seven times, but seventy times seven" (Mt 18:21-22, p.1116). Jesus is firm on 'forgiving the offender indefinite number of times'. It also means 'unconditional forgiveness'. In the episode of the woman found guilty in adultery, when the Pharisees were adamant on stoning her to death as per their law, Jesus responds with disarming compassion, "If anyone of you is without sin, let him be the first to throw a stone at her" (John 8.4-7, p.1216-17). While he categorically affirmed the wisdom of nonviolence by forgiving her, he also highlighted the eternal fact that one who is sinful or falls short of the ideal one has set, has no moral power to punish another, even in wrong is done. Jesus, after having received the worst of violence from the world, forgives his offenders on the cross "Father, forgive them, for they do not know what they are doing" (Lk 23.34, p.1201). This world-class statement of forgiveness is in fact the climax of his spirit of nonviolence. There is no better example for goodness of heart, forgiveness and nonviolence possible. There is no higher level of human attainment and spiritual excellence in this world, either.

3.9. Nonviolence as Serving Others

Serving the other is love in action and is the proof of love. Service is the practical aspect of love, where as love is the theoretical part of service. But, in order to serve, one needs to have a frame of mind that suits service. Usually what comes on the way of serving others is the sense of self. It is natural for anyone to feel important and to aspire to be considered the first. But, with the importance and the ego, the ambition to be served by others also may develop. Then, serving the other would become difficult.

Therefore, Jesus says, "If anyone wants to be the first, he must be the very last and the servant of all" (Mk 9:35, p.1148; Mt 20.26-28, p.1119). This is because service requires a sense of being humble before others. Ego blocks service. When one is able to extend humble service to others, all sense of violence dies out. Jesus demonstrated a perfect example of serving. On the night before he was executed, Jesus bent down and washed the feet of each of the disciples. He proceeded to explain the sublime act thus, "Now that I, your Lord and Teacher, have washed your feet, you also should wash one another's feet" (John 13.14, p.1225). This was the height of service in a symbolic form. Normally, the teacher or the Guru commands service from his students or disciples. Jesus pioneered a new tradition of brotherly-sisterly service with a sense of equality and humility. Jesus is noted for this exceptional act of serving, in which no violence is possible, even in imagination. This also is a 'Jesus style' that goes much beyond all discussion of nonviolence. Further, he urged his disciples to serve one another, especially the least, narrating an eloquent and uncompromising parable of the last judgment. He says, "Come, you who are blessed by my Father; take your inheritance, the kingdom prepared for you since the creation of the world. For I was hungry and you gave me something to eat, I was thirsty and you gave me something to drink, I was a stranger and you invited me in, I needed clothes and you clothed me, I was sick and you looked after me, I was in prison and you came to visit me" … "Whatever you did for one of the least of these brothers of mine, you did for me" (Mt 25.34-40, p.1128). Those who failed to do such service to others would receive punishment, too (Mt 25.42-43, 45-46, p.1128). With these words Jesus summarised the entire Christianity, human life, religion and spirituality. Service extended to others is a conclusive proof of nonviolence and much more that cannot be described in words.

3.10. Nonviolence as Standing by the Side of the Weaker Sections of the Society

The human society constitutes institutions and organisations for better social order. These establishments, in the process of their growth, have the tendency to go out of proportion and then to be unsympathetic towards others. Consequently, inequalities are formed and society gets divided. Polarisation of resources, ideologies and interests cause distance between communities. Political, economic and social concerns tend to guide the destiny of the society. The rich and the powerful dictate terms to the running of the society. The weaker sections get pushed aside to the margins. They lose their voice in matters of social life. After-effects of this phenomenon are dissatisfaction, disturbances and violent outbursts in social life. In order to maintain a spirit of nonviolence, it is imperative to support the deprived sections of the society. The poor, the lowly placed and the voiceless of the society have to be brought to the mainstream of social life. Only then, a state of nonviolence can be maintained. Jesus always stood with the poor, the so called low caste, the sinful, the unsociable, the lost and the least. He presented God the Father as one who is extra merciful and loving to the helpless. Therefore, he promoted a preferential commitment to the lowly placed and the marginalised. He himself shared solidarity with the poor in being born in a manger. He experienced the pain of the oppressed and the impoverished. He exhorted his disciples to practice voluntary poverty (Mt 5.3, p.1097). He insisted on storing "treasure in the heavens that does not fail, where no thief approaches and no moth destroy; for where your treasure is, there will your heart be also" (Mt 6.19-21, pp. 1099-1100). He presented several parables to communicate the message, like that of the 'lost sheep, lost coin and the prodigal son' (Lk 19.1-10, p.1193; Lk 16.19-31, p.1190; Lk 15.1-32, pp.1188-89; Lk 5.30-32, p. 1170; Lk 23.34, p.1201; Mt 5.43-48, p.1099; Mt 18.1-5, p.1115; Jn 8.1-11, pp.1216-17; I Cor 1.26-29, p.1297). The special concern for the weaker sections of the society is a great symbol of love in action and an effective measure for celebrating the fruits of nonviolence.

3.11. Non-Violence as Promoting Peace

Peace is the fruit of nonviolence. Only when all violence is surrendered, stillness and serenity can emerge. Peace can be celebrated only when nonviolence flowers. The gospel of Jesus is good news of nonviolence and peace. Jesus proclaimed the God of peace. He walked the way of peace. He spoke the message of peace. He acted for peace. He suffered for peace. He died and rose again so that the humanity might live in peace. His clear-cut message "Blessed are the peacemakers, for they will be called sons of God" (Mt 5.9, p.1097) speaks volumes on the peace-centred understanding of God and human life. Military might and strength cannot establish peace on earth. No amount of battle and violence can settle the problems and struggles of the world. The spirit of nonviolence only can set up peace. The birth of the messiah of nonviolence was announced with the gift of God's peace to all humanity, "Glory to God in the highest, and on earth peace to men on whom his favor rests" (Lk 2.14, p.1164). Even when Peter acted on behalf of Jesus, he rebuked him saying, "Put your sword back in its place, for all who draw the sword will die by the sword" (Mt 26. 52, p.1130). Jesus greeted his disciples often with the divine sentiment of peace, 'Peace be with you' (Jn 20.21,26, p.1235). His parting message to his disciples was 'Peace I leave with you; my peace I give you' (Jn 14.27, p.1227). Jesus was certainly a prince of nonviolence and peace, par excellence.

3.12. Nonviolence as Behaving Ethically

Ethics have to do with principles, ideals, policies, values, standards, morals, and the like. Human life is impossible if these basic ingredients are missing in life. Nonviolence has the characteristics of all the above components. The spirit of nonviolence is the foundation for the above qualities that constitute a human life. Benevolence in oneself and gentleness towards others are shorelines of a meaningful human life. These morals and values are to be lived and practiced towards either side. Jesus made a series of ethical captions – "Do not judge, or you too will be judged", "with the measure you use, it will be measured to you"; "do not condemn, and you will not be condemned"; "forgive, and you will be forgiven" (Mt 7. 1, p.1100; Lk 6.37, p.1172). He asked his disciples, "why do you call me, 'Lord, Lord' and not do what I say?" (Lk 6.46, p.1172). Jesus cautions, 'only the sinless has the right to throw a stone at the guilty' (Jn 8.7, p.1217). On another occasion, the authorities approached him and asked, "Is it right to pay taxes to Caesar or not? Should we pay or shouldn't we?" His answer left them amazed. "Give to Caesar what is Caesar's and to God what is God's' (Mk 12.14-17, p.1152). He made a summary statement of his ethics in the words, "In everything, do to others what you would have them do to you" (Mt 7.12, p.1100).

4. NONVIOLENCE IN THE BIBLE – MULTI-FAITH POSSIBILITIES

4.1. Nonviolence Ushers in God's Reign

The entire story of the New Testament is Jesus emerging as the gospel or good news of God's reign on earth. Jesus was installed as messiah of the good news by the approval of his Heavenly Father, in the words, "This is my son, whom I love; with him I am well pleased; listen to him" (Mt 3.17, p.1096; Mt 17.5, p.1114). His realisation as the Messiah of good news was expressed through his preaching "the time has come; the kingdom of God is near. Repent and believe the good news" (Mk 1.15, p.1136). The details of his messianic duties were elaborately presented at his inaugural speech at the synagogue of Nazareth, when he exclaimed, quoting the words of the prophet Isaiah, "The Spirit of the Lord is on me, because he has anointed me to preach good news to the poor. He has sent me to proclaim freedom to the prisoners and recovery of sight for the blind, to release the oppressed, to proclaim the year of the Lord's favour". And he boldly declared, "Today this scripture is fulfilled in your hearing" (Lk.4:18-19, 21, p.1168). His consciousness as a 'missionary of human rights, justice, nonviolence and peace' inaugurated God's kingdom and reign in human lives. All God-incarnations, prophets, great men and women are endowed with such a mission of bringing the presence of God alive in the world. It can never be denied that the vision and mission of Jesus has something very unique about it. All the same, there are several universal experiences and values that are similar with the founders of other religious and spiritual traditions. Therefore, a dialogical and inter-relational approach has to be appropriated between Jesus and other divine men and women in establishing God's reign on earth, especially with special reference to the universal implications of nonviolence and peace.

4.2. Nonviolence is the Wisdom of Life

Human life has immense limitations. There are a lot of aberrations and violations in day to day life. Cut-throat competition seems to be the distinguishing feature of the highly globalised world of today. People are all the more obsessed with power and so-called cleverness in order to win the race. 'Victory by hook or crook' is the motto that leads the wave. Principles and policies do not attract many today. Convenient logic and pragmatic ways appear to guide the destiny of the day. The idea of a God, who surrenders and dies on the cross, as in the case of Jesus, do not catch the attention of many. People want to see the deity or God powerful and capable of tearing the opponent into pieces, just like the modern heroes of the present-day movies. No wonder, if the nonviolent way is looked upon as a terribly weak and foolish idea. Paul draws a striking comparison between the human and divine angles of foolishness and wisdom. He exclaims, "For the foolishness of God is wiser than man's wisdom, and the weakness of God is stronger than man's strength" (1 Cor 1.25, p.1297). This analysis is grounded on the logic of incarnation that culminates on the cross on which Jesus died. The wisdom that underlies the seeming foolishness is 'what looks like the weak way is actually the strong way and what looks like foolishness is actually amazingly brilliant'. The world has to get purified and become spiritual in order to penetrate into this divine and eternal way that Jesus lived and presented to the world. The wisdom of the strength hidden in the weak and the wisdom concealed in nonviolent and peaceful ways are to be explored and propagated. Similar ideas and examples from other faith traditions and their scriptures are to be investigated and such parallels could initiate a movement of promoting the divine wisdom that are scattered in the diverse ideologies of the world.

4.3. Nonviolence is a Spiritual Way

There is a massive confusion that exists among people as regards spirituality. They entertain the thought that following a particular God-man or woman, subscribing to certain doctrine and dogma, believing in some myths and stories, engaging in some rituals and pious activities and belonging to a particular community is what it means to be having spirituality. Religious leaders that are functionaries of religions see their advantage in such confusions. Certain ambitiously emerging mini-gods support and perpetuate such understanding of spirituality and thrive on the benefits of such superstitions. While all these pious activities, though many of them blindly pious, may be called 'religious', there is a dire need of distinguishing the difference between religiosity and spirituality. 'Spirituality is a perspective of life' It is an attitude to life. It is a mindset that is infused with eternal values of life. It is the way one understands and conducts life. Spirituality is living a life that is prompted and guided by the Spirit. When one is fully human, one becomes divine. An on-going celebration of the sense of the divine is spirituality. Spirituality is dying to oneself and rising to others, as Jesus did. It is self-realisation attained in enlightenment or nirvana, as *Gautam Buddha* did[18]. It is being totally detached as *Mahaaveer* did. It is being completely surrendered to the will of God as Muhammad did. It is becoming aware of the presence of God in all directions as *Guru Nanak* did. Spirituality is living one's human life entirely oriented to the divine. Spirituality is living one's life totally nonviolent in one's thoughts, desires, feelings, imaginations, words and actions. Nonviolence is being fully humane and spiritual in life. Nonviolence is spirituality by itself. It is beyond the boundaries of all faith traditions and is universal in its outreach. Nonviolence takes one to that height in life.

4.4. Nonviolence Facilitates Harmonious Living

Diversity is the hallmark of the creation, especially of the human society. The ethnic traits, races, castes tribes, languages, ideologies, professions, social customs, religious traditions, faiths, nationalities and cultures present a spectacular spectrum of diversity. There is no denying the transparent fact that each of these streams is endowed with a specific character. All the same, all of them have a common origin. Great men or women emerged in different historical and cultural settings, with the mission of making human lives more and more nonviolent and peaceful. The world classics as well as Sacred Scriptures of all faith traditions are the processed product of divine promptings. They are gifts of the same Creator to the world. They are the common cultural heritage of the human society, too. They belong to each other and belong to the Creator together. They are like a 'rainbow'[19]. Together they radiate a singular beauty. Together they stand and divided they fall. In spite of the individual identity all these items have, there is a shared social identity that all of them have to be conscious of possessing. They have to explore the universal human and spiritual values that are inherent in the respective faith traditions. 'Making a More Harmonious Society' has to be the common motto of all faith-based individuals, organisations and communities. Therefore, sustained efforts have to be made for ensuring harmony in social life. Faith-based organisations and communities have to initiate a culture of interaction, understanding, dialogue, collaboration and harmony among individuals and groups in the society. Human beings have to be motivated and empowered to meet each other as human beings and not as individual and communities with tags of mutually separating identities of diverse types. Building bridges of understanding, friendship and fellowship among people of different affiliations only can contribute a nonviolent way of dealing with each other. 'Leave the place better than you found it' is a dictum that motivates one to a creative commitment to one another and to the human society at large. Communal tension and violence have to stop and 'harmony in social life' has to lead the way of human progress and wellbeing. Such a spirit of nonviolence will foster the 'humane and spiritual culture of harmonious living'.

CONCLUSION

The 'sacredness' of the Sacred Scriptures is in its inner capacity for awakening their readers towards a 'sense of the sacred' that is present within oneself and all over in the creation. The 'Sacred' or the 'Divine' reflects itself in the eternal values of life, which pave the way for the humans to unceasingly travel towards being spiritual. All the godly men and women of the world have infused the holy books with the brilliant wisdom they obtained from the same Divine Power in different times and contexts. Jesus Christ, grounded on his exceptional divine endowments and founded on his sublime and elevating divine experiences, lived and taught certain mysterious and original ways of 'being nonviolent' for the 'harmonious co-existence of the humans'. The nuances and implications of such a 'humanely human and spiritual life' that is recorded in the Bible need to be explored and learnt from. This has to be done in a spirit of togetherness with the singular universal values enshrined in the 'Sacred Books of other faith traditions and ideologies'. A more 'multi-scriptural, multi-faith and secular approach' to attaining the divine reality and living one's human life, I am sure, can facilitate a human world that is more worth living.

Endnotes

1. Joan Valerie Bondurant, Conflict: Violence and Nonviolence, New Jersey, 1971, p. 176
2. *Ibid,* p. 177
3. *Ibid,* p. 192
4. *Ibid,* p. 117
5. *Ibid,* p. 177

6. *Ibid,* p. 211
7. *Ibid,* p. 119
8. *Ibid,* p. 45
9. Terrence, J. Rynne, Gandhi and Jesus: The Saving Power of Nonviolence, New York, 2008, p. 84
10. *Ibid,* p. 91
11. *Ibid,* p. 107
12. *Ibid,* p. 119
13. Joan Valerie Bondurant, Conflict: Violence and Nonviolence, New Jersey, 1971, p. 219
14. The Holy Bible, NIV, Michigan, 1994
15. Joan Valerie Bondurant, Conflict: Violence and Nonviolence, New Jersey, 1971, p. 87
16. *Ibid,* p. 18
17. *Ibid,* p. 146
18. Terrence, J. Rynne, Gandhi and Jesus: The Saving Power of Nonviolence, New York, 2008, p. 84
19. *Ibid,* p. 236

(Published in Third Millennium (Quarterly Journal), Rajkot, Vol. 25, pp. 75-101 – in July-September 2022)

Chapter - 9

The Bible and Inter-Scriptural Dialogue

INTRODUCTION

The Holy Books, obviously, are those books that are considered sacred by some community or other in the society. They, may they have originated in any language, geographical area or cultural context, cannot, in any way, be considered the private property of any given community. They are the common heritage of the human society. They belong to each other as well as exist together. They are complementary to each other. Together they give a sense of completion to the sacred world of the Religious Scriptures.

The real holiness of the Holy Books is to be searched for in their inner capacity for universal application as well as in their mutually inclusive character. Universality of the Holy Books would mean one crisscrossing the other with similar implications. It would mean being permeated by each other and being overwhelmed by a spirit of togetherness. It would mean being inclined towards a centripetal process, in order to make a single effect of ameliorating the human life spiritually.

Approaching the universal spirit of the diverse Sacred Scriptures is necessitated by the dynamics of the dialogical way of understanding the texture of human life, which is fundamentally multi-dimensional. It is all the more a dire reality in the uniquely multi-Scriptural context of Asia, and especially of India. 'Inter-textuality of the Holy Books' is the fundamental perspective, which is capable of making this integral, collaborative and comprehensive approach to the Sacred Scriptures successful. An honest attempt to re-read and re-understand one's own Sacred Scripture is the first step to this imperative and inevitable religious mission of life. Such a mission only can assure the possibility of a joint pilgrimage towards the divine.

Here is a humble attempt to re-read and re-understand the Christian Bible from a pluralistic and multi-Scriptural point of view. The general and particular dimensions of the Bible discussed below present a broader and a contextually applied understanding of the Bible. It also suggests immense scope for wider as well as comparative understanding of all the Sacred Scriptures, which only can usher in a relevant and auspicious spiritual future for the human society.

1. THE BIBLE IN GENERAL

'The Bible in general' attempts a symbolic understanding of the Bible. The symbolic implications of the Bible could very well be applied to any Religious Scripture. This perspective, certainly, would go a long way in situating the diverse Sacred Scriptures of the human society in a creative and harmonious relation to one another.

1. The Bible is the 'word' of God. The word 'Bible' comes from the Hebrew word *'biblos'*, meaning 'book' or 'the books'[1]. This general meaning, of course, applied to the religious context, proposes broader alternatives and paves the way for Inter-Scriptural Dialogue. Even though it is the 'Sacred Book' of the Christian community, its content addresses the entire human society. The core message of the Bible stands in some way singular amidst other Sacred Texts, too. Its origin is attributed to the same super-natural power, which can be expressed in a variety of ways, like 'the Infinite', 'the Ultimate Reality', 'the Absolute Truth', 'the Real', 'the Way', 'the Divine' and 'the Higher Power' as well as 'God'. The Bible, in sum, is a message from the divine.

2. The Bible is the 'written' word of God. When defined and documented, it acquired the status of a Scripture. But it is only an attempt to articulate the inexpressible experience of several individuals or a community, of its own time. The authors, undoubtedly, wrote it down, prompted by the divine power. Therefore, it is an inspired message. It is preserved in the written form and is communicated to the future generations. It is written by human authors, in human language; and so, it is limited as well as symbolic. It is conditioned by historical factors and remains in the need of being interpreted at all times and all situations. The reality it stands for is certainly much richer than the virtual expression of it. In other words, the God of the Scriptures is greater than the Scriptures! The Bible, as a written word, needs to openly and honestly dialogue with the written parallels of other religious traditions, in order to make it intelligible and relevant[2]. This endeavour is required for doing better justice to the great reality expressed therein.

3. The Bible is the 'unwritten' word of God. Basically, it was an oral tradition. The promptings of the divine come very informally and in the natural context of life. Any tradition evolves from the womb of a particular culture, at a particular time. The Biblical message evolved from the Jewish religious culture, in close interaction with the Greek Philosophy. The content of the Bible was the experience of the people of the community of the Jews before the time of Jesus and of the community of the disciples of Jesus, with the fundamental experience of Jesus at the core[3]. Only later, the above religio-cultural experience was interpreted, inherited, written and handed over. As an unwritten word of God, the Bible was a lived reality. It is the live story of the people of that tradition, here and now, too. It has inevitably to keep interacting with similar unwritten experiences and messages of God everywhere.

4. The Bible is the 'voice' of God. It is an unfolding of the divine mystery, in a given historical setting. It is the recorded or unrecorded form of the divine wisdom. It is a spiritual treasure, par excellence. It reveals, awakens, inspires, motivates, changes, transforms, re-creates, and saves the humans. It is an ulterior force, which liberates them from all that is enslaving, which helps them go beyond and which introduces them to eternity. It is a perennial source of insight and meaning in life. It is the basis of enlightenment and strength. It is dynamic and evolving. It is ever-growing and ever-new 'good news'. It becomes the conscience of the individual or the community, which has known the essence of it from within[4]. As an ever-speaking voice, it gives a sense of direction in life. All the same, the Bible has to remain tuned to other Scriptural voices of God received in the diverse spiritual traditions, in order to prove its *raison d'être*.

5. The Bible is the common heritage of the human society. Its message has a universal significance. It is meant for the whole humanity and the whole creation. Its central message does not contradict but complements other Scriptures. It derives from a common foundation. It has to remain ever open to other Scriptural approaches to human life. It is the shared property of the human community. It is no way to be monopolised by the Christian community. To narrowly interpret the Bible would be nothing less than a crime against the comprehensive message of Jesus[5]. Considering the Bible as belonging to the human society in a shared way would not only broaden the horizons of the Bible, but that of all the Religious Scriptures of the world. That would be the beginning of a new culture of religious dialogue and spiritual harmony through the Sacred Scriptures.

6. The Bible gains full meaning when it is in dialogue with other Scriptures. The interpretation of the Bible should not be in terms of myths and cults. It should be understood in a liberating sense. The understanding of the Bible should take one beyond all the boundaries. Its message should facilitate one to extend oneself in relation to the other, in a spirit of brotherhood. It has to be applied to the multi-dimensional context of our society, which has characteristically diverse languages, ideologies, castes, classes, creeds, faiths, cultures, nations, traditions, customs, practices, etc. in it. Inter-Scriptural study, comparative understanding and contextually applied interpretation need to be promoted. Commonalities are to be searched for[6]. Such a multi-Scriptural approach will not only enrich one's own faith, but also make it relevant. The concept of life will become much broader then. The understanding of religion and spirituality will become more realistic and worthwhile, too.

7. The Bible is the 'symbol' of the word of God. Such an understanding of the Bible is more inclusive and respectfully accommodates other Religious Scriptures of the world as co-symbols. It also allows legitimate importance to the other Christian symbols, like cross and sacraments. The religious, moral and social traditions of the world have numerous Scriptural symbols, like Quran, *Bhagvat Gita*, *Dhammapad*, *Guru Grandh Sahib*, *Avesta*, *Tora*, Teachings of *Mahaveer*, Teachings of Bahaullah, Teachings of Confucius, Tenets of Taoism, Tenets of Shinto, Atheistic Code of Behaviour and Tribal Beliefs and Practices. The symbolic value of the Bible is to be understood in relation to the symbolic value of these equally rich pieces of spiritual heritage, which the majority of the humans cherish and derive motivation and strength from. Respect has to be paid to and inspiration has to be drawn from other 'Scriptural Symbols' of the society[7]. A genuine and really spiritual search in life can, in no way, compromise with such a holistic understanding and approach to 'Sacred Scriptures'.

THE BIBLE IN PARTICULAR

'The Bible in particular' would mean concentrating the attention on the key message of the Bible. This would highlight its core message and underline its genius, in such a way that its singularity can be more effective as well as be understood as brighter and broader. Besides, it would facilitate a creative dialogue with the core messages of other Religious Scriptures, which will be helpful in promoting the universal implications of the human and spiritual values inherent in them.

1. The Understanding of God proposed by the Bible is 'God as Father'. This understanding is based on the personal experience of Jesus. Although the term 'father' used is that of the male gender, the implication is beyond the scope of the gender mentioned, meaning parent (father and mother both). This is clear from the fatherly and motherly qualities reflected in the person of the 'Father' as understood by Jesus. This concept is based on the 'dualistic' concept of life, i.e., the Creating Reality and the created realities, and makes it easy for the humans to relate to the divine in a personal way. The word 'father' highlights a relational approach to God. Among the relational ways, this is the widest and the most sober concept. It is like a large umbrella, which can gather the whole humanity, even the whole creation, together[8]. This concept has a personal touch and offers a sense of elevation, security, other-oriented love, and the like, to the one who pursues it.

But, there is no one single, uniform and fool-proof understanding of God possible in this large human society of incomprehensible diversity. There may be, perhaps, so many shades of understandings as there are human beings. There is also a 'non-dualistic' concept of life, quite different from the dualistic one, i.e., there is only One Reality. That concept admits a non-relational understanding of God. 'Self-realisation' is the response to this concept. This concept is the most basic and leading concept of God found in the Indian sub-continent. This concept has its singular standing in the world context, too.

The relational concept of God includes also a variety of dimensions of the relation. They are different relational ways that are humanly experienced, but applied to the divine context. The Semitic traditions, like Jewish, Christian and Islamic, and some Indian traditions consider 'God as Male'. The Sufi and some Indian religious streams conceive 'God as Female'. *Ganga Maiya, Mahalakshmi* and *Durga/Shakti/Kali* are some of the female deities. God is understood as a 'Composite of Male and Female' by the main-stream Indian tradition. *Shiv-Shakti/Parvati*, *Laxmi-Narayan*, *Sita-Ram*, *Radha-Krishna*, etc. are some examples for the same. There are also other relational understandings of God, either in male or female form. *Krishna* in relation to *Balram* reflects 'God as Brother' whereas *Krishna* in relation to *Sudama*, 'God as Friend'. The 'Child form of God' is highlighted by the relation of Jesus to Mary and Joseph and the relation of *Krishna* to *Yashoda* and *Nand* and to *Jankee* and *Vasudev*. The disciples of Jesus find in him God as '*Guru*'. The saint poet *Kabeer* sees the divine mainly as his '*Guru*'[9]. There are also other relational ways of understanding God, which do not come under the category of gender. Japanese and Chinese traditions conceive and relate to the divine in yet other ways.

These pluralistic ways of conceiving the Divine/God, which are experienced and defined by the diverse religious cultures of different times and places are not contradictory to each other. They are mutually inclusive and complementary to each other. Together they attempt to draw the picture of the divine, which is much larger and even incomprehensible. The humble fact stands that the divine is still much more beyond all these perceptions and experiences of all the human cultures put together. Hence a dialogical interpretation of the Christian understanding of God as 'Father' is required.

2. The filial experience of God was the core experience of Jesus (Mk 3.17; 17.5; Jn 5.19; 14.9, 10,11; 15.1; 17.10,11; Lk 10.22; 14.36; 23.34, 46). This filial experience is the natural response to the understanding of God as Father. Experiencing oneself as the son of God by Jesus is fundamental to the Christian understanding of God as Father. Filial experience is a very deep and meaningful way of experiencing the divine and it is open to all (Lk 22.34-40; Mt 6.4, 6,8,18,26,30, 32; 10. 29-31; 12, 7; 20.1-16). A spirituality of freedom evolves from this experience (Jn 18.35). This filial experience is beyond the boundaries of gender and it includes also experiencing oneself as a daughter of God. This filial spirituality has immense scope for an extensive application in the society, beyond the boundaries of caste, class, creed, gender, profession, language, culture, and the like[10]. This filial spirituality is charged with great possibilities of multi-religious interaction and unity. The Biblical understanding needs to be broadened.

3. A fraternal way of life logically follows the above filial experience. The filial experience of Jesus spontaneously found its expression in a fraternal fashion of thought and behaviour. Considering the other one's brother or sister in a universal manner is a new way of being human. Loving the enemy, as if he is a friend, is the beginning of a revolutionary movement. That is the new culture that was initiated by Jesus. It surpassed all boundaries (Mt 5.43-48). The radical values of social commitment proposed by Jesus are capable of taking the humans towards total liberation (Lk 22.34-40; Mt 7.12; 5.9; 25.31-46). Jesus lived a life of preferential concern for the oppressed and the marginalised (Lk 19.1-10; 16.19-31; 15.1-32; 5.30-32, 23.24; 23.34; Mt. 5.43-48; 18.1-5; Jn 8.1-11; I Cor. 1.26-29). Establishing a loving relationship with every human being one meets in life and being of all possible service to him or her across all the boundaries is what is meant by the culture of love and service, which is implied by the fraternal way of life Jesus inaugurated. This fraternal way of life has unlimited universal possibilities as well as implications[11].

4. The Trinitarian style of life is considered the mainstream tradition of Christianity. 'Three-in-one and one-in-three' is the reality reflected in the terminology of 'Father, Son and Spirit' or Trinity in the Christian tradition. This concept has its clear roots in the Gospels and is grounded in the experience of Jesus. This concept, as interpreted as a superb model of self-giving, other-orientedness, love and communion, is a source of great inspiration for human life. It proposes a democratic and communitarian style of human life. It suggests a relational and spiritual approach to one-another. It not only agrees with the cultural genius of India, i.e., 'diversity in unity and unity in diversity'[12], but gives a new meaning to it. It upholds religious pluralism and dialogue between different spiritual streams, irrespective of geographical and other considerations. The communitarian style of human life, emerging from the Trinitarian concept, is capable of a great deal of multi-Scriptural and multi-religious understanding and communion.

5. The 'God-centredness' was the foundational vision of Jesus. The basic aspiration of Jesus is found in the prayer Jesus used to constantly utter, i.e., 'your will be done' and 'your kingdom come'. Both his God-centredness and Kingdom-centredness are clearly expressed in this prayer. He relied on God totally and was committed to establishing his kingdom. The 'I' sayings of Jesus do not ever smack of a self-contained and self-centred attitude, not even in the least. His God-centredness is obvious from his constant reference to the Father. The self-emptying attitude to life expressed in his suffering and death is ample proof to the above fact[13]. A common belonging to the divine is the underlying message for all. People of all Scriptural persuasions and religious affiliations should be able to realise the common foundation of life as well as the common origin and destiny of all human and other forms of life.

6. The harmony model of creation 'One body, many parts' is the fundamental key to human life (1 Cor. 12.12-28). This is a common place example. Paul elucidated its details from different angles and highlighted its radical implications. The parts of the body are different in their identity as well as many in number. But they exist as one body. The different parts have equal duties and equal rights. They all have their own singular importance and dignity, which is not only shared by all but is beyond the scope of comparison. One part cannot be replaced or superseded by another. Joy or pain and achievement or failure of one part is felt and shared by all the parts. It is an existence in togetherness. In other words, it is unity in diversity and diversity in unity at the same time. There cannot be a more powerful model for harmony[14]. This natural example for harmony speaks volumes for multi-Scriptural dialogue, which, in its turn, will enable a multi-dimensional style of life for the human family and the whole creation.

7. Biblical values are the sum and substance of the Bible. Christian values derived from these Biblical values. The narrative and descriptive element of the language is at the service of the communication of the message. The mythical setting of the stories is for the purpose of situating the message. The spiritual values, human values, social ethics and living policies of life that emerge from the Bible are intended to enhance the personal and social quality of life. Evolving a mission statement, based on the Biblical values, and living it with a sense of commitment would be the most worthwhile endeavour of a Christian. Attempt to single out the universal values from the Bible by the Christian should be a source of motivation for other believers to search for similar universal values in their own Sacred Scriptures[15]. This will definitely go miles and miles in initiating a creative and on-going dialogue of values, which emerge from the diverse religious Scriptures of the world.

CONCLUSION

The humans of today are greatly privileged to live in an age, when the society has a large variety of Sacred Scriptures. All these Sacred Scriptures are the common heritage of the human culture. To follow one of them exclusively and to remain totally untouched by the others would be a very naïve understanding of the one in hand. It would be as if not following any of them. It would be equal to being totally atheistic in life, with no faith at all! It would be a negation of all fraternal human sentiments, too. That is, undoubtedly, pathological and tragic as well as irreligious. One should be firmly rooted in the Sacred Scripture of one's own affiliation. There is no compromise to this. At the same time, one should be creatively related to the Sacred Scriptures of the other traditions. 'One is mine in special; the others are mine in general'—that is the multi-Scriptural perspective, which is certified by a genuinely spiritual and human outlook in life. Therefore, a culture of multi-Scriptural studies should be the normal attitude to religion, especially in the third millennium we are shouldering the responsibility of.

Besides, in addition to the classical Holy Books, there are several 'holy books' of different levels, which emerge from the diverse historical events as well as from the great men and women of all communities (who are considered saints and sages), at different times and in different places. The concept of holy book gets updated and broadened as newer editions of the traditional Holy Books appear. They present a more relevant interpretation of the socio-spiritual values of life. One needs to be spiritually tuned enough, in order to discern the worth of them and to imbibe the best from them. One has to update one's heart and mind, in order to appropriate a more creative, experiential and relevant approach to the diverse editions of the Sacred Scriptures of the society.

A Christian believer, to be genuine, has to re-read the Bible with an open mind. He or she has to recognize, first and foremost, the symbolic character of the Bible as its most significant message. The understanding of the same has to be such that it liberates and elevates the believer, in every way. It should facilitate him or her to go beyond, to go higher and to go across to the other humans as well as to the other Sacred Scriptures. The basic filial experience and the fraternal mission of Jesus are to receive the right focus once again. The Biblical message is to be interpreted in terms of the inescapable multi-dimensional context of the human society. Inter-Scriptural study should be encouraged and comparative understanding of the emerging unifying elements should be promoted. The human and spiritual values of life, commonly found in the diverse Sacred Scriptures, are to be duly highlighted. The right vision and spirituality of the Bible is characteristically dialogical and that needs to govern the destiny of a every Christian. Students and disciples of the Bible have to honestly attempt understanding its core message in relation to other Religious Scriptures. The multi-Scriptural understanding of the Bible will, certainly, usher in a culture of 'united human spirituality', which, in its turn, will facilitate the spiritual art of living the human life. This is the challenging but glorious future the humans are inevitably to travel towards.

Endnotes

1. John Barton, A History of the Bible: The Book and Its Faiths, London, 2019, p. 03
2. *Ibid,* p. 07
3. *Ibid,* p. 11
4. *Ibid,* p. 19
5. Stephen, E. Fowl, Engaging Scripture: A Model for Theological Interpretation, Eugene, 2011, p. 87
6. *Ibid,* p. 91
7. John Barton, A History of the Bible: The Book and Its Faiths, London, 2019, p. 11
8. *Ibid,* p. 115
9. Stephen, E. Fowl, Engaging Scripture: A Model for Theological Interpretation, Eugene, 2011, p. 206
10. *Ibid,* p. 186
11. *Ibid,* p. 222
12. Sadhu Santinath, Encyclopedia of Philosophy of Indian Religion, New Delhi, 2001, p. 527
13. Stephen, E. Fowl, Engaging Scripture: A Model for Theological Interpretation, Eugene, 2011, p. 311
14. *Ibid,* p. 356
15. *Ibid,* p. 428

Chapter - 10

Fraternity and Social Friendship—The Mission of Harmony

INTRODUCTION

The Christian mission, grounded in the vision and mission of Jesus the Christ on earth, covers a large gamut of activities across the globe. In the course of the history, it has imbibed multifarious dimensions and directions. For sure, it has benefited the humans in terms of purpose, meaning and fulfilment in life, in various proportions. Without doubt, the future times will invent immense ways and means of reaching out to the humans and the entire creation with ethical, spiritual, social and cultural fibre, still further. But, the vision and mission of Jesus is too eternal to be exhausted and therefore innovation in the visionary and missionary frontiers has to be a continuous process. From that angle, every missionary aspect has its own genius and can never be compared with each other. All the same, the destination of the Christian mission is a 'sense of harmony' with the human fraternity as well as with the divine paternity (maternity included), in a degree that is beyond compare. Besides, the paternal spirit of the divine has to be translated into the 'fraternal' character of the humans, taking expression in 'social friendship' with all brothers and sisters as the destiny of the Christian mission. This article proposes to discuss fraternity and social friendship as the mission of harmony, in the context of the Encyclical *'Fratelli Tutti'* by Pope Francis.

1. Conceptual Nuances

The first section of the essay analyzes the key concepts involved in it, along with their root meanings and nuances, in view of making the exposition of the theme in question clear.

1.1. Fraternity

The word 'fraternity' derives from the Latin root *'frater'*[1], meaning 'brother'. It means 'sister' also, inclusively so. Thus, 'fraternity' would mean 'brotherhood' or sisterhood. Fraternity also means a fraternal organisation, society, club or order, which is an association exclusively of men or women or both mixed, for religious or secular purposes. The female religious orders and societies wholly for women are sometimes specifically known as sororities. 'Fraternity' is mostly a Western concept. It developed in the Christian context as a religious order of the Catholic Church. The concept was eventually further extended with medieval confraternities and guilds. In the early modern era, these were followed by fraternal orders, such as Freemasons and Odd Fellows, along with gentlemen's clubs, student fraternities and fraternal service organizations. Members of the fraternity are often referred to as 'brothers', *'frater'* or friar', mostly in the religious context. Today, connotations of fraternities vary according to context, including companionships and brotherhoods dedicated to the religious, intellectual, academic, physical or social pursuits of its members.

1.2. Friendship

'Friendship' is a relationship between friends. It is the state of being connected, one to another. It is the way in which two or more people or groups regard each other and behave towards each other. It means 'being familiar'. It is the liking of each other's mind and ways. People who are friends talk to each other and spend time together. They trust one another and also help each other when they are in trouble or are hurt. Friends are people that can be looked up to. Usually, friends have similar interests. Friendship is the state of mutual confidence and support between connected persons or allied nations. Someone who is a true friend stands up for his friend. When others try to hurt you emotionally or physically, they do everything they can to make sure that you stay safe. They don't care who is trying to harm you. They will defend you anytime, anywhere. If they can help you, they will do it without reservation or reward. Such state of affairs defines what friendship is all about and applies to persons, organisations or nations. Friendship makes life meaningful; may it be between or among persons or institutions[2].

1.3. Social Friendship

Social friendship is the relationship between or among those who meet each other at social occasions. They may accompany each other to social gatherings. It is not necessary that they have a personal relationship between them. Social friends may know about each other much more than among mere acquaintances, but much less than between personal friends.

All the same, there could be personal friends among social friends. Some of the values that would accompany personal friends are affection, sympathy, empathy, honesty, altruism, mutual understanding and compassion. They would enjoy each other's company, have trust in the other and will have the ability to be their own selves. They would express their feelings and make mistakes without fear of judgment from the friend. Good friends are loyal and accept each other during the good and bad times. Good friends are also honest, honest enough to tell the other that he or she is not being a good friend. In social friendship the qualities of personal friendship may be available in more or less degrees. Social friendship has larger dimensions, while personal friendship has deeper dimensions. Social friendship is the state of a general friendliness with one and all, irrespective of variations in characteristics and identities. Social friendship has the capacity of covering the entire society[3].

1.4. Mission

The word 'mission' derives from the Latin words *'mittere'*[4] and *'missio'*[5], meaning 'to send', obviously with a 'task that is special'. Mission is a 'call from above' or a 'commission from a higher power' and it involves a person or a group of people. It could also be 'a call with in a call' or a 'higher mission' when it is remarkably insightful and original in its character. As an undertaking, it evolves from the 'vision' that is intrinsic to the mission and that vision, in its turn, emerges from the one who commissions and from the quality of commissioning by him. Engaging one's self with a profound 'commitment' explores the 'deeper' meanings of the mission and 'reaching out' headed for far and wide as well as to every person opens its 'larger' shades of meanings. In any case, a 'sense of mission' is the core of any mission and that motivates one to invest oneself to a cause with the 'whole heart, mind and spirit'. That decides the enhanced 'quality' of whatsoever is undertaken and performed in life, as well. Attaining 'higher dimensions or altitudes' as well as 'larger dimensions or magnitudes' in life, for oneself and for others, is the outcome of a mission in life, of course to the credit of the divine being, who motivated, enlightened and empowered the missioner. Noticeably, the inner meanings of the Christian word 'mission' blossom forth and crisscross the diverse units of the larger society, by way of a 'sense of mission' or 'purposefulness' at the hub of life that applies to one and all[6].

1.5. Harmony

The old French *'armonie'*[7] and Latin-Greek *'harmonia'*[8] indicate 'agreement, accord, concord, order, integration, co-ordination, fastening, joint, fitting together, unity, balance', and the like. The Hindi synonym for the word 'harmony' is *'samanvay'* and it has two parts, *'sam'*[9] and *'anvay'*. *'Anvay'*[10] means 'agreement, co-ordination', etc. and *'sam'* means 'on equal footing' or 'equally' and 'in totality' and 'completely'. Further, harmony is a word grounded in the world of music. It is the 'pleasing effect' that emerges from a group of musical sounds as they are sounded all together[11]. A single note cannot produce harmony. The concord among many notes does. Solo players conduct themselves in such a way in the orchestra that they make a single musical effect and create fine and sublime sentiments. The co-ordination of melody and rhythm offers a perfect model for harmony of faiths as well as harmony in all the social elements of life. Further, the sense of harmony includes the human-divine context in the vertical line as well as among the human communities and groupings in the horizontal line.

2. THE ENCYCLICAL 'FRATELLI TUTTI': THE BACKDROP

The second part of the article examines the Encyclical of Pope Francis, *'Fratelli Tutti'*. It elaborates in brief its various chapters and highlights its genius, in terms of the theme in question.

2.1. *Fratelli Tutti*: Its Roots and Meaning

The title 'Fraternity and Social Friendship' emerges from the Encyclical of Pope Francis, with the name *'fratelli tutti'*. The first part of the Latin phrase 'fratelli'[12] literally means 'brother, fellow, neighbour', etc. The second part 'tutti'[13], when in a musical concert means 'with all voices or instruments together'. In the human sense, it means 'the entire fraternity, without exception'. It implies, 'all brothers' or 'all brothers and sisters', well, as a direction. It comes from the 'admonition' of Saint Francis of Assisi (1181–1226) to his Franciscan brothers and sisters to 'follow a way of life marked by the flavour of the Gospel'[14]. An admonition is the lightest punishment under Scots law. It occurs to an offender who has pleaded guilty or who has been found guilty, but is not given a fine, considering the minor infringement of the law by him or her. As an alternative, he or she receives a lesser penalty, in the form of a verbal warning. The conviction is recorded 'Fratelli tutti' or 'All brothers and sisters' or 'brothers and sisters all'.

2.2. The Abu Dhabi Declaration: Momentum for the Encyclical

The 'Abu Dhabi Declaration'[15] on 'Human Fraternity for World Peace and Living Together', signed by Pope Francis, head of the Catholic Church, and *Sheikh Ahmed el-Tayyib*, Grand Imam of *Al-Azhar*, in Abu Dhabi, United Arab Emirates, on 04 February 2019, gave the momentum for the Encyclical *'Fratelli Tutti'* or 'Fraternity and Social Friendship'. It was a milestone of interreligious dialogue. The appeal proposes 'dialogue to be adopted as the way, common cooperation as conduct and mutual knowledge as method and standard of fraternity. The document addresses the diverse issues of the current society, such as moral deterioration, soulless materialistic development, unequal distribution of resources, manipulation and misuse of power and decay of religious sense. The document aspires also give and take between the east and the west, interactive learning between the different ideologies, faiths, cultures and social traditions, and the like. Pope Francis and *Imam Sheik Tayyib* have jointly invited the world society to collaborate across the human-made borders and to make a human society that is characterised by the spirit of fraternity, friendship, world peace and living together. This significant declaration has been the boosting spirit for Pope Francis to proceed into making the Encyclical 'Fraternity and Social Friendship'[16].

2.3. The Encyclical: Its Whereabouts and Objectives

The Encyclical *'Fratelli tutti'* was signed by Pope Francis on 03 October 2020 in Assisi[17]. The text was made public the following day, 04 October. This is the third encyclical of Pope Francis. It is a 'social encyclical', as rightly called by Pope Francis. The immediate background of the Encyclical is the corona pandemic, technically called 'Covid-19', which 'unexpectedly erupted'. He proposes concrete actions to restore the world and overcome the ills generated by the crisis of the pandemic. The crisis has health-related, economic, social, anthropological, political and various other dimensions. As a result, harmony and peace of the world is disturbed. The global health emergency was an invitation to realize that 'no one can face life in isolation' and that the time has come, for sure, to 'dream as a single human family', as 'brothers and sisters all'. Besides, Pope Francis emphasizes that the humans ought to be living as one family in the common home of the earth. In other words, he envisages a way of restoring the balance, harmony and peace of the world. The Encyclical 'Fraternity and Social Friendship' is geared towards building a better, more just and peaceful world. Realisation of this objective is possible with the contribution of all people and institutions. An emphatic 'no' to war and to globalised indifference is a necessary component of realizing the target. The encyclical proposes to present the 'toolkit' for building a more just and fraternal world in their ordinary relationships, in social life, politics, institutions, and the like. The Encyclical underscores the universal aspiration towards fraternity and social friendship.

2.4. The Dark Clouds over a Closed World

The first chapter of the encyclical discusses the 'dark clouds over the closed world and sees them as 'distortions of the contemporary era'[18]. The current world is characterised by the manipulation and deformation of concepts, like democracy, freedom and justice. As a result, the meaning of the social community and history is getting lost. Selfishness and indifference toward the common good are rampant. The market logic based on profit is prevalent everywhere. The culture of waste is so powerful that there is hardly any sensitivity about wasting anything. Unemployment, racism and poverty are found in an unbridled form. Rights are disparaged to such an extent that its aberrations, like slavery, trafficking, subjugating women and then forcing them to abort and organ trafficking are uncontrollable. The Pope sounds 'alarm' against the 'culture of walls' that favours the explosion of organised crime, fuelled by fear and loneliness. These global problems call for global actions, manifestly so.

2.5. Strangers on the Road

The second chapter of the Encyclical discusses the 'strangers on the road'[19] in the world of today. The chapter is dedicated to the ever powerful figure of the 'Good Samaritan'. The Pope calls the current society 'unhealthy', seeing it turning its back on the suffering. It is 'illiterate' in caring for the frail and vulnerable. As the Good Samaritan proved himself a 'neighbour' to the one left abandoned on the street, so too are all believers invited to be a 'neighbour' to one and all, especially the needy. This calls for overcoming prejudices, personal interests, historic and cultural barriers. It is the duty of the humans to build a mutually inclusive society, by being co-responsible with others. Creating a society that is able to include, integrate and lift up those who have fallen or are suffering is not a choice, but a divinely oriented duty. Love builds bridges and 'we were made for love', underlines the Pope. Christians in particular have to recognise Christ in the face of every abandoned and excluded person, he emphasises strongly. The Pope advocates a life style for Christians in particular and all human beings in general to leave no one on the road of life as a stranger, but to recognise one's neighbour and brother or sister with love, to be true to the human duty to the divine.

2.6. Vision of an open world

The third chapter focuses on the capacity to love according to a universal dimension, namely 'envisaging and engendering an open world'[20]. Pope Francis exhorts us to go 'outside' 'the self' in order to find 'a fuller existence in another'. This would require opening ourselves up to the other according to the dynamism of charity, which makes us tend toward a 'universal fulfilment'. In fact, 'the spiritual stature of a person's life is measured by love'. Love, far from selfishness, leads us to seek better for the life of the other. The sense of solidarity and of fraternity begins within the family and this has to be safeguarded and respected in its 'primary and vital mission of education'. The right to live with dignity cannot be denied to anyone, the Pope affirmed. Since rights have no borders, no one can remain excluded, regardless of where they are born. In this context, the Pope underscored the 'ethics of international relations'[21]. Every country belongs to foreigners also. The goods of the territory cannot be denied to those who are in need and come from another place. The natural right to private property is secondary to the principle of the universal destination of created goods. The Encyclical places specific emphasis on the issue of foreign debt. Subject to the principle the debt must be paid, the growth and subsistence of the poorest countries should not be compromised.

2.7. Heart open to the world

The fourth chapter of the Encyclical discusses the theme of migration, in terms of 'a heart open to the whole world'[22]. Pope Francis argues for the 'lives at stake', who are forced to flee from war, persecution, natural catastrophes and unscrupulous trafficking. Migrants, who are ripped from their communities of origin, are to be welcomed, protected, supported and integrated. Unnecessary migration needs to be avoided, by creating concrete opportunities to live with dignity in the countries of origin. All the same, the right to seek a better life elsewhere has to be respected. In receiving countries, the right balance will be between the protection of the rights of the citizens and the guarantee of welcome and assistance for migrants. Several indispensable steps for those who are fleeing on account of grave humanitarian crises have to be considered. Increasing and simplifying granting of visas, opening humanitarian corridors, assuring lodging, security and essential services, offering opportunities for employment and training, favouring family reunification, protecting minors and guaranteeing religious freedom are some of those steps. What is needed above all is global governance and an international collaboration for migration, which implements long-term planning, going beyond single emergencies, on behalf of the supportive development of all peoples, the Pope argues.

2.8. Better politics

The fifth chapter considers 'a better kind of politics'[23]. Since good politics is placed at the service of the common good, it represents one of the most valuable forms of charity. It recognises the importance of people, who are available for discussion and dialogue as an open category. Attracting consensus in order to exploit them for its own service and fomenting selfishness in order to increase its own popularity is a crime of the first order.

On the other hand, a better politics is the 'essential dimension of social life'. The best strategy against poverty is to promote them in the perspective of solidarity and subsidiarity. The task of politics is to find a solution to all that attacks fundamental human rights, such as social exclusion, marketing of organs, tissues, weapons and drugs, sexual exploitation, slave labour, terrorism and organised crime. Human trafficking is a 'source of shame for humanity'[24] and has to be eliminated. Hunger is 'criminal' because food is 'an inalienable right', Pope Francis affirmed. The politics we need is a politics centred on human dignity and not subjected to finance, because 'the marketplace, by itself, cannot resolve every problem'. Hence, popular movements must be engaged in society with greater coordination. In this regard, the Encyclical proposes a reform of the United Nations, in view of giving substance to the concept of 'family of nations' working for the common good, eradication of poverty and protection of human rights. The UN must promote the force of law rather than the law of force, as well.

2.9. Dialogue and Friendship

The sixth chapter talks about 'Dialogue and friendship in society'[25]. This would mean a concept of life as the 'art of encounter' with everyone, even with the peripheries of the world and with original peoples, because 'each of us can learn something from others'. No one is useless and no one is dispensable. The 'miracle of kindness' Pope refers to is like a star 'shining in the midst of darkness' and 'frees us from the cruelty ... the anxiety ... the frantic flurry of activity'[26] that prevail in the contemporary era. Pope Francis proceeds to the issue of 'death penalty' and asserted that it is 'inadmissible and must be abolished worldwide'. Not even a murderer loses his personal dignity. God himself pledges to guarantee this. It is necessary to respect 'the sacredness of life'. No part of the human family can be readily sacrificed. The unborn, the poor, the disabled and the elderly have to be ensured their dignity.

2.10. Paths of Renewed Encounter

The seventh chapter proposes 'Paths of renewed encounter'[27]. Peace is connected to truth, justice and mercy. Far from the desire for vengeance, it is 'proactive' and aims at forming a society based on service to others and on the pursuit of reconciliation and mutual development. Peace is an 'art' that involves and regards everyone and in which each one must do his or her part in 'a never-ending task'. Forgiveness is linked to peace. Loving an oppressor means helping him or her to change and not allowing him or her to continue oppressing his or her neighbour. Forgiveness means renouncing the destructive power of evil and the desire for revenge. The 'horrors' of history, like persecutions and ethnic massacres, must be remembered always, anew, so as not be become anaesthetised and to keep the flame of collective conscience alive. Besides, the Pope focuses on war as a 'constant threat' that represents 'the negation of all rights', 'the failure of politics and of humanity' and 'a stinging defeat before the forces of evil'. 'Never again war' has to be vehemently reaffirmed. The total elimination of nuclear arms is 'a moral and humanitarian imperative'[28]. The Pope suggests the establishment of a global fund for the elimination of hunger, instead of investing money on weapons.

2.11. Religion and Fraternity

In the eighth and final chapter the Pope advocates that 'religions have to be at the service of fraternity in our world'[29]. Terrorism is not due to religion but is an erroneous interpretation of religious texts as well as 'policies linked to hunger, poverty, injustice, oppression'[30]. A journey of peace among religions is possible. Therefore, it is necessary to guarantee religious freedom, a fundamental human right for all believers. In addition, Pope Francis underlines the role of the Church. The Church should not 'restrict her mission to the private sphere'. While not engaging in politics, the Church does not, however, renounce the political dimension of life itself, attention to the common good and concern for integral human development, according to evangelical principals.

3. THE MISSION OF SOCIAL FRIENDSHIP

The third segment of the paper explores the Christian grounding of the topic, especially the Bible (New Testament), the Second World Council of Vatican and the subsequent Papal decrees. It proceeds to apply the theme to faith, the Constitution of India, catholicity of the mission and the mutual relatedness of either part of the theme under discussion. It further arrives at the conclusion that 'fraternity and social friendship' is the brilliance of the Christian mission, par excellence.

3.1. Fraternity grounded in the Paternity of God

Jesus presented to the world a God who is 'Father' or 'like a father'[31]. The term 'father' is inclusive of motherly qualities, too. Father of the creation would mean 'source of life', which gives, nourishes and sustains it with love. All human beings are his children and he loves them without any condition. He takes care of them with a 'sense of equality'[32] and with a 'sense of all'[33], certainly with a special concern for the weaker ones. He does not discriminate even between the good and the evil. He sends his sunshine and the rains to both, in an equal measure. Even in defections, he forgives, overwhelmed by total love, and as if nothing wrong has taken place. He is head of the 'large divine family' of human beings, along with the entire creation. The notion of God as Father in Christianity, without a shred of doubt, defies all divisive considerations, in terms of religious and other affiliations. Obviously, human fraternity and the brotherly-sisterly relations among the humans are firmly grounded in the paternity, maternity as well, of God.

3.2. The Landmark Realisation of the Second World Council of Vatican

The Second World Council of Vatican[34] of the Catholic community, in the 60s of the 20th century, initiated the vision and mission of dialogue, interaction and fellowship with communities of other faiths. This epoch-making event marked the new wave of 'inter-faith relations, fraternity and social friendship' in the history of the world. The foundational document called '*Nostra Aetate*'[35], meaning 'In Our Time', certified that the Catholic Christian community became an adult in age and faith. Accordingly, 'if Christians treat other individuals, groups and peoples in a manner that is not befitting sisters and brothers, they have no right to call God their Father'. That would amount to losing the filial status with God, once and for all. Catholics would cease to be Christians, as well. Therefore, Catholics and Christians are bound to think as large as the world and to engage in fostering relations, fellowship and collaboration with people of all communities, lest they cease to be Christians. The Encyclical 'Fraternity and Social Friendship' is firmly in line with the declaration of the Vatican Council and is advancing the realisation miles and miles afar.

3.3. Papal Decrees on Harmony with other Faiths, Ideologies and Cultures

The subsequent pronouncements of the Popes on harmony among faiths categorically articulate its all-embracing implications. Convening the Second Vatican Council in 1962, Pope John XXIII declared, "we have to look at what unites people rather than what divides them"[36]. "We… have to meet as pilgrims and start…searching for God…in the hearts of humankind"[37], added Pope Paul VI, at the Meeting of religions at Bombay, India, in 1964. He continued, "Man must meet man, nation meet nation, as brothers and sisters, as children of God"[38]. Pope John Paul II, during his visit to Manila in 1981, exhorted, "Christians will…join hands with all men and women of good will and work together in order to bring about a more just and peaceful society, in which the poor will be the first to be served"[39]. During his first visit to India, he stated at Madras in 1986, "by dialogue we let God be present in our midst, for as we open ourselves in dialogue to one another, we open ourselves to God"[40]. "Either we learn to walk together in peace and harmony or we drift and ruin ourselves and others"[41], he affirmed at World Day of Prayer for Peace at Assisi, 1986. "Dialogue is an act of love, which has its roots in God himself"[42], he emphasised during his second visit to India at New Delhi in 1999. "Different religious traditions of India are a hope for a better future for the human family"[43], he further stated then. He caught the imagination of people of all religions as he pronounced categorically then that "religion should be what God intended it to be a source of goodness, harmony and peace"[44]. All these Papal pronouncements are grounded in the statement of Ecclesia in Asia, 26, that "the dialogue, which the Church proposes, is grounded in the logic of the incarnation"[45].

3.4. The Triangular Dynamics of Faith and the Sense of Harmony

Faith has a three-sided dynamics – faith in oneself, faith in the other and faith in God[46]. Trusting oneself or the core of one's being is 'individual faith'[47]. Trusting another person as the extension of one's own being is 'social faith'[48]. Elevating one's trust in oneself and in others and applying the same to God or the spiritual power is 'spiritual faith'[49]. These triangular realities of life together make a complete faith. The inter-connectedness of these aspects as well as the quality of faithfulness makes faith balanced and worth the while. In other words, faith can be described as self-confidence, confidence in the other and confidence in God, all at the same time. When any of these facets of faith is missing, faith becomes insipid and fruitless; faith ceases to be faith, as well. Manifestly, the triangular dynamics of faith affirms the sense of being related to other human beings within the very frame of faith. The social aspect of faith is geared towards fraternal relations and social friendship. The comprehensive relation of faith to the creative, paternal and divine principle establishes the orientation of faith to the sense of harmony, as well.

3.5. The Rootedness of the Three-sided Faith in the Teachings of Jesus

The teaching of Jesus illustrates this triangular texture of faith in a very lucid manner. First and foremost, the 'parable of the talents'[50] motivates one to attain one's self, to the fullest stature, by doubling or multiplying the original gift. This is what Jesus said about himself, 'I have come, so that they may have life, life in its fullest measure'[51]. Secondly, the golden rule of Jesus advocates 'doing to the other what one would have the other do to you'[52]. Such a measure, for sure, maintains the equilibrium of social life. Thirdly, the last judgment illustrates how 'what is done to the other human being, however little he or she may be, reaches God'[53]. This is a perfect blending of the human and divine logic of life. Such a perception of faith composes a total definition of life and establishes faith as a multi-faceted and all-inclusive occurrence between human beings and God as well as among the humans. The three-sided character of faith is rooted in the life, mission and teachings of Jesus and gives an authority and dignity to the fraternal, social and friendly dynamics of human life.

3.6. The Fraternal, Social and Friendly Implications of Faith

Faith leads a believer to see in the other a brother or sister and friend to be appreciated, supported and loved. God has created the universe, creatures and all human beings equal. Believers are called to recognise and express this human fraternity by safeguarding creation and the entire universe. Faith motivates believers to support all persons, especially the poorest and those most in need. Faith empowers one to make a friendly and fraternal atmosphere for sharing the joys, sorrows and problems of our contemporary world. The scientific and technological progress, therapeutic achievements, the digital era, the mass media and communications have to be considered in terms of faith, too. Faith makes believer reflect on the level of poverty, conflict and suffering of so many brothers and sisters in different parts of the world. Faith helps one address the arms race, social injustice, corruption, inequality, moral decline, terrorism, discrimination, extremism and many other problems. It is faith in God and faith in human fraternity that helps people unite and work together. Faith is the agent that creates an awareness of the great divine grace, makes all human beings brothers and sisters and advances a culture of mutual respect[54]. Finally, faith is geared towards the profound hope in a bright future for all human beings.

3.7. Social Friendship knows no boundaries

True friendship, social as well as personal, knows no boundaries. It has no limits of time and space. There is hardly anything off-limits in conversation, depending on the degree of closeness in friendship. Both parties can peel back their layers and lay out their broken pieces without judgment and without holding back. A friend would never want to see his or her friend hurt or watch you fail. A friend is a special companion who cares about the wellbeing of the other. A friend is someone you rely on when things seem blink and most times, they are your source of reasoning when confused. A friend is always there through thick and thin. True friendship involves sacrifice. It can be sacrificing time, money and even life for ensuring the safety and happiness of the friend. True friendship means giving up something or everything dearest to one for another willingly, like Jesus Christ[55]. A friend stands by one and defends one even when one is not present. A friend is one's ally who would go any length to put a smile on the other's face. Friendship calls for mutual appreciation, thoughtfulness and reciprocation. Social friendship is geared towards building a better, more just and peaceful world. These characteristics of personal and social friendships is to be applied into persons of all affiliations, like caste, clan, creed, culture, ethnicity, language, gender, food habits, dress habits, social traditions and nationalities. Social friendship has to be developed and maintained across all the human-made boundaries[56]. That is what is meant by the Encyclical.

3.8. Fraternity in the Preamble of the Constitution

Fraternity in the Preamble of the Constitution declares two things: the dignity of the individual and the unity and integrity of the nation[57]. Fraternity is the binding element between unity and equality. It gives birth to new rights, which facilitate the constitutional goal of an egalitarian society. Fraternity assures the right to live with dignity and respect, free from oppression and unsociability. Fraternity is a feeling of brotherhood and sisterhood. It is a sense of belonging to the country and its people. '*Bandhuta*'[58] is a beautiful and shining word derived from Sanskrit, reflecting the idea that we are all bound to and with each other. Fraternity or *bandhuta* is the most radical and important idea of our times, the necessary foundation to fight all the world's injustices, hate and inequalities. Fraternity in the Constitution gives a dignity to the nation. Fraternity gives meaning to the mosaic of diversity and difference in the individual, social and cultural characteristics of the individual citizens and communities of the country. Fraternity is the hub of the nationhood of the country as India.

3.9. Fraternity is the Essence of Socialism, Democracy and Secularism

The Constitution of India gloriously proclaims its credentials as 'socialist, democratic and secular'[59] country. Socialism is to recognize the humans as social beings. Democracy acknowledges the rights and duties of every citizen. Secularism, far from negating affiliation to all religious traditions, gives due space to all religious, social and cultural streams. An 'all-inclusive spirit'[60] is the genius of socialism, democracy and secularism. 'Leaving no one behind'[61] and caring for the weaker, voiceless and marginalised are at the nub of the triple provisions of the Constitution. It is not the game of the majority, but every person, every voice, every right and every entity have and should have the due space allotted in the Constitution. All the above provisions vouch to secure the identity and dignity of every citizen, family, institution, community, religion, ideology, culture, ethnicity, gender, language, food habit, dress pattern, and the like. It is fraternal spirit that motivates the citizens and the state to honour the provisions of socialism, democracy and secularism. In other words, fraternity is the essence of socialism, democracy and secularism enshrined in the Constitution of India.

3.10. The Dire Need of Fraternity in India and the World Today

Dr Bhim Rao Ambedkar, after having added the clause on 'fraternity' in the Preamble, submitted the draft of the Constitution to the President of the Constituent Assembly, *Rajendra Prasad*, on 21 February 1948. He stated then, 'the need for fraternal concord and goodwill in India was never greater than now' [62]. The people of India, much of the world too, are now living through deeply troubled times, marked by rising hate and inequality. A new leadership is gaining strength and electoral support in India and certain countries around the world. These are leaders who are authoritarian, divisive and polarising, who reflect, amplify, legitimise and indeed valorise 'bigotry, prejudice and targeting of minorities' of many kinds. Besides, there is simultaneously a sheer decline in the civility of our public discourse, in which bullying and blotting one's adversaries are seen as markers of high oratory and political muscularity. These together constitute in India a grave threat to our constitutional values, and most of all to fraternity. Fraternity remains the least understood, least discussed and doubtlessly the least practiced of the four pillars of constitutional morality spelt out in the preamble of India's Constitution: justice, liberty, equality, and fraternity. India today stands more divided than it ever was since the assassination of Mahatma Gandhi amidst the bloodbath of Partition[63]. *Ambedkar* was too right that the imperative for fraternity was never greater, since the birth of India's constitution.

3.11. Fraternity and Social Friendship: Two sides of the Coin

The word 'fraternity' suggests not only 'brotherhood', but also 'friendship, community and cooperation'. Derivatively and contextually, it means 'sisterhood', as well. Both 'fraternity' and 'social friendship' have shared roots and implications. 'Fraternity' signifies a sense of common brotherhood of all Indians. Indians, therefore, have to be seen as being one people. They are bound to consider and hold each other in a spirit of brotherhood and sisterhood. Fraternity is the principle that gives unity and solidarity to social life. Without fraternity, equality and liberty will be no deeper than a layer of paint. Without fraternity, liberty and equality cannot become the natural course of things, too. Fraternity and Social Friendship are a collective call to recognise and love others as brothers and sisters, without borders[64]. It is an invitation to overcome all distance and every temptation to engage in disputes, impositions or submissions. It is a summons towards a new civilisation of love, justice, solidarity and care for our common home. It is a double-sided address to all men and women of goodwill of all communities to take up a shared spiritual and moral leadership for fraternity, friendship, peace and living together. In sum, Fraternity and social friendship means that all human beings are brothers and sisters, one to another, and that the shared fraternal and friendly relations correspond to the paternal-maternal sense of the sacred, divine and creative power.

3.12. The Down-to-earth Edition of Inter-religious Dialogue

Thanks to the Second World Council of Vatican, there emerged the new wave of inter-religious or inter-faith dialogue[65]. As the word 'dialogue' had classical and scholarly connotations, dialogue became 'theological dialogue', meaning discussions of theologians of diverse religions on the respective doctrines and dogmas religions. The negotiation on the theories of religions did not make a headway, obviously so, due to the set academic implications. Only a handful of theological scholars could attempt this, because of the technical knowhow it required. Prayers or recitations from the corresponding scriptures used to end up in a ritual, as well. Dialogue was broadened to include 'dialogue of life, dialogue of ideas, dialogue of deeds and dialogue of spiritual experience'. It did some good only. Discussions on social concerns from the various religious perspectives among people diverse disciplines, perceptions and communities made a great relevance and impact. Of late, 'inter-faith relations'[66] came up as a more realistic version of inter-religious dialogue. The articulation of 'fraternity and social friendship' makes real sense as regards promoting relations and fellowship among persons of all affiliations. At the end of the day, religions, rituals, theologies and ideologies matter less. Promoting good relations and friendship among persons and communities will take the humans a long way in harmonious and peaceful living as human beings who are well-tuned to the divine creative power and care.

3.13. The Catholicity of Mission

Believing in God as Father would clearly mean being part of a family or a community as large as people of all religious, non-religious and humanistic ideologies. This is what fraternity and social friendship is all about. The all-inclusive and universal disposition is intrinsic to being 'catholic'. The catholicity of mission is recognizing the fraternal and friendly character of the human society, national, regional or global. Promoting such a mindset is the catholic mission, as well. Implicitly, not opening one's self to others without boundaries and conditions is to run the risk of remaining closed against God, too. The other and God are like two sides of the same coin. One does not exist without the other. One cannot be approached without entertaining the other. Both directions have to be understood in relation to the other. An interactive faith would demand interaction between the horizontal lines as well as between horizontal and vertical lines, without any condition and limit. To be catholic is not a communal makeup. To be catholic is to be performing the mission of fostering being rooted in the paternal-maternal quality of God. In other words, promoting fraternal and friendly sentiments to one and all and taking up activities that strengthen a family culture is intended and mandated by being catholic[67]. This is the catholicity of the mission Christians are invited to perform in life.

3.14. The Mission of Harmony as Interfaith and Intercultural Relations

The mission Jesus performed on earth was one of promoting unity and harmony between the divine power and human beings. He presented God as a loving Father and the humans as his children. That would necessarily follow that human beings are brothers and sisters to each other. He himself was Son of the Father and told his disciples that they were sons in the line of his son-ship. That would amount to state that he was and is elder brother to all human brothers and sisters. He was and is friend and companion to one and all, too. Besides, he healed the sick, gave new life to the dead. He continues to do the same now as well. The filial life he inherited was translated into a fraternal life. The fraternal fibre he lived on earth is oriented to making friendships with persons of all communities and groups. Goodwill, equality, respect and cooperation are the four steps towards attaining harmony. Deeply grounded in the filial relationship with God the Father, promoting the fraternal and friendly relations to one and all is the very mission the Church has inherited from Jesus. All other dimensions of the mission of the Church are secondary to this mission of harmony or they have to be understood within the purview of the mission of harmony. In sum, the Christian mission is a mission of fostering interfaith and intercultural relations[68].

3.15. Fraternity and Social Friendship: The Mission of Harmony

As already been discussed, 'fraternity' means brotherhood, that is to say, 'the sense of being brotherly and sisterly. It is the quality of being a social group with persons with shared interests and experiences. Fraternity or brotherhood promotes unity and integrity in the nation and binds its people. Fraternity stands for standing up for fellow citizens and it fosters the integrity of the nation or of the society. Fraternity is committed to celebrating together our shared values of acceptance, openness, empathy and love towards other human beings, as well. Human fraternity is grounded in the divine paternity. The creator God is origin and life-giver, sustainer and care-taker and destiny and destination. The human and other beings are filial to the Creator and are necessarily fraternal to each other. Human fraternity is the way of being related to each other, without borders. Human fraternity is the very way to be related to the paternal Creator, too. The spirit of human fraternity is the right response to diversity of ethnic traits, gender, caste, clan, class, creed, and the like. Fraternity is the true solution to problems related to differences in language, ideology, culture, social traditions, food habits, dress patterns, etc, too[69]. 'Fraternity and Social Friendship' is the spirit of the family culture of the human society, which in India is typically stated as '*Vasudhaiv Kutumbakam*'[70].

CONCLUSION

Fraternity is the nucleus of life. It is the core principle of the Constitution of India. Fraternity is the essential spirit of religious systems and social communities. Fraternity is the universal human quality underscored by the United Nations Organisation. Fraternity is the sum and substance of human life, as well. Social friendship is the result of the fraternity. Furthermore, the antidote to hate is human fraternity, which embodies compassion, solidarity, unity and mutual respect. 'Cultural diversity and freedom of belief' are part of the 'rich tapestry' of humanity. Promoting peace, love and fraternity has been a consistent message from religious figures throughout history. Therefore, more commitment towards promoting cultural and religious tolerance, interaction, understanding and collaboration is called for. Living like brothers and sisters, one to another, gives dignity to humanity and the divinity in, around and above us. Promoting the spirit of 'fraternity and social friendship' is the mission of harmony ahead of a Christian, for that matter, every believer and human being.

Endnotes

1. Joseph Esmond Riddle, A Complete English-Latin and Latin-English Dictionary, London, 1870, p. 303
2. Peter, C. Phan, Being Religious Inter-religiously: Asian Perspectives on Interfaith Dialogue, Michigan, 2009, p. 116
3. *Ibid,* p. 127
4. Joseph Esmond Riddle, A Complete English-Latin and Latin-English Dictionary, London, 1870, p. 377
5. *Ibid,* p. 378
6. Peter, C. Phan, Being Religious Inter-religiously: Asian Perspectives on Interfaith Dialogue, Michigan, 2009, p. 116
7. Harrap's French-English Anglias-Francais Mini Dictionary, New Delhi, 1998, p. 03
8. Stuart Brown, N. J. Fox, Historical Dictionary of Leibniz's Philosophy, Lanham, 2006, p. 188
9. Ramchandra Verma (Ed.), *Maanak Hindee Kosha*, Vol. 5, Allahabad, 1993, p. 280
10. *Ibid,* p. 103
11. Walter William Skeat, A Concise Etymological Dictionary of the English Language, New York, 1882, p. 270

12. Joseph Esmond Riddle, A Complete English-Latin and Latin-English Dictionary, London, 1870, p. 207
13. *Ibid,* p. 506
14. Steven Rosefielde, Daniel Quinn Mills, Democracy and its Elected Enemies, New York, 2013, p. 05
15. Dane Munro, Ian McIntosh, Nour Fara Haddad (Ed.), Peace Journeys: A New Direction in Religious Tourism and Pilgrimage Research, Newcastle upon Tyne, United Kingdom, 2020, p. 59
16. *Ibid,* p. 63
17. Pope Francis, *Fratelli Tutti*: On Fraternity and Social Friendship, New York, 2020, p. 01
18. *Ibid,* p. 05
19. *Ibid,* p. 26
20. *Ibid,* p. 39
21. *Ibid,* p. 42
22. *Ibid,* p. 57
23. *Ibid,* p. 69
24. *Ibid,* p. 71
25. *Ibid,* p. 91
26. *Ibid,* p. 93
27. *Ibid,* p. 102
28. *Ibid,* p. 105
29. *Ibid,* p. 124
30. Rajendra Vora, Suhas Palshikar, Indian Democracy: Meanings and Practices, New Delhi, 2004, p. 27
31. Robert, H. Stein, An Introduction to the Parables of Jesus, Philadelphia, 1981, p. 122
32. Peter, C. Phan, Being Religious Inter-religiously: Asian Perspectives on Interfaith Dialogue, Michigan, 2009, p. 116
33. *Ibid,* p. 118
34. Walter, M. Abbort, SJ, Documents of Vatican II, New York, 1966, p. 03
35. Edward Bristow (Ed.), No Religion is an Island: The *Nostra Aetate* Dialogues, New York, 1998, p. 07
36. Thomas Cahill, Pope John XXIII: A Life, London. 2002, p. 79
37. Paul, M. Collins, Christian Enculturation in India, New York, 2007, p. 157
38. *Ibid,* p. 158
39. George Weigel, Witness to Hope: The Biography of Pope John Paul II, New York, 2001, p. 619
40. *Ibid,* p. 619
41. *Ibid,* p. 623
42. *Ibid,* p. 629
43. *Ibid,* p. 639
44. *Ibid,* p. 637
45. https://www.ewtn.com/library/papaldoc/jp2asia.htm
46. Daniel, L. Migliore, Faith Seeking Understanding: An Introduction to Christian Theology, Third Edition, Cambridge, 2014, p. 156
47. *Ibid,* p. 201
48. *Ibid,* p. 207
49. *Ibid,* p. 211
50. The Holy Bible, NIV, Michigan, 1994, Mt 25.14-30, p. 1127
51. *Ibid,* Jn 10.10, p. 1220
52. *Ibid,* Mt 7.12, p. 1100

53. *Ibid,* Mt 25.41, p. 1128
54. Daniel, L. Migliore, Faith Seeking Understanding: An Introduction to Christian Theology, Third Edition, Cambridge, 2014, p. 109
55. David R. Smock, Religious Contributions to Peacemaking, New York, 2019, p. 254
56. *Ibid,* p. 263
57. Iqbal Narain, Secularism in India, New Delhi, 2000, p. 79
58. *Ibid,* p. 117
59. *Ibid,* p. 26
60. *Ibid,* p. 53
61. *Ibid,* 109
62. Aparajita Baruah, Preamble of the Constitution of India: An Insight and Comparison with Other Constitutions, New Delhi, 2007, p. 64
63. Mujibur Rehman (Ed.), Communalism in Postcolonial India: Changing Contours, Abingdon, England, 2020, p. 11
64. Pope Francis, *Fratelli Tutti*: On Fraternity and Social Friendship, New York, 2020, p. 109
65. Peter, C. Phan, Being Religious Inter-religiously: Asian Perspectives on Interfaith Dialogue, Michigan, 2009, p. 117
66. *Ibid,* p. 109
67. Jenny Daggers, Postcolonial Theology of Religions: Particularity and Pluralism in World Christianity, London, 2013, p. 146
68. Jonathan, Y. Tan, 'Missio Inter Gentes: Towards a New Paradigm in the Mission Theology of the Federation of Asian Bishops' Conferences (FABC), Mission Studies, 21.1, 2004, p. 88
69. *Ibid,* p. 150
70. *Brihadaranyak Upanishad* 1.4.14, Swami Satchidanandendra Saraswati, The Method of the Vedanta: A Critical Account of the Advaita Tradition, New Delhi, 2007, p. 492

(Published in 'Jeevadhara' (Monthly Journal), Kottayam, Vol. LII, Issue No. 309, pp. 68-87 – in May 2022).

Chapter - 11

Interactive Dynamics of Christian Mission

INTRODUCTION

The idea of God as Father, along with the universal values that emerged from Jesus, clearly composes the idea of a 'family' on earth. Christian mission is firmly grounded in this idea of family. A 'sense of mission' is the hub of that mission, which, in turn, is motivated by a vibrant faith in Jesus. As diversity is the all-pervasive character of life, the world over, engagement with one another in a complementary and mutually enriching manner becomes the multi-way process of life. That would amount to state that mission as well as faith is an interactive reality among persons and people of diverse affiliations of faith, ideology, culture and other social traditions. Therefore, the dynamics of the Christian mission is out and out an interactive and evolving one.

This essay, in the process of arguing out the above thesis, analyzes the related key notions first and foremost and establishes faith as an interactive reality. Having compared the fabric of diversity in Asia in particular as well as in the planet in general with the universal and familial mindset of the Christian world, it searches for a paradigm that does full justice to bridging and balancing diversities. Finding the *Ad Gentes* paradigm of mission too self-centred and heavily-loaded with colonial and institutional overtones, it convincingly arrives at the paradigm of Inter *Gentes* mission, which is centrally rooted in the Second World Council of Vatican and is in perfect tune with the mind of Jesus. The conclusive finding of the author in this article is 'making the family of God on earth' is the happy outcome as well as objective of the Christian mission.

1. KEY NOTIONS

1.1. Mission

Mission[1] is a 'special task' given to a person or a group of people. It denotes a 'higher power', which has commissioned the missioner. As a 'calling from above', mission is an undertaking that is either just provisional or that transcends the limits of time and space. The latter involves one's entire life, whereas the former, a short period. Reaching out to one and all as well as far and wide affirms its larger nuances, while engaging one's self with a profound commitment confirms its deeper meanings. Mission evolves from the vision, universally conceived but locally applied.

Besides, a 'sense of mission'[2] is the core of any mission and it is that sense of mission, which motivates one to invest oneself to a cause with the whole heart, mind and spirit. It is the same sense of mission that decides the enhanced 'quality' of whatsoever is undertaken and performed in life. Attaining 'higher altitudes' as well as 'larger magnitudes' in life, for oneself and for others, is the outcome of a mission in life, of course to the credit of the one who empowered the missioner.

1.2. Christian

The term 'Christian'[3] derives obviously from the name 'Christ'. Christ or Messiah is 'the anointed one'[4] and he is anointed for the spiritual uplift of the entire world. Christ Jesus as 'Immanuel' is the embodiment of 'God with us'[5], in diverse dimensions. To be a Christian is to be 'like Christ' and to 'follow Christ' in being 'God with us', for all those who come in touch with one's life. Being Christian, in the right sense of the word, never admits a passive, idle and cozy idea of worshipping Jesus, which contradicts the mind and mandate of Jesus, too.

The mission of a Christian necessarily emerges from the mission of Christ Jesus. It is not exactly preaching the message of Jesus. It would mean 'living the values' lived and taught by Jesus, at all times and in all places. It would imply making a living example out of one's self in facilitating the process of enhancing the quality of human lives, environmental, ethical and spiritual. Being a member of the Christian community does not necessarily make a real Christian missioner, but one who qualitatively 'radiates the character of Christ' in one's life, may be even off the specific campus. The brilliance in following him makes the difference.

1.3. Dynamics

'Dynamics'[6] implies technicalities as regards the process of forces acting on each other. It covers the entire range of properties that motivate change, development and growth within a group or a system. It is the 'dynamism' that stimulates a movement and expresses itself in dynamics. It not only regulates relations among the components of social life but also maintains the balance, poise and dignity within the given composition. It is an enthusiastic and progressive phenomenon that is oriented to an intense play of energy among all the elements of the collection or the organism.

Dynamics is the essence of interaction in all living entities and is the inner principle that supplies meaning and newness to life. In this context, dynamics in the Christian mission undertakes to maintain the 'Mission Quotient' (MQ) of the Christian missioner, as well as of mission in general. It also balances the diverse ingredients of the mission in the given human society, such as divine logic and human commitment, along with all the connected cultural characteristics.

1.4. Interactive

The word 'interactive'[7] has three components – 'inter', 'interact' and 'interactive'. 'Interaction' is the spinal reality that these words intend to compose. 'Inter' connotes 'between', when the dynamics affect two persons or entities and 'among', when the dynamics involve more than two people or things. 'Interact' refers to two or more persons 'influencing each other'. 'Interactive' signifies a 'two-way flow that acts upon each other'. 'Interaction' implies an 'interface', dealings or relations between/among persons or things. It is a double-sided stream of ideas, feelings, insights and experiences.

Interaction is a reciprocal engagement between/among persons of diverse backgrounds and affiliations. The interplay of information between the computer and the computer-user could be a case in point. Interaction covers a large gamut of areas, like gender, language, ideology, culture, faith, economy, business and other social associations. It implies all types of 'give and take' as well as 'sharing'. Interaction takes the form of its adjective 'interactive' as the heart of its process and dynamics. In the current context, the term 'interactive' modifies, enhances and elevates the quality of the missionary engagement of the missioner, whatever may be its place, mode and area of operation.

2. FAITH AS AN INTERACTIVE REALITY

2.1. Faith – a blend of sacred and secular

The term 'faith'[8] means 'belief, confidence, trust', etc. It is a complete belief in the truth, value and trustworthiness of a person, idea or a thing. Faith takes shape as a result of a series of ideas, feelings and deeds, like drops of water come together to form a flow. It does not have any essential connection with any religious doctrines and dogmas. It is grounded in the personal experience of the human being and is primarily oriented to a living reality, human or divine. It surpasses ceremonial stereotypes and theological categories. It does not contradict the secular, not even the least. On the contrary, it celebrates a 'sense of the sacred' in an all-encompassing manner, deeply applied to the human context as well as nature.

One's faith is naturally geared towards the source and destiny of life in the vertical context and towards the human and environmental realities in the horizontal context, both at the same time. The sacred sentiment of faith is deep and all-pervasive as well as replete with human and divine experiences in a dynamic and inventive fashion. Manifestly, faith, as a wide-ranging phenomenon of the world, is clearly secular and has in its niche the sacred in a more applied and realistic form than what is claimed in a fanciful way by the goody-goody and showy religious sector. That would amount to say that faith, in the right sense of the term, is a perfect blend of the secular and the sacred. No doubt, the traditional notion of faith, as contrary to the secular and the sacred as the monopoly of religion, requires being radically revisited.

2.2. Faith – its triangular dynamics of oneself, the other and God

Faith has a three-sided dynamics[9] – faith in oneself, faith in the other and faith in God. Trusting oneself or the core of one's being is 'individual faith'. Trusting another person as the extension of one's own being is 'social faith'. Elevating one's trust in oneself and in others and applying the same to God or the spiritual power is 'spiritual faith'. These triangular realities of life together make a complete faith. The inter-connectedness of these aspects as well as the quality of faithfulness makes faith balanced and worth the while. In other words, faith can be described as self-confidence, confidence in the other and confidence in God, all at the same time. When any of these facets of faith is missing, faith becomes insipid and fruitless; faith ceases to be faith, as well.

The teaching of Jesus illustrates this triangular texture of faith in a very lucid manner. The parable of the talents[10] motivates one to attain one's self, to the fullest stature. This is what Jesus came to the earth for, too[11]. The golden rule[12] advocates measuring out to the other what one would have the other due to one. Such a measure, for sure, maintains the equilibrium of social life. The last judgment[13] illustrates how what is done to the other human being, however little he or she may be, reaches God. This is a perfect blending of the human and divine logic of life. Such a perception of faith composes a total definition of life and establishes faith as a multi-faceted and all-inclusive occurrence.

2.3. Faith – its religious and non-religious dimensions

Faith has two dimensions[14] – religious and non-religious. When a certain religious system is the locus of faith, there is a religious faith. On the other hand, when an ideology, a culture, an experience or a certain branch of science is the context of trust, faith is positively non-religious or humanistic. Religious faith entertains philosophy, doctrines, dogma, myths, stories, fasts, pilgrimages, symbols and rituals, in view of experiencing the eternal reality. Non-religious faith relies on all available realities in the world, engages in scientific research and evolves truth in diversely innovative ways. Faith, as a perspective and an approach to life, can be both theistic and humanistic or non-theistic. The two aspects of faith are not contradictory poles, but are complementary aspects of faith and therefore require being dovetailed.

In addition, faith does not become religious when a collection of people share certain beliefs and performs certain rituals together. But, it does, when a community of people stays tuned to each other in trust, care for each other and join hands to live together harmoniously. Further, the value of a faith is not to be judged by the number of people pursuing it, but the volume and quality of contribution it makes to the community or society, towards enhancing its worth. In addition, a stream of faith is powerful not when it is rigid in what it professes and proclaims it in superlative terms, but when it radiates the sublime values of love and brotherhood/sisterhood towards one and all, in a mutually inclusive manner.

2.4. Faith – a multi-way process of interaction

Faith, in its essence, is dynamic and interactive. Interaction is oriented to action between persons. It would mean 'people talking with each other or doing things with each other together'[15], as Merriam Webster Dictionary puts it. Being mutually or reciprocally active, it is a thorough crossing point between two or more persons. Similarly, faith is a two-way process of communication, when two persons or entities are involved and it is a multi-way process, when more than two persons or units are involved. Faith, as a perception, a conviction and an orientation, necessitates that the components influence each other or act on each other, in varied ways. It is a 'continual exchange of live information between or among persons'. Such reciprocity in the diverse areas of faith affirms the social character of faith.

Evidently, religion is a system and faith is abstract and neither of them can interact with their counterparts. Persons or believers interact, one with another. When human beings meet one another, faith becomes a live reality. In other words, the meeting of human beings is what is actually implied by 'faith meeting faith'. Moreover, faith is creative in its character. A single element cannot create anything. Faith in its spirit is a multifaceted and inventive reality and not a dead phenomenon of the cemetery. It cannot be an isolated and insulated entity, too. Faith is inclusive, participatory and collaborative as well as resourceful and insightful in disposition. It is equivalent to the very process of life, which is many-sided and interactive.

2.5. Faith – a relational way, like 'one body, many parts'

Faith, as a social experience, is a relational entity. It would mean 'being in close relation with other constituents of life', beyond all boundaries. 'One body with many parts'[16] is a perfect model of true faith. Faith is one, but has many aspects, just like spirit is one and has many manifestations. Humanity is one, but has many expressions. The body exists as one, but functions as many. All the parts of the body have their own singular identities and roles. They are equal in their dignity and status, as well. What happens in one part of the body, good or bad, necessarily affects other parts. The relational characteristics of the different parts of the body illustrate clearly the logic of a relational and interactive faith.

In a similar way, specificities and commonalities of the diverse aspects of faith require being harmonised. In fact, faith is a partnership of faiths, just like the body that is a shared existence of parts. That would amount to state that believers of diverse faiths, as a matter of fact, have a collective existence, even though they have specific identities, roles, dignity, status and functions. They are naturally other-oriented, one to another. Therefore, they need to learn from each other, enrich one another and celebrate fellowship with each other. They require walking together to the same divine, like a shared pilgrimage, and working together, like partners, to make human lives more humane and harmonious, as well.

2.6. An interactive faith – a blessing

Faith signifies surrendering one's entire being to the higher power, though in more or less degrees. However, trust or confidence can imply a stoppage of thinking. Therefore, faith is inclined to become a 'blind faith', which definitely is a liability, though ironically so. This is indeed tragic and suicidal, too. For that reason, faith stands in need of being examined, reconsidered and updated constantly. The active involvement of the mind and spirit has to be ensured, in favour of inventive insights and convictions that enhance the liberating quality of faith. Only a faith that is enlightened, settled, serene and sublime is a pure faith. A childish faith is a stagnant faith and is a burden and a thorough curse to life. It arrests the process of growing or blossoming up, which is vital for faith.

Faith, to be a good thing for one and all, has to grow along with one's age, education and life experience. Only a progressively evolving faith proves to be a blessing. This attainment is an outcome of an interactive process, both within oneself and with other believers. Faith is a spiritual drive, which permeates into all areas of life in an integrated manner. Besides, faith is a radical reality and has to be grounded in the 'roots or origin' of life. It has also to be founded on the fundamental values of human life that supply divine sap to faith and nourish it. Vitality is its hub and 'imbibing the quality of life' in an imaginative way is that which makes faith spiritually sound and meaningful. Networking with all streams of faith and life and celebrating a 'communion of faiths' with everyone, including the creation, is the core ethos of faith, worth its name.

3. DIVERSITY – THE CONTEXT OF THE WORLD

3.1. The plural fabric of life

Diversity[17] is the mastermind of the Creator. It is perhaps the most incontestable reality of the universe. It applies to all areas of the creation. The planets, the vegetation, the animals and especially human beings reflect immense dimensions of diversity. It is the foundational characteristic of all cultures and identities. The dimensions of diversity in human life are varied and subtle. Some of the general areas are – geographical environment, climatic conditions, historical backgrounds, ethnic traits, gender, languages and dialects, food tastes, dress patterns, ideas and ideologies, professions and crafts, civilisations, social customs and mores, cultural streams, faith perspectives and spiritual sensibilities.

Diversity has two elements in it – being many and being different. 'Being many' refers to the numerical strength and being different, to the uniqueness of the individual being. The former is quantitative and the latter, qualitative. The external and the internal poles together make diversity possible. In addition, in its functional dynamics diversity has several other facets, too. It has individual and social qualities in it. It is also singular and plural, at the same time. It is one and many in a composite form, like one body and its many parts. It is particular from one angle and general from another angle. It is vertical as well as horizontal. In sum, it is a blend of several components that make diversity function and make a collective effect.

3.2. The Asian-Indian fibre of diversity

The Asian continent and very specially the Indian sub-continent stand out for marked forms of diversities, even to minute details. Asia stands out as unique among continents as regards the content and details of diversity. It is significant as regards its brilliant contribution to the world in various philosophic and religious perceptions of life. Its highly pluralistic social texture and spiritual outlook to life has unearthed several new insights. Its imaginative and aesthetic approach to life has explored various mysteries and wonders. It has cradled all major religious traditions of the world. Well, it is a rich collection of cultural streams of life, as if one better than the other.

India is exceptionally a living album of singular and unlimited diversities[18]. It is perhaps the most pluralistic country in the world. India has homed all possible faith perspectives and practices of the world. Its musical, linguistic, literary and artistic tributaries make 'unity in diversity' a tangible reality. Its ethnic sources, philosophies, cultural heritage, spiritual traditions, together with its geographical, climatic and social varieties, compose a real 'rainbow' of life. Its constitution provides for a secular and democratic fabric of life, although there are various conflicting tendencies in action on the ground. India is indeed a living laboratory of major and minor diversities that are in the process of continuous interaction and fusion.

3.3. Difference and its complementary nature

Difference[19] is the distinguishing mark in diversity. It stands for the individuality of an item in circulation. It makes existence of many things and beings relevant. It has absolutely no negative connotation in it. It is a positive reality. It is the component of enrichment in any item. Difference is the creative element in any being, like male or female. It is the mark of singularity. It constructs and advances life. Difference implies the specific and un-interchangeable roles dissimilar beings are intended to play in the entire spectrum of life. Difference is the brilliance of life, especially of the humans. It affirms being special, even beyond similarities. It defies uniformity and sameness that are contradictory to being special, as well.

Difference is complementary in character, too. The different items and units are as if 'made for each other'. They do not contradict each other, not even the least. They are not one against the other, in any way. They cannot exist disconnected from each other, like islands. They cannot make sense unrelated to each other, like parallel lines. Differences are necessarily complementary, one to another. 'One completes the other' is the logic of difference. The quality of difference provides scope for interaction among the diverse components of life, human or other. It is difference that makes unity and harmony possible among the multifarious aspects of social life.

3.4. Engaging with various forms of diversities

The grass root realities of social life show up subtle forms of diversities, both positive and negative. The regional and local contexts of life unearth finer details of the diversities in life, whereas national and inter-national circumstances bring to light larger forms of diversities. Celebrations of festivals, social mores and modes of life and ways of co-existing in life highlight multifarious nuances of diversities. At the same time, economic disparities, caste polarisations, class divide and communal tensions also find their place in the social map of life. The educated and the illiterate, the rich and the poor, the liberated and the enslaved, the exploiting and the exploited, the ruling and the ruled, the corrupt and the genuine – all find their space within the range of diversities of life, for better or for worse.

Engaging with the above forms of diversities is the way to respond to the reality of diversity. Recognising the differences and problems connected to the diverse social contexts is the first step to engage with diversity. Tuning the various perceptions, convictions, persuasions and sensibilities is the interactive way of engagement. Commonalities among the groups as well as individuals require being identified. Problems related to harmonious living with different entities need to be sorted out and addressed. Freedom and rights as well as duties and responsibilities of all units and players have to be harmonised. The collective consciousness of belonging to each other and belonging together have to be celebrated with the spirit of goodwill, equal footing, respect, cooperation and harmony. Engaging with diversities is an ever-dynamic and continuous process of mutual interaction.

4. CHRISTIANITY AND ITS UNIVERSAL VISION

4.1. The Universal Values and Principles of Christianity

Christian values and principles, obviously, derive from the person, life and teachings of Jesus Christ. The idea of human beings as 'created in the image of God'[20] establish the universal fatherly character of God. The definition of human beings, as 'divine abodes' or 'living temples of God'[21], guarantees their inviolable dignity, too. On the whole, Christian values are grounded in the three-faceted and mutually related dynamics of life – oneself, the other and God. Investing oneself towards a life in full, as in the parable of the talents[22], justifies the incarnation and mission of Jesus [23]. 'Doing to the other what one would have the other due to one'[24] is 'naturally and systemically directed to God himself'[25] and thus completes the triangular cycle of life.

Besides, 'pursuing perfection by non-discriminating[26], loving enemies[27] as well as one another[28], forgiving the other unconditionally[29], washing the other's feet[30], considering one another as friends[31], reaching out to the weak[32], being 'good news' to one and all[33], honouring the other above oneself[34] and being a brother or a sister to everyone, after the fashion of Jesus[35], summarise the core values of Christianity. These principles underscore a culture of human life that is thoroughly humane and spiritual as well as universal and interactive. These values defy all boundaries, as well.

4.2. The Launch of an Interactive Faith in the Second World Council of Vatican

The Second World Council of Vatican[36] of the Catholic community, in the 60s of the 20th century, initiated the vision and mission of dialogue, interaction and fellowship with communities of other faiths. This epoch-making event marked the new wave of inter-faith relations in the history of the world. The foundational document called '*Nostra Aetate*'[37], meaning 'In Our Time', certified that the Catholic Christian community became an adult in age and faith. Accordingly, 'if Christians treat other individuals, groups and peoples in a manner that is not befitting sisters and brothers, they have no right to call God their Father'. That would amount to losing the filial status with God, once and for all. Therefore, Catholics and Christians are bound to think as large as the world and to engage in fostering relations, fellowship and collaboration with people of all communities, lest they cease to be Christians.

Believing in God as Father would clearly mean being part of a family or a community as large as people of all religious, non-religious and humanistic ideologies. Such an all-inclusive and 'catholic' disposition categorically defines Christian faith today. Pope John Paul II summarised this faith in his public meeting in Madras in 1986 thus, 'By dialogue we let God be present in our midst, for as we open ourselves in dialogue to one another, we open ourselves to God'[38]. Implicitly, not opening one's self to others without boundaries and conditions is to run the risk of remaining closed against God as well. The other and God are like two sides of the same coin. One cannot exist without the other. An interactive faith would demand interaction between the horizontal lines as well as between horizontal and vertical lines, without any condition and limit.

4.3. The Ground-breaking Implications for a Relational Fabric of Faiths

Being grounded in a Trinitarian monotheism of 'Father, Son and Spirit'[39] as God, a Christian is well-founded in the framework of 'one-in-three' and 'three-in-one'. He or she is bound to pursue the spirit of 'God with us', while following Jesus as 'Immanuel'. The implication of such a faith is to have a faith in the family or community of God the Father, which inevitably involves all civilisations of people, as 'many parts in one body'[40]. 'Making the family of God' on earth is the esteemed mission of a Christian and it involves humans of all communities and nations including the creation, with a preferential service to the voiceless, the weak, the least, the lost, the deprived ones and those on the margins of the society.

Motivated by the universal mandate of being 'good news to one and all', a Christian has to awaken in herself or himself the consciousness of a 'common origin, shared existence and a common destiny'[41], along with all people. This would mean reading the signs of the times'[42] in the extremely multi-religious, multi-cultural and multi-ideological context of the present day times and responding to it meaningfully. As Jesus observed, 'Sabbath is for man[43] and not vice versa' and faith has to be an agent of unity among peoples. That is what Pope John Paul II affirmed at Meeting of Religions, New Delhi, 1999, 'religion should be what God intended it to be – a source of goodness, harmony and peace'[44]. This exactly was the aspiration of Jesus as he prayed 'Father, that they all may be one'[45]. Pope John XXIII added to it a profound realisation, 'we have to look at what unites people, rather than what divides them' and 'what *we have* in common is greater *than what separates* us'[46].

4.4. The Mission of Being a New Christian

The brilliance of Christianity is its all-encompassing idea of God as the Father of all. The relational idea is the plinth of a universal family of the humans, along with the entire creation. It is like a 'large umbrella' under which the entire family of the humans and the nature becomes a united and an integral whole. Discrimination and considerations of high and low, familiar and strange, friend and enemy, and the like, are totally alien to a true Christian. The sense of 'equality and relatedness' constructs the dynamics of that family. The sisterly and brotherly spirit that makes the family of God is the essential character of a Christian.

An adult Christian is mandated to live this quality of faith by making a communion of communities, traditions and cultures with all groups of Christians and other faiths, the world over. One has to be a Christian anew by developing innovative and wide-ranging perspectives and attitudes towards people of all civilisations. Only in such a context, the universal values lived and taught by Jesus will really make sense. Sustained efforts for advancing interaction, collaboration, fellowship and harmony among people of all affiliations only can make the Christian a 'Christian', in the right sense of the word. This is precisely what Pope Francis meant sharply and ironically in his General audience, at St Peter's Square, Vatican City, in 2015, 'Churches, parishes and institutions with closed doors must not call themselves a church; they must call themselves museums'[47]. The mission of 'being a new and inclusive Christian' is the clarion call of the hour.

5. CHRISTIAN MISSION AND ITS INTERACTIVE DYNAMICS

5.1. The Best of *Missio Ad Gentes*

'Missio Ad Gentes'[48], meaning 'mission to the nations/peoples' is a 'mandate impelled by the love of Christ' and certainly is the continuation of the mission of Jesus as a pilgrim and missionary Church. It is admirably a step forward in extending pastoral care to all peoples, by reaching out to people of other religious communities. Going beyond the old idea of 'there is no salvation outside the church' and 'shedding the exclusive right over the salvific grace of God' are landmark shifts in the understanding of the mission.

Some of the exceptionally larger musings of *Missio Ad Gentes* are the following – 'being familiar with the national and religious traditions of fellow beings', accepting them as 'co-members of the same group of humans', 'being united with them in a sense of esteem and love', 'sharing in their cultural and social life', 'learning the treasures God has distributed among the nations of the earth', 'absorbing their ways and culture' and 'collaborating with people of other denominations and faiths'. Moreover, *Missio Ad Gentes* acknowledges 'the presence of God' in other traditions and 'living according to one's conscience'. Better relations with people of other Christian and religious communities are to be proudly credited to *Missio Ad Gentes*.

5.2. Beyond *Missio Ad Gentes*

All the same, the pastoral care of *Missio Ad Gentes* has as its objective 'founding new churches' and this smacks of a scheme of extending the boundaries of the Church towards 'potential Christians'. Its characteristic concept of being 'exclusive, superior and unique' as well as 'definitive, normative and absolute' reflects imposing overtones and is oriented to 'conquering and displacing the other'. One's faith in the centrality of salvation by Jesus and Christianity, however honest, shows up highhandedness, especially if and when indiscreetly imposed upon people of other convictions and affiliations. This certainly is not approved by Jesus, in anyway, and therefore requires being overcome, even the least of it. *Missio Ad Gentes* also has in it an institutional pedestal of pre-eminence and strategy for colonising the other.

Besides, the giver-complex of the missioners considers other believers mere beggars and violates the reality that 'God was already there in the world before the Christian missioners arrived'. As per Mission *Ad Gentes*, the missioner claims all importance and makes the other an object. Mission cannot be a one-way activity and for that reason *Missio Ad Gentes* lags far behind the interactive spirit vibrant at the heart of the Second Vatican

Council, too. A self-righteous notion of faith is bound to belittle others as well as contradict the spirit of interfaith dialogue. As a self-absorbed concept, it is a dominating, un-negotiable and outdated approach to mission. Obviously, the mission of Jesus and of the Church has to go much beyond *Missio Ad Gentes*, in line with the essential spirit of the Second Vatican Council. The noble, serene and unique values lived and taught by Jesus calls for revisiting the obsession of *Missio Ad Gentes*.

5.3. Towards *Missio Inter Gentes*

'*Missio Inter Gentes*'[49] signifies 'mission between or among the peoples/nations'. It is a mission 'of the people, by the people, for the people, with the people, from the people and among the people'. It implies that the 'mission emerges or evolves from the people'. '*Missio Inter Gentes*', as a term, was first proposed by William R. Burrows and, as a concept, was advanced by the 'Federation of Asian Bishops' Conference'. This model of the mission not only transcends '*Missio Ad Gentes*', but also is markedly different from it in essence. The new concept is brilliantly rooted in the vision of 'interfaith dialogue' that is the masterstroke of the Second World Council of Vatican, as well.

Missio Inter Gentes, as a mission that coils around the culture of 'inter', is truly the model of incarnation. It is grounded in the socio-cultural and religious landscape of plurality in Asia in particular and the world in general. Its approach to mission is one of an 'interactive' mode and recognises the identity and dignity of all major and minor streams of faith, ideology and culture. The realisation of *Nostra Aetate* of having 'a common origin, a shared life and a common destiny' with people of all religions, ideologies and cultures is the nucleus of *Missio Inter Gentes*. This is the expressway towards making the family of God the Father on earth. Evidently, expressway is expressly a two-way traffic and family is essentially a multi-way culture.

5.4. The Multi-Religious Implications of *Missio Inter Gentes*

The term that differentiates *Missio Inter Gentes* from *Missio Ad Gentes* is 'inter' and that term is common with inter-faith dialogue. Further, the word 'dialogue', meaning 'across, with, through, between and among' and 'converse or speak', respectively, also refers to the nuances of the term 'inter'. As dialogue is an 'exchange of ideas, views and experiences or conversation between two or more', so also *Missio Inter Gentes* affirms 'sharing in and sharing with' other ideologies and traditions as well as individuals and communities, in an equal and dignified manner.

Both *Missio Inter Gentes* and Multi-Religious Dialogue or interaction honour equal footing as a strategic measure in the process of interaction.

They do not admit superiors or inferiors. On the contrary, they allow the mission to occur as a two-way or multi-way process, in a spirit of partnership. Here, mission becomes an 'interface' or 'crossing point' between or among persons from different backgrounds, beliefs, persuasions and interests. Such a spirit of honest sharing calls for being free of prejudices, fixed positions and vested interests. More importantly, this paradigm of mission integrates the core values of Jesus that makes a Christian missioner stand ever upright on his feet. Evidently, the *Missio Inter Gentes* implies that both or all partners are committed to a mutually enriching and elevating journey of faith, in human as well as spiritual arenas. *Missio Inter Gentes* is truly a 'shared pilgrimage of faith' along and towards the same divine power.

5.5. Christian Mission as Celebrating the Spirit of Togetherness

Being plural is part of the inner dynamics of life. Balancing 'one and many' is the fundamental mission of every human being. The complementary and enriching character of male and female in the wise design of the Creator is a perfect model for harmonising all areas of social life. The diverse civilisations, histories, cultures, languages, philosophies, values and traditions do not in any way contradict each other; they are complementary to each other. Recognising the divine logic and design of diversity is the foundation of faith, which is interactive in its essence.

In addition, the creative interaction among the diversities contributes to the richness of their interactive and harmonious co-existence. When the basic identity of humanity is accepted by all partners further than secondary identities, even of religions, life is bound to become a celebration by itself. As diverse colours and shades of colours are in an exceptional fibre of harmony in the 'rainbow' and they radiate a 'unity and beauty in diversity', so are the diverse perceptions, philosophies, faiths, experiences and convictions, when harmonised, contribute to the 'spirit of togetherness'[50] in life. That defines the dynamics of an interactive faith, as well.

5.6. Christian mission as making the family of God

With a faith that stands firm on the pedestal of the universal Fatherhood of God, 'making the family of God'[51] with people of all peoples as sisters and brothers, along with the entire creation, highlights itself as the core of the Christian mission. People of diverse religious and other communities have to take initiatives to foster communal harmony. Leaders of the respective sectors have to facilitate those around them to share the concerns of their neighbourhoods, work places and other areas of their operation. Personal friendships with persons of other communities will assist collaborative efforts for addressing humanitarian concerns. The courtesy line among communities as well as individuals has not to be violated. The fundamental rights of anyone have not to be infringed upon, too. Anti-social elements have to be kept under control.

Faith-based organisations have to take initiative in interacting with the civil society. An open-ended exchange of views and collaboration with non-religious perspectives cherished by scientists, secularists, humanists and people of all sectors and professions has to be always in the swim. Bridge-building between conservatives and progressives has to be a regular exercise. All communities have to come together for resolving conflicts in the society. Both curative and preventive approaches have to be appropriated for making a harmonious society. Religious leaders, educationists, industrialists, businessmen, medical doctors, social activists and people of other service sections have to join their hands with each other and the administration for making the society more integrated.

Moreover, measures have to be taken for reducing disparities in the society. Discrimination and un-bashed inconsistencies in economic, social, civil, religious, caste and professional areas accelerate tension and turmoil in the society. Therefore, all communities have to join their hands to address the concerns of the displaced, the marginalised, the voiceless and the suppressed sisters and brothers of the country and of the society. Acting on the ideals of the Indian Constitution would be helpful for strengthening national solidarity and integration in India. A shared commitment to 'leaving the place better than one has found it'[52] will go a long way in ensuring the development and progress of the entire society or nation. The Christian mission is all about initiating and living a shared scheme of life that is geared towards making the family of God on earth, in the given society. Obviously, the mission of making the family of God on earth is a shared responsibility, both spiritual and social, along with people of all affiliations.

CONCLUSION

Mission is an ever-evolving happening. A 'sense of mission' is the essence of any mission. Christian mission, rooted in the perennial and stimulating values of Jesus, has to keep evolving according to the time and context of the given society. A fully blossomed Christian mission is never a one-way traffic, but is one that keeps emerging from the partners of faith in the given context, in a spontaneous and interactive fashion. When Christian mission as well as faith is interactive, participatory, collaborative and innovative, faith in God the Father of all, for that matter, in Jesus as well, makes full sense. The mission of Christ gets embodied in a new way of being Christian, every moment, in line with mission among persons and people of all times and places.

'Faith meets faith' is the road to 'harmony of faiths' as well as to spirituality with a fulfillment in life. Interactive processes among the diverse facets of faith pave the way for larger magnitudes as well as higher altitudes in faith and life, at the same time. Faith becomes here an all-inclusive phenomenon that addresses the entire spectrum of human life. Interactive dynamics of life with people of all religious, ideological and cultural persuasions, along with all walks of life, makes the mission of life fully relevant for all. Such is the pedestal of a faith, Jesus Christ conceived, lived and taught; such is the interactive dynamics of Christian mission a Christian disciple shoulders; and such is the mission that would usher in a family of God on earth!

Endnotes

1. J. Andrew, What is Mission?: Theological Explorations, Minneapolis, USA, 2000, p. 13
2. Titus Leonard Presler, Horizons of Mission, Boston, 2001, p. 38
3. William Carl Placher, Jesus the Savior: The Meaning of Jesus Christ for Christian Faith, London, 2001, p. 13
4. Alden Thompson, Who's Afraid of the Old Testament God?, Florida, 2004, p. 86
5. Holy Bible, NIV, Michigan, Mt 1.23, p. 1094
6. Girifalco, Dynamics of Technological Change, New York, 2000, p. 27
7. Angus Stevenson (Ed.), Oxford Dictionary of English, Oxford, 2010, p. 937
8. *Ibid,* p. 628
9. Paul Tillich, Dynamics of Faith, New York, 2001, p. 22
10. Holy Bible, NIV, Michigan, Mt 25.14-24, p. 1127
11. *Ibid,* Jn 10.10, p. 1220
12. *Ibid,* Mt 7.12, p. 1100
13. *Ibid,* Mt 25-41, pp. 1127-28
14. Hugh Nicholson, Comparative Theology and the Problem of Religious Rivalry, New York, 2011, p. 13
15. Merriam Webster Dictionary, Massachusetts, 2004, p. 991
16. Bruce, A. McDowell, Faith in the Mosaic: Finding a Biblical Focus in a Pluralistic World, Washington, 2016, p. 112
17. Beatrice, S. Brown, Case Studies in Evangelism: Effective Principles in Reaching Others, New York, 2008, p. 13
18. T. K. Suman Kumar, India: Unity in Diversity, California, 1992, p. 15
19. Alison, Bailey, Paula, J. Smithka (Ed.), Community, Diversity, and Difference: Implications for Peace, New York, 2002, p. 103
20. Holy Bible, NIV, Michigan, Gen. 1.27, p. 2
21. *Ibid,* 1 Cor 3.16, p. 1298
22. *Ibid,* Mt 25.14-30, p. 1127
23. *Ibid,* Jn 10.10, p. 1220
24. *Ibid,* Mt 7.12, p. 1100
25. *Ibid,* Mt 25.40, p. 1128
26. *Ibid,* Mt 5.45,48, p. 1099
27. *Ibid,* Mt 5.44, p. 1099
28. *Ibid,* Jn 13.34, 35, p. 1226
29. *Ibid,* Lk 23.34, p. 1201

30. *Ibid,* Jn 13.14, p. 1225
31. *Ibid,* Jn 15.15, p. 1228
32. *Ibid,* Lk 15.3-7, p. 1188
33. *Ibid,* Mt 4.23, p. 1097
34. *Ibid,* Rom 1.12.10, p. 1291
35. *Ibid,* Jn 10.30, p. 1222, Mt 25.40, p. 1128
36. Douglas Pratt, The Church and Other Faiths: The World Council of Churches, the Vatican, and Interreligious Dialogue, New York, 2004, p. 13
37. Edward Bristow, Edward W. Bristow (Ed.), New York, 1988, p. 3
38. George Weigel, Witness to Hope: The Biography of Pope John Paul II, New York, 2001, p. 619
39. Holy Bible, NIV, Michigan, Jn 15.26, p. 1228
40. *Ibid,* 1 Cor 12.12-31, p. 1306-07
41. Walter Kasper, Jesus the Christ, New Jersey, 1985, p. 215
42. Holy Bible, NIV, Michigan, Lk 12.56, p. 1185
43. *Ibid,* Mk 2.27, p. 1138
44. George Weigel, Witness to Hope: The Biography of Pope John Paul II, New York, 2001, p. 519
45. Holy Bible, NIV, Michigan, Jn 17.21, p. 1230
46. Thomas Cahill, Pope John XXIII: A Life, London. 2002, p. 79
47. http://www.catholicnewsagency.com/news/churches-families-must-be-places-of-welcome-pope-says-13552/
48. Austin Flannery (Ed.), Ad Gentes Divinitus: Decree on the Church's Missionary Activity, Dublin, 2014
49. Jonathan Yun-Ka Tan, *Missio Inter Gentes*: Towards a New Paradigm in the Mission Theology of the Federation of Asian Bishops' Conferences, Hong Kong, 2004, p. 9
50. L.M. Singhvi, Towards global Togetherness, New Delhi, 2002, p. 21
51. Daniel Bush, Noel S. Due, Embracing God as Father: Christian Identity in the Family of God, Bellingham, 2014, p. 9
52. Jon Gordon, The Hard Hat: 21 Ways to Be a Great Teammate, New Jersey, 2015, p. 72

(Published in Re-visiting Pastoral Care (Book) – published by Orient Publication, Orient Theological College, Shillong – in September 2017)

Chapter - 12

Christian Contribution to Harmonious Living in India

INTRODUCTION

Christianity in India meant a 'large worldview' and an 'all-inclusive way of life'. Its motto of 'universal love and service of all' was foundational not only to the sectors of education, medical care, social welfare, special care, etc, but to 'harmonious living' among communities of diverse affiliations. The versatile characteristics of the Christian community facilitated 'harmonious coexistence with other communities', by way of reaching out to one and all, especially the unreached sections. The catch-phrase of the above 'rainbow culture' has been 'inclusive thinking and harmonious living' and this is capable of gearing all affiliations towards a common destiny as well as towards a rare 'beauty' inherent in 'unity in diversity'. Undoubtedly, the Christian community, through its very being and mission, has contributed immensely to the spirit of *'Vasudhaiv Kutumbakam'* in India, by filtering through the diverse faith traditions and social ideologies as well as the rich variety of cultures.

It could be stated with hardly any exaggeration that the advent of Christianity in India brought a 'culture with a difference', in several respects. The Christian culture, in the general sense, meant mostly a 'larger way of looking at life'. Ideas about God, life, creation, human relations, society, nature, development, ethical values, spirituality, etc. composed for the country fairly a comprehensive tradition.

The notion of 'universal love and service of all' contributed immensely to a variety of vital sectors, like literacy, education, art, literature, medical care, social welfare, special care, religion and ideology. One significant area of Christian contribution that is less observed but is the finest as well as the most integral is the 'promotion of harmonious living among diverse communities' through interaction and personal relations as well as through service and collaboration. Obviously, this is an area that has both particular as well as general implications.

1. CHRISTIAN FOUNDATIONS FOR HARMONIOUS LIVING

1.1. God as Father

Thinking large, as large as the world is, is innate to being a Christian. Christian worldview is grounded in its notion of God as 'father', as experienced by Jesus[1]. The word 'Father' is from the family sector and it stands for the largest relational network in the world. It is like opening a large umbrella, under which the entire human society can gather together. This idea is the religious, ideological and cultural foundation for 'harmonious living' in the context of the world as well as within the Christian limits.

Whether God is father or mother, male or female, how he or she generates children, etc are irrelevant questions. What makes sense is, human beings can reach out to him in a relational way as if he is father. Such a 'father' is the point of reference above all and for all. Human beings enjoy the 'freedom of the children of God' in terms of God, in a vertical way. At the same time, this notion has comprehensive implications towards making a large 'family' out of the human society, in the context of the entire existential reality.

1.2. God reflected in human beings

God is reflected in human beings in a two-dimensional manner. First and foremost, man is created in the 'image and likeness of God.'[2] As a piece of art reflects the artist that is inherent in it, so does creation in relation to the Creator. Human beings radiate the characteristics of God, in terms of life, light, spirit and relations as well as of the diverse and complementary genders that share in the creative role of God.

The very fact that the likeness of the Creator is found in the creation, it necessarily follows that the entire creation as well as the individual items is the 'dwelling place of God'. Human beings, in a very special way, are 'living temples of God,'[3] by virtue of the rational, volitional and spiritual character they bear. The places of worship of all religious communities are mere symbols made of brick and stone and are mere indicators of the real temple of God. The harmonious setting of the human society emerges from the living presence of the divine being spread all over the creation as well as in living beings. The 'spirit of harmony' that prevails in the human society and in the creation is the ever-living testimony of the presence of God.

1.3. The 'Catholic' brotherhood of man

The Christian understanding of God as Father has direct bearing on the 'fraternal attitude' among human beings. The implication of the vertical idea makes sense only in terms of a horizontal application. Christian culture is basically 'catholic' in character and that would mean 'universal', 'general', 'whole', 'all-embracing' 'liberal', 'inclusive', 'having larger interests', 'beyond the boundaries', etc[4]. The universal outlook that emerges from an 'inclusive thinking' is the corresponding parallel between relation to God and relation to other human beings and to the creation.

There is no separate track for devotion to God in the Christian tradition. 'Loving one's brothers and sisters is equal to loving God'. The eternal mandates of Jesus 'love your neighbour,'[5] 'love your enemy'[6] and 'do to the other what you wish the other do you'[7] establish this truth in a categorical manner. In the backdrop of these mandates, it clearly follows that one's way to the heavenly father is through one's brothers and sisters only. This calls for a fundamental duty to strive for 'harmonious living' with other individuals and communities.

1.4. Preferential option for the weaker sections

Option for the weaker sections was the basic maxim that motivated Christian activities in favour of those who were pushed to the margins of the society. The source of strength for extending a preferential space for the poor, the voiceless, the suppressed, etc in the horizontal context of life is the words of Jesus 'whatever you did for one of the least of these brothers (and sisters) of mine, you did for me.'[8]

Schemes for reaching the unreached, as in liberating the tribals from money-lenders and landlords and helping the *dalits* rise above the clutches of suppression, are notable examples of the groundbreaking contribution of the Christian community at the level of grassroots. Such measures, no doubt, were geared towards social transformation that accelerated 'living in harmony' with each other as well as putting the society back to its social equilibrium.

The poor and the downtrodden in villages have been organised by the Christian community and were empowered with strategies for self-advancement, like liberating themselves from oppressive forces, collective action, saving for tomorrow, income-generating projects, self-help groups, etc. No wonder, such initiatives earned the anger of the rich and high caste groups, who, in the disguise of religious freedom and the so-called conversion, dared to attack and attempted to demoralise Christians, in order to re-establish their hegemony.

All the same, it could be stated without any exaggeration that if Christianity is anything special and stands to this day, it is the 'preferential concern for the weaker sections'[9] of the society, to a very great extent. Through such painstaking efforts, Christianity has contributed immensely to fostering 'social harmony' in the country, as well.

1.5. Silent and unassuming style of work

Much of the contribution the Christian community has been making, especially in rural as well as special areas of social uplift, remain unobserved. This is because of the fact that the Church has been shying away from publicity and preferred to work silently as the leaven. This has also been motivated by the teaching of Jesus 'let the left hand not know what the right hand is doing.'[10] No wonder, such humble and spiritual ways go very much unnoticed in a world, which has an extra sense of ego and a high degree of publicity-mongering.

Besides, the Church has not been politically and economically tuned enough to command visibility and power in the society. The involvement of the Church in the political and corporate sectors was almost nil or insignificant. Unlike the way adopted by most NGOs, it has not been the strategy of the Church to seek high profile propaganda, especially for services at grass root levels. [11]

All the same, it cannot in any way be denied that the unassuming and even invisible contribution of the Church has been making, though in a gradual manner and in limited contexts, fairly a commendable impact towards transforming the society in India, that too of a qualitative level.

2. COMMUNITY CHARACTERISTICS FOR HARMONIOUS LIVING

2.1. The Community mindset of St. Thomas Christians

Saint Thomas, one of the prominent disciples of Jesus, made history as he landed at the coastal areas of Kerala in the early fifties of the first century. The Christian community that emerged over there had certain unique characteristics. In other words, Saint Thomas Christians or Syro-Malabar Christians represent a single ethnic group, very much tracing back to Brahmin origin. It was known for its capacity for 'harmonious living' with people of other cultures[12].

The Christian culture of Saint Thomas Christians has been a harmonious blend of East Syrian influences and local customs, along with elements derived from indigenous Indian and European colonial contacts. They adopted Malayalam, the local language of Kerala, for day-to-day means of interaction. Living in harmony with others was one of the top priorities of their life.

St Thomas Christians co-existed harmoniously with the local Hindu community, commendably well. Many of the religious, social and cultural traditions of Saint Thomas Christians are the adapted forms of the local Hindu heritage. The values of hospitality, toleration and acceptance of others lived by the community made way for a pleasant blending of the East and the West, too.

The singular record of 'harmonious coexistence among diverse religious communities' in India Kerala has been proudly celebrating is to be credited to the account of Saint Thomas Christians, to a great extent[13].

2.2. The larger setting of the Roman Catholic Christian community

Francis Xavier came to India in the 15th century and started his mission from the western belt of the country. The Roman Christian tradition that took off with him made several landmark contributions to the mainstream culture of India, especially in the educational, social and cultural fields.

Reaching out to the remotest villages of the country with service schemes, in addition to establishing in the cities and towns of the country, was a master-plan the Roman Catholic Church implemented[14]. Establishing the Christian presence far and wide as an indispensible part of the country was the most observable achievement of the above tradition.

2.3. The organisational set-up of the Christian community

The catholic community is known to be the most organised society in the world. This reality applies to the rest of the Christian community in a general sense, as well. The fact that it stood the test of time for the last 20 centuries certifies the statement very convincingly. The most local unit of the community is parish. There are town level units called vicariates or *forane* churches. The city level unit is called diocese. There are also archdioceses, regional or state level units and national apex body. There are also several hundreds of congregations of committed men and women, who have been pioneers in outstanding contributions in almost all areas.

Democratic processes are applied in the functioning of the community from top to bottom. Each level has office bearers for administration, departments for coordination, experts for technical assistance, inclusive bodies comprising of men, women and youth, training centers called seminaries, catechists at the grassroots, and the like. It is the strength of the organisation that is really responsible for accountability, quality, efficiency, etc. Many communities and organisations, including RSS, have copied or learned from the organisational dynamics of the catholic community. The organisational set-up of the Catholic Church has influenced, to a great extent, the organisational dynamics of the country in various respects and has contributed to a related manner of living, as well[15].

2.4. The spirit of service in the Christian community

The spirit of service is a quality that is innate to the Christian community. The foundation for the same is the motivating words of Jesus 'whatever you did for one of the least of these brothers (and sisters) of mine, you did for me'[16] and 'if anyone wants to be the first, he must be the very last, and the servant of all.'[17] By washing the feet of the disciples, Jesus presented an outstanding model of service and exhorted them to 'wash one another's feet.'[18] The 'fibre of service' reflected in the Christian community evolves from the ever-living source of the deeds and words of Jesus.

Christian approach, on the whole, to other communities was notably inclusive, in terms of service. All the service sectors, educational, medical, social, special and other, were 'extended to all communities', without any discrimination[19]. The deprived sections, like low castes, women, prisoners, lepers, the old, the orphans, the dying, the disabled, the addicts, the mentally challenged, the exploited, etc., received even extra care, too. All these services, at the end of the day, have been oriented to making a 'better and more harmonious' society.

2.5. Exceptional models of harmonising

Christian culture, from the roots, has been greatly non-reactive, peace-loving and even forgiving. The words of Jesus 'blessed are the peace-makers, they will be called sons of God'[20] coupled with the greatly inspiring gesture of Jesus 'Father, forgive them, for they do not know what they are doing'[21] are the exceptional foundation for a peace-filled way of conducting one's life.

The Christian community has been accommodative, tolerant and capable of restraint, even in cases of deep-seated discrimination and brutal attacks. The Christian community did not retaliate in a violent way either, after the random attacks on priests, nuns, churches and institutions of the church that have been taking place time and again or even after the terrible atrocities perpetrated against it in Orissa. Instead of reacting, the Christian community chose to appropriate only non-violent measures in response to the same.

Further, the Christian community demonstrated commendable models of transforming the society in the positive manner, in line with the genius of its basic tradition. Extending 'forgiveness to the murderer of Steins by his wife' and 'tying *raakhee* on the wrist of the murderer of Sister

Rani Maria in the jail by her sister' are two exceptional and spiritually motivated instances of the truly 'Christian' way of treating even the offender positively[22].

Mother Theresa emerged as an icon of service of the poorest of the poor, the orphaned, the disowned and the dying and the ensuing congregation of the Sisters of Charity[23]. She received a 'call within a call' to pick up human beings from the dust bin, from the railway tracks, from the road sides and the dark corners of the world. It was not important for her what community they came from. The only thing that mattered to her was that she saw Jesus on their face and therefore she wanted to extend to them the dignity they deserved as human beings and as children of God the Father. Hers has been an elevated and highly laudable contribution to harmony in social life, on behalf of the Christian community.

Without a doubt, through such outstanding 'Jesus-like' attitudes speak volumes of the Christian response to balancing the derailed situations of the society. Such gestures contribute to fostering 'peaceful co-existence' and harmonious living, in a larger and effective manner, too.

2.6. Community-minded culture

The Christian community is a worldwide community; it is international in character and reach-out; and it is the largest single community in the world. In other words, Christians are oriented to and have the privileged facility to think larger as a community and as a world society. Mixing with other communities as well as nations is mostly in its basic dynamism. Interacting with people of other languages, ideologies, faiths and cultures is more natural to it.

Christian culture is very much 'community-minded'[24]. The social dimension of life is perhaps the strongest in the Christian tradition. The spirit of world-level brotherhood emerges from the relational understanding of God. Worship in the church is communitarian. There is no discrimination in principle among the different social strata of the community. Church-going is not only for prayer and worship but also for socialising. Christianity, especially Catholic Church, is the most organised religious community in the world. 'Community-consciousness' is an exceptional strength of the Christian community. 'Harmonious living with all communities' is an extended form of the sense of being a community[25].

2.7. Churches are open to one and all

Churches are basically a place frequented by Christians for worship and prayer. They are also symbols of an all-inclusive goodwill. They are welcoming places for people of all persuasions of faith and ideology. There is hardly any restriction for anything. Entry is allowed even with shoe-*chappal* on. There is no mandatory head-covering required for anyone. Shooting a video or film also is allowed in the Church. Church campuses also are often well-kept with good gardens and they attract people of all affiliations.

Churches are widely accepted as places where peace, neatness, order, artistic presentations, etc are regular features. People of all faiths come to churches, all over and in large numbers, especially at Christmas times. There are individuals and families from other communities who come to the church to pray and to light candles on occasions that are important to them. Among places of worship of all religions, Churches are the most popular spots for people of all religious persuasions. According to a social survey, Christmas, as a religious festival, brings people of all communities together the most, worldwide and India included[26].

2.8. A fairly enlightened and integrated community

The Christian community is a community that is fairly educated and enlightened. Primary education is highly stressed and promoted free of charge, especially in rural areas and therefore, only a small percent of people are deprived of it. The enrolment system of the Christian community in its smallest units called parishes and the regular Sunday gatherings for worship and religious education not only keeps the community together, but also fosters its level of general enlightenment. The number of beggars or very poor people is considerably low, in relation to most communities, as well.

Besides, the Christian community is an integrated community from various angles. It does not normally have too rich and too poor people in it. If there are a few highly well off people, they also mostly have some way of sharing their riches with the poor. Similarly, it does not have many people of too high and too low profile. Ruling out either extreme, the Christian community remains fairly an integrated one. Moreover, it receives hardly any financial scheme from the government. The Christian community has a system of regular contribution to the church from within, which makes it self-supportive and integrated further[27].

2.9. Quality of the Christian ethos

The Christian ethos is comprised of certain significant elements, like respect for life, dignity of life, dignity of work, fundamental rights, justice, service, love, equality and special concern for the disadvantaged sections[28]. Christians, by and large, are open-minded enough not to stick to their own group. They do not make Christian colonies, like Muslims, if I can say so. The degree of superstitious behaviour is relatively much less in the

Christian community. Besides, the freedom and capacity for open thinking is perhaps the highest in the Christian community, in comparison to almost all the religious systems of the world. Moreover, there is lot of scope for self-criticism in the Christian community.

The Christian community has been conducting institutions and centres for people of all communities, without any discrimination. Two-thirds of the educational and other institutions conducted are in the rural areas. There are also professional, technical and vocational training institutes and colleges run by it. The scheduled castes, scheduled tribes and other backward classes are the most taken care of by the Christian community. Programmes for the poor and the downtrodden, like self-help groups, employment schemes, rehabilitation centres, centres for lepers, centres for the terminally ill and counseling centres, highlight the quality of the Christian ethos, in a special way[29]. Mother Theresa remains a champion of the superb quality of Christian ethos in the most realistic way.

2.10. Extra-ordinary traits

What is extra-ordinarily praise-worthy of the Christian, especially of the catholic community is, in spite of being a tiny minority; it has been making significant contribution to the all-round development of the country in diverse areas[30]. On account of the widely acclaimed traits of self-respect, dignity, hard work, honesty, simplicity, straight-forwardness, justice and fairness, Christians are mostly preferred even in high profile offices of the country, at the centre and the states alike.

Christians are on the whole law-abiding and fair-behaving citizens of the country. They are more 'secular' in the way they conduct themselves in social life. They are relatively less in number in the crime sector. They are mostly not found in the notorious areas of the country, like corruption, rape, terrorism, adulteration, breaking laws, etc. Christians are not very politically tuned as a community. Though they are politically literate, they do not cluster themselves into parties or unions normally. Besides, Christian contribution to development and progress of the country is immense, both from the west as well as from India[31].

2.11. Leadership and contribution of the committed class

The religious personnel of priests and nuns, approximately 1.3 million of them, who are committed to the service of the society on a life-time basis, have been making an unparalleled contribution to the country[32]. They work in different fields of social engagement and live a peaceful life themselves and promote a mindset of peaceful life. A considerable percentage of priest and nuns works in the remotest areas of the country. They share in the basic struggles of the people. Their contribution to agriculture, horticulture, infrastructure for basic needs, etc is immense.

A good number of priests and nuns are qualified to the first degree in some discipline or other and most of them are professionally qualified in some sector or other. Some of the most scholarly books in the areas of philosophy, politics, sociology, culture, art, literature, religion, spirituality, etc have been written by Christian missionaries from India as well as from other countries[33]. Learning the local language, developing script, writing grammar books and dictionaries, inventing printing press, etc have been an exceptional achievement of Christians. All these amount to Christian contribution to building up of the nation and to harmony in social life.

2.12. Orientation towards education and social change

It requires no mention that the Christian community made an impressive contribution to literacy and primary education. The literacy rate was 14 during Independence and the current rate is above 60%. Christianity can be proud of having played a vital role in it. What is more praiseworthy is the fact that among the schools run by the catholic community 70% is in rural areas and they directly serve the interests of the poor, especially the *dalits*, the *aadivaasees* and other deprived groups[34]. Another noteworthy fact is that nearly 80% of the students in Christian institutions are from other communities. They belong to all religions, castes, classes, tribes and cultures.

The Educational endeavour made a historical breakthrough into the caste system of the country by 'breaking the monopoly of a single privileged caste and by decentralising and democratising education'. This achievement made it possible for *dalits* and tribals to attain social mobility in life. Education of the masses in urban and particularly in rural areas has been the backbone of the development of India. This was a new paradigm for social change in India that contributed immensely to a modern era for India[35]. No doubt, the contribution of the Christian community in this sector stands significant.

2.13. The large mosaic of diversity in the Christian community in India

India is a land, with a singular mosaic of immense landscapes, climates, races, ethnic origins, creeds, colours, castes, classes, dress patterns, food tastes, ideologies, languages, cultures, traditions, and the like, is an unparalleled laboratory of give and take, hybrid blending and composite existence[36]. This extra-ordinary characteristic is reflected in the Christian community in India, as well.

The Christian community in India is spread over the entire country and is immensely diverse in its characteristics. It comprises of people with different ethnic traits, caste or tribal backgrounds, languages and dialects, ideologies and cultures, food and dress habits, social customs and traditions as well as levels and types of faith practices. Though the Christian community in India is one, it is indeed a celebration of 'unity in diversity', after the fashion of the genius of the country, so much so that no community in India appears to be as diverse as it is[37].

2.14. Higher degree of women empowerment

Though the Christian community has a long way to go yet in empowering women, the position of women in the Christian community is fairly commendable. Several women of the Christian community find themselves among the noted administrators, leaders, thinkers, educationists, professors, writers, medical professionals, legal experts, industrialists and social workers and activists[38]. Pathological anti-women practices, like female feticide, gender discrimination and dowry-related casualties, are almost nil in the Christian community.

Kerala stands a role model and is the only state where the number of girls exceeds the number of boys, 1084 girls for 1000 boys, as per the census of 2011[39]. There is hardly any girl in Kerala who does not go to school because she is not a boy. The nursing profession took off in Kerala from the Christian community as a female movement. The sense of equality in gender in Kerala is basically a contribution of the Christian community, that too, of the Saint Thomas Christian community[40].

The organised and conscious efforts for making an inclusive society with women is clearly reflected in the formation of Church structures, like parish council, Diocesan Pastoral Council, etc. This was in view of ensuring equal representation in policy-formulation and decision-making in micro, semi-macro and macro structures. Such drastic measures for empowering women by the Catholic and Christian communities are commendable models for making participatory and harmonious society.

Working for the abolition of girl child feticide, education of girl children in schools, conducting adult education classes for women, supporting women to fight against discriminatory practices, empowering women through self-help groups, fostering the on-going education of women through awareness programmes, etc are schemes that are directly oriented to empowering women and thus balancing the genders.

The fact that almost half of the catholic colleges of the country are for women and one third are mixed as well as a very high percent of them are staffed and even managed by women is enough proof for the significant space accorded to women in the Christian community.

2.15. Secular outlook and national consciousness

Christian community has significantly contributed to strengthening the secular outlook enshrined in the Constitution of India[41]. The secular character of the Republic is a positive force for peace and communal harmony in a multicultural and multi-religious society that India is.

Using national anthem in educational institutions and at programmes, hoisting national flag at schools, colleges, churches and other institutions on the occasion of national festivals and celebrating national festivals and dates of importance at almost all Christian centres are common practices seen in the Christian community. The secular outlook paves the way for national consciousness.

2.16. Church gives way for national interests and public good

In 1962, the Indian National Committee for Space Research (INCOSPAR) was established. *Homi Bhabha*, then the father of India's nuclear programme, along with *Vikram Sarabhai*, took into consideration number of sites situated in Kerala to construct a rocket station. After long discussion they both finalised Thumba as the appropriate place. Thumba was a small village, until then, known only for fishing and situated near the Thiruvananthapuram airport in Kerala. The site for the newly built rocket launching pad was located amidst coconut groves.

St Mary Magdalene's Catholic Church was situated there. It served as the main office for the scientists. The bishop's house was converted into a workshop. A cattle shed became the laboratory in which the young Indian scientists worked on the first sounding rockets. The first sounding rocket (Nike-Apache) was launched on 21 November 1963. That marked the beginning of a new era for India, with multi-national collaboration and over 350 rockets from Thumba[42].

I have the pleasure of having heard the genius scientist and former President of India *APJ Abdul Kalam* a few times from dignified platforms profusely appreciating the parish priest who not only gladly agreed to transfer the Church from the spot but also facilitated the entire process in converting the site from religion to science. He is never tired of appreciating the larger faith of the Christian community that is capable of giving way for national interests and is ready to highlight that model for a faith that enables public good.

3. INTERACTIVE PROCESSES FOR HARMONIOUS LIVING

3.1. Learning the languages of other communities

Christians, especially those of the Syro-Malabar community from Kerala, are known for their migrant character. They have migrated to most of the countries of the world as well as to almost all the cities and towns of the country. They pick up the local, regional and national languages and get fairly well-settled in the respective area[43]. Christians who have migrated from other areas share this quality, as well. The language of the place facilitates them to get networked with the people of the area and to get culturally adapted in all aspects of social life. Learning the language of the other is 'dialogue of tongue' or 'dialogue of letters' or 'dialogue of language'[44].

Learning Urdu offers a double benefit-socio-cultural and religious. Urdu is a tent language, born of '*Arabi*-Persian and Hindustani' languages. The emotional, poetic and musical appeal of Urdu has enriched Hindi so much that Hindi poetry today is one of the best poetries of the world. Urdu is gaining more and space in the country as well as in Hindi. Facility for Urdu by learning it as well as through Hindi enhances relations with Muslims and thus contributes to mutual understanding and harmonious living.

3.2. Indian Studies and Cultural Adaptation

Lots of priests and nuns as well as Christian people pursue higher studies in Indian disciplines. The Indian colleges and universities offer them opportunities for closer interaction with Indian ideas, symbols and categories. The personal contacts thus made serve very enriching opportunities of give and take in the area of cultural transaction. Such cultural exchange is 'dialogue of learning' or 'dialogue of adaptation' or 'dialogue of transformation' or 'dialogue of cultural integration'.

Specialising Indian languages and literatures, poetry, music, dance, art, philosophy, cultures and religions as well as live in interactions and exposures to the regional and local contexts served a natural setting for cultural adaptation in diverse areas[45]. The cultural adaptation has different dimensions, in line with the variations of the ethnic and social genius of the respective regions of the country.

3.3. Specialising the sacred languages of other religions

The ancient languages in which the different religious traditions evolved are considered sacred languages by the respective religious tradition. The original languages of the Sacred Scripture of the respective tradition too are the same as above. They are mostly called '*dev-vanees*' or 'God's languages'. Sanskrit, *Prakrit*, *Pali*, *Gurumukhi*, Hebrew, *Dari*, Arabic, Syriac, Latin, etc are sacred languages of different religious communities, in more or less degrees. Learning these sacred languages is 'dialogue of sacred tongues' or 'dialogue of divine messages'.

In the last decades of the 20th century, and in the 21st century in special, Christian interest in learning the sacred languages of other religious communities has produced a considerable number of scholars on Sanskrit, *Prakrit*, *Pali*, *Gurumukhi*, Hebrew, Arabic, etc[46]. This achievement has been contributing to the knowledge of those scriptures and of the universal values that are enshrined in it. It has also been a great strength for enhancing the mutual understanding and fellowship of the communities that hold those languages sacred and motivating sources for life.

3.4. Specialising other religious scriptures and tenets

The Catholic community in India in particular and the Christian community in general, have fairly a good number of scholars on other religions today. It is a heartening note that this number is gradually but steadily on the increase. The openness and commitment to the religious, social and cultural traditions of other communities is growing much deeper and wider in its dimensions and degrees. Specialisation of other religious scriptures is 'dialogue of research' or 'dialogue of sacred ideas' or 'dialogue of divine messages'[47].

Their personal friendships with people of other religions, learned discourses, scholarly articles and books and efforts for collaboration with them have facilitated not only bettering the relations with people of other religious communities but also in fostering harmonious living with them, in many ways.

3.5. Study of other religions at Christian Seminaries

Study of all religions has been introduced in Christian seminaries in India as mandatory. This is a trend that has been motivated by the liberal inter-faith perspectives of the Second World Council of Vatican (1964) and the same has been progressively considered a basic academic requirement for pastoral undertaking in the Church. Regular courses on other religions are offered to the students. Specialists on different religions are engaged as part of the staff, residential or visiting. Many students attempt dissertations on themes that research into the diverse aspects of other religious perspectives in a comparative way. Study of other religions is 'dialogue of religious learning' or 'dialogue of religious search'[48].

Besides, seminars and workshops are also organised involving experts and leaders of different religions on themes that highlight differences as well as commonalities and are enriching for all. Several students, guided by the staff, take up visits of places of worship of other religions and interactions with people of other religions, too. Such initiatives suggest better prospects for closer affiliations between Christians and people of all communities in the future[49]. Nevertheless, there is still a long way to go, it is heartening that lot of efforts in this area are in the process.

3.6. Indian Christian Ashrams

The initiatives of the Christian community in developing Indian Christian spirituality took shape in the launching of Indian Christian Ashrams. Several priests and nuns emerged as *Gurus* and *Achaaryas* after close interaction, study and even religious initiation (*diksha*) from noted Hindu ashrams and Gurus[50]. These ashrams adopted Indian categories and symbols into Christian rituals and prayers. They adapted Christian concepts to the genius of Indian cultures, as well. Christian ashrams are examples of 'dialogue of applied religious living' or 'dialogue of alternative spiritual experiences'.

The Christian ashrams are many-sided centres. They have often large plots of land and they cultivate whatever they need in their land. The inmates enjoy unpolluted produce of their land. They share the same with people who lived around them, as well. They are also harmonious environments for a large variety of animals and birds that are grown there. They are a home for lot of other living beings, too. The ashrams maintain friendliness with not only their neighbourhoods, but also with all those who visit them[51]. With its free atmosphere, homeliness is characteristic of the Indian Christian ashrams.

Moreover, Christian ashrams are substantial centres of study, research, hard work, discipline and spirituality. They are powerful centres of interaction and unity among various religious communities. They radiate an Indian and acceptable picture of Christianity for all. By and large, Indian ashrams are significant centres of fostering good will and harmony as well as environmental harmony. Most of the Christian ashrams of the country have been making far-reaching and outstanding contribution to the country.

3.7. Interaction on religious themes among communities

The new wave of inter-faith dialogue is to be attributed to the revolutionary perspective that evolved in the Second World Catholic Council of Vatican. It is grounded in the Christian worldview of considering God as Father and human beings and the rest of the creation as brothers and sisters. The main focus of the perspective is dialogue between traditions of religion and faith. Later, it also included dialogue with people of non-religious ideologies, as well.

Faith has both personal and communitarian dimensions. Interaction among people on themes that are related religion and faith, in terms of one's perspectives, experiences, aspirations, doctrines and practices, has been the core focus of the exercise. This is 'dialogue of interface' or 'dialogue of ideas' or 'dialogue of sharing'[52].

Dialogue on religious matters opens new windows and corridors in the religious sector. A new way of looking at life and its details is the spontaneous outcome. Dialogue involves listening to each other, understanding each other, sharing with each other, getting transformed to each other and getting enriched.

Interaction also takes the partners ahead through working together and making a joint journey of life to the same divine destiny. It is a spiritual journey. Interaction among persons of diverse communities on religious themes has helped eliminating prejudices and distance. It has facilitated fostering a spirit of peaceful and harmonious co-existence[53].

3.8. Personal friendships with persons of all communities

Personal friendship with people of other communities, religious and other, is the most down to earth, practical and effective measure for peaceful co-existence. This is 'dialogue of friendship' or 'dialogue of love'[54]. Everything happens among friends. Getting into a friendship is a gradual process. It could be compared to mighty and long-lasting banyan trees. When mutual understanding develops, barriers disappear. Besides, differences of perceptions, convictions and commitments get transformed into factors of enrichment.

People of all sectors of the Christian community are seen getting into thick friendships with people of other communities of faith, caste, language, culture, and the like. This phenomenon applies to other communities also, in varying degrees and dimensions. But, for the Christian community, it is more a wide-spread happening.

Often, the affection, sharing, fellow-feeling and collaboration seen among friendships between people of different communities are stronger than that with the same kind. This personal friendship, spread over the country and the society, is a less visible but a time-tested and large network that balances the communal disturbances in favour of harmonious living[55].

3.9. Neighbourly relations with other communities

Christians are not inclined to make their private colonies and they normally stay amidst other communities. This is in fact 'dialogue of life' or 'dialogue of relations' or 'dialogue of sharing life situations'. This is a commendable approach as regards establishing neighbourly relations with people of all ideologies and affiliations. Residing in a cluster, Muslims are often seen doing that, causes distance from other communities, instigates prejudiced attitudes and invites unnecessary tension.

The Christian faith in God as Father of all and the resulting attitude of considering all human beings and other items of nature brothers and sisters, coupled with its logic of extending service to one and all has enabled them to extend good neighbourly relations with people of all affiliations[56]. Harmonious living is the positive outcome of such an approach to life.

3.10. Working together with people of other communities

Christians rub shoulders with people of all communities in offices, factories and other places of work. They are often seen freely mixing with their collaborators, irrespective of their personal affiliation. They work together with others with fairly a high degree of facility. Certain qualities of hard work, efficiency, integrity and broad-mindedness contribute to the excellence of the group work as well as to the sense of being well-integrated in the work place.

Working together with others is in fact 'dialogue of deeds' or 'dialogue of action' or 'dialogue of working together'[57]. Group work is dialogical in its basic character. Unity of purpose is a foundational factor for the quality of output. The friendly atmosphere in the work place contributes to good results in work. Besides, the meeting of ideas, traditions and cultures that takes place spontaneously through informal interaction and friendly ways, without a doubt, influences harmonious living among diverse traditions. The Christian presence in this area has been significantly noteworthy, so much so that Christians command a considerable degree of preference in several prestigious offices.

3.11. Inter-community marriages

Marriage between persons from different communities of faith and cultures is very much a modern phenomenon. Exceptions of the earlier times have become an increasingly usual practice today, though majority of people is still for the traditional way. Arranged marriages seem to pave the way for or rather accommodate love marriages as a manner with a substantial logic in it. The few events of honour killings that are found in certain groups need to be considered only pathological instances that are born of insecurity, illiteracy and vested interest. These instances are only a passing phenomenon.

Since love is the most common and basic denominator in life, the sense of harmony that can be attained through the same is capable of guiding the destinies of the society that is more harmonious as well as more inclusive and interactive. This is 'dialogue of love' or 'dialogue of creativity' or 'dialogue of intimacy'. Inter-faith marriages are blessed both in Churches and in other places of worship[58]. What is required in these happenings is a maturity that can make the couple and the respective families withstand the changing times. The natural ice-breaking, if not shock-treatment, that is involved between communities is destined to break open the traditional taboos and eventually usher in a culture of harmonious living among the humans.

3.12. Partnership in social concerns and joint initiatives

Christians engage in partnerships with persons and organisations of other communities in several enterprises. People from other communities compose majority of people who work in Christian institutions. This endeavour involves sharing the concerns of life with each other as well as sharpening unity of purpose. The stronger the mutual understanding, the more effective is the partnership between them. Joining hands with the other for addressing the concerns of the society is an opportunity for sharing with each other one's faith, perspectives, values, experiences and aspirations of the other. Christian partnership with people of other communities that stands the test of time has been a great contributor to social harmony.

'Joint schemes for human wellbeing' is indeed emerging as the focal point in inter-faith engagement in India, too. The question is 'how to enhance the quality of human living in the country and in the society?' This becomes possible when one is rightly motivated and empowered by one's faith. 'Joining hands with other believers and human beings' in view of humanitarian purposes is, in its turn, is the test of faith, as well. A communion of perspectives enhances the quality shared action and the welfare of the human society. This is in fact a 'dialogue of partnership' or 'dialogue of unity of purpose' or 'dialogue of social commitment'[59].

3.13. Impact on the Hindu religious revival movements

The Hindu religious revival movements that emerged in the pre-independent India seem to be considerably influenced by Christian ethos. The Christian models of thought had a regular interplay with the social, economic, political and cultural arenas of the Hindu life style. The natural outcome of this cultural transaction served an effective answer to the existential needs of the people, too. The series of reformers who emerged on the religious and social spectrum articulated this fact. The impetus for the revival movements was definitely Christian worldview[60], values and practices. The proponents of the revival movements had profuse exposure to the Christian west, through personal education and interaction, and the same occasioned them to imbibe lots of values of life that are different from that of India.

First and foremost, ***Raja Ram Mohan Roy***, who founded *Brahmo Samaj*, reinterpreted Vedas and reformulated Hinduism; in the light of several elements from the Western and Christian models he had assimilated[61].

While stressing monotheism, he denied the theory and system of caste. He downplayed child marriage and *Sati,* which was the practice of burning the widow in the funeral pyres of her husband. He not only advocated Western education, but ran several schools himself. He did not have any feeling of antagonism towards other religions and cultures, either.

The second icon of reform in the Hindu tradition was ***Dayananda Saraswati***, founded *Arya Samaj*[62]. He revisited Vedas and as a result condemned idolatry and highlighted monotheism. He ruled out caste-system and child-marriage as having nothing to do with Vedas. All the same, he instigated a militant spirit of Hinduism, which wouldn't tolerate anyone to even talk against it. Stress on Vedas slipped into an aggressive as well as arrogant attitude.

Ramakrishna Paramhansa was very much influenced by Jesus Christ and Christianity[63]. He confesses to have had a vision of Jesus. He took a 'vow of *sanyasa*' on Christmas Eve. This fact motivated *Ramkrishna Mission* to celebrate Christmas on 24 December. Besides, *Ramakrishna* contended that 'love of one's neighbour' is the only form of adoring God. *Swami Vivekananda* held *advaitic* principle for the basic unity of God and creatures and introduced the idea of social service to mankind. He founded Ramakrishna Mission on Christmas Eve in 1897, too. Several schemes of charitable and social work are being pursued by Ramakrishna Mission, today.

Ram Krishna Mission has imbibed a very high degree of inspiration from the Catholic community, especially of its priestly system. The idea of mission, seminary studies, the triple vows of celibacy-obedience-poverty, social service schemes, transfer of duties and place, etc are some of the major visible influences RK mission has appropriated from the Catholic community, though minor adaptations are made by it in course of time[64].

Swami Vivekananda, who was previously known as *Narendranath Datta*, was inspired by *Ramakrishna Paramahamsa* and struck a balance between the reformatory character of *Brahmo Samaj* and the militant spirit of *Arya Samaj*[65]. The complementary character of religions and the ecumenical spirit among them articulated his attitude towards other religions. The overtones of Hindu-Christian cultural transaction in such an outlook are more than clear. He underlined mystical experience as the validating factor amidst the different sectarian Hindu gods and cults as well as the religious rivalry between Christians and Muslims

Brahma Kumari *Eeshwareey Viswavidyaalay* is an Indian edition of the priest-nun system of the Catholic Church[66]. Though, they have *sari* and *kurta-pijama* as their dress, they have adopted the traditional white dress of the priests and nuns. They have appropriated the vow of chastity for *brahma kumars* and *kumaris*, which is not the basic tradition of the land. They seem to have been inspired by the Catholic Church in view of a life time service and the subsequent effectiveness. Though their chief administration is women-centred, the general style of conducting themselves to various details is obviously influenced by the missionary perspectives of the Catholic Christian community.

Modern Hindu religious movements and sects, like *Sai Baba, Satya Sai Baba, Amritanandamai, Art of Living, Iscon, Brahma Kumari, Ramkrishna Mission, Swami Narayan, Niramkari Mission and Dera Sacha Sauda Baba*[67]. They have established themselves in hundreds of countries outside India for propagating themselves and for gaining money and power. To say the least, they have been influenced greatly by the Christian community, especially the Catholic Church, in terms of their organisational set-up, dynamics and methodology of expansion.

Raastreey Swayamsevak Sangh (RSS) and the organisations affiliated to it is a replica of the Catholic Church in terms of its organizational set-up, to the details[68]. They survive and thrive on the funds from Christian countries and organisations, much more than the Christian community in India. Attacking the Christian community for its special commitment to the oppressed and the abandoned sections of the society, after having profusely benefitted from the Christian community, is the tragic irony of the matter. All the same, the Christian influence on the RSS and affiliated organisations are more than obvious.

3.14. Christian impact on Mahatma Gandhi

Mahatma Gandhi was very much inspired by Jesus Christ. He did his law in England and practiced it in South Africa. He had to face a lot of ill-treatment from the white. All the same, Bible had a great influence on him[69]. The exceptionally sublime ethical values of the Sermon on the Mount left an indelible print on the heart and mind of Gandhiji. His political values, his non-violent methodology of life and his preferential concern for the suppressed sections of the Indian society were grounded in the Christian ethos[70]. It could be said without exaggeration that Christianity has greatly contributed to his becoming the Mahatma.

4. SPECIFIC ENGAGEMENTS FOR HARMONIOUS LIVING

4.1. The beginning of the enlightenment

Thanks to the great enlightenment during the Second World Council of Vatican, Christian attitude to people of other faiths changed radically. Recognizing the work of the spirit in all communities, entering into dialogue with people of all religious and non-religious faiths, making enriching and friendly relations with them and collaborating with them to make a better society were a few of the salient features of that realisation.

Christians share a consciousness in having a 'common origin, a shared existence and a common destiny' and it prompts them to 'walk and work together' with others[71]. This awakening facilitated conceiving one's identity on three levels in a progressive fashion: an 'individual identity', a 'social identity' and a 'spiritual identity' or an 'identity beyond all identities'. Such an elevated realisation, though in limited circles, paved the way for 'inclusive thinking and harmonious living' together with people of all affiliations.

4.2. The journey of the realisation

Ever since the sixties of the 20th century, the catholic community and other Christian communities have been putting in lot of efforts worldwide for ushering in a society, which is capable of understanding their faith in terms of being members of a larger family. India, as a land of diverse faith traditions and social ideologies, has immense scope for living the national maxims 'unity in diversity' and *'Vasudhaiv Kutumbakam'*[72].

In order to make the 'composite' character of our land a reality, all communities have to get awakened towards a 'spirit of togetherness'. This would assist the nation to develop a 'rainbow' culture. This would mean 'recognising the beauty of each colour and shade of colour' and 'sticking together in order to make an effect of collective beauty'[73]. Narrow outlooks and private interests require giving way for the larger good. The pathological instances of narrow outlooks, petty interests and communal disturbances are indeed opportunities for awakening positive initiatives, as well.

4.3. The schemes for fostering understanding

The schemes and activities that have been in the process for fostering interaction and mutual understanding could be categorised as personal friendships with people of other communities, workshops, seminars, lectures, messages, interviews to electronic and print media, research, study, articles and books[74]. These efforts have been pioneered by individuals and organisations in different parts of the country.

These schemes have a double effect. They have an impact on other communities and they have an impact on one's own community as well as those involved in the process. Fostering harmonious relations with other communities is the external effect and opening up from within, as individuals and as communities, towards a world large enough to accommodate all ideologies, traditions and communities is the internal effect. The mutual understanding, along with third option/s that emerges is the positive outcome of the exercise[75].

4.4. Centres of Religious Dialogue and Harmony

Centres of inter-faith dialogue and harmony have been established in the different parts of the country ever since the second world council of Vatican in the sixties of the twentieth century[76]. They have been organising get-togethers to celebrate religious festivals of all religious traditions and days of national importance on a collective basis.

The centres have also been conducting workshops, seminars and symposiums to explore the comparative implications of all faith traditions as well as to study the deeper meanings of the religious tenets of the respective tradition. Some of the centres also have been publishing news bulletins, souvenirs and books, in order to disseminate the concept further[77].

4.5. Special efforts for bettering relations with the Muslim community

The endeavour of interfaith interaction does not seem to have made much impact on the Muslim community. Some efforts could be highlighted here. Christians (Jesuits) were part of the court of *Mughal* Emperor *Akbar*, in the 16-17th century, who fostered 'discussions on matters concerning religion and philosophy.'[78] It was an opportunity to accelerate a culture of interaction in the arena of governance and religion.

Henry Martin, an Anglican priest and missionary, made a commendable effort at harmonious living in the 18-19th century with the Muslim community[79]. He organised sessions of 'personal sharing' of Christian faith in small circles of interested Muslims. The stress on 'sharing the forgiveness and peace', 'recognizing and appreciating the activity of God in what is good in Muslims and their faith', 'studying both the Bible and the Quran' and 'fostering good friendship' between Christians and Muslims made a positive difference.

Launching Henry Martin Institute (HMI) in the early 20th century as an ecumenical Christian organisation for inter-faith relations, especially with Muslims, was a great venture[80]. As a well-equipped centre, it is a milestone in the above area today. In the second half of the 20th century, All India Seminar, Bangalore, All India Consultation, Patna, and National Consultation, Agra, were landmarks in fostering the Christian-Muslim relations. 'Islamic Studies Association' and the journal 'Salaam' were results of the same.

The National Commission Religious Harmony of CBCI conducted a National Consultation on 'Christian-Muslim Endeavours for a Better

Society' in New Delhi in 2005, after a series of Regional Consultations in the country in 2004[81]. Having shed considerable light on the inner construct of the Christian-Muslim faiths, the Consultations presented major insights for re-fashioning the approaches to Christian-Muslim dialogue and for developing down to earth models of partnerships that improved harmonious living with Muslims.

4.6. The efforts of the Commission for Religious Harmony, CBCI, New Delhi

The national Commission for Religious Harmony, CBCI, on behalf of the catholic community in the country, has been taking initiatives for promoting dialogue and harmony among religious communities and social groups as well as other Christian communities, since the early 70s of the last century[82]. The Commission has a three-tier system of national, regional and local levels. Accordingly, there are 165 local units in the country, 13 offices of coordination at the regional or state levels and over 30 specific centres or institutes in different cities. The Commission has been putting in painstaking efforts for dialoguing with people of all religious communities.

The first decade of the third millennium has been significant for the Commission in pioneering a major break-through into establishing harmonious relations with all communities. There was a major shift of emphasis in the mission of dialogue and harmony. 'Harmony' was fixed as the end result of the efforts and 'dialogue' as the means and the process. Along with religious communities, social groups also were included in the regular process of interaction and relations[83].

4.7. New avenues in the new millennium

The Commission appropriated Hindi, the national and the most spoken language of the country, as the chief medium for interaction[84]. This brought the Christian community closer to the civil public. A secular and all-inclusive language of the inter-faith mission also was developed, both in Hindi and in English. The journal 'Fellowship', with a circulation capacity of over 10,000 copies and with lots of information and knowledge of the heritage of all religious communities disseminated the larger outlook of the mission to all sectors and walks of life of the society[85].

The Commission also reached out to new avenues of sensitizing people as regards the harmony perspective of life, by way of guest lectures at departments of universities and colleges, seminars for school and college teachers and extension lectures at seminary institutes, in addition to lecture and messages at thousands of platforms in India and abroad with a composition of people from all communities. Visiting places of worship and pilgrim centres of all religions, participating in their worships, addressing gatherings of the respective religions, and the like, have been other schemes that were oriented to fostering interaction, friendly relations and harmonious living with people of all communities[86].

4.8. Towards a language that is common and intelligible

An incident speaks volumes to elaborate the point under discussion here. There was an interfaith prayer service organised by Salwan Public School, New Delhi, immediately after the 'Tsunami' tragedy in 2004. Representative leaders of all religions presented some excerpts from their respective sacred scriptures in their respective '*dev-vaanee*'. When the turn of the Christian leader came, he thought of making a condolence message, a *bhajan* of divine invocation and a spontaneous prayer-all in Hindi, since Christianity has no special sacred language and since Hindi was the language that the gathering understands. The response of the public to this Christian approach was widely applauded[87].

The simple message of this event is God has no special language and all languages are of God[88]. The original languages in which the divine experiences were written by different seers have relevance only in the historic and social context of the place of origin. The followers of the respective religious tradition have to appropriate the language of the place of their existence.

The language people understand is the sacred language proper or the language of God that is intelligible and common to all. Faith is ultimately a question of language only. Christian community that has been adapting to all the languages and dialects of the world are pioneers in this initiating interfaith perspective[89]. This is perhaps the most important lesson the Christian community can teach other communities in India.

CONCLUSION

Living harmoniously with the second largest population, largest democracy and the most diverse country in the world, by way of characteristics, like geographical conditions, climate, ethnic origin, language, caste, class, creed, ideology, food tastes, dress patterns, social mores and culture, the Christian community in India has the resources and potential as well as opportunity to develop a singular model of harmonious living.

Though the Christian community in India has miles and miles to travel by way of more significant contributions, it has presented several noteworthy modules to its credit, with reference to living its faith in an inclusive and dialogical way and to presenting to the world more active and outstanding models of harmonious living with other communities, religious and social.

The Christian community has to further its initiatives and efforts in exploring and living more and more interactive, participatory, inclusive and innovative ways of assimilating and getting assimilated in the ideological, social, spiritual and cultural traditions of the country, in view of ushering in a tomorrow with a richer and an enriching culture of 'harmonious living'.

Endnotes

1. The Holy Bible (New International Version), Michigan, 1994, Psalm 103:13, p. 682
2. The Holy Bible (New International Version), Michigan, 1994, Gen1.27-28, p. 02
3. The Holy Bible (New International Version), Michigan, 1994, 1 Cor 3.16, p. 1298
4. Kathleen Engebretson, Catholic Schools and the Future of the Church, Bloomsbury Publishing, London, 2014, p. 19
5. The Holy Bible (New International Version), Michigan, 1994, Mt 19.19, p. 1117
6. The Holy Bible (New International Version), Michigan, 1994, Mt 5.44, p. 1099
7. The Holy Bible (New International Version), Michigan, 1994, Mt 7.12, p. 1100
8. The Holy Bible (New International Version), Michigan, 1994, Mt 25.41, p. 1128
9. Rebecca Samuel Shah, Joel Carpenter, Christianity in India :Conversion, Community Development, and Religious Freedom, Fortress Press, Minneapolis, Minnesota, 2019, p. 146
10. The Holy Bible (New International Version), Michigan, 1994, Mt 6.8, p. 1099
11. Rebecca Samuel Shah, Joel Carpenter, Christianity in India :Conversion, Community Development, and Religious Freedom, Fortress Press, Minneapolis, Minnesota, 2019, p. 153
12. George Poikail, St. Thomas Christians and Their Eucharistic Liturgy, *Christava Sahitya Samithi*, New Delhi, 2010, p. 33
13. *Ibid,* p. 112
14. Leonard Fernando, G. Gispert-Sauch, Christianity in India: Two Thousand Years of Faith, New York, 2004, p. 187
15. Leonard Fernando, G. Gispert-Sauch, Christianity in India: Two Thousand Years of Faith, New York, 2004, p. 93
16. The Holy Bible (New International Version), Michigan, 1994, Mt 25.41, p. 1128
17. The Holy Bible (New International Version), Michigan, 1994, Mk 9.35, p. 1148
18. The Holy Bible (New International Version), Michigan, 1994, Jn 13.14, p. 1225
19. Rebecca Samuel Shah, Joel Carpenter, Christianity in India: Conversion, Community Development, and Religious Freedom, Fortress Press, Minneapolis, Minnesota, 2019, p. 91
20. The Holy Bible (New International Version), Michigan, 1994, Mt 5.9, p. 1097
21. The Holy Bible (New International Version), Michigan, 1994, Lk 23.34, p. 1201
22. Rebecca Samuel Shah, Joel Carpenter, Christianity in India: Conversion, Community Development, and Religious Freedom, Fortress Press, Minneapolis, Minnesota, 2019, p. 92
23. Rebecca Samuel Shah, Joel Carpenter, Christianity in India: Conversion, Community Development, and Religious Freedom, Fortress Press, Minneapolis, Minnesota, 2019, p. 15
24. Leonard Fernando, G. Gispert-Sauch, Christianity in India: Two Thousand Years of Faith, New York, 2004, p. 112
25. *Ibid,* p. 204
26. Leonard Fernando, G. Gispert-Sauch, Christianity in India: Two Thousand Years of Faith, New York, 2004, p. 228

27. Alaine, M. Low, Robert Eric Frykenberg (Ed.), Christians and Missionaries in India: Cross-cultural Communication Since 1500, William B. Eerdmans Publishing Company, Michigan, 2003, p. 91
28. *Ibid,* p. 123
29. *Ibid,* p. 234
30. Rebecca Samuel Shah, Joel Carpenter, Christianity in India: Conversion, Community Development, and Religious Freedom, Fortress Press, Minneapolis, Minnesota, 2019, p. 36
31. *Ibid,* p. 48
32. *Ibid,* p. 104
33. *Ibid,* 207
34. *Ibid,* p. 221
35. Leonard Fernando, G. Gispert-Sauch, Christianity in India: Two Thousand Years of Faith, New York, 2004, p. 287
36. *Ibid,* p. 307
37. *Ibid,* p. 308
38. Rebecca Samuel Shah, Joel Carpenter, Christianity in India: Conversion, Community Development, and Religious Freedom, Fortress Press, Minneapolis, Minnesota, 2019, p. 109
39. www.census2011.co.in
40. Rebecca Samuel Shah, Joel Carpenter, Christianity in India: Conversion, Community Development, and Religious Freedom, Fortress Press, Minneapolis, Minnesota, 2019, p. 97
41. *Ibid,* p. 154
42. Hari Pulakkat, Space, Life, Matter: The Coming of Age of Indian Science, Hachette India, Gurgaon, 2021, p. 186
43. Leonard Fernando, G. Gispert-Sauch, Christianity in India: Two Thousand Years of Faith, New York, 2004, p. 109
44. *Ibid,* p. 132
45. *Ibid,* p. 207
46. *Ibid,* p. 231
47. Leonard Fernando, G. Gispert-Sauch, Christianity in India: Two Thousand Years of Faith, New York, 2004, p. 251
48. *Ibid,* p. 256
49. Rebecca Samuel Shah, Joel Carpenter, Christianity in India: Conversion, Community Development, and Religious Freedom, Fortress Press, Minneapolis, Minnesota, 2019, p. 109
50. *Ibid,* p. 201
51. Rebecca Samuel Shah, Joel Carpenter, Christianity in India: Conversion, Community Development, and Religious Freedom, Fortress Press, Minneapolis, Minnesota, 2019, p. 209
52. Alaine, M. Low, Robert Eric Frykenberg (Ed.), Christians and Missionaries in India: Cross-cultural Communication Since 1500, William B. Eerdmans Publishing Company, Michigan, 2003, p. 129
53. *Ibid,* p. 187
54. Alaine, M. Low, Robert Eric Frykenberg (Ed.), Christians and Missionaries in India: Cross-cultural Communication Since 1500, William B. Eerdmans Publishing Company, Michigan, 2003, p. 95
55. *Ibid,* p. 124
56. *Ibid,* p. 154

57. Rebecca Samuel Shah, Joel Carpenter, Christianity in India: Conversion, Community Development, and Religious Freedom, Fortress Press, Minneapolis, Minnesota, 2019, p. 212
58. Leonard Fernando, G. Gispert-Sauch, Christianity in India: Two Thousand Years of Faith, New York, 2004, p. 251
59. *Ibid,* p. 287
60. Sisir Kumar Das, The Shadow of the Cross: Christianity and Hinduism in a Colonial Situation, Munshiram Manoharlal Publishers, New Delhi, 1974, p. 109
61. Abidullah Al-Ansari Ghazi, Raja Rammohun Roy: Encounter with Islam and Christianity and the Articulation of Hindu Self-Consciousness, Xlibris Corporation, Bloomington, 2010, p. 91
62. Sisir Kumar Das, The Shadow of the Cross: Christianity and Hinduism in a Colonial Situation, Munshiram Manoharlal Publishers, New Delhi, 1974, p. 110
63. *Ibid,* p. 113
64. *Ibid,* p. 114
65. *Ibid,* p. 120
66. Lenore Manderson, Matt Tomlinson, Wendy Smith, Flows of Faith: Religious Reach and Community in Asia and the Pacific, Springer, New York, 2012, p. 88
67. *Ibid,* p. 89
68. *Ibid,* p. 109
69. B. Srinivasa Murthy, Mahatma Gandhi and Christianity, Long Beach Publications, California, 1998, p. 19
70. *Ibid,* p. 57
71. Rebecca Samuel Shah, Joel Carpenter, Christianity in India: Conversion, Community Development, and Religious Freedom, Fortress Press, Minneapolis, Minnesota, 2019, p. 202
72. Balmiki Prasad Singh, India's Culture: The State, the Arts, and Beyond, Oxford University Press, New Delhi, 2011, p. 123
73. *Ibid,* p. 206
74. Rebecca Samuel Shah, Joel Carpenter, Christianity in India: Conversion, Community Development, and Religious Freedom, Fortress Press, Minneapolis, Minnesota, 2019, p. 107
75. *Ibid,* 209
76. Rebecca Samuel Shah, Joel Carpenter, Christianity in India: Conversion, Community Development, and Religious Freedom, Fortress Press, Minneapolis, Minnesota, 2019, p. 232
77. *Ibid,* 233
78. Charles Herbert Payne, Akbar and the Jesuits: An Account of the Jesuit Missions to the Court of Akbar, Routledge Curzon, Oxfordshire, 2004, p. 18
79. Clinton Bennett, In Search of Understanding, Wipf & Stock Publishers, Eugene, 2019, p. 15
80. *Ibid,* p. 29
81. Suhas Pereira, The Challenges of Vatican II for an Authentic Indian Catholic Church, Lit Verlag, Münster, Germany, 2020, p. 159
82. Suhas Pereira, The Challenges of Vatican II for an Authentic Indian Catholic Church, Lit Verlag, Münster, Germany, 2020, p. 161
83. *Ibid,* p. 162
84. Baptist Rodrigues, Authority as Service: Mission of the Church in India, Dhyanavana Publications, Bangalore, 2011, p. 306
85. *Ibid,* p. 307
86. *Ibid,* p. 308

87. Baptist Rodrigues, Authority as Service: Mission of the Church in India, Dhyanavana Publications, Bangalore, 2011, p. 311
88. Rebecca Samuel Shah, Joel Carpenter, Christianity in India: Conversion, Community Development, and Religious Freedom, Fortress Press, Minneapolis, Minnesota, 2019, p. 11
89. *Ibid,* p. 107

Chapter - 13

The Popular Saints of India and Their Message of Liberation

INTRODUCTION

The human society, on the one hand, has always had established forms of selfishness, exploitation and bondage. But, there have always been, on the other hand, saints and sages, who emerged from the common folk as powerful prophets, whose life and message have immensely contributed to the on-going reformation of the human society. These saints and sages of India were not mere symbols of holiness but were unique agents of spiritual liberation and social renaissance. Their being born in to the society is a matter of great pride and blessing for the humanity. They remain perennial sources of inspiration and their message of liberation contributes immensely to the various details of life. The following lines, in brief, are attempting their story.

1. POPULAR SAINTS OF INDIA

1.1. Who is a saint?

A saint is one who is regarded as a holy person. Outward appearance or religious following, or even capacity to foretell future happening, does not necessarily make a saint. Professing a dogma and falling in line with certain so-called infallible traditions are not required either, in order to be a saint. Belonging to a certain religious community and practicing a system of rituals are not the signs of a saint, too. 'Being holy' is the mark of a saint. "True holiness is simply the presence of God reflecting itself in the goodness of a person's character and action"[1]. That would mean to say, a saint has to be endowed with a good human nature, first and foremost. He or she needs to be characterised by a spiritual flavour of life. He or she ought to be recognised as a saint in terms of social relevance, i.e., the message of liberation he or she imparts.

1.2. 'Saint' in different religious traditions

Different religious traditions have different understandings of a saint. For some religious traditions, saint is one who, having died, is among the blessed, i.e., one who has merited favour with God by the quality of religious living on earth. Accordingly, a person is considered a saint when he or she is declared by the head of the community to have won a place in heaven and so is worthy of veneration on earth. Some other religious traditions do not consider it necessary for someone to be declared a saint by a certain official. While on earth, one can be accepted as a living saint by virtue of one's quality of living. The spiritual genuineness gives a glowing account of one's saintly existence.

1.3. The word 'saint'

The word 'saint' is understood in two ways – general and particular. The general understanding evolves from the basic meaning of the word whereas the particular understanding, from its sectarian application. The word 'saint' derives from the linguistic roots *sat, san and shaant*, which mean 'true', 'calm', 'still', 'serene' 'quiet', 'peaceful', 'silent', etc. Accordingly, the inherent features of a saint would be being devout, wise, truthful, gentle, pure, noble, generous, and serviceable as well as having faith, good conduct, and the like[2]. The Hindi word *sant* almost tallies with the English word 'saint', in both pronunciation and meaning. The word 'saint' was used in this general meaning till it received a particular application later.

1.4. The sectarian application of the word

The word 'saint' was used in a sectarian sense beginning with *Gyaneshwar* of *Varkari* sect of Maharashtra in the 14th century. The sectarian understanding of the word developed in to its full capacity in the context of *Kabeer* in the 15-16th century. The 20th century literary criticism almost sealed this particular sense of the word. Now, it is not applied to the *sagun* devotee poets like *Tulseedaas, Soordaas, Meerabaayee,* etc. but to the *nirgun* devotee poets like *Kabeer, Ravidaas, Dadoodayal* and the like. The sectarian use of the word accommodates the *Soofee* saints also, in a certain sense. Anyway, the word 'saint,' in our context, entertains a different and wide understanding of God, even wider than the traditional understanding of *nirgun* God. Quite many *sagun* sages have maintained various dimensions of broader thinking, too. Some aspects of their message also fall under the *nirgun* or beyond *sagun-nirgun* concept of being a saint.

Having approached life from their own given situations, they have even re-defined the word 'saint' by the unique way they lived their lives. In them, the word 'saint' stands for various dimensions of continuing liberation in life. Key words like 'saint', 'saint literature', 'saint tradition', and 'saint vision' and 'saint sect' are discussed here from this perspective.

1.5. Popular Saints

These saints are known as popular saints, because they belonged to the people. Their popularity can be seen from various angles. Most of these saints hailed from the so-called lower strata of the caste-ridden society of the time and belonged to the discriminated lot of the general public. They represented the cries and sentiments of the 'voiceless'. They suited the tastes, needs and level of the masses. They shared the problems, struggles and life-situations of the ordinary people. They were liked by the common folk for their genuineness and were admired for their relentless search for the Higher Power. They presented a simple form of *bhakti* and spirituality to the common person and the same was highly appealing to them. They were appreciated for the liberative life they lived and for the inspiring message they communicated. They spoke in the dialect of the general public. In their discourses, the language was adjusted to the audience in hand. Their utterances were not only spontaneous but also poetical and musical. They preferred the simple, straightforward, colloquial, mixed, and the country way of speech, which was used by the common folk, to the refined, classical, polished, symbolic and systematic style of language that was used by the educated. At a time, when Sanskrit monopolised all knowledge and media of communication, to attempt the popular dialect for communication was nothing less than a crime, which wouldn't easily be pardoned. This was the revolution these saints pioneered. These saints could whisper volumes of spiritual message to the hearts of the general public. That is why; their lines are often found ready at the tips of tongues of people, especially of the general public. Though they had to face many odds in their respective life-situations, eventually they were accepted by the masses to the core, as great men–fully liberated and capable of facilitating liberation. In this sense, they were 'popular saints'.

1.6. A few names

Let me name a few of these saints from different parts of India– *Kabeer, Ravidaas, Tukaraam, Gyaaneshwar, Naamdev, Eknaath, Jaanaabaayee, Muktaabaayee, Narsee Mehtaa, Meerabaayee, Sree Naaraayan Guru, Sarvagy, Thiruvalluvar, Purantardaas, Jaitraam, Chattambiswaamikal, Basveshwar, Chaitanymahaaprabhu, Ghaaseedaas, Guru Naanak, Raamdaas, Annamaachaary, Periyaar, Pothana, Molia, Thyaagraaja,*

Sundaradaas, Kutban, Manjhan, Bhaarteeyaar, Jotibaa Phule, and the like. Most of them were renowned poets, too. Their poems are available in the national and regional literatures. Translations, commentaries and research findings on them in the form of books and articles are found in Hindi and English, and also in many Indian and non-Indian languages.

1.7. Indian saints with a universal character

The popular saints of our interest here, definitely, belonged to the sub-continent of India. They had their birth in different geographical settings, at different times of history. They are Indian not merely by way of their nationality, but because they were deeply involved in the concerns of the Indian society – its traditions, values, struggles, problems, needs, ambitions and aspirations. Their hearts and minds were fully alive to the spiritual, cultural, ideological and behavioural patterns of Indian life. They were deeply committed to the diverse dimensions of the genius of Indian worldview, such as spiritual outlook, individual freedom, plurality, integration, philosophical concept, experiential approach, aesthetic attitude and poetic expression. They were Indian thus, through and through. But, to be Indian meant for them, in no way, a mind divided by linguistic, communal and national boundaries. Their life and message had ample implications for the whole humanity, even though their poetical lines were addressed to themselves, as they were rooted in their given contexts. Their 'being Indian' communicates a symbolic value for the welfare of the whole humanity. Its perennial value travels across the boundaries of caste, creed, profession and community. It has a universal bearing. But for this quality of universal application, their relevance as saints would have been insignificant. Their Indian character would have had hardly anything liberative, either. Their message is for all people and is for all times; and that is their uniqueness.

1.8. A powerful message

These saints have a powerful message for the humanity. Their message was not merely social, moral and religious tenets. It was not just processed in the mind; it evolved from their experiences of life. Their poetical expressions were not intellectual or verbal exercises. Their speech was the communication of a lived reality. These saints never relied on others' utterances or on pieces of hearsay. They counted on their own personal experience. Naturally, their sayings radiate genuineness. It is tested by the truth of life and would stand the challenge of time and space, too. Their message does not merely present good ideas. It is an invitation, which cannot be escaped from. It is an earnest request, which could not be denied. It is a teaching, which penetrates in to the heart of the listener. It is an inexhaustible treasure of inspiration for all ages to come. Their message speaks volumes, effectively so, to the one who is a seeker of human and spiritual heights.

1.9. Capacity for liberation from diverse forms of bondage

The life and message of these popular saints had a great capacity for the all-round liberation of the human kind. Liberation is setting someone free from slavery or bondage of any sort. Human society, often, gets stagnant in the realm of ideas, feelings or practices. The saints could not close their eyes against the rampant forms of enslavement their respective human society was afflicted with. There were bondages of understanding, like ritualism, fundamentalism, fanaticism, communalism and terrorism. Attitudinal forms of slavery like prejudice, hatred, and ill feeling were strongly prevailing. Several wrong habits developed in to behavioural ruts. Discrimination based on caste, class, sect, office, social status, profession, language, region, etc., was the most commonly found social malady. Forms of enslavement were thriving in almost all areas of life. The saints attempted a campaign of liberation, in view of freeing the humans from the clutches of diverse bondages. Only the one who is liberated can facilitate another to get liberated. The saints possessed enormous spiritual powers, which they received from the Almighty. Their personal lives had a considerable in-built spiritual capacity for awakening reformation in societal life as well as spiritual transformation in personal lives. Their message of liberation was processed in their own social contexts, and it was in the light of the personal experience of the divine they were brimming forth.

The multi-sided **message of liberation** propounded by these popular saints could be analyzed under two heads – spiritual and social. The salient features of their liberative message will certainly highlight the quality of their saintliness and the universal character of its application to human situations, beyond temporal and geographical considerations.

1.10. Message of Spiritual Liberation

Religion is a double-sided phenomenon. On the one hand, it is a system of faith, which takes care of the spiritual factor in life. It is supposed to be an agent of all-pervasive liberation. But, on the other hand, it is a sad fact that the followers get enslaved to a certain perspective, an interpretation, a code and a ritual expression. It is a certain type of conditioning. It is intended to unite human beings. But nothing else has divided the human society so appallingly as religion. It takes the credit of all attempts at peace and harmony in the world. But the worst of the wars and tensions in the world have taken place in the name of religion. The pages of the world history go thus. No doubt, it has facilitated the humans in the search for the Divine. But the institutionalised and sophisticated details of the religious systems have made the spiritual journey of the followers not only bothersome but also next to impossible, in many respects. There is a large number of self-styled leaders, who claim to have been 'anointed to rule over the people'. They have no scruple in manipulating the religious fabric in order to suit their private interests. Pseudo-orthodoxy and discriminatory attitudes based on caste, class, language, ideology, profession, sect, etc. gain undue power. No wonder, the general public feels suppressed and pushed aside. This is more or less the story of religion the popular saints found themselves encircled by, in their respective life setting. Most of these saints and sages had their roots in the discriminated sections of the society, but they emerged in different areas as extra-ordinary men and women. They had deep personal experience of the Divine and were capable of a spiritual leadership. The positive character of their response to the situation evolved as a spiritual message. They were considered saints in terms of this message. Some of the salient features of the same are being discussed here.

1.11. Simplicity of Religion

The Saints understood religion in a very simple manner. Their spiritual insights were natural. They were accessible to all. They were more appealing to those who were downtrodden and alienated in the matter of religion. The texture of religion suggested by these saints included such simple threads, like remembering the Higher Power in any form that suits, entertaining sentiments of faith in that Power, singing *bhajan* or praises to that Power in one's own way, engaging in *satsang* (good company) or in acquaintances which are conducive to a divine atmosphere, being of service to the other, etc. These attempts at self-realisation were coupled with values of social behaviour, too. The practice of religion was made simple for the common folk. Spiritual experience was brought within the easy reach of the general public. This form of religion, which was lived and highlighted by these popular saints, goes beyond the barriers of caste, creed, traditions, community, ideology and sect. This is an approach of religion, which incorporates all faith positions and perspectives of life, in some fashion or other. It is like a world religion for the humanity, which could easily be accepted by people of all times, with minor modifications. This understanding of religion, which is universal as well as simple, is capable of liberating the humans from the clutches of the prevailing system of religion, which is highly complicated as well as degenerated in many respects. This is, perhaps, the most significant message of liberation communicated by the popular saints.

1.12. Personal experience

Experience is personal by its very nature. 'Personal' pertains to the core of one's being. When processed by one's own personal involvement, experience becomes genuine and reliable. That is precisely what *Kabeer* means when he says '*anbhai saancha,*[3] i.e., experience is true, and true experience is personal. He does not rely on *lekhaa lekhee*, i.e., what is written or narrated by others, but on *aankhin dekhee*,[4] what he has seen with his own eyes. He exhorts, 'you think for yourself (i.e., experience); then you will become wise'.[5]According to him, 'seeing, hearing and touching the reality oneself, thinking and feeling it oneself, experiencing and knowing it oneself, gives one a joy, that is special'.[6] He continues, 'the story of love is indescribable; hardly anything can be said about it; it is like a dump person who has taken jaggery and is not able to express what he or she feels about it, but just smiles'.[7] That would amount to say experience defies expression. God is a matter of personal experience, as love is; one has to know him for oneself. *Kabeer* proceeds to a mystical experience and tells the Lord: 'pondering you again and again I became you; now there is nothing left in me'.[8] His experience of the divine reaches an exquisite culmination when he says, 'I am so full of your presence; wherever I look you are seen'.[9]

The deeper the experience, the richer it is. Pearls are not found at the shore but at deep sea. The personal experience of *Meerabai* makes her affirm, '*Girdhar Gopal* is mine; I have no one else other than him'. [10]About the depth of her yearning for the Lord, she says, 'only the one who is wounded knows the pain of a wounded person'.[11] She exclaims, 'O Lord of *Meera*, when will you come to me; I cannot live without you';[12] 'I am longing for you, O my Lord, make me your own'.[13] *Ravidaas* expresses his personal relationship with the Divine in these words: 'Lord you are *chandan*, I am water; you are lamp, I am the wick'.[14] Similarly, *Tukaraam* expresses his deep God-experience: 'God is now in my heart and mind, within me he does dwell. I see God's face; I feel his presence near. I think of him and touch his feet so dear. As I gaze on this fantastic sight, all mental cares and spiritual woes depart… I live with him; he lives within my heart'.[15] *Raaman Maharshi* approaches this mystical experience in silence, peace, stillness and perfect serenity of mind; and he attains self-realization, thus.[16] The personal experience of the mystic saints goes to the point of ecstatic communion and is often expressed in striking analogy between 'drop and sea', 'wife and husband', 'fish and water', 'bird and air', 'pea cock and mountain', '*chakor* and moon beams', 'waves and sea', etc.

This characteristic of personal experience highlighted by these saints could be compared to Paul: 'for to me, to live is Christ' (Phil.1.21), and

'I no longer live, but Christ lives in me' (Gal.2.20). It can be paralleled with the experience of Thomas, who, having seen the Risen Lord for himself, exclaimed 'My Lord and My God' (Jn 20.28). The experience of Jesus 'I and Father are one' (Jn 10.30) seems to be a culmination of such sentiment. Jesus' question 'who do you say I am' (Mt 16.15) further underlines the importance of the personal experience of the Ultimate Reality, without which religion remains almost untouched.

1.13. Purity of Heart

Purity of heart makes one eligible for attempting an experience of God. Since the Divine is pure, only a pure state of mind can assure an encounter with him. That is why *Meerabaai* prays, 'make me pure as you are pure, beloved'.[17] Purity of heart would mean simplicity. Simplicity is the absence of duplicity, which scatters the energies. It rules out crooked ways and advocates straightforwardness, too. *Kabeer* says, 'One is capable of meeting the Ultimate Reality only when the mind clears its crookedness off'. [18]'A sound mind is as pure as the holy *Ganga*[19]', says *Ravidaas*. *Meerabaai* proceeds further in saying, 'externals do not matter, if but your heart is pure'[20]. Transparency is synonymous to purity of heart.

This fundamental characteristic of spirituality can be compared to the Jewish way of thinking. The Psalmist affirms, 'who may ascend the hill of the Lord? Who may stand in his holy place? He who has clean hands, and a pure heart' (Ps 24:2-4)! Jesus puts it characteristically: 'blessed are the pure in heart, for they shall see God' (Mt 5.8). Purity of heart is holiness and that is the starting point of spirituality, which is worth any name.

1.14. Indwelling of God

The presence of the Creator in the creation is a fact too obvious to be negotiated. This common belief underlines the constant awareness of his abiding presence in all the beings. *Nam Alvaar's* attitude to the Divine can be summarised thus: 'my lord of the celestials, thou hast made my heart thy tabernacle; so intimate and close is thy union with me. That I beseech thee never more to leave me, me so lovingly clinging to thee'! That is to say, the human heart is the special abode of the divine. *Gyaaneshwar* considers the whole universe as the home of God. All the man-made abodes of God on earth are compared by *Ravidaas* to the human body: 'the body is the Temple, Masjid and Gurudwaara'[21]. *Meerabaayee* used to pray to the Lord to cleanse her of sin, so that she may be a worthy dwelling place of the Lord. Kabeer has many categorical sayings to establish the fact: 'as the whole subsists in the part'[22], 'as musk resides in the deer', [23] so dwells God in every being; 'mind (*man*) is *Mathura,* heart (*dil*) is D*waarika* and body (*kaayaa*) is *Kaashee'*.[24]

Similar spiritual realisations are found in the Bible: 'man is the temple of God / the Holy Spirit' (2 Cor 6.16, Cor 6.19, 1 Cor 3.16-17) and 'man bears the image and likeness of God' (Gen 1.27, 5.1). The indwelling of God is materialised in an experience of self-realisation, which is a personalised form of the universal presence of God. It makes the existence of the Divine real and meaningful. It permeates in to the diverse dimensions of life, making it effective to the details.

2. MESSAGE OF SOCIAL LIBERATION

2.1. Social Liberation

The saints found themselves amidst staring contradictions of social life. Social behaviour was in stark incompatibility with the prevailing theories and policies. The general public was being crushed by the clutches of the hierarchical structure of caste and class. The ways of discrimination and exploitation were beyond any logic. Brahmins and high classes monopolised the religious, social and educational arenas. The low-placed people in the realms of caste and class found themselves dominated over and deprived of their right, which was assured even by basic justice. The saints were products of their own respective social situations. Their spiritual insight enabled them to recognise the seriousness of their awkward social predicament and its tragic implications. They were charged with a great sense of social consciousness. They felt the pang of being challenged by the social evils prevailing around them. They experienced a passionate urge to respond to them positively and creatively. No matter how unjust and trying their situations were, they proved their spiritual mettle. Like lotus, which remains in dirty conditions but produces immaculate flowers, the saints rose to such spiritual height in life that their very presence became a living symbol of social resurrection.

The saints campaigned against evil forces like selfishness, hypocrisy, discrimination, exploitation, manipulation, suppression and fatalism. They were genuinely committed to reforming the society. They advocated the basic principle of equality in life pausing arguments like 'the image of God is in all'[25] and 'the divine power is present in all'[26]. Personal values like genuineness, honesty, sincerity, love, service and respect were emphasised, too. Their saintly way was 'living up to this alternative value system', which they themselves proposed. They propagated their message in a subtle poetic language. The values were applied to the respective life setting of the people. The saints placed a clarion call to the practice of social values. They were avowed to making the society a better place to live in. This reformative character of the message of the saints is like an ever-flowing fountain, which contributes immensely to better quality of life in the society.

2.2. Co-ordination between theory and practice

The most reliable test of one's social fitness is the co-ordination between theory and practice. It is the proof of one's genuineness in life. It reveals the level of maturity a person has achieved. The individual fruitfulness and social relevance of one's life is hidden in this hard reality. The life of the saints has always stood the test of the theory they upheld. Their behavioural integrity was not only beyond doubt but was highly inspiring for others.

The poetical utterances of the saints shed light on the details of the problem of disagreement between theory and practice that prevailed in their respective society. *Kabeer* asks, 'what is the use of that speech which does not correspond to action?'[27] According to him, 'theory is empty, practice is the essence of life'.[28] 'Many are those who say things but few are those who do accordingly'[29]. *Tulseedaas* also expresses the same idea, 'many are those who give advice to others, but those who translate the same into action are very few'.[30] *Kabeer* appropriates a satirical approach to those who preach without practicing; 'you haven't got water with you; but you pretend to distribute milk to others. Your own mind is not at peace; and you seem to be enthusiastic in consoling others'[31]. *Dadoodayaal* adds another dimension to the argument, 'You aren't pure yourself, but you give advice to others![32]' *Rajjabdaas,* while realising the double-sided play of the reality of speech and action, poses the basic predicament of spiritual attainment: 'to do is difficult, to say is easy; but without living the life yourself, how can you attain the Divine'?[33] *Kabeer* analyses the phenomenon further: 'the speech is sweet like jaggery, action is like poison; but if you leave speech and do action, then you will attain nectar, in the place of poison'.[34] He observes the sad plight of the learned and categorically suggests an effective treatment to the problem of disharmony between theory and practice: 'the world has (generations have) gone by perusing large volumes and no one has ever become learned. The one who learns the single word of love only will really become learned'.[35]

Biblical ideas also highlight this crucial problem of life. Verbal expressions, if they do not correspond to what they imply, are a futile exercise. Jesus commands: 'not saying lord, lord, but doing the will of his Father is heaven is the ideal act, which merits the kingdom of heaven' (Mt 7.21). He also presents a paradox: 'one who does not translate the word in to practice is like a foolish man who builds his house on sand' (Mt 7.24-27). 'Faith has to be accompanied by action, otherwise it is dead', says James (James 2.14-17). He continues, 'one who does not care for action is like a person who sees his face in the mirror, but does not want to improve his look' (James 1.23-25).Jesus has a parable about the talent, which has the following implication. When received from God, it is just a theory; when invested upon and developed, it is practice that is worthy of appreciation and reward (Mt 25.14-30).John says, 'the one who claims to love God and does not love his neighbour is a lair' (1 Jn 4.20-21). Loving God is theory and loving one-another is practice.

Disagreement between theory and practice would mean having a divided heart. That is why *Tukaraam* says: 'a single-minded man cannot hate another; if he sees God in all, his foe becomes his brother'.[36] Co-ordination between word and deed and as well as thought and action is the sign of integrity. That is why the saints condemned oral knowledge and appreciated behavioural knowledge. Their utterances are as if they are addressing themselves! They used to speak out only that which was experimented by them in their personal lives. They gave evidence to their own words by their actions. They presented the ideal before others through the witness of their own lives. Only the one who has practiced the message beforehand has the right to preach to the other. That which has come to one's own experience only is worthy of any importance. As the words interpret the action, so the action bears witness to the words. The conflict between theory and practice proves one's state of being disorganised in life, which is to be regretted. Moreover, word and deed are complementary to each other. They are like two sides of the same coin. The saints highlight co-ordination between theory and practice as the most radical social message. This aspect of the saints' message of social liberation seems to be exceptionally relevant for the world of today.

2.3. Equality

The measure adopted by the saints to re-organise the society, which was scattered by discriminatory behaviours, was the ideal of equality. Different standards were being applied to individuals and communities; and superior-inferior attitudes were maintained in the society. The approach of the saints to this mentality of inequality and discrimination was basically spiritual. *Dadoodayaal* exhorts, 'contemplate the whole Divine (*Brahm*), then you will find all the individual spirits on the same plane; if you concentrate on the quality of the body, then you will see diverse colours'. [37] The quality of the spirit is to be imbibed in order to see the basic oneness. A non-dualistic experience is the basic requirement for equality. It is the divided mind, which discriminates on the basis of caste, colour, language, profession, class, creed, faith, conviction, ideology, nationality, etc. The foundation for human equality is faith in the same divinity. The characteristic of 'rainbow' inspires one to comprehend the mystery of divine oneness. The rainbow presents seven colours, one different from the other. The diverse colours expressed in the rainbow are all hidden in the sunlight. It is the same sun and the same sunlight at the root of all these colours. So is the divine spirit

– basically one in experience and different in expressions. The different colours are different expressions and they are not to be compared with and discriminated against each other. Each has its own singular quality. Together they radiate a beauty. This aesthetic outlook of life is the spiritual motivation for equality. This has been the subtle experience of the saints.

An awareness of the **common roots** elicits a sense of common belonging. By going deeper into the experience of the Divine, one comes to the realisation that all beings essentially belong to the same Divine. That is the supreme truth *Dadoodayaal* expresses in these simple words: 'all beings are of the same God'.[38] All human beings are the children of the same God. All are members of the same family of God, the same family of humanity. All have the right to live. The differences are just artificial and they are superimposed. *Gorakhanaath* says, 'A Hindu approaches temple and a Muslim, masjid; but both contemplate and find the same Higher Power, that knows neither temple nor *masjid*.[39] The high and low feelings are based on merely external differences. The quality of the human person is more important. The inner quality is the invisible basis of an attitude of equality. To be carried away by the visible world would mean to lead a life on the level of the body, which is not life proper. All beings share the same Creator and the same creation. 'All share the same water, the same air and the same light. It is because of one's foolishness one makes a difference between persons,' says *Rajjabdaas*[40]. Sorrows and joys, hopes and disappointments, sufferings and struggles, successes and failures, dreams and achievements are a common experience for all. In fact, there is no reasonable ground for discrimination and unsociability. The basic reality of life is just equal for all. The so-called leaders of the society erected a system of classification of human beings, where they can satisfy their selfish interests. But, such a division has no logical basis.

A religion of **good social conduct** is *dharma*. Good behaviour towards one another is that which makes a real human society. Kabeer challenges the proponents of the caste system, who undervalue others and thus fall short of a social conduct, which is humanly dignifying. He asks in an ironical tone, 'you *Brahmin*, why haven't you taken another way to be born[41]'? He means that if both Brahmina nd *Shoodr* have taken the same way to be born in to the world, what is the difference between them? Both have blood of the same colour; both have hunger and thirst as well as needs and problems. *Paltoosaheb* settles this problem in his own way: 'I have cancelled the whole system of castes and erected a basic path of devotion for all. I am now like a flower blossomed in the garden of *Govind'*[42]. The system of caste-discrimination is a hindrance to a meaningful social life. What is important is a spirit of equality in the garden of life, which is created and maintained by the same God. That is why *Muni Devsen* conclusively and categorically affirms; 'there is but one religion of good conduct and no Brahmin, no *Shoodr*.[43]

Such a morality of good behaviour to one and all establishes perfect equality among the humans. Unity of the human society is dependent on the behavioural equality in life. Equality takes care of the right approach to life. This attitude does full justice to the human dignity and to the dignity of life. It rules out all narrowness of thinking. It also proves one's genuineness and nobility. Such an open, transparent and realistic disposition assures the right orientation to life. It liberates the humans from all that is unworthy of the human spirit and promises a healthy tuning to one-another. The welfare of the whole humanity (*Sarvoday*) is inherent in this elevated state of mind.

2.4. Integration of values

Integration is combining different parts to form a single whole. It is like bricks, stone and the other requisites brought together to erect a wall. It is like different letters fixed together to form a word in the block. It is like different words put together to make a piece of poem. It's like a harmony of various notes to make music. It is like a body which functions as one unit while having many parts (1 Cor 12.12-31).The many parts exist as one. There is no contradiction between the parts; there is no discrimination among them. There is equal importance and dignity shared among the parts. There is mutual understanding and agreement. This is an example, which speaks volumes on what integration would mean. Integration, thus, is an existence in togetherness. It is a holistic vision of life and can rightly be described in the terminology of Indian culture: 'unity in diversity and diversity in unity'. It is like a family or a community, in whom the members exist in mutual communion. All the basic values of life merge in to this reality of communion. Integration is the positive outcome of the dynamics of human values, which make social life possible. A well-knit social life is dependent on the inter-play between the values the humans live by.

The saints not only underlined the need of integrating the values of social life but their own lives were a lofty example for the same. They were persons of great **integrity**. They were honest and upright in character. They were simple and straightforward in heart. They were fully committed to the society. The sole mission in their life was an all-out attempt at making the human society a better place to live in. They started this campaign with themselves. They proved themselves to be people of character – human and spiritual. The physical, mental, emotional and spiritual components of their persons fitted together well. It is this personal achievement of theirs which make them being remembered as inspiring models. Shree *Naarayan Guru* suggests a highly imperative single-doze medicine for the disorganised and disintegrated human society: 'one caste, one religion, one God for the humanity.'[44] Only a person of sublime integrity can conceive such a concept, which can integrate all that the humans hold on to. For him, following a particular religious tradition or ideology, belonging to a particular social caste, class or community, holding a particular profession or position, etc., is not important. Becoming a good human being is the most meritorious achievement in life. Such an approach to life organizes life values into an integral whole.

2.5. Qualitative approach

A **qualitative approach** to life is the right perspective for integration. Quality and quantity are like two sides of the same coin. Both are equally important. Quantity stands for the body, while quality represents the spirit. Quantity elaborates the visible world, whereas quality searches for the invisible world. Quantity is the dimension of expression with regard to the reality, and quality is the dimension of experience of the same. Quantity is the external aspect, whereas quality, the internal. Since they are complementary components, the mutual equilibrium needs to be maintained. But the general inclination is to give priority to the quantity component. The saints realised that the sad predicament of the society was because of too much importance given to the quantity factor and too little importance, to quality. So they felt the need to stress the quality factor more. By doing so they did not mean to underrate quantity, but only wanted to re-establish the right balance between the two. This is what *Ravidaas* means when he underlines the importance of the quality of the mind in comparison to the ritual purity *Ganges* is believed to accord.[45] Moreover, the human society has accumulated a lot of junk in the name of tradition. Much of it is just a burden, a futile heavy weight, for the human being. There is a dire as well as a continuous need to examine, discern and discard what is out-dated and irrelevant. *Kabeer* gives a categorical exhortation: 'accept the substantial and reject the insubstantial'[46].The primary things are to be attended first in comparison to the secondary things. The inner element has to get priority in relation to the outer. Quality should gain the first importance. That only can help life progress. That only assures a bright future for the human society. Quality takes care of a sense of perfection in life, which is the greatest human motto possible. The motivation for being perfect and the best model of perfection is God the Father, because he never discriminates between the good and the evil, witnesses Jesus (Mt 5.48). 'The quench for perfection is life's greatest adventure'.[47] This divine characteristic of perfection can be imbibed only by an honest commitment to quality in life.

Integration of values is to be searched for in **the quality of concord** one maintains with the divine and with the other human beings. The Unseen is reflected in the seen. Creatures are the images of the one same Creator. The Divine is to be encountered in the human and in the natural. Commitment to the Creator is to be expressed towards commitment to the creatures. The latter is the measure of the former, too. That is what *Tulseedaas* says, 'there is no religion like doing well to the other and there is no irreligion like doing harm to the other'[48]. Doing well to the other is the right worship of the Divine. Jesus says, 'whatever is done to the other is done unto me' (Mt 25.25-40).To love one's neighbour is to love God. To live in harmony with one's co-creatures, especially the humans, is to achieve harmony with the Creator. This is the Truth of God and the God of Truth –the two-in-one. When *Guru Ghaseedaas* declares that 'God is truth and truth is God'[49], he inter-twines the visible and the invisible dimension of the Higher Reality in an unparalleled way. This superb form of integration summarizes all values in life.

2.6. The Popular wisdom presents a basic ethic for all

A piece of popular wisdom is found being traditionally communicated to the younger generations of the general public. The texture of the message gives an impression that some popular saint has composed it. It is found in poetical form in *Hindi* and of late is available in cassette form with a musical rendering. It is like a formula of social values. It seems to be a lived reality of the saints. It highlights their value system, in an ironical rhetoric. It is an effective preamble to the practice of the values. The following is a free translation of the same in English.

Doing well to others is a noble ideal, but not doing harm to anyone is more noble an ideal. Being a flower to someone is meritorious, but not becoming a beast for another is more meritorious. Not being able to keep good conduct is a failure in life, but going into sin is a greater failure. Speaking truth is the golden motto, but avoiding telling a lie is more golden. Silence is better than poisonous speech. Weigh before you speak. Open your mouth only when you have a kind word to speak. Building a house for someone is a gesture of generosity, but not burning another's hut is more generous a gesture. Bandaging someone's wound is an act of mercy, but not putting alkali on the wound of someone is much more a merciful act. Trying not to add to darkness is more important than becoming a lamp and burning for others. Consoling another in his or her misery is a heavenly deed, but not causing pain to anyone is more heavenly a deed. Hence, do not become a thorn to another.[50]

3. EMERGING MISSIOLOGICAL PROSPECTS

3.1. Missiology

The above analysis of the spiritual and social message of liberation of the popular saints invites one to pursue the immense missiological possibilities that emerge from it. Missiology, when not addressed to the context, is bound to fail. Its foundation cannot be just a dead message from a Scripture of the remote past, but it has to be founded on the recent past and more so on the present living realities of the society here and now. Missiological reflection in India should not entirely rely on the imported religious and cultural affiliations of the west, but has to draw the sap of life from the spiritual resources of the social milieu within the national and regional boundaries of India. It is encouraging to note that the recent centuries have witnessed a tremendous shift of emphasis in Missiology by way of thinking for Indian context. A lot of attempts have been made in missiological research in line with the cultural riches of the country of our inheritance. Several experts have evolved from several Indian disciplines of research and have specialised in related educational affiliations. They have immensely contributed to opening new routes in missiological application. But the above saints and sages bring us to a humble realisation that missiological endeavour has miles and miles to go before it can consider itself sufficiently situated in the Indian context. It needs to open new avenues of understanding and living one's faith. These saints awaken a new taste in those who have a mission to perform for India. That would mean to say that missiological insights should spontaneously evolve from the spiritual and social heritage the above sages have experienced in their noble lives. The comprehensive message of liberation these saints have highlighted thus speaks volumes. It provides one with various valuable insights while in the mission. A disciple-like following of these sages will assure a deeper understanding of them. That will facilitate their life and message to inspire a continuing inter-action with one's own faith tradition, too. Such a missiological engagement, certainly, will open up new vistas of living one's Christian mission as well as theologising on it, which is suited to the genius of our country.

3.2. Spiritual and social commitment

A few missiological possibilities could be pinpointed, in response to certain emerging questions. The first question is: *does spiritual and social commitment necessitate a withdrawal from the normal course of life?* Most of these sages were married men and women and were true to family responsibilities. They proved by their own life that withdrawing from life is not essential for a spiritual pursuit, even for excellence in the same. Their dedication to the task of reforming the society with regard to its unbecoming ways did not make it necessary to escape from life-duties, either. Combining successfully the basic life reality of sex, marriage and family life with a saintly and social career was an exceptionally meritorious achievement they highlight by their lives. Such combination gives a touch of realism and balance in processing one's life, too. It is noble to follow the motto—'one is called to be saint'. But, it is an undeniable fact that real saints aren't those who are alienated from life realities. Only those who are well integrated in the diverse situations of life can be thought of traveling a saintly track. The above sages present a living definition of who a saint is, in the right sense of the word. This dimension of the popular saints addresses the missiological thinkers on the compulsory discipline of the Catholic Church, which detaches the spiritual and social pursuit of life from the normal divine design of being a man and woman wedded to each other.

3.3. Absolute claim?

The second question is: *can any person or community place an absolute claim on the spiritual resources and service of the society?* The Creator has intelligently distributed the life resources among his creatures. Attempting to monopolise any item of the divine gift and to sideline others as less important is because of sheer selfishness. To think in a manner, which gives importance to one self seems to be natural for every being. Animals are inclined to be selfish by instinct, whereas human beings are so by virtue of their intelligence. But, when selfishness goes to the extent of suppressing other dimensions of life, the very purpose of intelligence stands defeated. Besides, one runs the risk of losing some of the best spiritual aspects of life. Spiritual pursuit is like an open book. All human beings have equal access to it. Imbibing the qualities of the Spirit and attaining spiritual excellence are the achievements of any individual or community who pursues that track honestly. No one can claim to monopolise the same. This is true about the service of the society also. To love and serve the other is part of the basic nature every human being is endowed with. It is an invitation addressed to all. It is the sacred duty of every individual, too. Discerning the same and acting upon it in a sublime manner is one's personal merit. Therefore, no single person, religious community or cultural group can make an exclusive claim on spiritual or social excellence. The popular saints belonged to diverse traditions and communities. The superb spiritual fruits they achieved and the reformative social contributions they have rendered are highly inspiring and elevating. The fruitful life and the powerful message of the above sages invite the traditional Christian community to revise the absolute claims placed on the unique heights of spiritual experience and social service. Appropriating a humbler disposition, even after doing the best in the above arenas, would be a better response.

3.4. Harmony

The third question is: *how can harmony of life be maintained if any person or community refrains from relating to the other and being integrated to the other?* Harmony is the basic spirit of life, which affirms the commonalities of the origin, maintenance and destiny of life. The success of one's life is to be evaluated by the capacity for and the achievement of a spirit of harmony. Harmony in all aspects of life is inevitable. Special mention needs to be made of the harmony of different faiths and cultural streams. No religious or social tradition can afford to remain detached from the other and run the risk of being ineffective, it not fossilised. Such disintegration results in disharmony. Disharmony is present in our society today, much more than before. The life and message of the popular saints place a clarion call to the agents of ill will, hatred, violence and disorder, to rise above the petty and man-made boundaries and divisions in the name of caste, class, creed, language, ideology, profession, nationality etc. As these sages do not belong to any particular group, so are their poetic lines, which are addressed to all human beings of goodwill. Attempting anew a bridge building, which promotes goodwill, love, friendliness, service, cooperation and harmonious togetherness is the only way that does justice to the sublime life and message of the popular saints and sages. The above sages invite missiologists to advance anew the dialogical perspective of life, by involving in the life of the other persons and communities, by finding good in the other, appreciating the other, learning from the other and by promoting the other traditions, especially that of India.

3.5. Missiological prospects

The fourth question is: *can missiology claim any bright prospects for India without significantly incorporating the spiritual and social resources of the popular saints into the chunk of its reflection and practice?* Missiology is, in fact, reflection on the life of the humans of various traditions. Reflection makes full sense when applied to the context. The details of the context one lives in as well as the rich heritage one cherishes cannot remain untouched. Along with various field realities of India, the spiritual and social vision of these popular saints should become a significant basis of missiological reflection. Prayer habits are to be tuned in line with the superb poetical and spiritual lines of these saints. No spiritual and social endeavour worth the name is possible in India without experiencing, learning from and appropriating the sublime spirit of these sages. There is a good collection of books and articles available on these sages. Lot of research has been done in this area, too. Father Lesser, in spite of his non-Indian origin, has made a noble and praise-worthy attempt to popularise the message of these saints. The research on *Kabeer* done by Father William Dwayer and Father M.D. Thomas could be mentioned here as further efforts in this line. But, missiologists have to step in to this important field and have to experience for themselves these great sages. These sages will definitely add a new chapter in the direction of articulating an 'applied missiology' for India. A commitment of these saints and sages of India will certainly situate the missiological endeavour in a new way in the great spiritual and social resources of the Indian context. Such a new trend in missiology is the need of the hour.

CONCLUSION

More than being a holy person, wise and enlightened, a saint is one who is oneself liberated – spiritually and socially – and has a powerful message of liberation for the humanity of all times, of all places. Such were the popular saints of India. They enriched the humanity by their being in it. They had the inner stamina to flow against the current. They struggled against the various forms of discrimination, slavery and abnormalities of the respective society they were born into. They not only expounded the real spirit of religion but also lived it. They were endowed with a special *charism* of being human as well as spiritual. Their life encompassed the diverse dimensions of spiritual and social liberation. Their spiritual and social message is a clarion call to liberation in the diverse realms of human life. They have highlighted a universal spiritual foundation for human integration. They have facilitated a revolution for renewal in view of promoting integrity and quality in social behaviour, too. The process of liberation initiated by them needs to be responded to with a whole-hearted commitment, by way of imbibing its spirit and promoting it. That will, necessarily, usher the world towards a more liberated family of the humans, which, certainly, will be more conducive for living. The spiritual and social message of liberation, lived and poetically uttered by the popular saints of India, present immense missiological prospects. Imbibing the spirit of the rich spiritual and social heritage these sages has left for the humanity will definitely guide the destinies of a 'context-applied missiology' for India. Thinking anew in this direction, along the logic of Incarnation will, I am sure, not only assure a new meaning to Christian existence and mission in India, but also set a new trend in missiological reflection in India.

Endnotes

1. Sir David Goodall, Farward, R.H. Lesser, Saints and Sages of India, Intercultural publications, New Delhi, 1994, p. xi

2. Dr Rajdev Singh, *Shabd aur arth Sant Sahity Ke Sandarbh Mein*, Nand Kishor and Brothers, Varanasi, 1968, pp. 51-53
3. *Kabeer Granthavalee*, Dr Shyam Sunder Daas (Ed.), Nagree Prachaarinee Sabhaa, Varanasi, VS 2045, *Saakhee* 5.4, p. 10
4. *'Too kehtaa kaagad kee dekhee, mein kehtaa aankhin kee dekhee' – Kabeer*
5. *'Aap bichaarei so gyanee hoi' – Kabeer Granthaavalee, Padaawalee*, 52, p. 79
6. *'Aap hee aap vichaariye, tab kaisaa hoi anand re'* – Kabeer
7. *'Akath kehanee prem kee, kachu kehee na jai, goonge keree sarkaraa, baithe muskaai' – Kabeer*
8. *'Too too kartaa too bhayaa, mujhmein rehee na hoom'* – Kabeer
9. *'Jit dekhoom tit toom' – Kabeer*
10. *'Mharo to girdhar gupaal, doorsaro na koi' – Meerabai*
11. *'Ghaayal kee gati ghaayal janai' – Meerabai*
12. *'Meera ke prabhu kab re miloge, ye bin rahyaa na jai' – Meerabai*
13. *'Meim tere liye taras rehee hoom; he prabhu too mujhe apnee banaa le' – Meerabai*
14. *'Prabhu too chandan, meim panee; too Deepak, meim batee' – Ravidaas*
15. R.H. Lesser, Saints and Sages of India, Intercultural Publications, New Delhi, 1994, p. 67
16. C.C. Jung (Foreword), The spiritual teaching of *Ramana Maharshi, Shambhala*, London, 1988, pp. 48, 61
17. R.H. Lesser, Saints and Sages of India, ibid, pp. 22-23
18. *'Jab man cchod kutilaayee, tab aayee milei raam rayee' – Kabeer*
19. *'Man changaa kasautee mein Gangaa' –Ravidaas*
20. R.H. Lesser, Saints and Sages of India, *ibid*, p. 28
21. *'Sareer hee mandir musjid gurudwaaraa' – Ravidaas*
22. *'Khaalik khalak khalak mein khaalik' – Kabeer Granthavalee*, ibid, *Padaavalee*, 51, p. 81
23. *'Kastooree kundali basei' – Kabeer Granthavalee*, ibid, *Saakhee*, 53.1, p. 64
24. *'Man mathuraa dil dwaarikaa, kayaa kaasee jaanee' – Kabeer Granthawalee, ibid, Sakhee*, 23.10, p. 35
25. *'Jyoon bimbahi pratibimb samaanaa' – Kabeer*
26. *'Ghati ghati rahyo samaayee' – Kabeer Granthaavalee*, ibid, *Padaavalee* 18, p. 111
27. *'Kethne Kethee tou kya bhayaa, je kernee na thahray' – Kabeer Granthwali, ibid, Sakhee* 18.1, p. 29
28. *'Kethnee thothee jagat mein, kernee uttam saar' – Kabeer*
29. *'Kehtee to bahut milaa, garta milaa na koi' – Kabeer*, Sant Sudhaa Saar
30. *'Dar updes kusal bahutere, je aacharahi te nar na ghanere' – Tulseedaas* (*Ramacharitmanas*)
31. *'Paanee mile na aapko, auran baksat ccheer; aapan man nichal nahin, auran banthawat dheer'* – Kabeer, *Sant Kavy*, Parasuram Chatruvedi (Ed.), p. 241
32. *'Sodhee nahim sareer ko, auran ko updes' – Dadoodayal kee baanee*, Swami Mangaldaas (Ed.), p. 117
33. *'Kernee Kathin re bandagee, kehne sab aasaan; Jan Rajjab rehnee bina, kehaa milei rehmaan' – Sant Sudha Saar* (*Rajjab*), Part 1, p. 531
34. *'Kehnee meetha khaand see, kernee vish kee loy; Kethnee taj kernee karei, to vish se amrut hoi'* – Kabeer, *Sant Baanee Sangrah*, Part 1, p. 47
35. *'Pothee padi padi jag muvaa, pandit bhayaa na koi; ekei ashir peev ka, pade so pandit hoi' – Kabeer Granthavalee*, ibid, *Sakhee* 19, 4, p. 30
36. R.H. Lesser, Saints and Sages of India, *ibid*, p. 62
37. *'Daadoo poorn brahm vichaariye, tab sakal aatma ek; kaayaa ke gun deshiye, to nana baran anek' – Dodoo dayal Granthavalee*, Parsuraam Chaturvedee (Ed.), pad 27, p. 274

38. *'Sanyee ke sab jeev hain, keeree kunjer doi'* – *Daadoo Dayal Granthavelee, ibid*, p. 161
39. *'Hindu dhyavei dehura, musman maseet; jogo dhyavei parampad, jahan duhura na maseet'* – *Gorakhbaanee*, Pectambardatt Badthval (E), p. 25
40. *'Ekahi pavan ekahi panee, budhi bina beech bairtaa thaanee'* – Rajjabdaas, *Sant Sudhaa Saar*, Part 1, p. 32
41. 'Je too banbhan-banbhanee jaayaa, to aan baat hvei kehee na aayaa?' – Kabeer Granthavalee, *ibid*, p. 79
42. *'Chaari baran metike, bhakti chalaayaaa moo; Guru govind ke baag mein, Paltoo pholaa phool'* – *Sant Sudhaa Saar* (Paltoo Saheb), Part 3, p. 100
43. *'Ehu Dhamm jo aacharay, banbhanu suhuvi koi'* – Muni Devsen, *Sant Sudhaa Saar*, Viyogi Hari (E), part 1, p. 4
44. Dr K. Sreeniwasan, Sree Narayan Guru, Jay Sree Publications, Thiruvanthapuram, 1989, p. 97
45. *'Man changa to kasautee mein ganga'* – Ravidaas
46. *'Saar Saar ke gahee rehein, thothaa de uday'* – *Kabeer*
47. A French quote
48. *'Par hit saris dhamm nahin bhayee; par peeda sam nahim adhmayee'* – *Tulseedaas*
49. *'Satya hee eeshwar hei, eeshwar hee saty hei'* – *Guru Ghaasidaas*
50. *'Bhalaa kisee ka kar na sako tum'* – Satsangee Keertan (cassette), Shishodia Electronics, Nagpur, Vol.12

(Published in FOIM series on 'Creative Ministries' (Book), Mumbai, pp. 186-212 – in March 2004).

Chapter - 14

Mysticism in Kabeer and Jesus

1. INTRODUCTION

1.1. Mystery

'Mystery'[1] is 'something of which the cause or origin is hidden'. It is 'not exposed to all'. It is 'that which cannot be described'. It is the 'inner meaning or wisdom' of the ultimate reality. For ordinary human beings, it is 'impossible to understand'. One has to be eligible for that knowledge. 'Only special persons are privileged for divine endowment'. 'Persons of pure mind and heart only can know the supernatural truth'.

1.2. Mysticism

Mysticism[2] is a philosophy or a line of thought or an inclination of mind that has to do with 'mystery'. It is about 'hidden meaning or spiritual power'. It emerges from 'feelings of awe and wonder'. Mysticism would mean 'seeking union with God, and through that, attempting to realise truth that lies beyond the ordinary capacity of understanding'. It is founded on a belief that 'knowledge of God and of real truth can be attained through meditation or spiritual insight'. It is the 'spiritual experience of the divine'. It is 'love for the divine' that springs in the heart or conscience of human beings. It is a 'leaning towards the ultimate truth'. 'Curiosity for the supreme higher power' is its core factor. It expresses itself in the 'craving of the human heart for intimate union with that power'.

1.3. Mysticism beyond margins

Mysticism is a spiritual phenomenon that defies all bounds. It is a category by itself. Different religious traditions have different streams of mysticism. They cannot be cut off from each other like 'islands'. They are not independent currents like 'parallel lines', either. For the convenience of understanding one may say Hindu mysticism, Sufi mysticism, Christian mysticism, Buddhist mysticism, and the like. But, as a matter of fact, they are not compartmentalised units. They are only diverse dimensions of the same mystical phenomenon. They are sublime spiritual experiences that transcend the multifarious traditions[3]. They make a complete sense in colloquium of mystical experiences. Mysticism admits no borders. Only such an understanding can do full justice to the very concept of mysticism.

1.4. Dualistic-non-dualistic grounds of mysticism

Mysticism is grounded on the philosophy of non-dualism[4] that believes that the ultimate reality is one and only one. On the other hand, devotion or *bhakti* is founded on the philosophy of dualism[5] that considers two realities, one absolute and one relative. Accordingly, mysticism and devotion are two separate trends. But, actually, in most of the instances, devotion and mysticism are seen intertwined in some degree or other. In spite of the fact that different religious traditions have different philosophical foundations, various mystics seem to have combined devotion and mysticism meritoriously well. Their worldview gives the impression that they transcend dualistic limits and embrace non-dualistic positions. Similarly, their spiritual journey seems to have proceeded from devotion to mysticism. Devotional sentiments are more functional and ultimately mystical experiences only reach real spiritual altitude[5].

1.5. Mysticism has social implications

The basic drive of mysticism, obviously, is oriented to the divine. But, it cannot be, perhaps as traditionally understood, confine itself to individual ecstasies. It has social implications, as well. In other words, mysticism has social dimensions. Human beings are individuals and social beings at the same time. They cannot be otherwise. Individual mystic experiences have to overflow towards social mystic expressions[6]. It is an inevitable interplay between vertical and horizontal dimensions of divine experience. It is also an interaction between the social dynamics of human life. Elevated spiritual experiences have, and they have to have, a bearing on the social lives of human beings. It is the same logic of life that works in double directions. Therefore, mysticism combines social dimensions along with individual dimensions[7]. The relational network of human life, longing for one another, intimate friendships, telepathy, whole-hearted sharing, etc are proofs for the same.

1.6. Mystics and their unique contribution

Time and again, the human society has been endowed with great men and women who have left the indelible imprints of their personalities. They were capable of pioneering new currents of life, even by flowing against the challenging currents. No wonder, they changed the course of human life. Obviously, remarkable achievements of the world are to be credited their account. Saints and sages have been exceptional human beings who were finely tuned to the divine. They were not merely devotees. They emerged as great mystics on the merit of their elevated experience of the divine. Their extra-ordinary life and penetrating insights have immensely contributed not only to the spiritual uplift of the humans, but to the transformation of the human society[8]. Kabeer and Jesus were among such significant and extremely estimable mystics, who enriched the human society in an incomparable way through their novel and complete grasp of the reality of life, both the creating and the created[9].

2. *KABEER* – THE MYSTIC

2.1. *Kabeer* – a profile

Kabeer was a saint, a poet, a mystic, a great thinker, a social reformer, and the like – all rolled in one[10]. He was a product of the 15th century. He lived in *Kashi* and went to *Meghar* towards the end of his life, in order to challenge the traditional belief that 'to die in *Kashi* would merit entry to heaven and to die in *Meghar*, would lead to hell'[11]. He belonged to the *Julaha* community. He supported himself and his family by hard work.

He hailed from the so-called lower strata of the caste-ridden society of his time. Belonging to the discriminated lot of the general public, he voiced the cries, sentiments and aspirations of the 'voiceless' as well as the struggles of the ordinary people[12]. He spoke in the dialect of the general public. He moved with the common folk and lived like them. Weaving was his profession and weaving the human society into a 'well-knit human network' in all its facets was his life mission. *Kabeer* was not scientifically educated. But his ideas and insights were revolutionary as well as wise. His utterances were spontaneous, poetical and musical, simple, straightforward and colloquial. His thoughts were genuine. His experiences were practical and his expressions were bold. A new 'saint tradition' was initiated after his fashion. The exceptional blend of devotion and mysticism was its characteristic mark.

The poetic character of Kabeer was intimately linked to his mystic accomplishments. His insights were a spontaneous overflow of his deep union with the divine[13]. The categories were from the day to day life and the images from the nature. Poetry was the natural and effective tool for *Kabeer* in communicating the mystical experience. He lived a poetical spirituality and he uttered spiritual poetry. Poetry added quality to his mystic elevations. His poetical lines were mostly addressed to himself, but they communicated the diverse dimensions of his mystical ecstasy. No wonder, those mystical delicacies are of perennial value across the boundaries of caste, creed, profession, community and nationality[14].

2.2. The foundations of *Kabeer*'s mystical heights

The spiritual insights of *Kabeer* were grounded in the natural settings of human life. He understood religion in a very simple manner. Remembering the Higher Power, cherishing sentiments of faith in that power, singing *bhajan* or praises to the power, engaging in divinely conducive *satsang* (good company) or in acquaintances, rendering service to the other, etc. were some of the threads through which he composed the texture of his religion[15]. The mystic realisations he acquired through these ways not only crisscrossed the boundaries of caste, creed, traditions, community, ideology and sect but also rose above the limits of all earthly affiliations. It could be better said that he was less religious, but more human and spiritual. The message of *Kabeer* was oriented towards the re-construction of the society into a harmonious whole. 'Accept the substantial and reject the non-substantial' (*Saar-saar ko gahee rehein, thothaa de udaai*) [16] was his watchword in this spiritual process. The mystic journey of *Kabeer* was inclusive and integrated.

2.3. Indwelling of God as the mystical premises

The presence of the Creator in the creation is a fact too obvious to be negotiated. Mystical insights can emerge from the constant awareness of his abiding presence in all the created beings. *Kabeer* highlights the human heart as the real abode of the Divine. Therefore, intimate union with the Divine is the right response. The whole universe is the home of God. His categorical sayings establish the fact: 'as the whole subsists in the part' (*Khaalik Khalak Khalak mein Khaalik*) [17], 'as musk resides in the deer' (*Kastoori kundali basei*) [18], 'so dwells God in every being' (*aise ghati-ghati raam hei*)[19]; mind is *Mathura,* heart is *Dwaarika* and body is *Kaashee*' (*Man mathura dil dwaarikaa, Kayaa kaasee jaanee*)[20]. *Kabeer* advocated the universal presence of God relying on the indwelling of God. Kabeer argued further, 'the image of God is in all' (*Jyoon bimbahi pratibimb samaanaa*) [21] and 'the Divine power is present in all' (*Ghati ghati rahyo samaayee*)[22]. *Kabeer's* spiritual consciousness establishes the fact that the human heart is the temple of the Divine.

2.4. Eligibility for divine union

'Purity of heart' makes one eligible for attempting the path of divine nearness, a much more, of union with the divine. The Divine is pure and only a pure mind can encounter him. Purity of heart would mean first and foremost simplicity, i.e., the absence of duplicity. That is why *Kabeer* says 'One is capable of meeting the Ultimate Reality only when the mind clears it crookedness off' (*Jab man chhod kutilaayee, tab aayee milei raam rayee*)[23]. 'Transparency' is synonymous with purity of heart. Purity of heart is holiness or spirituality, which is capable of radiating the inner reality. This is akin to the concept of *'safa'*[24] in Sufism, which means purity of heart, mind and body. This quality of mental purity also makes one accountable in life, to both the divine and the human directions.

2.5. Approach to the mystic experiences

Personal experience was the approach to the mystic world of *Kabeer*. It emerged from the core of his being. '*Anbhai saancha*'[25], i.e. experience is true and genuine. He does not rely on '*lekhaa lekhee*'[26], i.e. what is written or narrated by others, but on '*annkhin dekhee*'[27], what he has seen with his own eyes (*Too kehtaa kaagad kee dekhee, mein kehtaa aankhin kee dekhee*) [28]. He exhorts, 'you think for yourself (i.e. experience); then you will become wise' (*Aap bichaarei so gyanee hoi*) [29]. According to him, seeing, hearing and touching the reality oneself, thinking and feeling it oneself experiencing and knowing it oneself gives one special joy, that is mystical (*Aapahi aap bichaarei, tav kaisaa hot annad re*) [30].

2.6. The indescribability of the divine as love is

Kabeer delved into the depth of the mystic ocean and affirms the indescribability of love, 'the story of love is indescribable; hardly anything can be said about it; it is like a dumb person who has taken jaggery and is not able to express what he or she feels about it, but just smiles' (*Akath kehanee prem kee kachoo kehee na jai, goonge keree sarkaraa, baithe muskaai*)[31]. That would amount to state that 'experience defies expression'. God is a matter of personal experience, as love is; one has to know Him for one self. Human language is not adequate for verbalising it and it is bound to fail. The inexpressible quality underlines the depth of his spiritual knowledge[32]. Only 'smile-like' signs can radiate the inner story.

2.7. Imbibing the divine identity

Mystical ecstasies of *Kabeer* proceed to obtaining a divine identity. He tells the Lord: 'pondering you again and again, I became you; now there is nothing left in me; and I am not in myself any more' (*Too too kartaa too bhayaa mujhmein rehee na hoon*)[33]. He continues, 'meditating on the red colour of my beloved, I also became red' (*Lalee meree laal kee...mein bhee ho gaya laal*) [34]. He seems to have lost his human identity; or better, he attained a new divine identity. Having emptied his human identity[35], his experience of the Divine reaches an exquisite culmination when he says 'I am so full of your presence; wherever I look, I see You' (*Jit dekhoom tit toom*) [36]. His complete vision seems to be taken over by the divine reality. His divine experience took the entire human and created reality in its custody. The social aspect of the mysticism in Kabeer becomes observable here.

2.8. The mystical culmination of *Kabeer*

Pearls are not found at the shore. *Kabeer* probed deep into the world of mystical delicacies. His personal experience reaches the point of an 'ecstatic communion with the divine'. He describes his mystical status decisively when he exclaims, 'I surpassed the limits and gone to the world of the unlimited (*had chhodi behad gayaa, hua nirantar vaas*) [37]. He attained the *niraakaar* divine totally. That is his final destination. The mystical caliber of *Kabeer* encompasses the universal spiritual content of the divine. Some of the analogies that are characteristically expressive of the mystical communion are 'drop and ocean', 'wife and husband', 'fish and water', bird and air', 'peacock and mountain', '*chakor* and moon beams', 'waves and sea', etc[38].

2.9. The social implications

As discussed above, the mystical ecstasies of *Kabeer* were clearly reflected in his social applications. Mystical world is one that knows no discrimination. *Kabeer* could not accommodate in any way the superior-inferior considerations among human beings in the name of birth, caste, class, ideology, profession, etc[39]. He not only outright disowned and argued against such positions, but also lived a life that is worthy of human beings. He questioned the caste-sick Brahmins 'if you are superior, why were you not born through a way other than that of the so called inferior (*Aan baat se kyoon aayaa*)? [40] He also condemned the disparity between theory and practice, which makes life incredible. He asks 'what is the use of saying things that are not done?' (*Kethnee kethee to kyaa bhayaa, je karnee na thahraay*) [41]; he continues, 'Speech is empty, action is the essence of life' (*Kethnee thothee jagat mein; karnee uttam saar*) [42]. These and many other down-to-earth insights of *Kabeer* is oriented to the transformation of human lives and they highlight the social dimensions of mystic experiences in the life of Kabeer.

3. JESUS – THE MYSTIC

3.1. Jesus – a profile

Jesus Christ is visible to the whole world by the world Christian calendar, which measures the human history as Before Christ and After Christ. Though researchers dispute the actual year of his birth as between

4 and 7 BC, what is fixed is admitted and used at the world level. The story of Jesus Christ is known to the world today mostly through the four Gospels of the Bible[43]. His auspicious birth in a stable in Bethlehem, his emergence as a great teacher with miraculous powers of healing sicknesses, performing miracles, foretelling the future, his close association with his twelve disciples, his betrayal by the apostle Judas, his crucifixion by the Romans, his death on the cross and his resurrection are the major events of his story. His birth from Mary is celebrated on December 25 as Christmas Day[44]. The date of his crucifixion is now marked as Good Friday and of the resurrection is celebrated as Easter[45].

The word 'Jesus' is the English word for Hebrew word *'Yeshua'*, which means 'one who saves'[46]. Jesus is also called 'Emmanuel', meaning 'God with us'[47]. 'Christ' refers to the *'Messiah'* in Hebrew, which means 'the anointed', 'the chosen one' and 'the promised one of Israel'. Jesus Christ is the foundational and central figure of the Christian tradition. He is known to be 'the Son of God' as per the Bible. He is considered 'the Divine living within human flesh'[48] and 'the Lord of the universe'. He is understood to be the fulfillment of the promise of the Old Testament. He was a revolutionary thinker. He was endowed with divine powers.

Jesus Christ is known for the New Testament he introduced in the world. Researchers and knowledgeable people agree that Jesus Christ has made an exceptional impact on the world, so much so that he is considered the person who has influenced the human history most[49]. Jesus Christ is known to have touched hundreds of millions of lives in the world. A vast number of people in the world, Christians or others, claim to have had a personal relationship with Jesus Christ and to have gained a new meaning and purpose for living. The 'filial experience of God'[50] he had was his utmost strength. He claimed to have experienced God, as his own Father, and himself, as God's son, to great mystical heights and details. His filial mystical ecstasies were all-inclusively applied to the human scenario, as if God became human being in a literal sense. This perspective and experience contributed to the elevation of the human being to a divine status, par excellence.

3.2. 'The image of God' as the foundation

The first chapter of the Bible vividly highlights the origins of the creation, especially the human race. 'God created man (human being) in his own image... male and female he created them'[51]. This is the foundation for the spiritual experience of human existence and for the relation between human being and God. The piece of art reflects the personality of the artist. The writer can be understood from the book or write up. The piece of poetry or music speaks of the heart of the poet or of the musician respectively.

It makes perfect sense to say that the image and likeness of the creator is inevitably found in the creation, especially in the human beings. Jesus appeared as the image of God the Father, as evident from the following citations – 'the Word was with God from the beginning' and 'through him all things were made'[52]; 'the Word became flesh and dwelt among us… came from the Father, full of grace and truth'[53]; Jesus made the Father, whom no one had seen, known[54]. The reality of 'being the image of God', nay, Son of God, was the foundation of his mystical journey.

3.3. 'Temple of God' the premise of mystical experience

The reality of the image and likeness of the Creator in the creation and human beings proceeds into a more subtle understanding of the indwelling of God in human beings in a personal way. Paul underlines this idea while writing to the Corinthians. 'The human beings are God's temple' and 'God's spirit lives in them'[55]. This concept is advanced and applied to the community, as well. 'God dwells in the community', 'he would walk among them' and their mutual relation will be 'God and his people'[56]. The mystical experience of Jesus is firmly grounded in the consciousness of indwelling of God in him. While the concept 'image and likeness of the Creator'[57] awakens a 'cosmic consciousness'[58] of the all-pervading presence of God in the universe, the awareness of being the 'temple of God'[59] where 'God dwells' facilitates a mystical realisation that human beings are the living and dynamic abode of the divine on earth. This insight made a transforming difference for the spiritual world of Jesus.

3.4. Personal experience for mystic heights

Personal experience is the mainstream of the Biblical world of spirituality. Jesus is at the core of that tradition. Jesus asks his disciples as regards the impressions of other people about him. But, he affirms the prime importance of what do they think about him in the words, 'who do you say I am'[60]. When Peter, one of the disciples, confessed his personal knowledge of Jesus, he affirmed that 'this was revealed to you…by my Father in heaven'[61]. One's experiential knowledge only stands the test. In the episode of going to the Father to prepare rooms for his disciples, Thomas, one of the distinguished disciples of Jesus, confesses his ignorance about the way to the place where Jesus was going. In response to his query, Jesus asserts 'I am the Way, the Truth, and the Life'[62]. Jesus himself is the way to the Father and therefore knowing Jesus would mean knowing the Father and the way to reach him[63]. Here also personal knowledge through one's own experience is stressed. Again, in the account of Jesus' appearance to Thomas after resurrection, the refusal of Thomas to believe without seeing and the personal appearance of Jesus to Thomas confirms the singular importance of personal experience for mystical elevations. This is all the more underlined by the incomparable quality of the outburst of Thomas as he saw Jesus with his own eyes. The confession of faith Thomas makes through the words 'My Lord and My God'[64] is indeed a superlative witness of the mystical heights that a personal experience can accord with the one who passes through it.

3.5. Understanding 'God as Father'

The word 'father' symbolises the basic relation between the creating and created realities[65]. In the general sense, 'father' is the life-giver. In the specific sense, it is a relational term. It stands for the widest relational category of life and is inclusive of all other relational categories in human life. 'Father' is like a large umbrella that brings together the entire creation in one single fold[66]. This realisation is logically founded in the human phenomenon of father begetting children and the children recognising their father as the source of their life. There is a personal touch in the entire idea. The concept of 'God as Father'[67] is open to all the sectors of the society. It is beyond the boundaries of gender, caste, class, creed, profession, language, culture, and the like. It is an all-inclusive and complete concept. Understanding 'God as Father' by Jesus is not a mere abstraction of the above creative or relational idea, but is rooted in his personal experience and in line with the messianic prophecies of the Jewish tradition[68].

3.6. The filial experience of Jesus

'Experiencing oneself as the son of God' is the natural response to 'the understanding of God as Father'[69]. Filial experience encompasses the entire gamut of the life of Jesus on earth, from birth to resurrection. His relation with his Father was so intimate that human language fails to express it adequately. He hears the voice of the Father from heaven, both at the time of the baptism and transfiguration, that accepts him as his son in the words 'this is my Son, whom I love; with him I am well-pleased'[70]. He felt that Father loves him as the Son[71] and repeats this realisation again and again. He admits that 'as the Son he does what the Father does'[72] and does nothing of his own. He explains his relation with the Father through the metaphor of 'the vine' and the 'vinedresser'[73]. His consciousness that the 'Father has sent him to the world'[74] and 'the Father loved him before the creation of the world'[75] was the pivot of his mystical life.

3.7. The mystical yearnings of Jesus

Jesus emphasised seeking and acting on the will of his Father in heaven as the eligibility for heavenly bliss and not merely taking his name[76]. This is a striking reference to an ethical code for mystical privileges.

Jesus expressed his total surrender to the will of his heavenly Father all throughout. Some of his characteristic prayers elaborate his ardent longing for the will of the Father. He is seems to be dealing with the Father as regards the hour of agony he was going through towards the end of his life. He prayed, 'Father, if you are willing, take this cup from me; yet not my will, but yours be done'[77]. Even after having been betrayed by one of his disciples and having received the worst of the behaviour from the society and its governance of the time, Jesus prayed 'Father, forgive them, for they do not know what they are doing'[78]. This is a brilliant example for the mystical elevation of Jesus that wouldn't discriminate between the good and the bad. At the end, Jesus made a total surrender of himself, saying 'Father, into your hands I commend my spirit'[79]. These are obvious instances of spiritual loftiness Jesus celebrated in his life.

3.8. The mystical ecstasies of Jesus

Jesus confesses the source of whatever he has by saying 'all things are committed to me by my Father'[80]. He also affirms his closeness with the father saying 'Father knows me and I know the Father'[81]. That is an inner knowledge, which only divinely tuned persons are gifted with. He reveals the mystery of his oneness with the Father by saying 'no one knows who the Son is except the Father, and no one knows who the Father is except the Son and those to whom the Son chooses to reveal him'[82]. He also confesses his shared ownership of everything with the Father in the words 'all I have is yours and all you have is mine'[83]. Jesus reveals his deep intimacy with and equivalence with the Father by asserting that 'one who has seen me has seen the Father'[84]. Therefore, knowing Jesus and the Father is one and the same thing[85]. He continues, 'I am in the Father and the Father is in me'[86]. He comes to the culmination of his mystical union with the Father when he says, 'I and the Father are one'[87]. He hits the highest point of his mystical ecstasy in his intense desire 'that all of them may be one, Father, just as You are in me and I am in you'[88]. Observably, the above sensitivities and details declare Jesus as having reached the zenith of his spiritual journey.

3.9. The Trinitarian dimension of mystical experience

The mystical experience of Jesus has a Trinitarian dimension. Jesus' reference to the Father is elaborately discussed above. He also referred to the Spirit or Counselor, whom 'Jesus will send from the Father'[89]. He adds, 'all that belongs to the Father is mine… the Spirit will take from what is mine and make known to you'[90]. The relation between Jesus and Father seems to be extended to the Spirit or Counselor. This seems to be a 'three-dimensional communion'. 'Three-in-one and one-in-three' is the reality reflected in the terminology of 'Father, Son and Spirit'[91]. This concept is a veritable model of self-giving, other-orientedness, love and communion, which has a singular touch mystical uniqueness[92]. This three-sided communion is more sublime than the union between two and has such unfathomable depth. This Trinitarian mysticism speaks volumes as regards the mystery of the divine, the human and the natural and the mutual relation between them[93]. It also has significant implications for the inclusive, interactive and participatory dynamics of family and community. The idea of 'diversity in unity and unity in diversity' gets a deeper meaning from the above style of mysticism, as well.

3.10. The broader dimensions of the mystical experience of Jesus

The wider application of the Fatherhood of God gives an extra credibility for the unique claim of the filial mystical union of Jesus with the heavenly Father. Jesus made his personal and relational approach to the divine open and accessible to all. While speaking to his disciples, Jesus refers to God as their Father, as well. The reference 'your Father'[94] is an all-inclusive approach to the mystical relation with God. The filial experience of Jesus was a spirituality of freedom. He did not monopolise it in an exclusive way. His filial experience was all-embracing. It was beyond the boundaries of gender and includes also experiencing oneself as a daughter of God. The basic eligibility to see God was being pure of heart, as in the beatitude[95]. It was inclusive of the poor, as cited in the beatitude of Jesus 'blessed are the poor in spirit, for theirs is the kingdom of heaven'[96] and the story of the rich man and Lazarus[97]. The filial bliss is open to the lowly placed in the society, as in the story of Zacheus[98] and the sinners, as in the story of the adulterous woman[99]. It also included the persecuted for righteousness[100] and the lost, as in the prodigal son[101]. The heavenly happiness was also open to the sick[102] and the hard-working, as in the parable of the talents[103]. This filial approach to the divine has immense scope for an extensive application in the society beyond all human boundaries of affiliations and categories.

3.11. The fraternal implications of Jesus' mystical height

The horizontal aspects of the mystical delight of Jesus were distinctively marvelous. The filial experience of Jesus spontaneously found its expression in a fraternal fashion of thought and behaviour. He wanted 'those who were given to him also to be with him to partake of the glory given by the Father'[104]. By stating 'I am the vine and you are the branches'[105] he referred to the level implications of communion. Considering the other human being one's brother or sister in a universal manner is a new way of being human. Loving the enemy, as if he is a friend[106] is nothing less than performing a revolutionary act. His role model was the Father who is perfect and does not discriminate between the righteous and the unrighteous[107]. The fraternal implications of the mystical experience of Jesus contain unlimited universal possibilities. They celebrate 'the spirit of heavenly togetherness'[108] in global consciousness. 'The other'[109] is not really the other. He or she is part of me. He or she is my 'brother' or 'sister', 'neighbour' or 'companion' in life[110]. Reaching out to the other in love and service, especially to the inimical and unfriendly as well as to the weaker and the disadvantaged of the society, is the true result of mystic experiences.

3.12. The mystic blend of divine union and human communion

Mysticism can be complete only when its vertical and the horizontal dimensions are harmonized[111]. To be socially reconciled is a fundamental requirement for spiritual rising. The instruction of Jesus to those who appear before God is clear-cut. 'One has to make sure that one's brother or sister (other human beings) has no complaint against one, before one proceeds to offer gifts before God'[112]. One cannot effectively relate to God mystically without being mystically related to human beings. Some of the world-famous teachings of Jesus are highly telling in this regard – 'do to others what you would have them do to you'[113]; 'love one another as I have loved you'[114] and 'whatever you did for one of the least of these brothers of mine, you did or me'[115]. These are certain culminating points of combining the divine and human implications that are barefaced in the mysticism of Jesus. In Jesus, there is a complete equalising of loving service to human beings and filial devotion to the Heavenly Father. The 'new mystical culture' inaugurated by Jesus is one of a perfect blend of the 'mystical union with God' and 'communion with human beings', in a spirit of family and community[116].

4. COMPARATIVE UNDERSTANDING OF THE MYSTICAL CHARACTERS

4.1. Similar traits

Kabeer had non-dualism as his philosophical base. All the same, he started his spiritual journey with *bhakti* or devotion, which is founded on the dualistic perspective of life. He proceeded to an exceptional mystical gracefulness that was supported by non-dualistic outlook and thus culminated his spiritual journey[117]. Jesus was rooted in the dualistic worldview of the Semitic traditions. All the same, he rose to the mystical heights of union with the Heavenly Father and touched upon non-dualistic peak points in an unsurpassed manner[118].

The mystical experiences of *Kabeer* were applied to the social context of the time and they contributed to the uplift of the society of the time.

The mystical pinnacle of Jesus was capable of establishing a complete 'communion' with other human beings that was equivalent to 'union' with the heavenly Father[119]. The social dimensions of the mysticism are resultant of the individual supernatural attainments and they are highly vibrant in both *Kabeer* and Jesus[120]. The mysticism of *Kabeer* and Jesus, while being distinct from each other in its singular characteristics, are similar in its general frame of mind, with more or less degrees[121].

4.2. Special traits

The mysticism of *Kabeer*, on the one hand, proceeds from the dualism-based devotion to the non-dualism-based mysticism and culminates there[122]. On the other hand, the mysticism of Jesus has a continuous interplay between dualistic relation and non-dualistic mystical union and communion[123]. The social dimension of the mysticism of *Kabeer* is not so extensive in its outreach, where as the social application of the mysticism of Jesus is comprehensive and complete in its full length.

CONCLUSION

This discussion, in its process, approach and findings, has attempted to research into the worldwide phenomenon of 'mysticism that is without bounds'. The innovative nuances of mysticism in *Kabeer* and Jesus highlighted here are the fruits of comparative consideration of the diverse angles of the phenomenon of mysticism. The social implications of mysticism as well as the interplay between dualistic devotion and non-dualistic mysticism are a special contribution of this endeavour. All the same, this research is not exhaustive and proposes to advance the research into greater altitudes of mystical implications and applications.

Endnotes

1. William, B. Parsons (Ed.), Teaching Mysticism, Oxford, 2011, p. 03
2. *Ibid,* p. 04
3. *Ibid,* p. 09
4. Randall Studstill, The Unity of Mystical Traditions, Boston, 2005, p. 167
5. *Ibid,* p. 190
6. Janet Ruffing, Mysticism and Social Transformation, New York, 2001, p. 23
7. *Ibid,* p. 53
8. William, B. Parsons (Ed.), Teaching Mysticism, Oxford, 2011, p. 253
9. *Ibid,* p. 260
10. Prof. Shrikant Prasoon, Knowing Sant Kabir, New Delhi, 2009, p. 04
11. *Ibid,* p. 27
12. *Ibid,* p. 29
13. *Ibid,* p. 53
14. *Ibid,* p. 109
15. *Ibid,* p. 47
16. Ramkishor Verma (Ed.), *Kabeer Granthaavalee*, Allahabad, 2008, p. 39

17. *Ibid,* p. 15
18. *Ibid,* p. 317
19. *Ibid,* p. 96
20. *Ibid,* p. 225
21. *Ibid,* p. 33
22. *Ibid,* p. 241
23. *Ibid,* p. 279
24. Randall Studstill, The Unity of Mystical Traditions, Boston, 2005, p. 59
25. Ramkishor Verma (Ed.), *Kabeer Granthaavalee*, Allahabad, 2008, p. 634
26. *Ibid,* p. 88
27. *Ibid,* p. 581
28. *Ibid,* p. 261
29. *Ibid,* p. 211
30. *Ibid,* p. 170
31. *Ibid,* p. 399
32. Prof. Shrikant Prasoon, Knowing *Sant Kabir*, New Delhi, 2009, p. 207
33. Ramkishor Verma (Ed.), *Kabeer Granthaavalee*, Allahabad, 2008, p. 123
34. *Ibid,* p. 175
35. Prof. Shrikant Prasoon, Knowing *Sant Kabir*, New Delhi, 2009, p. 119
36. Ramkishor Verma (Ed.), *Kabeer Granthaavalee*, Allahabad, 2008, p. 121
37. *Ibid,* p. 149
38. Randall Studstill, The Unity of Mystical Traditions, Boston, 2005, p. 109
39. Prof. Shrikant Prasoon, Knowing *Sant Kabir*, New Delhi, 2009, p. 269
40. Ramkishor Verma (Ed.), *Kabeer Granthaavalee*, Allahabad, 2008, p. 67
41. *Ibid,* p. 212
42. *Ibid,* p. 347
43. Luke Painter, Finding the Roots of Christianity: A Spiritual and Historical Journey, Eugene, 2017, p. 06
44. *Ibid,* p. 07
45. *Ibid,* p. 08
46. The Holy Bible, Michigan, 1994, Mt 1.23, p. 1094
47. *Ibid,* Mt 1.21, p. 1194
48. Luke Painter, Finding the Roots of Christianity: A Spiritual and Historical Journey, Eugene, 2017, p. 06
49. *Ibid,* p. 109
50. *Ibid,* p. 43
51. The Holy Bible, Michigan, 1994, Gen. 1.26, 27, p. 2; Col. 3.10, p. 1342; James 3.9, p. 1381; Mt 19.4, p. 1117
52. *Ibid,* Jn 1.1-4, p. 1205
53. *Ibid,* Jn 1.14, p. 1206
54. *Ibid,* Jn 1.18, p. 1206
55. *Ibid,* 1 Cor. 3.16, p. 1298; 2Cor 6.16, p. 1316
56. *Ibid,* Ex 25.8, p. 90; 2Cor 6.16, p. 1316
57. Luke Painter, Finding the Roots of Christianity: A Spiritual and Historical Journey, Eugene, 2017, p. 72
58. Robert Crookall, The Interpretation of Cosmic and Mystical Experiences, London, 2011, p. 63
59. Luke Painter, Finding the Roots of Christianity: A Spiritual and Historical Journey, Eugene, 2017, p. 07
60. The Holy Bible, Michigan, 1984, Mt 16. 13-14, p. 1113
61. *Ibid,* Mt 16.15-17, p. 1114

62. Luke Painter, Finding the Roots of Christianity: A Spiritual and Historical Journey, Eugene, 2017, p. 117
63. The Holy Bible, Michigan, 1994, Jn 14.1-7, p. 1226
64. Luke Painter, Finding the Roots of Christianity: A Spiritual and Historical Journey, Eugene, 2017, p. 146
65. Correna, R. Barzey, Steps to Knowing God: A Spiritual Journey, Bloomington, 2018, p. 33
66. *Ibid,* p. 70
67. *Ibid,* p. 72
68. *Ibid,* p. 80
69. *Ibid,* p. 109
70. The Holy Bible, Michigan, 1994, Mt 3.17, p. 1096; 17.5, p. 1114
71. *Ibid,* Jn 5.20, p. 1211
72. *Ibid,* Jn 5.19, p. 1211
73. *Ibid,* Jn 15.1, p. 1227
74. *Ibid,* Jn 17.20, 1230
75. *Ibid,* Jn 17.24, p. 1230
76. *Ibid,* Mt 7.21, p. 1101
77. *Ibid,* Lk 22.42, p. 1199
78. *Ibid,* Lk 23.34, p. 1201
79. *Ibid,* Lk 23.46, p. 1201
80. *Ibid,* Lk 10.22, p. 1180
81. *Ibid,* Jn 10.15, p. 1220; Jn 8.55, p. 1218
82. *Ibid,* Mt11.27, 1106
83. *Ibid,* Jn 17.10, p. 1230
84. *Ibid,* Jn 14.9, p. 1226
85. *Ibid,* Jn 14.7, p. 1226
86. *Ibid,* Jn 14. 9, p. 1226
87. *Ibid,* Jn 10.30, p. 1221
88. *Ibid,* Jn 17.21, p. 1230
89. *Ibid,* Jn 15.26, p. 1228
90. *Ibid,* Jn 16.15, p. 1229
91. Luke Painter, Finding the Roots of Christianity: A Spiritual and Historical Journey, Eugene, 2017, p. 109
92. Randall Studstill, The Unity of Mystical Traditions, Boston, 2005, p. 136
93. *Ibid,* p. 118
94. The Holy Bible, Michigan, 1994, Mt 6.4,6,8,18, p. 1099; Mt 6.26, p. 1100; Mt 10.29-31, p. 1105
95. *Ibid,* Mt 5.8, 1097
96. *Ibid,* Mt 5. 3, p. 1097
97. *Ibid,* Lk 16.19-30, p. 1190
98. *Ibid,* Lk 19.1010, p. 1193
99. *Ibid,* Jn 8.1-11, p. 1216
100. *Ibid,* Mt 5.10, p. 1097
101. *Ibid,* Lk 15. 11-24, pp. 1188-89
102. *Ibid,* Mk 5. 21-34, pp. 1141-42
103. *Ibid,* Mt 25.14-23, p. 11250
104. *Ibid,* Jn 17.24, p. 1230
105. *Ibid,* Jn 15.5, p. 1227
106. *Ibid,* Mt 5.43-44, p. 1099
107. *Ibid,* Mt 5.45-48, p. 1099

108. Randall Studstill, The Unity of Mystical Traditions, Boston, 2005, p. 132
109. *Ibid,* p. 109
110. *Ibid,* p. 213
111. *Ibid,* p. 119
112. The Holy Bible, Michigan, 1994, Mt 5.23-24, p. 1098
113. *Ibid,* Mt 7.12, p. 1100
114. *Ibid,* Jn 13.34, p. 1226
115. *Ibid,* Mt 25.40, p. 1128
116. Randall Studstill, The Unity of Mystical Traditions, Boston, 2005, p. 287
117. Prof. Shrikant Prasoon, Knowing *Sant Kabir*, New Delhi, 2009, p. 207
118. Luke Painter, Finding the Roots of Christianity: A Spiritual and Historical Journey, Eugene, 2017, p. 101
119. *Ibid,* p. 104
120. Osho, The Revolution, Mumbai, 2007, p. 163
121. *Ibid,* p. 139
122. Prof. Shrikant Prasoon, Knowing *Sant Kabir*, New Delhi, 2009, p. 219
123. Luke Painter, Finding the Roots of Christianity: A Spiritual and Historical Journey, Eugene, 2017, p. 193

Chapter - 15

Education as Building Human Beings

INTRODUCTION

Kabeer, the renowned mystic and popular saint poet of the medieval period, was a giant stalwart of the Guru tradition in India, as well. His characteristic lines '*Guru govind dou khade, kake lagu pau; Bali hari guru aapne, govind diyo batay*' pays the best respect to those who are privileged to be teachers as well as the gurus of the world. Guru shows the way of life. Guru is God incarnate! Therefore, I salute Guru first!

Education is not a syllabus-bound close circuit of imparting ready-made information or processed knowledge. It would mean learning to think and act, applied to the context. It is the continuous process of growing towards larger dimensions and degrees of life. It is an unending journey of becoming more and more inclusive through interaction with diversities. It is the art of culturing human beings in order to facilitate the spirit of living in harmony with the natural, the human and the divine and at the same time and at the same time to celebrate it in life.

1. THE EDUCATIONAL SECTOR TODAY – AN OVERALL PICTURE

1.1. Education in India

The present system of education in India and its wide and popular form are to be attributed to the British rule. Both public and private sectors provide education in India. Central, state and local levels regulate and support the endeavour. The Indian Constitution affirms education as a fundamental right. It is pleasing to note that the literacy and primary education rate has considerably risen today.

1.2. Better financial prospects

The educational sector today is more attractive in terms of its financial returns. For instance, a lecturer of a degree college was drawing just Rs 1,000 in 1967. After 35 years, thanks to the 6th pay commission, he or she is drawing Rs 35,000, i.e., an increase of 35 times.[1]

1.3. Some basic challenges

Approximately one-third of the population of the country is illiterate still. There is a very high percent of drop outs in higher education at different levels. The qualification of a considerable percentage of the teachers is inadequate. Roughly one-fourth of the teaching positions seem to be vacant. The national vision of education is not inclusive and effective enough.

1.4. Poor quality of education

The quality of education in India is on the whole poor. Excellence in education is seen only in certain pockets, i.e., some creditable institutions as well as in a large number of brilliant individuals. The general low quality of education in India is certified also in comparison to other major developing nations.

1.5. Educational content is highly theoretical

The syllabus of education in the country is overloaded by theories and concepts. Students have to busy themselves with too much of abstract and imaginary content. Very little of it is applied to the varied situations of life. It is insufficiently oriented to practical life as well as to the job ahead. Most of the problems of the country and of the society are hardly studied and therefore most of the degree-holders are incapable of suggesting a way forward. The educational content needs to be much more realistic and field-based.

1.6. The third national policy of education

Recently the HRD Minister, *Mr Kapil Sibbal*, announced the commitment of the government to revise the national policy of education, in the context of globalisation and the changes in the area of education.[2]

This is going to be the third revision of the policy in the independent India, after the policies of 1968 and 1986. Will there be in the new policy a due emphasis on the basic information of the diverse religious-social traditions and on the universal human, ethical and spiritual values as well as on the secular ethos of the Constitution? Is it going to address the deficiencies of the present system?

1.7. The dismal picture of education on Bollywood films

Hindi films 'Three Idiots', *'Taare Zameen par'*, etc present the character of the teacher or the role of educational sector in a bitter taste.

They are indeed a mirror to know the impact of education today. Hardly any step seems to have been taken by the educational and administrative sectors, in view of addressing the concerns highlighted in these films.

1.8. Low image of the teacher in the society

The image of the teacher in the Indian society today has considerably fallen and even shattered. The vast majority of the students seem to just use the service of the teachers, as much as they need. For the rest, the teacher hardly matters to them. Scandals, like 'marks for sex' of the Jabalpur University, lack of commitment of the teachers to the students, etc could be a few reasons.

1.9. The teaching profession do not attract the students

Students of exceptional calibre mostly are not inclined to follow the suit of the teachers. The teaching profession seems to have lost its charm and attraction. The number of qualitative teachers is significantly coming down. Is it that teachers today are no more inspiring or very little inspiring? Has teaching become like the 'salt that has lost its saltiness'?

1.10. Teaching a last resort?

A high per cent of teachers today seem to have become teachers because they could not qualify themselves for any other job. The chunk of the teaching staff all over the country seems to be so. Is it that teaching is the easiest job? Is teaching just fulfilling the syllabus? Is this fact a highly discouraging phenomenon?

1.11. Teaching in the class rooms or outside?

Justice *Markanday Katju* observes, 'much of the real education takes place in private coaching institutes and at the residence of teachers who make much more money there than in their institutions'.[3] Is it because proper teaching is not taking place in the class rooms? Or is it that teachers have become increasingly commercially motivated?

1.12. Concerns of the teachers

In the words of Justice *Markanday Katju*, 'in many of the staff rooms of our educational institutions, teachers, instead of discussing academic matters, often discuss petty politics, often of a casteist nature, or matters pertaining to their service conditions'.[4] Why advancing knowledge as well as problems connected to teaching does not occur to the teachers? Are the teachers getting more and more disoriented?

1.13. 'Teachers' Day' a mere ritual

'Teachers' day' is being celebrated since 1962, when *Sarvpalli*

Radhakrishnan became the second president of the country. Honouring a few teachers with an award by the president, publishing a write up or two in newspapers exalting the guru tradition of the country and having a programme of paying respects to the teachers of the respective schools are some of the routine rituals of the day. 'Teachers' day' seems to be just one of the formalities of the festival-loving country of ours, with very little outcome.

1.14. Why not a day of re-charging or introspection?

Teachers need to be technically equipped and professionally empowered time to time. But, our country, tragically so, does not seem to feel the need of a day or a few days every year for such a re-charging exercise or even introspection. The morale of the teachers needs to be strengthened as well as the quality of education has to be improved. But who will bell the cat?

2. CERTAIN IRONIC OUTCOME OF EDUCATION

Shashi Tharoor notes as regards the real outcome of education, 'education wasn't just exams; it was what's left behind in their minds when they have forgotten what they learned for exams!'[5] But, what is left behind is definitely intended to be positive. But, something contrary seems to emerge.

2.1. Education makes people more individualistic and selfish

To think for oneself is basic to everybody. But, 'the educated seem to be more self-centred and individualistic' than others. As a matter of fact, the education and the opportunities they received from the society should make them feel more accountable for the society, as a gesture of paying back what they have received. Education is oriented to making responsible social beings. But the educated on the whole seem to seek their own career and security and they have hardly any concern for the rest of the society. The creation of a highly consumerist, competitive, intolerant and oppressive high class and upper middle-class society is the natural outcome of this dangerous unsocial or anti-social phenomenon.

How could education make people so ungrateful to the society for what they have received? Why does education fail in making socially aware and awakened citizens? How could education make them so introvert, deep down in their hearts? How could knowledge make the educated highly arrogant and indifferent to the masses? Is not the system of education defective somewhere?

2.2. Educated people tell more lies

Telling lies, per se, is a bad attribute, because it is a way of deceiving others. It creates a moral dilemma. But, ironically though, it seems to be an essential characteristic in human beings. All people tell lies. Some people are naturally better at lying than others. A certain survey states that men lie more than women. While men seem to lie thrice a day and women lie twice a day. Extroverts tend to lie more often than introverts, too.

All categories of people tell lies. But, according to a study, 'educated people tell more lies'. The educationally and socially skilled people make better liars than uneducated and simple people. Uneducated and simple people also tell lies. But, since they are more genuine, honest and tactless, they often fail to justify themselves and are highly inclined to get trapped. The educated are smart and successful, because they are capable of presenting lies more convincing than truth itself. Advocates are educated and are known to be liars by profession. They fabricate arguments in order to reach a target of conclusion set earlier. 'End justifies the means' is the logic that guides the destiny of liars.

Education per se is oriented to culturing the human beings. It is supposed to inculcate values. Therefore, the tendency to lie has to be reduced at least in some degrees. But, education mostly creates expert lairs. *'Satyamev jayate'* is the national motto of the country. But, Indians in general are acclaimed for being naturally exceptional at their capacity for being privately smart and therefore for intelligent ways of lying. No wonder, sugar-coated lies are a commonplace occurrence.

Therefore, while affirming the importance of education, considering the negative role of education in intensifying the ethical tragedy of lie, the fundamental question arises, is education the ultimate value in life? I suppose, teachers could answer this question the best.

The great poetess Elizabeth Wordsworth (Dame) observes, 'If all the good people were clever, And all clever people were good, The world would be nicer than ever, We thought that it possibly could'. But, the clever, by virtue of their cleverness, fabricate lies after lies and cheat good people who considerably are hesitant to tell lies.

What does education produce – clever people or good people? I suppose, mostly clever people and not good people! This is in fact disorientation of education. What are the possible measures for striking a balance? Can education stop producing liars and bad people? When does education succeed in producing a considerable percentage of good people?

2.3. Education adds to the creamy layer

Educated people, as a result of their education, manage to get job in high-ranking sectors and secure substantial envelopes. They conveniently seem to join the class of the creamy layer. They enjoy themselves in an exclusive close circuit of life. They join the class of the rich and thus substantially contribute to widening the disparity between the rich and the poor. They do not seem to be interested in sparing anything from their comfort zone of life. They do not show any interest in supporting the uplift of the masses in any way.

Ironically though, the educated seem to push the ladder away after having climbed up the roof with its support. How does education make them unsociable and irresponsible beings? Is not education helping them belong to the class of oppressors? Is not education failing in terms of the overall development of the society? Is not then the very purpose of education defeated? Is not education doing a disservice to human beings by making them what they are not supposed to become?

2.4. Education fails to teach basic human values

A large majority of the educated young people do not appear to be grounded in a solid system of values. Consumerist tendencies are very strong in them. Enjoying life by way of food, sex and amenities of life seems to be their motto. They seem to have lost the basic sense in the art of dressing as well as the way they conduct themselves in life. Their public behaviour is so funny, showy and boisterous. There is very little regard for the senior generation, including the teachers. Fabricating stories to suit their purpose is a commonplace thing.

Most of those who have got educated in schools, colleges and universities practice hardly any sense of etiquette in public life. Often the great number of the educated youngsters gives the impression that they are not educated at all. Very many of them seem to have got derailed from the value-track of life. No wonder, there is a higher grade of suicides and mental break down in the psychological and sociological graph of the society. A substantial percent of them do not seem to have any commitment in life.

While granting some margin for the generation gap as well as the influence of modernistic thinking, do we not see a topsy-turvy of education itself? Doesn't it follow that education has failed to teach them the basic human values of life? If education does not lay a solid value-foundation in their life, how could the entire educational engagement be justified?

2.5. Education in a religious country pathetic in ethical values

India is world-acclaimed as a religious country, as if an absolute truth. Almost all the religious traditions of the world are in India. No country can ever compete with India in terms of the ritual beliefs, traditions and practices Indians are habituated with. The number of places of worship in the country makes a world record, even outnumbering many times the educational, medical and social facilities as well as rendering insignificant basic needs, like toilet. The amount of time people in India engage themselves for the religious cause defeats all calculation. The religious sentiment flows in the form of cash, gold and silver, beyond all measures. All the same, the religious traditions and practices have not taught the followers of religions the basic ethical and spiritual values of life. Recently, *Mr Jairam Ramesh* underlined the need of toilets in comparison to temples and some people even reacted from a fix of blind, emotional and fanatic faith.

Has not education added to the heavy failure of religions in sharpening ethical consciousness in the students? Has not education bypassed teaching fundamental lessons of life, like the sense of being humane, being socially sensitive, keeping public hygiene, caring for public property, loving beyond the set boundaries, serving all communities, thinking inclusive and living harmoniously? Has not education by and large contributed to a disoriented and under-cultured citizenry and society? Has not education contributed to the ethical bankruptcy of the society and the country?

2.6. Education leaves people in their weak integrity

Sociological thinker *V. Raghunathan* in his book 'Games Indians Play' elaborates twelve characteristics as a mark of our 'Indian-ness'. They are – 'low trustworthiness, being privately smart and publicly dumb, fatalist outlook, being too intelligent for our own good, abysmal (extremely bad) sense of public hygiene, lack of self-regulation and sense of fairness, reluctance to penalise wrong conduct in others, mistaking talk for action, deep-rooted corruption and a flair for free riding, inability to follow or implement systems, a sense of self-worth that is massaged only if we have the 'authority' to break rules and propensity to look for loopholes in laws'.[6] The weak sense of integrity that is reflected from these features is obvious.

India is notoriously one of the most corrupt countries of the world, and in some aspects, the most corrupt. *Sharad Yadav*, Leader of *Raashtrey Janata Dal* Party, once said, 'corruption is in our blood'. 'Compromise' is the watchword of the country. People in India are capable of compromising anything. It can accommodate everything, even the worst of the evils and give the evil-doer a clean chit. Adulterating things is counted as a means to maximum profit and therefore success. '*Chalegaa*', '*chaltaa hei*', '*theek hei yaar*', etc are a few of the symptomatic commonplace maxims. Transparency is not understood as a value. Attempting integrity is a sure way to failure in life. These mainstream tendencies and practices seem to be some of the national traits of Indians.

What does education do to change the worldview or improve the sad predicament? Does not education add to the junk? Why education is incapable of strengthening the moral fibre of the students? What is the percentage of students who become citizens with basic integrity of life? What answer the teachers of the country have with regard to this anomaly?

2.7. Education does not promote civilised public habits

The uncivilised habits in public are a clear proof for this dilemma of the Indian character. Tearing off a page from a library book, skipping classes without permission of the teacher or the school authorities, leaving the school and college campus dirty, etc. are certain uneducated ways among students and teachers. Writing their names on the walls of Taj Mahal or lifts and at bus stops is a market-level behaviour seen among very many educated boys and girls. Jumping the red lights and queues, overtaking from the left, covering the road with vehicles from one side, not honouring the zebra crossing and traffic signals, being un-courteous even to an aging pedestrian or a child to cross the road, not caring for the closed gate at railway crossing, etc. are some blatant public habits of uncivilised nature. These misdeeds are most committed by educated people.

Polluting the air through noise, running the tap full blast while shaving, illegitimately occupying others' seats in the train, disturbing others through microphone at night by violating the Supreme Court verdict and choking and dirtying public places are symptoms of illiterate behaviour of the so called educated. Mostly the educated are responsible for irrational behaviours, like taking marriage processions to the road and even at the late hours of the night and taking religious processions at festivals and blocking the traffic and leaving the road a carpet of garbage. That is why *V. Raghunathan* states 'we are largely a less-civilised people than most other major nationalities and hence we need to take a fresh look at ourselves'.[7]

How could it not occur to the educational system in India that awakening a sense of civilised behaviour in the students is central to education? How could educational system be so deaf and dumb to the sociological mess of the country? What is that bookish education for if it does not produce any fruit in day-to-day life?

2.8. Wrong models from the elder generation make education fruitless

Whatever religious instruction and good education one may receive, good example of the seniors, especially of those placed in high pedestals, is the best teacher. There are very many teachers who in their person are opposite to what they teach in their classes. A considerable percent of teachers do not reflect in their person what they teach. Only a small number of teachers stand out as good models. However, best education the youngsters may get from their class rooms, most of the models they see in the political, administrative, commercial, social, corporate, religious and educational fields are sharp counter-witnesses. The youngsters imbibe successful ways as per the standards of the world. Even innocently they are more negatively influenced by the society than positively.

No wonder, the time-consuming, energy-consuming, expensive and laborious process of education get badly defeated by the scandalous behaviour of the senior generation in the society. It seems to be a tragic vicious circle. Is there a way out? If there is, what is the way out?

2.9. Sin of Omission of the educated

Doing and not doing are two poles of life. Popular thinking places more emphasis on commission and less on omission. But, actually, the sense of omission is more serious than the sense of commission. Only a small minority of people engages or commits. Vast majority of people are accustomed to evade or omit. *Raghunathan* refers to this symptom of social malady as he quotes in his book the German Pastor Martin Niemoller, who made a famous statement about the inactivity of German intellectuals, following the Nazi rise to power and the purging of their chosen targets, group after group – ‘First they came for the communists and I didn’t speak out because I wasn’t a communist. Then they came for the Trade Unionists and I didn’t speak out because I wasn’t a Trade Unionist. Then they came for the Jews and I didn’t speak out because I wasn’t a Jew. Then they came for me and there was no one left to speak for me’.[8]

This statement perfectly applies to the Indian mindset of fatalism in a more severe manner. Fatalism seems to be ingrained in the Indian psyche and it is reflected in the day to day actions of people, as if they are genetically encoded to be like what they are. Have the gods of the religious country genetically doomed their devotees or predestined them?[9] Unlike most other nations, there is a high degree of passivity, sense of omission and lack of self-regulation in India.

The silence of the educated is more serious than the noise of illiterate crimes. Their sense of omission is in fact sin of omission. Is education of this great country seems to be infertile with regard to making the educated rise above the fatalist mindset? How is that the educated turn out to be incapacitated and passive in becoming the brain for the illiterate and the exploited and the voice for the voiceless! How is that educated people do not get awakened to the problems of the society? How on earth the educated do not get trained in becoming leaders of the society, in the right sense of the word? How could the tragic outcome of Indian education be justified? What is the way forward for such a phenomenal and symptomatic education?

3. THE PERSON AND MISSION OF THE TEACHER

3.1. The stone-cutter who was 'building a temple'!

Let me narrate 'the story of three stone-cutters', which I heard some time ago. I think, the story does a god job in scanning the mindset of the teachers. There was a gentleman who was known for his positive and interactive disposition in life. Once, after a heavy day in the office, he went out for a stroll. Before long, he reached a place where he saw some men breaking stones. He asked the first man he met, 'friend, what are you doing?' The man shouted at the gentleman, 'can't you see what I am doing? I am breaking stones.' Realising that the man was in a bad mood, he moved on without showing any reaction.

As the gentleman reached another man, he asked the same question, 'friend, what are you doing?' He answered in a helpless tone, 'Sir, I have a wife and three children. I am earning my livelihood and that of theirs'. The gentleman nodded, 'I do understand and appreciate it'. Having said this, he moved on.

The gentleman reached the third man. At the very sight, he was fascinated by seeing him hammer the stones gently with a smile and shake his head, as if humming a tune. He asked him the same question, 'friend, what are you doing?' The man replied with a broad smile, 'Sir, I am making a temple'. The gentleman, enthusiastically exclaimed, 'Is it so? Great indeed! I wish your dream come true and your effort blossom up very soon'.

As the gentleman went on, he couldn't help reviewing the instance. The first man was angry with himself, with the world, with life, with the stone and even with the wayfarer. The second man was badly weighed down by the compulsions of his life. The third man was really enjoying his work to all details.

Besides, the world of the first man was as small as the piece of stone he was breaking. The world of the second man was as big as his family. The world of the third man was as large as a temple, which he believed, will be the dwelling place of God.

Moreover, as regards the spirit of work, the first man was almost displaced in his life, where as the second man was on the track of his duties. But, the third man, rich with a very large and other-oriented perception of life, was relishing his work, with his mind and soul immersed in it. His positive disposition not only motivated himself in his work but also was boosting and soothing as well as a joy for others.

3.2. The teacher who 'builds human temples'!

The above story, though simple, speaks volumes! I think, the story is a perfect mirror to the battalion of those people who are called and are privileged to be 'teachers'. I see three types of teachers.

The first type is a set of 'displaced teachers'. Having been unable to find a space elsewhere or having found themselves incompetent in other areas or thinking that teaching is the easiest career, they approach teaching as a work. But, since they have not been tuned to the skill of the trade, they are full of complaints – about the educational system, the syllabus, the administration, the students, the premises, and the like. They are literally displaced and misplaced. Obviously, it is for the students and the educational institutions to pay for the dull end result. Without doubt, they need to be put into their right track, but not necessarily teaching.

The second type of teachers is there for earning a living. They perform their teaching duties fairly well, but their primary interest is the returns of their work, for them and for their families. Teaching is only a means for their livelihood. There is hardly any creativity or initiative. Evidently, they need improvement towards the sacred demands of the work in hand as well as towards the right motivation and focus of the same.

The third type of teachers means business. In fact, they are there because they are teachers, in the right sense of the word. With interest and creative initiatives, they put their heart and soul into educating the children. Palpably, they are on their right track. They enjoy teaching and teach the young girls and boys as if they are 'building human temples'. No wonder, they not only inspire and motivate the students, they leave a print in the mind of the students that is impossible to remove. Proudly so, they are not only builders of human beings, but they contribute their mite to building nations and societies that are humane and full of wellbeing.

Regret to observe that the third category of 'genuine teachers' is the smallest in number in the world of educators. The first category forms the second largest section, while the second category composes the largest group. It is heartening to note that the third, though the smallest, is the ideal and the most effective in the educational sector. It is unpleasant to note that the second and the largest group of teachers are mediocre and lukewarm, with hardly any impact worth mentioning. It is highly shocking to realise that the first category is not only a burden to the educational area but also is fatally harmful to it.

3.3. A question posed to the Teacher!

Oh! dear teacher, do you see yourself in the large crystal clear mirror that is placed right in front of you? Where do you find your space? In which rung of the gallery are you seated? Have you really taught anyone so far? Or are you vegetating as a teacher? Have you found a niche in the inner recesses of any of your students? Or are you a failed teacher? Do you relish the job of making human temples as a sacred mission? Do you recognise the divine quality of a teacher in you? Do you deserve the great attribute 'teacher'? What is your fate?

3.4. Teachers – A Critique

How many teachers are able to find a space amid the chosen ones of the students? Is it because they do not consider it a value or they do not want it or are careless about that? Or is it that they do not have the academic calibre or that they do not have the human qualities required for the same? Why, after years and even decades of close acquaintance with the students, a vast majority of the teachers get derailed from the lives of the students? Why a large number of teachers get easily erased from the minds of the students?

Why, after elaborate and tireless teaching of lessons and lessons of the syllabus, most of the teachers fail to teach 'that lesson', which is the most fundamental in human life? Why, after passing millions of students to brilliant lives, *lakhs* of teachers get worn out as 'nobodies'? Why, after promoting the students class by class, above 90 percent of the teachers do not get promoted as 'gurus'? Why, teachers fail to live in the hearts and minds of the students and fail to guide the destinies of their lives in the 'class rooms' of life? What is that basic factor that blocks a teacher from being a 'genuine teacher'? This is a question that stares at every teacher, especially the one who fails in being a real teacher!

3.5. Inspiring Models of Great Teachers!

At this juncture, it is my great pleasure to recall to my mind a few teachers I am privileged to have had in my lifetime, as an exceptional and esteemed treasure. I do not venture to take their names now. To call them mere teachers would be too little for them, because they were 'great teachers' or better, 'gurus'. The very thought of those 'gurus' brings before me, even now, their moving picture that awakens in me spontaneously a sense of deep admiration and reverence. They literally taught me lessons of life. But more than that, they 'touched' me, at the core of my heart. I salute them for what they have been to me!

Those 'gurus' have extensively contributed to the making of what I am today. Even this very write up, I believe, has to be credited into their account. They will ever live in my heart till the end of my life and enjoy the credit of all that is good in me, in some way or other. Perhaps you are interested to know, why only those few are the 'chosen ones' and not others who would number, say a fifty if not a hundred? Though other teachers did teach me very well various syllabus-bound things, they failed to obtain a space in the niche of my heart! A real teacher is he or she who rises to the privilege of being a 'guru' and dwells in the hearts of the students, for all times!

3.6. Teaching is a calling and a mission

Unlike many teachers think, teaching is not a profession. It is not a job. It is not a career, either. It is a 'calling' of a superior character. If it is a job, it is higher than all other jobs. It is a mission of culturing human beings. It implies assisting the young minds to get informed, to understand, to assess, to think for themselves and to apply into their lives and that of others.

Teaching is a personal engagement with the students in view of cultivating their character in a value-based way. It would mean meeting the students in person and travelling with them in their search for life, as a trustworthy companion. Teaching is sharing with the students the lessons of life the teacher has learned for himself or herself. Further, teaching entails facilitating the young hearts to experience life for themselves, cross the boundaries, feel with the other and love him or her beyond measure.

3.7. Teaching is learning

The most fundamental misunderstanding that exists among teachers is that 'teachers are a breed who knows everything and is meant to teach and teach'. No wonder, such teachers literally fail to teach and even teach anything worthwhile. A teacher, first and foremost, is a learner and a humble learner. Such learners constitute the type of teachers who teach and teach much, in the process of learning.

O V Vijayan as a young Marxist went to a village to teach. He says, 'I went to teach, but I began to learn'[10] The teacher has to keep learning with the students. He or she has to learn the students, as well. In fact, the teacher, if attentive enough, learns more from the students than from books.

There is an interesting episode in the stories of *Mahabharat*. The gopis were passionately longing for *Krishna*, while he was deeply in love with *Radha*. *Uddhav* was sent to teach *gopis* lessons of moderation. To his utter shock, he came back totally changed in his outlook. Well, the teacher has several lessons to learn from the little angels whom they want to teach! Learning from children is an art, yes, the art of living especially for grownups.

Besides, many a teacher stop learning when they are through and through with the syllabus. This is a dangerous phenomenon. Ongoing learning has to be a regular habit of the teacher. The process of teaching requires unlearning various hard-learned lessons and re-learning them. Old perceptions and concepts are to be replaced by new ideas and viewpoints.

The world of data and approaches needs constant self-assessment, examination and re-examination. The teacher has to be up-to-date with dynamics of education as well as elevated as to his or her human tuning. This is unavoidable for placing the students on the track of learning, interiorising and thus of becoming enlightened and cultured.

3.8. Teaching is facilitating transformation

Treating the patients is a science as well as an art. A seasoned nurse knows the art of giving even the most painful injection to the patients. She engages in a friendly and warm chat with the patient. While relishing light moments with them, she does her job, so much so that the patient wouldn't know when the needle pierced him or her. Similarly, a skilled and experienced teacher imparts values and lessons of life in a spontaneous manner. The students wouldn't feel the pinch of learning. Such an approach is vital to the transformation the teacher intends to facilitate in the students.

The process of teaching is oriented to transform the lives of the students. The teacher facilitates the students and in that process he or she reaches them. He or she has to enter into a relationship with the students. The teacher not only teaches ideas but oneself – one's perceptions, attitudes, values, experiences, dreams and commitments. He or she has to be transparent, like a glass. The teacher has to make it easy for the students to see him or her through. The teacher himself or herself is the teaching proper. Only then teaching becomes transformative.

3.9. Teaching means getting relieved of the '*Gururin*'

Receiving and giving are two sides of the coin of life. Everyone receives and gives from birth to death. Normally, one receives more in the younger days and gives more in the elder days. Growing up is to be measured against the measure of giving.

Paying the *Gururin* back is the golden returns of education. Students have received from the teachers so much that it cannot ever be measured. One would never be able to duly pay the teachers back for what one has received. No doubt, students have to be taught to recognize the '*Gururin*', i.e., the obligation of having received knowledge and lessons of life from the teachers. But, teachers were students once and their being teachers is the best opportunity to pay the '*gururin*' back. Being a good teacher, even better than the teachers they had, is the challenge before this sacred job.

Getting relieved of the obligation could have practical implications, as well. The teacher has to pay the '*Gururin*' back to his or her teachers by 'investing a portion of his or her earning for supporting a poor child for schooling'. Such a noble gesture will certainly inspire his or her students to do likewise to set apart a portion of his or her earning for supporting a poor student for schooling when he or she is on job, if not while studying. The teacher who ventures into such humanitarian way of paying his or her '*gururin*' back will not only set a good model for others, but will 'teach definitely better'. This is a sure way of promoting social harmony as well as living human and spiritual values in life.

3.10. Teaching is 'building human beings'

A builder is a designer. He or she conceives an idea and develops it into a shape. He or she is a planner who sketches the draft of the idea. He or she is an engineer or artist who fashions the end product as a fine piece of artifact. What is to be built is a temple out of human ingredients. What makes the builder, the engineer and the artist eligible for building the human temple is a sense of reverence for the human person in the students. This concept applies to the teacher and to his or her dynamics of teaching.

Teaching would mean equipping the young students to search, research and find a large, multi-faceted and all-inclusive world. It implies empowering the students for learning to interact, inter-relate and co-exist peacefully with other persons and communities and nations. It would mean making the students capable of living their lives not only for themselves, but deeply committed to reconstruct the nation and the society at large. Teaching would mean assisting little human beings to become greater human beings who are humane.

Teachers have to be role models. 'Every reform needs examples more than advocates'[10]. Young people look for examples. Teachers need to be role-models, as good human beings, good citizens and persons who have a sense of mission in life.

Teaching implies 'building human beings'. Teaching means building 'builders of homes and families, neighbourhoods and communities, nations and the larger human society'. That is how teaching becomes the noblest job. That is why teaching is a mission, par excellence.

CONCLUSION

'Wiping the body after bath has to start with the head'. Otherwise, the process of wiping will never be complete or effective. Change has to start from the top. Teachers have to change first. The great Metroman, *Sreedharan*, retired and the condition of the metro system in Delhi has very much loosened. Teachers have to remain glowing role models in being ever-learning and innovative teachers. They have to be well-informed, enlightened, value-based and socially responsible. They have to be civilised citizens and cultured human beings. They need to be large-hearted, open-minded, empowered and transforming leaders. They are moulders of good human beings and of a culture of interaction and thus of a civilised nation and of a harmonious society at large. What is required is to have more and more teachers who are qualitatively equipped and morally empowered.

Endnotes

1. Hindustan, New Delhi, 05 September 2012, p. 08
2. Madan Jaida, '*Do Dashak ke baad Shikshaa par Banegee Nayee Neeti*', Hindustan, New Delhi, 26 October 2012, p. 11
3. Justice Markanday Katju, 'Professor teach thyself', The Hindu, 03 September 2012, p. 9
4. Justice Markanday Katju, 'Professor teach thyself', The Hindu, 03 September 2012, p. 9
5. Shashi Tharoor, Minister of State for HRD, The Times of India, New Delhi, 05 November 2012, p. 18
6. Raghunathan, V., 'Games Indians Play', Penguin Books, New Delhi, 2007, pp. 16-17
7. Raghunathan, V., 'Games Indians Play', Penguin Books, New Delhi, 2007, p. 17
8. Raghunathan, V., 'Games Indians Play', Penguin Books, New Delhi, 2007, p. 75
9. Raghunathan, V., 'Games Indians Play', Penguin Books, New Delhi, 2007, p. 13
10. Subhash Jeyan, Quiet polyphonies, The Hindu, Sunday, 04 March 2012, Weekly Edition, p. 01
11. John Kerry, US Senator, A thought for today, The Times of India, New Delhi, 06 November 2012, p. 20
12. Sadhu Santinath, Encyclopedia of Philosophy of Indian Religion, New Delhi, 2001, p. 527
13. Alister, E. McGrath, Christian Theology: An Introduction, West Sussex, U.K., 2011, p. 435
14. Angus Stevenson (Ed.), Oxford Dictionary of English, Oxford University Press, New Delhi, 1998, p. 572
15. *Ibid,* p. 379
16. Walter William Skeat, A Concise Etymological Dictionary of the English Language, New York, 1882, p. 398
17. Carl Sterkens, Interreligious Learning: The Problem of Interreligious Dialogue in Primary Education, Leiden, Netherlands, 2010, p. 203
18. Alister, E. McGrath, Christian Theology: An Introduction, West Sussex, U.K., 2011, p. 435
19. Victoria S. Harrison, Religion and Modern Thought, London, 2007, p. 199
20. *Ibid,* p. 205
21. Mark, S. McLeod-Harrison, Make/Believing the World(s): Toward a Christian Ontological Pluralism, McGill-Queen's University Press, Montreal Quebec, Canada, 1999, p. 227

(Published in 'AINACS News and Views' (Quarterly), pp. 30-45 – published by 'All India Association of Catholic Schools' (AINACS), New Delhi – in March-April 2013)

Chapter - 16

Societal Development: Need of Value-based Education

INTRODUCTION

Education is the characteristic mark of human beings. It refers to the growth, dignity, accomplishment and wellbeing of the human persons. It stands for the substance and level of the civilisations and cultures of the world, too. But, the meaningfulness, usefulness and effectiveness of education depend on the value-content of all the related constituents of the educational system. A value-based education only can contribute to the development of the communities, nations and the larger society, along with the battalion of individual human beings. This article elucidates this thesis, investigates into its various nuances and dimensions and establishes that education has to be necessarily value-based, especially in the current times of the country and of the world, when the erosion of principles and ethical values is at its peak. Value-based education is sure to usher in better days and years ahead, in the 21st century and much beyond.

1. CONCEPTUAL NUANCES

The first part of the article proposes to clarify the nuances of the concepts involved in the following article and in the general theme it is part of, such as 'value, education, value-based education, societal development and responsible'.

1.1. Value

The word 'value'[1] denotes 'how much something is worth compared with its price'. A few of its synonyms are 'merit, worth, use, gain, mileage, sense, good, avail, desirability and significance'. In ethics and social sciences, value stands for the degree of importance of something. It refers to the significance of an action, in terms of good, better, best, and even more. Value decides the intention and motivation of an action. Value affects the ethical behaviour of a person, too. 'What makes an action valuable' depends on the ethical principle that guides it. In other words, ethical significance increases, decreases or alters the value of an action. Values can be individual, social, aesthetic, political, cultural, religious, ethical, spiritual, ideological, and the like. Further, values are broad preferences concerning courses of actions or outcomes. Values reflect the sense of right and wrong of a person. Values influence attitudes, perspectives and actions. 'Excellence deserves admiration', 'equal rights for all' and 'people should be treated with respect and dignity' are a few notable values[2].

1.2. Education

Education[3] is the process of learning. This process involves both imparting and receiving knowledge. Knowledge received through schooling or instruction is formal education and that received or acquired in the natural course of life is informal education. Knowledge and development are the result of educating or of being educated. Human beings require education and every human being has a right to get it. The overall outcome of education is the discipline in life. Education makes human beings different from other living beings. Education enlightens, equips and empowers human beings and makes them capable of facing life. Critical thinking is the mark of education. Education boosts up creativity and managerial capabilities. It makes one capable of making informed and responsible decisions and of interacting with other human beings effectively. Education facilitates developing skills and making one eligible for job opportunities[4]. Education commands respect and esteem as well as success and fulfillment in life. Education helps the acquisition of experience, along with the formation of mind, heart, spirit and conscience. Right perspectives, proper attitudes, sound principles and good values in life are the marks of credibility in life and education is the means to acquire these qualities. An educated person is a socialised, refined and cultured human being who is well-suited for a civilised society, as well.

1.3. Value-based Education

'Value-based education'[5] is an approach to teaching that works with values. It creates an environment of learning that is conducive to academic excellence and skills along with the principles of meaningful living. Skills of good relationship between teachers and students and among students are vital to a value-conscious atmosphere. It is the duty of the school administration to promote educational ethos that is underpinned by core values of life. Training of the student takes place in a happy and purposeful environment. The entire curriculum and atmosphere has to be geared towards the human, social, cultural, ethical, moral and spiritual values of life. Individual freedom, respect, tolerance, democracy, rule of law, etc are introduced, discussed and lived out in the process of education. A consciousness of the values of life is central to education and its diverse components. Education helps students to develop self-worth, empathy, responsible personal behaviour, etc. The wellbeing of all the constituent sectors is important for the optimum effectiveness of education. The making of individuals who are self-led and capable of making choices, along with acting on them, is the outcome of education. A sense of connectedness with other human beings and the creation as well as with God or the Ultimate Being also is expected of good education. Having a good conscience, being trustworthy and responsible and being committed to the making of a better country and society is the result of values-based education, too. Reflective thinking, positive thinking, decision-making and ethically-tuned behaviour are landmarks of value-based or values-based education[6].

1.4. Societal Development

Societal development is the development of the society. It occurs through social development. Social development is about improving the wellbeing of every individual in the society. By way of defining it, social development is 'an upward directional movement of the society, from lesser to greater levels of energy, efficiency, quality, productivity, complexity, comprehension, creativity, choice, mastery, enjoyment and accomplishment'[7]. Social development becomes possible by assisting the humans to reach their full potential. The success of the society is inherent in the success of the individuals. This calls for investing the resources in people. Social development has several aspects, like social, political and cultural. Social development could also be understood as the change that occurs in the course of time in the individual as regards his or her understanding, attitude, behaviour, and the like. Social development is the marker of the overall development of the society. It includes freedom, respect, per capita income, sex ratio, female education, health facilities, employment, general education, etc. Social development ensures facility for language, interactive skills, capacity for relationships, knack for conflict resolution, and the like. Positive thinking and attitudes, along with self-esteem and dignified behaviour, is the net outcome of social development, as well[8].

1.5. Responsible

The word 'responsible' would mean 'liable to be called to answer'[9]. In other words, 'responsible' means 'liable to be called to account as the primary cause, motive, agent or a committee'. The word refers to 'someone or something that caused something to happen. Some of the synonyms of the word 'responsible' are 'accountable, amenable, answerable, liable, etc. Rather than the 'subject to being held to account', 'responsible' would further signify an office, duty or trust. 'Being responsible' provides a sense of purpose, too. The word is used as an adjective in the above context and it stands for the system of societal development, well, the person or persons who are the care takers or activists of the system[10].

2. DEMERITS OF A VALUE-DEFICIT EDUCATION

The second section of the essay investigates into the demerits of a value-deficit education and strongly negates it, in favour of a developed society, in the right sense of the term.

2.1. Education for a Profession

Education is understood to be geared towards making persons knowledgeable enough to take up the right career path and skilled enough to support one's life[11]. Every job requires some form of education or training about that particular job. Mostly students go to school in order to be educated, in view of securing some job. It is true that such a notion of education cannot be negated. But, job-oriented education is a utilitarian education and it has its drawbacks, necessarily so. Life is much more than a job or a good job and all that it brings. Of late, the syllabus of education is very much job-oriented. It addresses only certain aspects of life and not life in its entirety. This is a piecemeal education and the consequence of such an education is bankruptcy of values of life. The concept and system of education require being revised in the larger context of life, with its overall destination as making good, qualitative and value-based human beings[12].

2.2. Career-mania

Making a career is the spine of a purposeful education. The current society has immense possibilities and options. Every student has to be firmly oriented towards the career ahead of him or her, certainly so. Obviously, modern education is very much characteristic of a career mania[13]. When the consciousness of making a career becomes an obsession for the one who pursues it, along with the ones who runs the system of education, education becomes out of the track. When getting at the career becomes the only drive that governs the scheme of education, values are liable to be ignored. Along with the students, teachers and parents are responsible for such a state of affairs. Parents tend to impose on their children high ambitions in terms of income and position in the society. Very often, the over-charged ambition becomes a heavy weight for the children to pursue and achieve. As a result, human and spiritual values that make human life meaningful and happy happen to be trampled upon[14]. This trend is liable to make education one-sided and futile in the larger context of life. A major change is called for.

2.3. Consumerist Trend

Making a good career is oriented to the accumulation of a good or a high quantity of resources, obviously so. Good or high quantity of resources, along with acumen, ensures a handsome and prestigious status in the society, too[15]. Such a phenomenon increases consumption of goods as economically and socially desirable. People tend to possess even unnecessary things for maintaining the social status. The purchase of most educated and moneyed people is not based on need, but because they want it for the sake of social status. It is true that consumerism increased economic output, creates jobs and promotes competition between companies. Consumerism makes people work harder, borrow more and spend less time with the family. The craze to consume more and more gives rise to a materialistic society that neglects ethical principles and values of life[16]. A fundamental alteration in the design of education is imperative.

2.4. Selfish Mindset

Education has to take care of the individual and social culturing of the human person. But, the modern education in special very much creates selfish human beings, who are coiled around themselves and are interested in living their lives only. Through education a very high percentage of people become 'intelligent for themselves and foolish for others'[17]. It is not difficult to find a lot of educated people who are more concerned about themselves than the needs or wellbeing of others. 'Mobile telephone' is a perfect case in point. A very high percentage of literate people get lost in their mobile phones and do not bother to interact with others. Lots of educated people do not hesitate to manipulate life situations, in view of getting what they want. They look out for themselves above everyone else. Education makes lot of people clever and shrewd to take advantage of others, promoting themselves, taking undue credit and depriving others of their legitimate share of life. We can find plenty of educated people who have no empathy for others, i.e., the ability to understand and share in the feelings of others. When educated people are intelligent for themselves, they prioritise themselves by habit, are intolerable and manipulative of others, unconcerned and disrespectful of others, education gets defeated[18]. In fact, education should make social beings rather than self-absorbed persons.

2.5. Highly Competitive Spirit

The modern world is notorious for being highly competitive in anything and everything. A spirit of competition is indeed a positive factor, in view of enhancing quality or excellence[19]. But, when it becomes too much and more negative than positive, it has to be taken with a pinch of salt. Negative competition causes people to be trampled down and even pushed out of the track. In the right sort of competition, all the competitors run together, even though they are more or less by way of excellence. But, in negative competition, one does not hesitate to eliminate the other from the way. It is absolutely tragic that such a spirit prevails in the area of education and among educated people. Negative competition can cause stress, disappointment, depression, and the like. It causes also low self-esteem, breakage of relationships, etc. Undue competition is responsible for wrong means and cheating, in view of maintaining the rank or position in the area. High competitive spirit in the educational sector and among educated people proceeds to the spectrum of life and often spoils the art and fun of life[20]. There have to be values in place for keeping up the balance.

2.6. Theoretical Education

The greatest defect of the modern education system is that it is highly theoretical[21]. Students are forced to mug up a heap of bookish knowledge or abstract information. Lack of practical knowledge is responsible for the lack of human culturing that is supposed to take place in the process of education. Defective education system is responsible for a huge number of unemployed persons among the educated. Skill development of the students is not given sufficient importance. There is a huge heap of dead information of past things. Examination is like a memory test and not a test of the knowledge, intelligence, creativity, calibre, genius and character of the student. Gaining more marks is the criterion of success and not understanding and humaneness. More often than not, exams and grades lead to stress and anxiety, along with waste of time and money. Traditional system of education focuses on memorisation skills. Instead, the study of culture, traditions, customs and values has to be given utmost importance. Theories are certainly required. But, they have to be translated to interaction among the humans and between human beings and the rest of the creation[22]. Value-deficit theories are detrimental to life, as well.

2.7. Oppressive Education

Oppression is the hurt or harm inflicted upon others. It can be through insults, threats or physical violence. Many traditional ways of engaging in education contribute to oppression in the society as well as in schools. Oppressive education is reflected in curriculum, pedagogy, classroom management and the school culture[23]. Methods in education that violates or are not in agreement with common sense are not sustainable, however useful they may seem to be. The narratives of rulers, kings, high caste and class people alone are not sufficient material for the syllabus. The syllabus has to include narratives and realities and leadership of the oppressed and marginalised groups in the society. When too much of power symbols and power structures are discussed in the class rooms, students tend to be too much influenced by the political and powerful side of social life. Critical questioning, although it causes discomfort, has to be incorporated in the process of learning. The narrative system of education is often responded by students by receiving, filling and storing of information. This is a banking model of education that promotes deposits of information. This is very much in the line of the ideology of oppression, which sharply negates the notion of education as a process of inquiry. As the result, educated people get inclined to later become part of the oppressive system of the society. This is a major danger and it has to be carefully watched upon, avoided and rectified[24].

2.8. A Highly failed Education System at the Platinum Days of Independent India

It is 75 years since India has secured independence. It is not the Mughals or the British who rules India today. Indians rule themselves, by way of 'swashaashan'[25]. But, the question that arises today is, 'do the Indians have a better system of governance today'? Seeing the system of governance in India plagued with several mortal ills, one has to admit that the unrealistic system of education is mostly responsible for the rampant political, social, economic, cultural, religious and spiritual bankruptcy of the modern India. The grave lies that are being said in the public space, leave aside the private space, sharply insults the national ideal of the country *'satyamev jayate'*[26]. The wide-spread corruption, violation of human rights, communal hatred and divide and the lawless social life speak of a national society that is gravely sick. Where do the rulers and the citizens get values for life? The education system has very little of value-content in it. Lot of misfits rush into the governmental machinery. India is never tired of boasting that India is a religious country. But the human and spiritual values of religions are not included in the syllabus of education. The values of the Constitution are not really inculcated. Moral and ethical education, even in a secular way, is not stressed. As a matter of fact, education is basic to human culturing and ethical values have to be duly integrated into the system of education. Unfortunately, the stakeholders of the system of education and of the government are yet to get awakened to this fundamental reality of life as well as of the country[27]. The failed system of education, even at the Platinum days of independence, is a matter for serious introspection.

3. MERITS OF VALUES-BASED EDUCATION

The third segment of the article elaborates the merits of values-based education and advocates appropriating clear-cut and strong measures for ensuring societal development.

3.1. Education for Life

Education is the process of learning or the acquisition of knowledge, skills, values, beliefs and habits. Education helps one to learn to read and write. The goal of education is to make a person intelligent enough to make decisions logically. Education helps people become good citizens. It shows the difference between good and bad. It teaches the importance of hard work and helps one grow and develop in life. Knowing and respecting rights, duties, laws and regulations lead to shaping a better society. Good education is necessary for success in life. Education increases self-confidence and assists in developing the personality of a person. Education is the agent of change in one's life and in the society[28]. It promotes good health and decent livelihood. It contributes to social stability and all-round growth in life. Education facilitates thinking for oneself and becoming self-dependent. Education fosters political participation, social equality and environmental sustainability. Education upgrades the thinking level of the given society and helps uproot social evils. It helps uniform development and assists fight social evils. Most of all, education helps build character, by way of learning languages, cultures, ideologies, and the like. Education is naturally oriented to right thinking, right choice, right attitudes and right approaches. Education is for making good human beings, with ethical, human and spiritual values[29]. In the overall context, education is for life.

3.2. Civilised Citizens

A few of the synonyms of the word 'civilised' are 'enlightened, refined, polite, trained, idealised, socialized, advanced, polished, advanced and cultured'[30]. A civilised person is 'polite and courteous'. A civilised group of people is characterised by being socially and technologically advanced. A civilised society or country has a well-developed system of government, culture and way of life, too. It treats people who live there fairly. A fair and just system is basic to a civilised society. Civilised people respect other human beings and are tolerant, gentle and amenable. A civilised society is known for having advanced cities, specialised workers, complex institutions, record keeping and advanced technology. Advanced cities are marks of good civilisations, as well. A civilised society shows evidence of moral and intellectual advancement that is characterised by humane, reasonable and ethical values[31]. A civilised society should have a strong economy and a good infrastructure. It continues to accomplish new things, too. All the same, without the spirit of solidarity, cooperation and fraternity, a civilised society cannot exist. Moreover, the citizens of the country or the society have to imbibe the qualities of being civilised. Only then, the personal qualities of the citizens can make the respective society civilised. Only an education that makes civilised citizens is worth the while.

3.3. Critical Thinking

Critical thinking implies a 'critique'. It refers to the intellectual capacity for being able to discern or judge correctly. The concept traces back to Socrates and Plato. It stands for the intellectual discipline, by which one processes and articulates concepts. It analyzes, reflects, reasons and communicates a certain thought or action. Critical thinking delves deeper into the intentions, motivations and goals that are behind the ideas, concepts and actions[32]. It promotes personal growth and overall happiness. Well-thought-out, logical and reasoned judgments are the marks of critical thinking. Obviously, critical thinking involves principles, ideals, ethics, morals and propriety. It results in clarity and logical consistency. Critical thinking is an open-minded approach to life and is applied to the values of life. A sense of curiosity is at the core of critical thinking. It is geared to the solution of problems in social life. It is founded on a reflective attitude to life. An analytic approach to the matters related to life is the essence of critical thinking. Critical thinking is sign of a mature, creative, imaginative and inclusive mindset. Critical thinking makes one wise in life. Critical thinking is done in the light of values, principles, perspectives and attitudes. When critical thinking is applied to education, students are facilitated to the right formation of their brains. In short, critical thinking is a value-based approach to life as well as to learning[33].

3.4. Education for all

'Education for all' is a global movement led by UNESCO[34]. It aims at meeting the learning needs of all children, youth and adults by 2015. It is also a USA-based organisation that strives to provide free education to disadvantaged and underprivileged rural children, in line with the initiative of UNESCO. This is a non-religious, non-denominational and non-profit organisation, which attempts to provide quality education free of cost to all. It supports school education, tuition, nutrition, and the like. It reaches out to drop outs, too. This scheme is 'functional literacy', which focuses on ability to read and write and do the necessary calculations in the respective country. It includes addressing disadvantage, supporting weakest learners, providing learning resources, etc. Through this scheme, children with disabilities, children who speak minority languages and children from traditionally excluded groups, etc. It also fosters inclusive education, which ensures having children in the same class rooms and in the same schools. 'Education for all' is the right approach to education and to a societal life that is value-based[35].

3.5. Balanced Growth

'Balanced growth' is basically a theory of the economic sector. In development economics, balanced growth means the simultaneous and coordinated expansion of several sectors. The strategy of development depends on scale economics that calculates productivity and profitability of firms. Development of all sectors of economy is possible only in the long run. This is true about underdeveloped groups in a given society or country. Underdeveloped countries and groups start development either from zero level or from a lower level. There has to be a balance between agriculture and investment. In a similar fashion, there has to be balance between groups. When certain available resources and convenient ways run the show, inequality is bound to reign[36]. Consequently, some sectors of economy and groups will grow faster, while others remain neglected. All sectors of economy have to grow together simultaneously. It is like 'you can't do anything until you can do everything'. Similarly, all groups and communities have to grow together. Balanced growth aims at equality among rate of income, growth rates of output and growth rate of resources. Equality between growth rate of capital and labour force is the golden age of balanced growth. Underdeveloped countries and groups have low income, low investment, low capital formation and low productivity and that leads to low income again. Therefore, various sectors of the underdeveloped economy have to be developed. Growth and progress is possible only in a sense of togetherness. In underdeveloped countries and communities have low purchasing power and so their demand is low. Low income, low purchasing power, low investment and low productivity are the results. The idea of balanced growth calls for education for all, with special focus on the underdeveloped, illiterate, poor and marginalised sectors. Only good education can ensure a balanced society in the country and the society[37].

3.6. Disciplined Life

Discipline in life is a mark of character. Being disciplined would mean being honest, hard-working, motivated, encouraged, and the like[38]. It refers to a sense of time, sense of order, sense of work, sense of duty, sense of commitment, sense of devotion, sense of mission, and the like. Efficiency, concentration, punctuality, and the like are part of a disciplined life, too. Discipline provided people with principles and rules to live one's life successfully and effectively. Discipline creates habits, habits make routines and routines become who one is on a day-to-day basis. Identifying one's goals, visualising their outcome, starting small, having a mentor, etc are milestones of a disciplined life, as well. Self-discipline is the road to success in life. It makes one precise, focused and persevering as to securing one's targets and reaching one's destination. Discipline refers to inner strength and ethical fibre. Discipline is the proof of having an informed, enlightened, empowered and strong conscience. Discipline is the sign of will power. It signifies a law-abiding, ethical and moral life. Education is the key to a disciplined life. Discipline makes intelligent and motivated students, too. Discipline helps students focus on long-term goals in life and make wise choices. A disciplined person is value-conscious and value-based in life[39]. It is education that prepares disciplined, value-based and effective life possible.

3.7. Collective Progress

Human beings in a special way are social beings, while at the same time they are individual beings. As social beings, they act jointly. Collective progress is all about individuals acting together, in view of progressing in life[40]. It is oriented to improvement, development and growth in life. It would mean working together with others towards shared social impact goals. As a result, a huge number of different theories, approaches and frame work emerge. Each member would come out with his or her best genius, laying on the table principles and modules for the collective betterment. It is a shared exploration of the better, the best and even beyond. Multilateral approach is necessary for collective growth. Innovation, inclusion and investment are core principles of collective growth. Collective progress has to be of all groups and countries. This necessitates thinking and acting that is inclusive of all groups and sectors. It is like the human body in which all the parts grow together. Growing part by part or a few parts only does not make sense. In a similar fashion, the economic, social, ethical, political and spiritual sectors have to work together and grow together[41]. Education ensures such a realisation. Education for all makes it possible for all communities to grow together and promote the collaboration of all and the collective growth of the country and of the larger society[42].

CONCLUSION

Education is the process of learning and becoming accomplished persons. It expands and strengthens the social, ethical and spiritual culture of the society, too. It eventually contributes to the enhancement of the human condition, through better knowledge, health, living conditions, social equity and productivity. Well, all these are oriented to the development and progress of the human society. Social development is all about improving the well-being of every individual in the given society, by which he or she can reach his or her full potential. The development and growth of the society have to be responsibly monitored. This calls for an education that is value-based from all angles. Education has to make civilised and disciplined citizens who own enlightened mind, empowered heart, an elevated spirit and a responsible conscience. The modern times the need of value-based education and responsible societal development are vital for the bright future of the country, the larger society and of the entire creation, especially towards better prospects in the 21st century and beyond.

Endnotes

1. Kate Woodford, Cambridge Advanced Learner's Dictionary, Cambridge, 2003, p. 1109
2. Yojana Patil, Value Education: Need of the Hour, California, 2015, p. 17
3. *Ibid,* p. 03
4. *Ibid,* p. 09
5. Audrey Amrein-Beardsley, Rethinking Value-Added Models in Education, London, 2014, p. 13
6. *Ibid,* p. 12
7. A. Perret-Clermont, Alex Gillespie, Charis Psaltis (Ed.), Social Relations in Human and Societal Development, California, p. 19
8. *Ibid,* p. 27
9. Kate Woodford, Cambridge Advanced Learner's Dictionary, Cambridge, 2003, p. 713
10. A. Perret-Clermont, Alex Gillespie, Charis Psaltis (Ed.), Social Relations in Human and Societal Development, California, p. 89
11. Yojana Patil, Value Education: Need of the Hour, California, 2015, p. 21
12. *Ibid,* p. 33
13. Dr Arun Kumar Bapna, All Children are Equal Yes or Not, New Delhi, 2021, p. 133
14. *Ibid,* p. 143
15. Ashok Kumar, Current Trends in Indian Education, New Delhi, 2019, p. 60
16. *Ibid,* p. 66
17. *Ibid,* p. 51
18. *Ibid,* p. 53
19. *Ibid,* p. 17
20. *Ibid,* p. 22
21. Yojana Patil, Value Education: Need of the Hour, California, 2015, p. 33
22. *Ibid,* p. 34
23. *Ibid,* p. 57
24. *Ibid,* p. 63
25. Samar Verma, Sukhadeo Thorat (Ed.), Social Science Research in India: Status, Issues, and Policies, Oxford, 2017, p. 369
26. *Ibid,* p. 373
27. Yojana Patil, Value Education: Need of the Hour, California, 2015, p. 163
28. Audrey Amrein-Beardsley, Rethinking Value-Added Models in Education, London, 2014, p. 91
29. *Ibid,* p. 113
30. Audrey Amrein-Beardsley, Rethinking Value-Added Models in Education, London, 2014, p. 87
31. *Ibid,* p. 93
32. *Ibid,* p. 109

33. *Ibid,* p. 111
34. Rieckmann, Marco, Education for Sustainable Development Goals, Brussels, 2017, p. 03
35. Yojana Patil, Value Education: Need of the Hour, California, 2015, p. 97
36. Giulia Mennillo, Thomas Schlenzig, Elmar Friedrich (Ed.), Balanced Growth: Finding Strategies for Sustainable Development, New York, 2011, p. 18
37. Audrey Amrein-Beardsley, Rethinking Value-Added Models in Education, London, 2014, p. 127
38. *Ibid,* p. 53
39. *Ibid*, p. 41
40. Yojana Patil, Value Education: Need of the Hour, California, 2015, p. 53
41. Ashok Kumar, Current Trends in Indian Education, New Delhi, 2019, p. 109
42. Audrey Amrein-Beardsley, Rethinking Value-Added Models in Education, London, 2014, p. 207

Chapter - 17

Vasudhaiv Kutumbakam A 'Culture of Harmony and Peace' as Way Forward

Introduction

The recent times have been very much captivated by the ancient insight of the *Upanishad 'Vasudhaiv Kutumbakam'* and it is very much up in the skies, like a colourful and fascinating balloon. Without doubt, it is a great and unique ideal of the supreme order, wide-ranging, too. It speaks volumes of the true dynamics of human life. But, to be frank, most of it is yet to become a reality in India, i.e., the balloon hasn't really landed on the ground. Yet, it is interesting that the slogan has taken its space in the logo of G 20, 2023, along with the presidency of India. In line with the concerns of G 20, it is expected that India is sure to boost up the morale of the global society towards the all-inclusive implications of the maxim. In the process, I am sure India will be benefited at least in some measure by the echo of announcing the slogan to the world society. That bonus, I believe, will be a major 'restart' for India, towards ascending the ladder of greater heights along the lines of developing a culture of harmonious, peaceful and familial living for the times ahead.

1. *VASUDHAIV KUTUMBAKAM* AND ITS IMPLICATIONS

Part one of this article elaborates the notion of '*Vasudhaiv Kutumbakam*' from diverse angles and explores its implications in the diverse contexts of life.

1.1. *Vasudhaiv Kutumbakam*

'*Vasudhaiv Kutumbakam*'[1], the most concise Sanskrit phrase from *Maha Upanishad*, means 'the world is one family'. Well, 'all the living beings on earth are a family'. It is the most refined thought that can emerge from the human mind ever, divine as well as humane, too. It is the biggest truth about life. It is a symbol of positive thinking. It is the most leading moral value on earth. It is the most sublime social and spiritual principle. It is the core ethics of human life in this world. 'Living like a family' is the most balanced diet for the harmonious and peaceful living of the humans, as well. In sum, '*Vasudhaiv Kutumbakam*' is the best part of the human culture.

1.2. The Texture of Family

'Family' is the core idea in '*Vasudhaiv Kutumbakam'*. Family is a 'group of people who are related to each other', by birth, marriage, adoption, and the like[2]. It is a collection of persons, old and young as well as male and female. 'Living together' is the spirit of a family. 'Unconditional love and support for each other' is the character of a family. A sense of belonging to the family and to every member in it is its basic ethos. Love, affection, loyalty, trust, caring and relationship are the pillars of a family. The harmonious blend of parental, filial and fraternal sentiments is typical of a family. In other words, fatherly-motherly feelings are responded to by sonly-daughterly way of thinking and are further extended to a brotherly-sisterly mind-set. 'Unity in diversity' is the timeless logic of a family. Diversity is inherited as a legacy and unity has to be acquired and regularly sustained, too. Such a family spirit is the texture of '*Vasudhaiv Kutumbakam*'.

1.3. Family is the Most Sacred Space

Joseph Campbell, an American writer and professor of literature, observes, "Your sacred space is where you can find yourself again and again"[3]. Family is the sweetest resort, which the humans refer back to constantly during the entire journey of life. Family is the smallest unit of the society. Family is the place where life takes its form. Family is the 'home' of the humans. Family is the nursery of human life, where the humans begin to learn the fundamental lessons of life. Family is the natural niche of human life. Family, family members, family atmosphere, family memories, family experiences and family sentiments rejuvenate and energize every one. In addition, family accords a sense of belonging, harmony and peace to everyone. Applying the vision of Joseph Campbell to family, it could be stated without doubt that family is the most sacred place on earth. All these and much more of the spirit of life are implied by '*Vasudhaiv Kutumbakam*'.

1.4. *Udaarcharitaanaam*

'*Udaar Charitanam*'[4] makes '*vasudhaiv kutumbakam*' possible. In other words, '*udaar charitaanaam*' is the ethics of '*vasudhaiv kutumbakam*'. The full quote goes thus, 'one is a relative, the other is stranger, say the small-minded, *vasudhaiv kutumbakam*, live the magnanimous'. 'Be detached, be magnanimous, lift up your mind and enjoy the fruit of divine freedom' is the message. One has to cease to be low-minded, divisive and discriminative, which are diabolic in spirit. One has to keep travelling towards being good, noble, generous, upright and high-minded and thus humane, in view of being magnanimous enough to make a family out of the world feasible, as indicated by '*vasudhaiv kutumbakam*'.

1.5. Dynamics of *Vasudhaiv Kutumbakam*

Jesus the Christ presented the vibrant 'dynamics' of '*vasudhaiv kutumbakam*', as he revealed to the world that 'God is Father'[5], mother as well. We could also say that 'God is like our father'. This is indeed a revolution in the world history of conceiving God, very realistic and functional, too. It directly follows that all human beings are his or her sons and daughters. That, in its turn, would mean 'all human beings are brothers and sisters, one to another', irrespective of gender, caste, class, creed, culture, ethnicity, language, ideology, food habits, dress patterns, nationality and other social traditions. The family of the 'homo sapiens' is the extended biological family. Therefore, human society, whether it is regional, national or international, has to be characterized by the fatherly, filial and fraternal spirit put forward by '*vasudhaiv kutumbakam*'.

1.6. A Culture of 'Inter'

Besides, the Second World Catholic Council of Vatican initiated a 'culture of inter, interface and interaction' in the 60s of the 20th century, by affirming 'if we Christians discriminate human beings in the name of faith, religious practices, gender, caste, class, social mores, and the like, we cease to be Christians and believers'[6], tragically so. That makes it mandatory for every Christian to interact with people of all affiliations, both inside and outside, leading to brotherly-sisterly relations, in view of making the entire human fold into a one single family of God the Father. Similarly, the spirit of love and humble service has to be extended to all communities and individuals, starting from the neediest. I believe, 'the culture of inter'[7] reflected in the fraternal relations and service beyond borders fulfill the demands of '*vasudhaiv kutumbakam*'.

1.7. Ethos of the World Human Family

Furthermore, Jesus laid down the 'ethos' of the world human family, "Do to the other what you would have the other do to you"[8]. That is the 'golden rule' for an interactive familial living, illustrated by fulfilling the expectations of the other before expecting anything from him or her. Jesus continues, “When you have done anything to others, even the least among them, you have done to me”[9]. That means, what is done to the members of the human family is what is worthy of the head of the divine family, too. This is another golden rule, too. In addition, Pope John Paul clarified this horizontal-vertical dynamics of family life as he said in Chennai, the then Madras, in 1986, “In dialogue, we open ourselves to one another; for as we open ourselves to one another, we open ourselves to God”[10]. What’s more, Pope Francis, the most brilliant and revolutionary Pope of the modern times, added to the ethics of a human-divine family through a significant document titled “fraternity and social friendship”[11] in 2021, as well. The horizontal and vertical relations of human-human and the human-divine directions further elaborate the dimensions of ‘*vasudhaiv kutumbakam*’.

1.8. The Destination in Life

Henry Valentine Miller, an American novelist and writer of the 20th century, said “Your destination is never a place, but a new way of looking at things”[12]. Making an all-embracing human family out of life that is headed by God is our immediate as well as remote destination in life. Being confined to the small biological family is not sufficient for the human species. Having begun one’s life journey in the ethnic-genetic family, the humans have to transcend its limits towards the larger human family of human beings and that of the entire creation. In other words, in addition to being part of the natural family in a whole-hearted way, we require looking at our institutions, communities, nations and the larger society, along with the entire creation, in a new way, that is to say, in a familial way. That would mean, the ethos, ethics, integrity and dignity of the natural family have to be applied to the whole country, society and creation. This is the destination of humankind. Such a new way of looking at life is what is intended by ‘*vasudhaiv kutumbakam*’.

2. G 20, 2023, AND ITS RAMIFICATIONS

Part two of this essay examines the diverse aspects and issues connected to G 20. Further, it elaborates their ramifications from various angles and in a critical manner.

2.1. The Launch of the Logo, Theme and Website of G 20, 2023

The Prime Minister of India unveiled the logo, theme and website for the presidency of G 20, the inter-governmental forum comprising of 19 countries and the European Union[13]. The G 20 Logo draws inspiration from the vibrant colours of the national flag of India. The lotus construed as the national flower of India is placed adjacent to the planet Earth. It is officially understood as reflecting growth amid challenges. The Earth is believed to be a sign of the pro-planet approach of India, in perfect harmony with nature. Below G 20 logo 'Bharat' is written in *Devanagri* script. The theme of 'One Earth, One Family, One Future' signifies the need for unity of purpose as well as unity of action[14]. 'Supporting vulnerable people and economies, protecting the planet and harnessing the digital progress for all' are the projected priorities of the policy makers.

2.2. The Logo of G 20, 2023: Its Upshots

The official logo of the G 20 presidency of India includes 'lotus', the flag of *Bharatiya Janata Party*. This has been observed slightly as an objectionable choice. It could be recalled that Jawaharlal Nehru, the first prime minister of India, rejected the proposal of making the flag of the Congress party, the then ruling dispensation, the national flag of India. It is not difficult to observe that the current decision collides with the distinguished tradition of the country. Placing the Indian flag on the G 20 logo would have been nobler, inclusive and dignifying in its sentiments.

2.3. Situating the G 20 Presidency of India

It is too obvious that global economy is passing through delicate uncertainties. In this context, the projected strong performance of India is a bright spot. The meeting of the finance ministers of Group of Twenty, along with central bank governors, in Bangalore, is thus justified. In the wake of global growth slowing, the decline of inflation and bottoming out of growth are promoting projections. The emerging markets and developing economies seem to promise four-fifths of the global growth, out of which 15 percent is expected to be the contribution of India[15]. India is believed to be capable of being the global growth engine and thus of bringing countries together. Amid the multiple challenges faced by the world, along with geopolitical tensions, the leadership of India is believed to be critical.

2.4. 'One Family' of Solidarity, Protecting the Vulnerable

A major portion of the world human family has not come out of the shock and setback the corona virus has inflicted. A high percent of households around the world are struggling still to make ends meet, due to high cost of living. Millions fail to afford fuel for cooking and heating. Successive distresses have enlarged poverty and endangered progress. Some 400 million people in nearly 80 countries face acute food insecurity[16]. Supporting the vulnerable is vital in all countries. Economic measures have to reach the most in need. Procedures have to be appropriated for sustaining debts, even by resolving. Ensuring the stability of price and containing inflation are imperative. Emerging and developing economies have to be supplied additional financial support. Processes towards the over-all progress have to be made efficient and effective. Additional solidarity has to be ensured with the low-income and vulnerable members of the family of nations, in view of concessional IMF financing in times of distress and for guarding against future crises[17].

2.5. 'One Earth' of Protecting Our Planet, Our Home

The human family is victim of an increasingly severe and enveloping effect of climate change. This existential threat can be faced and mended only in a collective way. Banding together in defense of our earth is the only way of getting out of the prickly pickle we are in. The Paris Agreement is our collective goal and resources have to be geared towards green projects[18]. Incentivizing low-carbon investment, mobilizing private capital and financial innovations are a few effective measures. Helping vulnerable countries set up right policies and creating an environment conducive to climate-friendly investments were facilitated by the advice and financial support of IMF. Sharing of technology and green subsidies with the developing world and supporting them for green transition, without an attitude of protectionism, are a few pro-active measures[19]. The good health of our earth is the basis of our survival.

2.6. 'One Future' for Ensuring 'Everyone can Prosper'

Ours is an era of technological transformation. How policy makers manage the potential of digital progress is vital to a fair and inclusive future. Greater 'on line transaction' increases transparency and helps fight corruption. Central bank digital currencies, unified payments interface, push-button cell phones and crypto currency are some of the new devices that promote financial inclusion and accelerate digital progress worldwide[20]. At the back of certain collapses of crypto exchanges, market integrity and use protection have to be supported by right policies. This is inevitable for strengthening financial regulation and for maintaining global standards. In addition, 'one future' would mean sharing the 'common grounds', along with a spirit of travelling together towards a shared destination. It has to be ensured to everyone that 'all can prosper'[21]. This is the collective spirit called for making one shared future.

2.7. The Spirit of 'One': a Guide as We Move Forward

The spirit of 'one' is the common ground for the way forward, especially in the rear of the increasing geo-political tensions. The 'spirit of one' is not merely a sentiment, but a blueprint for action. This fact is supported by what the Indian Nobel Laureate *Rabindra Nath Tagore* once said, "You can't cross the sea merely by standing and staring at the water"[22]. This is a clarion call addressed to the policy makers to take up right decisions and actions, leading the society to a collective wellbeing. In this respect, the goalpost of India becoming '*Viksit Bhaarat*' by 2047 and several of the measures in the '*amrit kaal*', as announced, are worth being lauded. The maxim 'One Earth, one Family, one Future' contains a series of values, like diversity, freedom, justice, equality and fraternity, have their focus on the spirit of oneness, well, 'unity in diversity'[23]. These values are duly enshrined in the Constitution of India as signposts for the way forward, both in the national and global contexts.

2.8. G 20: A Great Opportunity for India

The G 20 presidency for India is a great opportunity for inventing new narratives, for chalking out efficient policies and for implementing effective practices, in view of the unity and integrity of the world human society as well as of India. Constructive dialogues and affirmative action have to be put in place, in view of revising the discriminative and divisive narratives in vogue. Conversations and actions require being harmonized. The expertise and experience of global level stakeholders are at the disposal of India. Merely improvising slogans and planning or announcing projects wouldn't be sufficient. The government of India, in partnership with the state governments and NGOs, has to prioritize socially, economically and geographically challenged regions and sectors, in favour of better quality of lives for one and all[24]. Inclusive development that would leave 'no one behind' has to be motivating force for the schemes[25]. It is a golden opportunity for making India a model of social justice. The opportunity will bear fruit only when honest and committed actions follow the projected plans and projects.

2.9. Reasons for Hope

As per the recent UNDP report on multi-national poverty 2022, some 415 million people exited from poverty[26]. This is not to be attributed to the generosity of anyone, as Nelson Mandela said, "Overcoming poverty is not a task of charity; it is an act of justice"[27]. Various schemes are geared towards addressing the problem, but also change of mindset, in line with social justice. Besides, some 1.4 million elected women *panchayat* representatives, perhaps the largest in the world and over 82 *lakhs* of self help groups across India are a sign of a huge potential to be game-changers in socio-economic development[28].

2.10. Call for Collective Action

'*Viksit Bharat*' calls for dissolving boundaries, fostering multi-sector collaboration and partnership. The slogan '*sabka saath, sabka vikas, sabka vishwas and sabka prayas*' has to be translated to action[29].

The corporate sector should re-imagine business in backward regions and create opportunities for more jobs. Rather than expecting the state to do everything, individuals have to re-awaken their social consciousness towards what one can do. India has to awaken itself towards the true spirit of democracy by living the values of inclusiveness, equality, prosperity and a human-centred approach to one and all. The destination is, as *Rabindra Nath Tagore* said, 'where the mind is without fear, and the head is held high, where knowledge is free – well, an India that is a heaven of freedom'[30]. This destination, without doubt, is the outcome of a collective action by all citizens, along with the responsible ones, who are committed to the realization of the dream for one and all, as our way forward.

2.11. Challenges before India

India has several challenges on the way forward. The subordinate trends of politics, like weak opposition, one-sided governance, change of political affiliation and frail national institutions are highly eating into the core fabric of democracy. While India is making a 'hop, step and jump' in the area of development in diverse sectors, the social sector seems to be highly shrinking, so much so that the distance between individuals and between communities seem to be alarmingly widening. The discriminative and divisive policies and practices, along with hate speech and brutal violence on other communities, tear away the spirit of communal harmony and national integration[31]. The ill will, distance and disharmony among individuals and communities have to be substituted by good will, respect, support and care for one and all.

Besides, the self-styled idea of exaggerated nationalism, along with the majoritarian sentimentalism, has to be rectified. The hazy and out-of-the-track idea of '*hindoo raashtra*'[32] and its terrorizing approach requires a major revision by rule of law. Aberrations, like addiction to the past, the idea of re-writing history books and the profuse slavery to myths, stories and superstitions require being brought back to the track[33]. The roughly 4/5th portion of the abject poor, the nearly half of the marginalized population and the high majority of the idiotic masses, along with the mental and emotional slavery of '*bheedchaal*' (crowd-like following) and '*bhedchaal*' (sheep-like following) require redemption[34]. The list goes on. India has to boost its will and stamina to rectify the wrong, in favour of overcoming these major challenges, at least to the bottom level.

3. TOWARDS A CULTURE OF HARMONY AND PEACE

Part three of this article elucidates the way forward towards a culture of harmony and peace, analyzing various applied realities and episodes of life.

3.1. National Pledge

Students at the school level make a pledge everyday as part of their educational curriculum. It reads, "India is my country and all Indians are my brothers and sisters"[35], and it goes on. This national pledge was composed by '*Pydimarri Venkata Subba Rao*', a noted author in Telugu and a bureaucrat, in 1962. This is not an ethnic statement. This refers to the spirit of brotherly-sisterly and friendly solidarity across the ethnic, linguistic, ideological, religious, social and cultural communities. This pledge is not a mere ritual for the school days. This is a value that is scheduled to accompany the students, even long after the school days are over, i.e., for the entire life as citizens of India. This is the diet required for the integration and integrity of the country. The national pledge ends, "In their well being and prosperity lies my happiness"[36]. One's happiness has to be tuned to the wellbeing of the other. Although this pledge is applied to the national context, the fraternal spirit and devotion that are professed includes the entire human society, as is implied by '*vasudhaiv kutumbakam*', as an extended family.

3.2. Rainbow

'Rainbow' is an 'arch of many colours that sometimes appears in the sky when the sun shines through rain'[37]. In other words, rainbow is a 'multicoloured arc made by light striking water droplets'. The most familiar type of rainbow is produced when sunlight strikes raindrops in front of a viewer at a precise angle, i.e., 42 degrees. Rainbows can also be viewed around fog, sea spray or waterfalls. The colours of the rainbow are 'red, orange, yellow, green, blue, indigo and violet'. Rainbow also signifies 'diversity, inclusivity, solidarity, oneness and an all-embracing image of love, friendship and fellowship. Rainbow is a sign of hope, beauty, good fortune and promise of better times to come, as well. Overall, rainbow signifies a 'culture of being together'[38], a culture of harmony and peace, in line with the spirit of '*vasudhaiv kutumbakam*'.

3.3. Honey bee

'Honey bee' is a eusocial flying insect, native to mainland Afro-Eurasia[39]. It is known for producing the most precious food item of the world called 'honey'. Honeybee is symbol of an exceptional discipline and hard work. Honey is deliciously sweet and there is nothing that can be compared to it. For that matter, jaggary or sugar also is sweet. But, jaggary is made of one agricultural product, called sugar cane when squeezed and processed. But, honey is made of juice from hundreds of flowers, not only of the same kind, but also of diverse types, that too from their nectar. The essence of different types of flowers together makes the difference. As a result, honey processed thus stands singular in the fineness and richness of its taste. If honey was processed from only one category of flowers, it would not have been so exquisite. In a similar fashion, human beings have to imbibe values from diverse ethnic, religious, ethical and cultural traditions[40]. If such multi-faceted approach to life becomes a reality, the outcome of the same will be humane and divine characteristics of social cohesion, harmony and peace, well, a foretaste of the 'heaven' ahead of us. Well, a 'honey-bee culture' is called for.

3.4. The Core ideals of the Seers of the World

The core ideals presented by the seers of the religions of the world suggest the various dimensions of the spirit of '*vasudhaiv kutumbakam*'. The *mantra* of the Vedic literature, 'Let noble thoughts come from all directions'[41] and 'let all be happy' or *sarve bhavantu sukhinah*[42] refer to an all-inclusive and holistic thinking. '*Maryaadaa purushottam Raam*'[43] refers to the 'upright discipline of remaining within one's limits'. The 'Middle path'[44] of *Gautam Buddha* implies 'striking a balance in life' by way of the '*saadhnaa*' of life. The 'non-violence'[45] of *Mahaaveer Jain* would mean 'refraining from violence in thought, word and deed'. The 'love, service, forgiveness, equality, sharing and peace'[46] advocated by Jesus Christ is the core life-style of being a family. The idea of 'brotherhood'[47] of Muhammad is the way of solidarity as members of the society. 'Good thoughts, good words and good deeds'[48] of Zoroaster's are the core principle of ethical living. The idea of '*sangat* and *pangat*'[49] *of Guru Nanak* is the way of knitting together. The notion of 'world citizenship'[50] by Abdul Baha is the worldview of universal fellowship. The concept of 'righteous living'[51] proposed by Moses is the basis of living together. The principle of ethical living[52] proposed by Confucius is the heart of daily life. *Sai Baba* affirmed '*sabkaa maalik ek*'[53], as well. All these top insights by the great seers of the world highlight the firm foundation of '*vasudhaiv kutumbakam*'. They are the tips for a culture of harmony and peace, too.

3.5. Temples

'Temples' of all religious traditions, to be specific, temple, church, masjid, gurudwara, synagogue, *vihar*, *ashram*, and the like, are vibrant symbols of the believed presence of God among the humans on earth[54]. In point of fact, it is the same God who is present in all places of worship. Besides, God is omnipresent, that is to say, he, she or it is present all over the world. God is all-pervading and is equally present wherever the humans gather, including the market places. "Where two or three are gathered together in my name, behold, there will I be among them"[55] reminds Jesus, referring to the wide-ranging presence of God. Moreover, God is present in the nature, as well. The degree of the presence of God in the temples is not more than other human dwellings as well as nature. In other words, God is not less present in places other than temples. The eternal truth of the all-pervading presence of God invites the humans to conceive a larger God, who is undivided by places of worship of different religious traditions. The idea of the 'God of one and all'[56] has to make it tenable for believers of all affiliations to visit, meet God and pray in all places of worship as well as natural places. Such a logical and realistic understanding of God will facilitate believers to transcend the human-made borders of faith and the consequent unsociable attitudes and behaviours. Such is the divine world of harmony and peace the spirit of '*vasidhaiv kutumbakam*' is inviting the believers to travel towards.

3.6. Preamble of the Constitution

The Preamble[57] of the Constitution of India highlights the principles of the Constitution and the sources of its authority. It presents all those central values the humans require for life. The Constitution secures its citizens liberty or freedom of thought, expression, belief and worship. These are fundamental to human life, whether it be an individual, family, institution, community, nation or any other organization. It also ensures social, economic and political justice. It assures equality of status and of opportunity. It promotes fraternity that ensures dignity of the individual, along with unity and integrity of the nation, which is a sovereign, socialist, secular and democratic republic[58]. These core values of the Constitution crisscross the universal values of all religious traditions, though in more or less degrees. The sublime values of the Constitution of India, along with those of the religious traditions, if lived honestly, are geared towards the realizing a 'culture of harmony and peace'[59], in line with the spirit of '*vasudhaiv kutumbakam*'.

3.7. Sustainable Development Goals 2030

'Sustainable Development Goals 2030 of the United Nations'[60] is a landmark scheme for the transformation of the world. 'Leave no one behind' is the central spirit of all the 17 SDGs. This is a revolutionary paradigm of a culture of being a family. Allowing 'no one to be left behind' is the family style of life. Family is a place where one who is weak in any respect is taken care of with preferential devotion. This family model has to be applied to the entire society. Those who are handicapped physically, mentally, psychologically, spiritually or ethically have to be attended to with favoured option. As family has a 'sense of home'[61] for every member, by way of leaving no one behind, so too, the human society should be having modules and provisions for taking care of the specially-abled of all kinds, towards the development of their maximum capacity. Therefore, preferential care has to be extended to the deprived or disabled sections of the society as well as for those pushed to the margins of the society, well, the homeless, the voiceless, the hungry, those needing clothes, education, medical care, and the like[62]. This is the ethics required by '*vasudhaiv kutumbakam*', which strengthens a culture of harmony and peace.

3.8. Secular Ethos

The 'secular ethos'[63] enshrined in the Constitution of India stipulates that the Indian state has no official religion. The principle of secularism goes with the notion of a 'nation', which is basically non-religious or irrespective of religion and religions. For that reason, ideas of a certain religious state can have no standing at all. All traditions of faith equally belong to the state. Secularism also means that one should not impose one's religious views on others. One shouldn't deprive the other of his or her right to pursue his or her religious convictions, too. The ethics of secularism provides ample scope for interaction and good relations among the multifarious traditions of faith or religions. It allows theistic and atheistic ideologies to survive and thrive side by side. It promotes learning from each other, give and take and a partnership between or among the diverse traditions of faith. In addition, secularism upholds '*sarv dharm sambhaav*'[64] or good will, dovetailing and harmony among traditions of faith, ideologies and cultures. Besides, the state is bound to extend equal treatment to all communities, irrespective of majority and minority. '*Vasudhaiv kutumbakam*' would mean such a culture of harmony and peace.

3.9. Inter-faith Relations

'Inter-faith'[65] means 'between or among', depending on the number or persons, families or communities involved in the process of interaction. It is a 'culture of inter, interface and interaction'[66] among the different traditions of faith. 'An inter-faith relation'[67] is the means to peaceful co-existence and social fellowship. Inter-faith would further mean realizing that we have 'a common origin, a common existence and a common destiny'[68]. Inter-faith would imply recognizing that "what unites us is far greater than what divides us"[69], as rightly observed by John F. Kennedy, Former President of the United States of America in his address to the Canadian parliament in 1961. Inter-faith signifies 'inclusive thinking, interactive learning, collaborative working and harmonious living'[70], which leads to a harmonious and peaceful human society. Inter-faith action brings the partners into one united world of shared living. 'Honouring the other above oneself'[71] is a module for an inter-faith style of life. Inter-faith unity refers to rising above considerations of majority and minority, high and low, rich and poor, familiar and strange and of this religion or of that religion. Inter-faith makes way for a community-based thinking and living as well as unity of the humankind as a family, across local, regional, national and global levels. Inter-faith unity and relations enhances the culture of harmony and peace, as envisioned by '*vasudhiv kutumbakam*'.

3.10. Value-based Peace-building

'Value-based peace-building'[72] is the ethics of '*vasudhaiv kutumbakam*'. 'Value'[73] is that which is valued by someone or an organization. Value is the worth of something or someone. Value decides the importance and usefulness of something or someone, too. Values are 'broad desirable goals that motivate people's actions and serve as guiding principles in their lives'. Besides, values, in essence, are universal and they apply to all, though in more or less degrees. They cannot be privatized or monopolized. They spill over the boundaries of caste, class, creed, culture, gender, language, ideology, nationality and other social traditions. Time-honored perceptions, world views, ideas, ideals, ideologies, attitudes, principles and truths are the crux of values. Further, values are a shared reality. They are the 'gifts of the same Creator'. They are the 'common cultural heritage of the human society'[74], too. Values are the foundation of peace-processes. They uphold the ethos and ethics of human life. They are best suited for making a society that can co-exist harmoniously and peacefully. Such peace-building processes are envisaged by '*vasidhaiv kutumbakam*'.

3.11. Social Cohesion and Harmony

Social cohesion and harmony'[75] is the larger and ultimate outcome of '*vasudhaiv kutumbakam*'. The human society gets its true dignity and integrity when it is cohesive and when it ensures the freedom and rights of all citizens. The human society loses its dignity when it is not ethical. It does not require a mention that India, the entire human society as well, is making strides in the area of technological development. But, on the other hand, the entire world, India in particular too, seems to be socially shrinking due to inter-community tensions, hate-speech, conflicts, violence, atrocities and the ensuing crack and distance between communities[76]. This tendency is extremely unfortunate and requires being mended with immediate effect, lest the development, education and progress as well as religions be rendered an anomaly and a contradiction as well as futile. Our country, along with the world society at large, requires a radical conversion towards a positive, creative and realistic outlook to life. In this direction of social cohesion, harmony and peace, our ultimate destination is the realization of the spirit of '*vasudhaiv kutumbakam*' in our day-today lives. No doubt, a 'culture of harmony and peace'[77] is the human ethics to be lived by one and all.

3.12. Peaceful Living

Peace is not merely an idea or a sentiment, but is a state of affairs. Peace is not just within, but is between and among individuals, families, communities and nations. Peace is not a state of being passive, but it is the quality of being active. Peace is not characterized by total silence, but by being fully alive. Peace is not a quality of the cemetery, but is of the dwelling together of the humans. Human life, in the right sense of the term, is distinguished by peaceful living, which, if not, is rendered futile. Peace emerges from the consciousness of humanity as the basic identity of the humans[78]. Peace is the 'conscience' of the human society[79]. Peace can be sustained only a shared faith. Peace ensures the onward journey of the humans towards its esteemed destination of humane and divine heights. The prayer of the Nobel Laureate *Rabindra Nath Tagore* highlights this eternal aspiration, "Into that heaven of freedom, my Father, let my country awake"[80], well, the world human society as well.

Conclusion

'*Vasudhaiv Kutumbakam*' is the most comprehensive and sublime ideal of the humankind. It is not merely a maxim or a slogan, but is the core of the ethos and ethics of living together, like a family. Even though human beings are born as individuals, they are social beings, in the full sense of the term. The social genius of human life is best pictured by the dynamics of a family. Therefore, one has to transcend the boundaries of one's biological, ethnic, linguistic, ideological, cultural and national family to a global human family of human beings, along with other living beings and the entire creation. While having the patent of the maxim '*Vasudhaiv Kutumbakam*', India has to go a long way before it can have a command over its heavenly spirit, adequately enough. The G 20 presidency is a great opportunity for India and the world beyond to imbibe the family qualities required of a humane life across the boundaries, in view of ascending to the humane and divine heights of human life. May our 'way forward' be '*udaar charitaanaam*', in view of a 'culture of harmony and peace' envisioned by '*Vasudhaiv Kutumbakam*'!

Endnotes

1. *Mahopanishad*, 6.72, Ramnarayan Vyas, Nature of Indian Culture, New Delhi, 1992, p. 155
2. Tim Delaney, Connecting Sociology to Our Lives--An Introduction to Sociology, New York, 2015, p. 337
3. Susan Smith Jones, How to Meditate, New York, 1998, p. 14
4. *Mahopanishad*, 6.72, Ramnarayan Vyas, Nature of Indian Culture, New Delhi, 1992, p. 155
5. The Holy Bible (New International Version), Michigan, 1994, Psalm 103:13, p. 682

6. Johnston R. McKay, Christian Faith and the Welfare of the City, North Ayrshire, United Kingdom, 2008, p. 21
7. *Ibid,* p. 27
8. The Holy Bible (New International Version), Michigan, 1994, Mt 7.12, p. 1100
9. *Ibid*, Mt 25.40, p. 1128
10. Address to Members of Other Religions, Madras, 5 February 1986, no. 4; L'Osservatore Romano, English edition, 10 February 1986, p. 14
11. Pope Francis, *Fratelli Tutti*: On Fraternity and Social Friendship, New York, 2020, p. 01
12. Henry Miller, Big Sur and the oranges of Hieronymus Bosch, New York, 1957, p. 25
13. https://www.g20.org/en/g20-india-2023/logo-theme/
14. *Ibid*
15. https://www.thehindu.com/business/Economy/india-remains-a-bright-spot-to-contribute-15-of-global-growth-in-2023-imf-md/article66540985.ece
16. https://press.un.org/en/2022/sc14894.doc.htm
17. https://www.imf.org/en/Blogs/Articles/2023/02/22/policy-priorities-for-the-g20-one-earth-one-family-one-future
18. https://unfccc.int/process-and-meetings/the-paris-agreement
19. https://www.imf.org/en/Blogs/Articles/2023/05/11/europe-and-the-world-should-use-green-subsidies-cooperatively
20. https://www.imf.org/en/News/Articles/2022/10/26/cf-how-indias-central-bank-helped-spur-a-digital-payments-boom
21. https://www.imf.org/en/Blogs/Articles/2023/02/22/policy-priorities-for-the-g20-one-earth-one-family-one-future
22. Jagdish Gupta, Book of Happiness, New Delhi, 2020, p. 36
23. T. K. Suman Kumar, India: Unity in Diversity, New Delhi, 2017, p. 12
24. Manjeet Kripalani, India in the G20--Rule-taker to Rule-maker, Oxfordshire, 2022, p. 57
25. *Ibid,* p. 97
26. https://timesofindia.indiatimes.com/india/415-million-exited-poverty-in-india-in-15-years- undp/articleshow/94927710.cms
27. Ken Wytsma, Pursuing Justice--The Call to Live and Die for Bigger Things, Rio de Janeiro, 2013, p. 79
28. Ajay Tankha, Banking on Self-help Groups--Twenty Years On, New Delhi, 2021, p. 58
29. https://www.mygov.in/campaigns/sabka-vikas/
30. B. L. Grover and Alka Mehta, A New Look at Modern Indian History, 2018, New Delhi, p. 491
31. Helmut Reifeld, Imtiaz Ahmad, Partha Sarathy Ghosh (Ed.), Pluralism and Equality: Values in Indian Society and Politics, 2019, New Delhi, p. 108
32. Ram Puniyani, Contours of Hindu Rashtra: Hindutva, Sangh Parivar, and Contemporary Politics, 2006, New Delhi, p. 29
33. *Ibid,* p. 51
34. *Ibid,* p. 109
35. Amita Gupta, Kulwant Rai Gupta, Concise Encyclopedia of India, New Delhi, 2006, p. 270
36. *Ibid*
37. Ronald Edsforth, A Cultural History of Peace in the Modern Age, New York, 2022, p. 102
38. *Ibid,* p. 104

39. https://en.wikipedia.org/wiki/Honey_bee
40. Ronald Edsforth, A Cultural History of Peace in the Modern Age, New York, 2022, p. 129
41. *Rig Veda 1.89.1, Reena Kapoor, Swaran Singh (Ed.), Revisiting Gandhi: Legacies for World Peace and National Integration, London,* 2022, p. 106
42. *Brihadaranyak Upanishad*, 1.4.14, Vatsala Sperling, Ehud Sperling, For Seven Lifetimes: An East–West Journey to a Spiritually Fulfilling and Sustainable Marriage, Rochester, 1996, p. 328
43. Kinkar Vitthal Ramanuja, Be Tension Free, Kolkata, 2011, p. 33
44. Robert M. Ellis, Middle Way Philosophy 1: The Path of Objectivity, Raleigh, 2012, p. 124
45. Ravindra Kumar, Non-violence and its philosophy, Meerut, 2003, p. 14
46. Jaroslav Pelikan, The Christian Tradition: A History of the Development of Doctrine, Volume 1, Chicago, 1971, p. 164
47. Carrie Rosefsky Wickham, The Muslim Brotherhood: Evolution of an Islamist Movement, Oxfordshire, 2013, p. 33
48. Jenny Rose, 'Zoroastrianism—an Introduction', New York, 2010, p. 17
49. Guru Nanak*, Aadi Guru Granth Sahib,* V. D. Mahajan, History of Medieval India, New Delhi, 2007, p. 360
50. Robert H. Stockman, The Baha'i Faith: A Guide for the Perplexed, London, 2012, p. 12
51. Stephen M. Brown, Higher and Higher: Making Jewish Prayer Part of Us, New York, 1985, p. 22
52. Lai Chen, Confucius and the Modern World, Oxford-shire, 2018, p. 39
53. Kinkar Vitthal Ramanuja, Be Tension Free, Kolkata, 2011, p. 59
54. Gurpreet Mahajan, Surinder S. Jodhka, Religion, Community and Development--Changing Contours of Politics and Policy in India, New Delhi, 2020, p. 53
55. Bethany K. Scanlon, Want to Find Your Mate?--Bible Study, New York, 2018, p. 111
56. Dil R. Banu, One God For All, Las Vegas, 2011, p. 11
57. Aparajita Baruah, Preamble of the Constitution of India--An Insight and Comparison with Other Constitutions, New Delhi, 2007, p. 03
58. *Ibid,* p. 109
59. Thoudam Damodara Singh, Towards a Culture of Harmony and Peace, Virginia, 2010, p. 13
60. Ajay Ahlawat, Sustainable Development Goals: Directive Principles for Sustainable India by 2030, New Delhi, 2019, p. 03
61. Helen James, A Sense of Home--Eat - Make - Sleep - Live, Dublin, 2017, p. 42
62. Ajay Ahlawat, Sustainable Development Goals: Directive Principles for Sustainable India by 2030, New Delhi, 2019, p. 157
63. Donald Eugene Smith, India as a Secular State, London, 2015, p. 53
64. Harish Sharma, Communal Angle in Indian Politics, New Delhi, 2020, p. 179
65. Frederic Ntedika Mvumbi (Ed.), Interfaith Dialogue--Towards a Culture of Working Together, Nairobi, 2018, p. 04
66. *Ibid,* p. 05
67. *Ibid,* p. 39
68. Jonathan Y. Tan, '*Missio Inter Gentes*: Towards a New Paradigm in the Mission Theology of the Federation of Asian Bishops' Conferences (FABC), Mission Studies, 21.1, 2004, p. 107
69. Dennis L. Kirkpatrick, American Racism!--The Big Weapon of Mass Destruction, Bloomington, 2013, p. 278
70. Frederic Ntedika Mvumbi (Ed.), Interfaith Dialogue--Towards a Culture of Working Together, Nairobi, 2018, p. 109

71. Jonathan Y. Tan, '*Missio Inter Gentes*: Towards a New Paradigm in the Mission Theology of the Federation of Asian Bishops' Conferences (FABC), Mission Studies, 21.1, 2004, p. 93
72. Mohammed Abu-Nimer, Renata Katalin Nelson (Ed.), Evaluating Interreligious Peace-building and Dialogue--Methods and Frameworks, Boston, 2021, p. 118
73. Ibid, p. 13
74. Gordon Wang, On the Culture of Harmony: Where Are Human Beings Headed?, Bloomington, 2013, p. 259
75. T. K. Suman Kumar, India: Unity in Diversity, New Delhi, 2017, p. 12
76. Helmut Reifeld, Imtiaz Ahmad, Partha Sarathy Ghosh (Ed.), Pluralism and Equality: Values in Indian Society and Politics, 2019, New Delhi, p. 108
77. Gordon Wang, On the Culture of Harmony: Where Are Human Beings Headed?, Bloomington, 2013, p. 259
78. Mohammed Abu-Nimer, Renata Katalin Nelson (Ed.), Evaluating Interreligious Peace-building and Dialogue--Methods and Frameworks, Boston, 2021, p. 209
79. Ibid, p. 211
80. Anthony Holden, Ben Holden, Poems That Make Grown Men Cry--100 Men on the Words That Move Them, New York, 2014, p. 107

Index

D

E

F

G

H

I

J

K

L

M

N

O

P

R

S

About the Book

The book 'Mission Religious Harmony', in seventeen chapters, researches into the nuances and dimensions of the related themes in an innovative, interactive and scholarly way. It explores the dynamics of the mission under discussion. It discusses the diverse aspects of harmony among religions, along with the various sections and sectors of social life. It also compares different religious branches of knowledge. It networks and dovetails the characteristic nuances related to harmony and peace among religions, in view of a better neighbourhood, nation and society.

The book vouches to travel through the high ways, streets and corners of all religions and faiths. It is committed to exploring the universal values that form the nerve hub of human culture. 'Inclusive thinking and harmonious living' among people of all affiliations is the ultimate destination of mission religious harmony. 'I have a mission to you', 'you have a mission to me' and 'we have a collective mission towards the country and the larger society' is the logic of life, of mission religious harmony, as well.

About the Author

Dr M. D. Thomas is Founder Director of Institute of Harmony and Peace Studies, New Delhi, and is deeply committed to 'inclusive thinking for harmonious living', which is the motto of the institute.

Ph.D. in Hindi Literature from Banaras Hindu University, Varanasi, on 'Kabeer and Christian Thought', he is scholar of religion, religions and harmony among religions. He has also specialized Hindustani classical music to Pradhma, Madhyama and B. Mus. (7 years) levels. He is also B. Th. in comparative religion from Urban University, Rome.

He deals profusely with education, cross-cultural perspectives, cross-scriptural values, constitutional values, interfaith relations, social ethics, communal harmony, national integration and social wellbeing.

He has been pursuing the above mission through lectures, messages, articles, books, video messages, social interactions, views at TV channels, and the like, for the last nearly 45 years, as a life-time commitment.

Dr Thomas worked as National Director at Commission for Religious Harmony in the national office of the Catholic Christian community, CBCI Centre, New Delhi. He was also Director of Institute of Religion and Culture, Ujjain.

By way of publications, he has to his credit 6 books, nearly 450 articles and 2 music albums of his composition. His books are '*Kabeer aur Eesaayee Chintan*', '*Moolya Bible Ke*', '*Desh Ek, Ek hein Hum Sab*', '*Fellowship of Religions*', '*Religion for Harmonious Living*' and '*Faith, Inter-faith and Spirituality*'. His music albums are '*Samanvay Dhaaraa*' and '*Moolya Bible Ke*'.

His contribution includes lectures at over 100 universities and colleges, Examiner of Ph. D. candidates and visiting professor at a few universities, special lectures at some 40 institutes of religion and lecture-series at seminars for school teachers in some 40 cities of the country.

Further, he had delivered some 80 keynote addresses at interfaith seminars, over 70 instances of views and interviews at TV channels and some 1500 addresses on interfaith and civil platforms, well, nearly 2000 appearances on public platforms in total, along with membership of over 20 organizations of diverse character.

What's more, he has a YouTube channel with over a 100 video messages on festivals of all religions, jayantees of great persons, regional festivals, days of national and international importance, interfaith, social, literary and cultural themes.

In sum, Dr Thomas has been making his contribution to the making of a better society as well as country, playing the roles of a versatile thinker, scholar, professor, writer, litterateur, poet, editor, musician, religious leader, social activist, spiritualist, and most of all, a harmony and peace promoter.

The leading awards he has received are 'Sahityik Kriti Sammaan', 'Swami Devanand Hindi Award', 'Communal Harmony Award', 'Lifetime Achievement Award', 'Maulana Mohammed Ali Jauhar Award', 'National Excellence Award', 'Icon of India', 'Manav Bhushan Samman', 'Gagan Swar Shree Samaman' and 'UN World Interfaith Harmony Week 2021 Award'.

Contact Details

Address: 102, Floor 1, Plot No 155, Pochanpur, Sector 23, Dwarka, New Delhi-110077

Websites: 'https://www.mdthomas.in' (p),
'https://www.mdthomas.academia.edu' (p)
and 'https://www.ihpsindia.org' (o)

Blog: 'https://drmdthomas.blogspot.com'(p)

YouTube:'https://www.youtube.com/@mdthomas53' (p)

Twitter: 'https://twitter.com/mdthomas53' (p)

Facebook: 'https://www.facebook.com/mdthomas53' (p)

Email:'mdthomas53@gmail.com' (p)

Telephone:9810535378 (p), 8447925378 (p)